RECORDS OF THE INTELLIGENCE DEPARTMENT

OF THE GOVERNMENT OF THE NORTH-WEST PROVINCES OF INDIA

DURING THE MUTINY OF 1857

RECORDS OF THE INTELLIGENCE DEPARTMENT

OF THE GOVERNMENT OF THE NORTH-WEST PROVINCES OF INDIA

DURING THE MUTINY OF 1857

INCLUDING
CORRESPONDENCE WITH THE SUPREME GOVERNMENT
DEHLI, CAWNPORE, AND OTHER PLACES

WILLIAM MUIR
THEN IN CHARGE OF THE INTELLIGENCE DEPARTMENT,
AND SUBSEQUENTLY LIEUTENANT-GOVERNOR, NORTH-WEST PROVINCES

EDITED BY
WILLIAM COLDSTREAM

IN TWO VOLUMES
VOLUME TWO

GYAN

Published by

Gyan Publishing House
5, Ansari Road
Daryaganj, New Delhi-110002
Phone: 011-47034999, 9811692060
E-mail: books@gyanbooks.com

Distribution Network
gyanbooks.com
India, USA, Canada, UK, Australia, France

ISBN : 978-81-212-3947-9 (Set)
ISBN : 978-81-212-5036-8 (PB)
First Published, Edinburgh, 1902

2nd Impression 2020

Printed at: Gyan Press, Delhi.

Records of the
Intelligence Department Vol. II
Author: William Muir

RECORDS OF THE
INTELLIGENCE DEPARTMENT

OF THE

GOVERNMENT OF THE NORTH-WEST PROVINCES OF INDIA

DURING THE

MUTINY OF 1857

INCLUDING

CORRESPONDENCE WITH THE SUPREME GOVERNMENT, DEHLI, CAWNPORE, AND OTHER PLACES

PRESERVED BY, AND NOW ARRANGED UNDER THE SUPERINTENDENCE OF

SIR WILLIAM MUIR, K.C.S.I., D.C.L.

THEN IN CHARGE OF THE INTELLIGENCE DEPARTMENT, AND SUBSEQUENTLY LIEUTENANT-GOVERNOR, NORTH-WEST PROVINCES

EDITED BY WILLIAM COLDSTREAM, B.A., I.C.S.

VOL. II.

EDINBURGH
T. & T. CLARK, 38 GEORGE STREET
1902

TABLE OF CONTENTS

VOLUME II.

RECORDS OF INTELLIGENCE DEPARTMENT, ETC

AGRA IN THE MUTINY.

INTELLIGENCE DEPARTMENT, AGRA.

MSS. VOL. VI.

NINTH SERIES.

THIS Volume contains the rough notes of intelligence collected daily by me from various quarters—Depositions of Spies or Messengers, purport of Native letters, Urzees, etc.

It was commenced on the 8th July (or three days after the action with the Neemuch Brigade, ending in our retiring into the Fort), and the early portion was written on the only loose sheets of paper available at the time.

The result was daily shown (so long as he was able to read it) to the Lieut.-Governor, a few of whose marginal notes will be found here and there.

The last entry is dated the 27th Oct. 1857.

W. MUIR.

DLXVI.

INTELLIGENCE DIARY, JULY 1857.

8th July, Wednesday.[1]—Chowbey Gunsham Singh reports that he received information from the Thannahdar of Secundra Rao, dated 5th July, to the effect that the 14th Irregular Cavalry from Nowgaon with 2 Pultuns and 3 guns were expected that day or the next on their way to Dehli. **14th Irregular Cavalry from Nowgaon.**

9th July, Thursday.—The Chowbey reports by Urzee that it will be advisable to gather together the plunder which is now cast forth by the people in the streets. **The Chowbey.**

[1] From 8th to 25th July these entries are written on sheets of small letter-paper.—W. C.

Isree Pershad.

Isree Pershad reports that the bodies of our Europeans killed in the action [1] are still unburied.

Neemuch force at Muthra have levied money from the bankers.

Chowbey Gunsham. Alexander and Burlton's Risala and Pearson's Battery.

Chowbey Gunsham Singh (in person), Alexander and Burlton's risala and Pearson's battery left Hatrass on the 3rd, and passed by Ferozabad on the 5th or 6th, plundering it; their route is through Mynpoorie by the metalled road; and thence they will go to Etawah.

The same person says that two Cossids with despatches from Dehli for the Lt.-Governor were seen at Hatrass, and that they were seen on the other bank of the river; but not being able to cross, went back to Poiya Ghat. Chowbey G. S. has sent to P. Ghat to bring them in.

It is reported they bring tidings of an action on the 3rd, in which the rebels were defeated with great loss—14,000.

10*th, Friday.*—Daniel despatched to Cawnpore and Allahabad with letters to Chester. Despatches through Dr. Clarke [2] to Meerut, Dehli, Nynee Tal, and Rajpootana.

Insurgents' army at Muttra.

Chowbey Gunsham Singh reports that the insurgents' army was at Muttra still, the day before yesterday, endeavouring to squeeze 3 lakhs out of the Seth.

. . . .

The Cossids with the letter from Dehli not yet heard of—may be murdered perhaps.

The Tehseeldar and Moonsiff of Futtehpore Sicri are in correspondence with the Neemuch Mutineers. Zâmin Ally has news on this point—will be sent for.

Seth's house surrounded. He flees.

The Seth's house was surrounded at Muttra by the Mutineers. He had fled to Bundrabun.

The Neemuch people have no ammunition, and are seeking to replenish their magazines.

Muttra records.

The Cucherries have been partially destroyed, but some records, English and vernacular, remain. These should be saved.

11*th July, Saturday.*—

. . . .

The Mutineers at Gwalior pacified by 3 months' pay, and remaining still.

C. G. S. brings Zâmin Ali, Mohurrir of Jugneyr, who has just returned *via* Futtehpore Sicri. He reports that the Neemuch

[1] The recent attack on Agra.

[2] Postmaster-General for the Province.

Mutineers have carried off the Tehseeldar Irshad Ally as a prisoner, and maltreated him so that one of his arms is broken. Tehsildar Irshad Ali taken prisoner.

The Moonsiff Md. Muazzam was appointed Tehseeldar of the Neemuch party, and Cazee Izzutoollah maintained as Thannahdar. A dak is kept up by Uchneyra. The last perwana from the Mutineers directed the administration to be kept up, but stated that the Mutineer army would not return till assistance came from Dehli. Mehndee Ally, a Sowar, was appointed by them Duffadar; and the Rissaldar maintained in his post at 150/ a month. The "Duftur"[1] is all destroyed, except the blank books which are used for current business. Defection of Native officials. Destruction of records.

Sayfoolla with his levy was at Jugneyr on Monday, so that he can have had no connection with the Mutineers. He was going on to Keraolee.

Reported that the Zemindars of Mundrakull had been called on to prepare 200 mds. of attah[2] for the Mutineer army. (Query—On their return march?)

12*th July, Sunday.*—The Gomashta of Deenanath Tewary, nephew of Sheo Churn Loll, Mahajan, brought a letter from Allahabad dated 8 days ago (4th July). It stated that the Company's arrangements are now excellent. Troops coming in *daily* from the East. That day troops had gone off towards Cawnpore. Budmashes being hanged daily after trial. All quiet: dak with Bengal regular. Allahabad.

. . . .

Gunsham Chowbey. The Neemuch Mutineers were at Muthra by accounts of yesterday. Some said they were going to Dehli, others going to remain.

News from Furruckabad, 13 days old: bazaar shut, and firing from Fort.

Dehli, 6 days old. Everything ready for the Hulla.[3] The Mutineers had all retired within the walls.

Hatrass all right yet.

The Gwalior Horse and guns, *en route* to Etawah, reported to be in confusion on this side Shekohabad. It is said they are surrounded by the villagers and have no ammunition, and are likely to lose their guns (Pearson's?). If this be true, it would be worth while offering a reward, say 1000 or 2000 rupees, for each gun brought in. Gwalior Mutineers surrounded by the villagers.

[1] Office records. [2] Meal. [3] Assault.

Chowbey Gunsham reports that a letter from Allahabad, dated the 2nd inst., has been received by the firm of Ram Ruttun Sheopershad, to the effect that, on the 2nd inst., a regiment of Sikhs and Europeans with 12 guns started that day (2nd) towards Cawnpore from Allahabad.

Sikh regiment and guns advancing on Cawnpore.

13th July, Monday.—Chowbey Gunsham brings copy of a letter (the one alluded to above), dated 2nd July, received by Ram Ruttun Sheopershad from Bukshee Ram Ram Ruttun in Allahabad. Great distress has been occasioned by the Sepoys, who, having mutinied, burned the Station, broke the Jail, plundered 30 lakhs of rupees, and made off for Lucknow. The Budmashes then looted the European and Native houses. After that a Moulvee came from Mehgaon and set up a Government (Thannahs and Chowkeys) in the city—which stood 5 days. Two or three times he tried to oppose the English in his (or against their) entrenchments. He and his adherents fled. The Europeans burned Kyd Gunge, and plundered the residents to the extent of 10 lakhs. Good arrangements have now been introduced. Martial law prevails. The adherents of the Moulvee, highway robbers, etc., summarily hanged.

Mutiny at Allahabad.

Moulvee from Mehgaon.

Troops regularly coming in. In 8 days 12,000 men will be here. A "pultun" of Sikhs and Europeans started with 12 guns. As forces arrive they will be sent on regularly west. In a month all will be right.

Examined the messenger who brought Deenanath Tewary's letter (see first entry of yesterday). He says: "Left Allahabad on Thursday, 3rd July. On the previous day a party of 500 Europeans, 600 Sikhs (100 mounted), left Allahabad; heard there were 6 guns; went with them by the regular stages as far as Lohunda, which they reached on Friday, 4th. Saw them at the toll there. The El. Telegraph wire was being mended; 7 coss had been completed."

After the detachment left there remained at Allahabad 500 Europeans and 500 Sikhs. But on Wednesday and Thursday (2nd and 3rd) 2 steamers arrived with 800 Europeans, and more were coming.

Nana's force.

At Cawnpore the Nana had 2000 or 3000 men.

At Nubbeegunge he passed a Risala of some 800 horse going to Dehli.

At Futtehpore passed a Calcutta Baboo, Punda Baboo (resident of Jumna Gunge here), who said he had the Governor-General's despatches for Lieutenant-Governor.

Gunsham Chowbey's intelligence from Muttra was that the Mutineers were still there. That from 1000 to 1500 Mussulmans had proceeded to them from Agra to complain of our alleged cruelties against them; spoke of the danger of razing the mosque as affecting the prejudices of the Mussulmans.

Gunsham Chowbey reports that a traveller just come from Muttra reports that the Mutineers have realised 1½ lakhs from the Muttra bankers by a "bâchh";[1] that many of the Sepoys are buying gold mohurs, and, having changed their dress and shaved their moustaches, have gone across the river to their homes. The Chowbey says that, from this man's statement, the object of the Sepoys is mainly to get money and go off to their homes or elsewhere. They have no apparent design. Conduct of Mutineers at Muttra.

14th July, Tuesday.—Chowbey Gunsham Singh reports the news from Muttra confirms the reports of yesterday. The women, camp-followers, and Sepoys of the Neemuch force are leaving in considerable numbers. They have no ammunition, and can get none. No troops at Futtehpore Sicri. No move at Gwalior; the M. Raja promises further pay if they will stay on to Katick. Maharajah holds the Mutineers in check at Gwalior.

Moorlee Muhajan of Bhurwul, a man from Furruckabad (he left 14 days ago, when fighting was still going on), reports that Madho Singh and Joher Singh, Aheers of Kaidra, brought 6 tôps (guns)—buried before—for the protection of the Tehseeldar of Mostufabad, but eventually turned off the Tehseeldar and took the treasure. Conduct of Ahirs Madho Singh and Joher Singh at Mostufabad.

The same man relates that near Nuseerpore (near the Tank of Futtehpore) the Aheers of Nuseerpore attacked the Sowars and Golundazes of the horse and Pearson's battery (probably directed by Koonj Beharee Canoongoe), took possession of the guns, and killed some of the Sowars as they crossed the bridge at Burra bagh near Butesur. Many of the Sowars went off to their homes towards Mhow, and the rest went on to Gwalior. Ahirs of Nusirpore. Pearson's Battery. Kunj Behari Canoongo.

Kulloo, a noted Aheer of Gorha near Naseerpore, and cousin of Khunsaya, has looted Sirsagunge. Kalloo, Ahir of Gorha. Sirsaganj looted.

Gunsham Singh brought Urzees from the Tehseeldars of Hatrass (Jeykishen, his brother), of Eglass (Abdoolla Khan, who has taken refuge in Hatrass), and of Allygurh (Md. Ally). Jeykishen, Abdulla Khan, Md. Ali, Tehsildars.

It appears that the Jhansi Corps passed through Allygurh for Dehli on the 8th, and plundered the city and the Tehseeldar's house. There were only 3 Companies and 3 guns, though some said more were behind. Jhansi Corps. Aligarh plundered.

[1] Assessment *pro ratâ*.

Troops returning from Delhi. Neemuch force breaking up.

Cafilas of troops daily pass, returning from Dehli.

Accounts of Neemuch force breaking up in this manner also confirmed by Allygurh Tehseeldar (who is in Moorsam, his letter dated the 11th). He says the day before 500 men went, and that day 300 passed.

Proceedings of Gwalior Mutineers. Madári Lál, banker. Jalesar plundered.

The Gwalior Horse and guns, when their officers left, threatened the Mahajans—plundered the treasury, and got some money from the bankers (including 2000 Rs. from Mudaree Loll, son of Beja Singh). They did not plunder the town. They treated Juleysur the same way.

Hatrass attacked. Gobind Singh and Tikum Singh act loyally.

Afterwards the Budmashes and butchers of Madhoogurhee (near at hand) attacked Hatrass on the 7th, and threatened Hatrass. On the 8th Gobind Singh, by Tekum Singh's direction, came to assist the Tehseeldar with a gun (from Berwan) and some 200 men, and preserved the peace. He sends an Urzee to the Lieutenant-Governor.

Subsequent Muttra messenger says they could not realise their assessment.

Pandit Durga Pershad.

15*th*, *Wednesday*.—No particular news. A letter was received by Gunsham Chowbey from a man called Pundit Doorga Pershad at Hatrass, who had been to Muttra and spoken with the Mutineer General and Brigade-Major of the Neemuch force. He says great numbers of Mussulmans were on the way to Muttra. The Tehseeldars of Agra and Furra were seen leaving with ten horse.

Tehsildars of Agra and Farra.

Composition of the Mutineer army.

The Mutineer army amounts to several thousand men. There is the Kota Contingent, the 72nd Native Infantry, the Gwalior 7th, and the 4th and 6th Gwalior Cavalry; also 4th troop of the Muheshpore 1st Risala. Two batteries, or 12 guns.

Officers of the Neemuch Mutineer force at Muttra: Sirdari Singh, Mutineer General; Hira Singh, Brigade-Major.

Sirdarie Singh, a Brahmin of the 1st Risala, a native of the Doab, is the Mutineer General; and Heera Singh of the Muheshpore Corps, the Mutineer Brigade-Major. They said that when they got 36-pounders from Dehli they would attack Agra. They had sent a Hurkara to Dehli.

The report from Dehli was that 8000 Europeans were coming from Surat with the "Jungee Lord Sahib"[1] against Dehli.

Lower Musulmans rise at Coel in rebellion. Jeykishen Das.

16*th*, *Thursday*.—Coel is in disorder. The fanatical lower Mussulmans, Joolahas, etc., raising the cry of "Deen—Deen." No traveller safe.

At Hatrass Jaikishan Dass has no magisterial powers; only

[1] Commander-in-Chief.

those of officer of Police. He cannot therefore punish. If invested with powers of special appointment, he could keep the town better in order.

25 Sowars are reported to have been sent from the Mutineers at Muttra to Bhurtpore for guns, but no arrangement made yet. **Mutineers at Muttra communicate with Bhurtpore.**

There is a bazaar report that a Moulvee and Rao of the Bhurtpore family have conspired against the Rajah of Bhurtpore and the Dhao; but have been seized and imprisoned.

. . . .

Dilsookh Jemadar has returned from Muttra. He says that the General has had his two hands shot off. Confirms report of attempt to get guns from Bhurtpore. **Dilsukh Jemadar.**

The Commr.'s Sowars with the Mutineers; he recognised four of them. **Commr.'s Sowars with the Mutineers.**

The Furra Tehseeldar Akbar Beg with them endeavouring to raise means. Knows nothing of Vikar Alee Beg being with them. **Akbar Beg, Tehsildar.**

(Isree Pershad.) Letter from Futtehpore Sicri: supplies got together for troops; some collections made for Sepoys. Troops (3 "pultuns" and 18 guns) expected from the Bombay Hata (direction). **Fattehpur Sikri.**

From Furra they say that Muttra force going on to Kosee (?).

16*th July*.—[From Major M'Leod. Through Kunhaie Lall, servant of Gunga Pershad, Muthra.] **Ganga Pershad, Muttra.**

The Cazee and Deputy-Collector and Cotwal have proclaimed the King of Dehli. When the Mutineers came next morning they were angry at the proclamation having been made without their order; whereupon the three officers ran away. **King of Delhi proclaimed at Muttra.**

The Mutineers are collecting money, and have looted several persons. The Seth has gone to Bhurtpore [Bindrabun ?]. **The Seth of Muttra.**

The Mutineers are not getting ammunition made up; and none is being made for them at Areeng. They have declined to go to Dehli. They are collecting boats on the river, with the intention of going away and dispersing. The Tehseeldar of Muhaban had paid to them all the revenue he had collected; but the other Tehseeldars ran away. **Tehsildar of Mahaban.**

The Jyepore force has left Kosee; and is *believed* to have moved towards Dehli. **Jyepore force.**

Their General's (the Neemuch men?) name is Sirdhara Singh (Cavalry man); and their Brigade-Major died (?) of his wound. **Sirdara Singh.**

Teekum Singh has kept the peace in Muat. **Tikum Singh at Muat.**

The above is a reply to a letter sent to Gunga Pershad

Mark Thornhill, C.S. through Tekum Singh by Mr. M. Thornhill, who regards the news as authentic.

17*th July, Friday.*—No official news yet from Dehli of the action of the 9th; but native report gives us the victory, with great loss to the enemy and little to ourselves.

Bhurtpore. Cheela Naee of Ackagurh in Bhurtpore left Bhurtpore yesterday after midday. Says that 25 Sowars and 8 Sepoys came four days ago from Muthra to Bhurtpore, and are pitched at Cudum Khunda. They demand guns—which if not given they threaten to fight. The Sirdars agree to give four guns; and it is said that they will be taken down from the Fort to-day. Guns are being mounted in the Fort and all round the City Wall. Doondee Khan, Feelban,[1] a man of great influence, and another Sirdar, went to the Neemuch force and are not yet returned. The Mutineers also ask for the troops called Huck Sahib, and the Infantry; but they declined to leave, as the Maharaja is too young to leave. Gyasee Ram, Dhaoo, Bhola Nath Dewan, and Goburdhun Singh Foujdar are the men chief in authority. Chowdree Churn Singh's influence is small at present. Mukoond Singh has a plot to put his sister's son, Rao Sahib, aged 12 years, on the Guddee. Major Morrieson is said to be at Bhosawur, 18 coss from Bhurtpore—surrounded by Sowars, but whether Mutineers or others is not known.

(Margin notes: Bhurtpore armed. Doondee Khan, Feelban. Bhurtpore officials. Conspiracy of Makund Singh. Major Morrieson.)

Chowbey Gunsham recommends three modes of action on the Bhurtpore Durbar.

Bhurtpore Durbar. First, a Khureeta, which might be sent by Pundit Bhowany Pershad of Cochesur in Boolundshuhur. He has a brother Risaldar at Bhurtpore. The Khureeta should threaten that any assistance given to the rebels will bring condign punishment on the Sirdars, if not on the State. Second, Thakoor Duryao Singh is a relative by marriage of Goburdhun Singh Foujdar, and might be used to dissuade the Durbar through him. He lives at Jawur, near Moorsam. Third, Gobind Singh is a relative of Churn Singh, not at present of much influence. But he might help.

17*th July.*—Tejraj, a man sent towards Dholpore, returned from 5 coss this side of it, and says there is no force coming this way from Gwalior. A Dholpore Goojur with 2000 men and 2 guns was plundering the country and coming towards Agra, but was turned back by the Zemindars about Kukooa.

Goojur plundering the country.

[1] Man in charge of an elephant.

Mirzapore.—A letter from Futteh Chund to Doorga Pershad Gooburdhun Dass, dated 4th July, says that yesterday Mr. Moore was killed in a fight with the Zemindars of Gopee Gunge. At Mirzapore there is great alarm. The European troops are on their way up, and order will soon be restored.

Mr. Moore killed.

Alarm at Mirzapore.

Furruckabad.—A man left Shahjehanpore 11 days ago; he passed through Furruckabad 7 days ago. Says, on report, that up to 3rd or 4th there was much fighting. On the last day many Sepoys who attempted to climb by ladders were killed by logs of wood cast on them. On that night the officers retired in boats to Kulyaree. The Nawab rules in the city. The Mutineers are pitched on the Parade.

Mutiny at Farakhabad.

At Shahjehanpore, he says, some (?) little girls of 8 or 9 years of age are said to be protected by Nizam Ali Khan. A Nawab of one of the old families rules.

Luchman Singh gives the bazaar report that the troops at Gwalior have proved too strong for Scindia and have plundered Gwalior, and declared their intention of joining Neemuch force.

18th July, Saturday.—Chowbey Gunsham Singh brings a Kuhar, Rudhay, who was at Muthra on Thursday, 16th: reached the Mutineers' Camp about 4 p.m.—left about 8 p.m. He declares that the general and immediate intention of the Mutineer army was to proceed to Dehli, as they could do nothing without ammunition. He states that they must all have gone by this time. They had realised one and a quarter lacs, and spoke of 1¾ being yet due to them. He met 50 Sowars of the Police, etc., which had been left at Futtehpore Sicri as an outpost, at Furrah, on their way to join the main force. The deserters from Syfoolla's Keraolee Sowars, and a body of Ulwur men who are carried against their will with the force, had been picketed in the direction of Bhurtpore. The Superintendent of Police, and Cotwal of Agra, and the P.S.A. had gone over the river. Their arms had been taken from their followers. They were plundered on the opposite side of the river.

Police Sowars join Mutineers.

Agra officials.

(The spy is a rough and plain bearer, but seems sufficiently intelligent; and, if not deceived by the Mutineers, may be relied on, I think.)

An Urzee from the Tehseeldar of Hatrass, two days old, states that the Ranee of Husain (widow of Narain Singh) is preparing to seize Cusba Mendhoo, a village about 4 coss from Hatrass, the purchased property of Mahmoud Alee Khan of Chutara, Boolundshuhur.

Sassni ruled by Mohan Singh.

Sassnee has not been plundered (as before reported), but the police have gone to Coel, and Mohun Singh (a freebooter of the vicinity) is ruling it.

Captain Alexander.

[States that his treasury was looted by the Sowars, when they went, of 975 rupees, and that 721 were paid away by Capt. Alexander's orders to a Jemadar of the Gwalior Horse. No receipt, however, was given. Capt. A. might be asked.]

Qazi-ul-Qazát of Agra.

Yesterday the Cazee-ool-Cuzát, who is going home, reported that a man who left Cawnpore on the 16th Zeehad—that is, 8 days before (9th of July)—reported that the Nana's force was going forth eastwards to meet ours (?).

Daryao Singh of Khaga flees.

The man saw our force at Khaga on the 10th Z.K.,[1] *i.e.* the 3rd or 4th of July, where it was to halt four days (to allow the main body to come up ?). Duryao Singh of Khaga had fled over the river.

W. E. Money.

A Cossid employed by the house of Moonna Lall was brought by W. E. Money. He left Agra 12 or 13 days ago—was 5 days on the road going, and 5 coming—stayed two days at Dehli, 11th and 12th (or 12th and 13th). It rained heavily all the time. And there was no fighting between the armies and no cannonade. He stayed with Chumput Roy Fakeer Chund in

Condition of Sepoys in Delhi.

Anár Gullee. The Sepoys are billeted about in the shops. They do not leave Dehli for fear of the Goojurs.

Agra reported at Delhi as captured.

Rajah of Balabgarh and Mutineers.

Sepoys at Delhi.

Describes an action in which our people retired. Spread money, etc., behind their entrenchments. The enemy came on and began to pick up the money, when we attacked them, killing 5000 or 6000. They have little money, only a lac;—their ammunition is in the Fort. On the day he left salutes were being fired—for the capture of Agra. A letter of the Rajah of Bullubgurh to us intercepted. He supplies no russud. The Sepoys have looted Bullubgurh. They speak against ——— and Jhujjur also.

The Sepoys in no case remain outside the gates. A great deal of horse does, especially at the Dehli gate.

The Bunnias say the Sepoys will never stand against us. In 13 or 14 battles they have uniformly been worsted. Yet the fight goes on as yet with no decisive result.

Jugganath Ray.—Native rumour says that Scindia has *dis-*

[1] *i.e.* Dzul-Kada.

banded some of the Mutineer Regiments who are marching to Furrah to join the Muttra Mutineers.

19*th July, Sunday.*—Abdoolla Khan, Tehseeldar of Eglass, writes under date 14th July. Hears distressing accounts of his home at Shahjehanpore, and has gone thither with the Sudder Sudoor of Agra, who passed through Hatrass. Made over his seal to J. K. D. of Hatrass. **Abdullah Khan, Tehsildar of Eglass.**

Jaikishan Dass sends an Urzee of Zuhoor Ahmed asking for two months' leave to go to his home at Bansa in Oudh. J. K. D. desired to use his discretion in granting the leave. **Jeykishen Das.**

No troops are at Biana; but some are by common report at Hindour.

20*th July, Monday.*—Pergh. Oreya, Etawah, and Bhudaick, Calpee.

Keshoo Singh of Motee Kutra was sent by Soorajbhan Sahookar to get tidings of a boat laden with salt and ghee. He found that Rajah Pareechit had taken the boat ashore at Bhudaick. He has planted two guns on his Gurbee, which commands the river; and is plundering about. **Rajah Pareechit of Bhudaick plundering.**

(Pareechit is the old Rajah of some 20 or 30 villages in Talooka Bhudaick, which have gradually passed from his hands from debt, etc.)

Any boats going down should be cautious here.

Keshoo Singh has been sent to Gwalior, but the true state of Gwalior cannot be learned by spies of this low caste: Gunsham Dass recommends a communication to Dinka Rao, through his purohits. Recommends re-establishment of authority in district.

25 Sowars are stationed at Oreya on the part of the Nana. **Nana's action.**

A city report, but loose, that the Gwalior Durbar troops, seeing the Contingent get so much advance, mutinied for more pay; and that the Maharajah has put some of the Sirdars in prison, and desired the troops to choose new Sirdars.

Pundit Kedarnath brings an arattea whose messenger came in yesterday from the east. He passed through Khaga on the 9th or 10th, and found there our army entrenched. One "pultun" Sikhs, and 1100 Europeans (Qy. 400 ?), 2600 Europeans (1200 ?), coming behind in two detachments with 28 guns.

A mile or so on this side Futtehpore he met the Nana's force going eastward,—2 "pultuns" and one "risala," with 8 guns. **Nana's force.**

Two days subsequently he heard at Cawnpore that there had

been a fight. The Europeans had made a feint, and led on the rebels to a bad position, where by a cross attack the latter were completely discomfited.

(The first part of informant's story seems true, though numbers exaggerated.)

21*st July.*—There is a report to-day in the Fort, proceeding from Jotee Pershad, I believe, that the Gwalior troops with Scindia are coming against us. I have not had it confirmed from any other quarter.

Mr. Chester's 2 Cossids from Allahabad reached this to-day. They got their despatches from Mr. Chester on Sunday the 12th; started early in the morning on an ekka; passed through Khaga, which they found deserted by the freebooter, Duryao Singh, who had fled across the river. Reached Belinda on Monday 13th, where they were told that European troops were ahead in Futtehpore, and that they would be killed if they went. Halted that night at Belinda (which is 4 or 5 miles on the Allahabad side of Futtehpore) in the Serai.

Khaga.

Daryao Singh.

Next morning, Tuesday the 14th, they left their ekka at Belinda and proceeded towards Futtehpore. About a mile or two on the east of Futtehpore they began to see signs of a battle: first the body of a Sowar and horse, and then as they approached Futtehpore 10 or 12 more bodies: and still nearer the city, by the Serai and Tank, bodies of men, bullocks, tents, coats of sepoys, etc. etc. In Futtehpore the report they heard was that on Sunday the 12th the Nana and army were in Futtehpore: the European army arrived the same day at Belinda. The Europeans sent on two companies towards Futtehpore, who retired before the Nana's force, which was drawn out of the city and then attacked by the whole European force, and completely discomfited.

. . . .

The Europeans marched early on Monday 13th (Tuesday 14th ?) to Mulwa, where they encamped, six coss from Futtehpore.

Mulwa.

The people were fleeing in great numbers from the G. T. Road towards the Kora Jehanabad Road; *i.e.* south.

. . . .

They started again early on Wednesday 15th, and passed through Kora Jehanabad. In the Serai, about 7 or 8 a.m., heard that the Deputy Hikmatoolla Khan (who had killed R. Tucker, and for whom 5000 rupees reward had been proclaimed at Allahabad) was there on his flight (probably from Cawnpore, where he may have fled with the rebels towards Banda); they saw his elephant ready, his carriage, and his myana (tent). Deputy Hikmatulla Khan. R. Tucker, C.S.

Passed through Moosanugger, where a police officer and two burkandazes were awaiting, as they said, who should be King, but longing for Company's rule. At Dowlutnugger—a Mussulman village—some 500 men were plundering. All quiet at Oreya. At Etawah the Muhajuns endeavouring to protect themselves, and keeping the peace. The Nana had two "pultuns," one "risala," 12 guns, and 7 lacs; he was going to Allahabad to take it. We had (*i.e.* about Futtehpore) our advanced force of 500 Europeans and 500 Sikhs (?), with the main body of 1100 Europeans, Sikhs, and 6 guns;—altogether some 2000 Europeans (?). We took all their artillery and treasure, etc. A short man with beard commanded,—name Williams—(Havelock?). The main body started on the Tuesday (7th) preceding the fight. Five hundred Europeans and two or three hundred Sikhs left behind, after our force left, in Allahabad. Heard that 1100 Europeans were immediately expected in Steamers. The Allahabad Moulvee rebel was at Cawnpore. Electric Telegraph wire being put up by a Sahib and beldars as far as Kutogurh. Plundering at Daulatnagar. Oreya quiet. Nana's force. Allahabad Moulvee.

Horse dak re-established to Futtehpore, and regular post running. Our Thannahs and police re-established. "Russud," etc., being got ready for our troops expected behind, and road all secure on the other side of Futtehpore. Dak and Police re-established.

22nd July, Wednesday.—Letters from Gwalior Durbar (20th July) announce arrival of our troops at Cawnpore on 16th, and occupation. Mutineers dispersing. From same source reported that 34 persons, male and female, killed at Indore—two at Augur (?), and as many gentlemen and ladies went to Holkar's house; they arrived at Mhow under care of Holkar's troops. Four lacs saved from plunder sent to Mhow by Holkar. Arrival of British troops at Cawnpore. Massacre at Indore.

Raikes and Alexander's, etc., horse and artillery reached Gwalior on the 20th.

Yesterday the Chowbey reported that he had intelligence from Mynpoorie (where he has relatives) that the Rajah was making good arrangements there; but that the Jhansi troops, passing through, burned bungalows and killed people in the town. Treasury safe. The Rajah has not spent a farthing. Loyal action of Rajah of Mainpúri. Jhansi troops in Mainpúri.

23rd July, Thursday.—A Mullah who had taken his boat to Allahabad, but could not get farther west owing to the disturbed state of the river, left it there, and started from Allahabad early on the 11th, Saturday; reached Belinda on Monday, 13th, night. Passed through Futtehpore on Tuesday. Says the fight was on Monday, when the Nana was defeated. Saw 11 guns, four carts (native) filled with ball, and other stores, under charge of an English officer, and some 250 Sikhs. Heard that we took two lacs from the Nana. The town was given up to plunder. An elephant of the Nana's was killed in the fight. The Nana fired guns on the Sunday, but the fight was next day. The two "pultuns" of English troops went on on Tuesday, and the Sikh troops remained with the guns.

On Tuesday the European troops were at Kullianpore.

Heard that the Futtehpore Deputy had fled to the "Dukhun."[1] Heard that the Nana had broken the bridge over the Pandoo on the G. T. Road and guarded it with entrenchments. Thannahs established, and suspicious characters searched, from Allahabad to Futtehpore. Dak runs regularly to our army.

Gunsham Chowbey.—Tejraj, a messenger of the Chowbey's, went to within 3 or 4 miles of the Hindun, where he was taken before Harvey as a spy, but was let off on telling his story. Harvey with two other officers would be at Futtehpore Sicri to-day.

Mewattis help Khadims of Fattehpur Sikri. They had some Sowars with them. They may be in some peril at Futtehpore Sicri, as the Khadims have got a party of Mewattees to help them. Any way of helping Harvey at Futtehpore Sicri?

Rajputs and Jats fight near Hatrass. *Near Hatrass.*—At Bisana there was a fight between the Rajpoot Zemindars and the Jats, who attacked them, assisted by a nephew of the Rajah of Moorsam (but acting without his authority) and a freebooter, Narain Singh. The Rajpoot repelled

Narain Singh. the Jats, and killed some fifty of them. Narain Singh was doing great injury by attacking well-affected villages. The Tehseeldar of Hatrass has him in custody, and solicits orders about him. I told the Chowbey to send up a keyfeut (report) on the subject. (Native reports that we have lost the "Puhari"[2] at Dehli, and that the King has stopped the advance of the Neemuch force towards Dehli, as they are to have reinforcements and a siege train to attack Agra with.)

[1] South. [2] Ridge.

24th July, Friday.—Ikram Hosen, in an Urzee dated the 20th July, confirms the victory at Futtehpore, and adds that on Friday the 17th our force entered Cawnpore, fought the Nana, put him to flight, and took his guns and all his effects. Our authority completely re-established there. Ikram Hosen. British authority re-established at Cawnpore.

Statement of a man who left Dehli on Monday the 20th.—On the 21st, Tuesday, met the Neemuch Mutineers between Hodul and Pulwul, and was told by them that they had neither ammunition nor leader. There were daily fightings at Dehli. From 4000 to 6000 Europeans there. The rebels were lying outside the town (?). "Russud" went out to them from Bullubgurh and Shahdera. Meeran Buksh (Kaghazee Muhullah) had restored the bridge. From 40 to 50 Sepoys, after cutting off moustaches, endeavoured to escape, and were stopped and imprisoned. Our balls were falling in the Loll Diggee. Neemuch Mutineers. Condition of things at Delhi.

Chowbey Gunsham says that a man named Eesra left Dehli on the 19th: saw that Meeran Buksh Chowdry has repaired the bridge; it consists of 125 boats, by which they get chief "russud." They also get some from Kosi and Bullubgurh. Met the Neemuch force at Hodul going to Dehli.

Reports threatened collision between Mahmoud Ali Khan of Chuttaree and Nawab Muzhur Ally of Purrawul (some of whose estates the former had obtained). The Nawab was collecting 10,000 men to overwhelm the former.

Luchman Singh has a letter from Rajah Pertabnugger.

Lucknow.—The troops are in Belee guard, and keep off the enemy by a cannonade and shells.

Second battle with Nana on the 16th. English have 12 H.A. guns;—confirms former account.

25th July.—A letter from Imdad Allee, Tehseeldar of Kosee, dated the 22nd, says Neemuch force has gone on: under command of Heera Singh and the Mahomedan who lost his hands. Dr. Wazeer Khan is with them. Neemuch force.

Eglass records kept by Kehree Singh and others of M[a] Kurtulla—a perwana of approval sent.

Fifty thousand rupees collected chiefly by supply bills in the city.

Gwalior news that we have followed up the "Baba Sahib" to Bithoor, and are hanging Sowars and Sepahis at 50/ on the former and 25/ for the latter.[1]

[1] Here end the entries on letter-paper.—W. M.

Note of some Expenses of the Intelligence Department, Agra.

13th July.—Received Rs. 20.	13th.—To Benares messenger Rs. 5
	20th.—Imdad Ali's man . . 3
	22nd.—Cawnpore Cossids . . 1
	24th.—Etawa man . . . 1
	25th.—Shekoabad to Mynpoorie 1
	25th.—Kosie man . . . 5
	27th.—Messenger to Cawnpore . 4
	Rs. 20

Things at Aligarh.

25*th July* 1857, *Saturday.*—An Urzee from Allygurh, dated the 24th of July, saying that the Mewattees and Goojurs rule there. There is a new Cotwal every day.

The old Cotwal has gone. The native Doctor of the Regiment (9th) was chosen Cotwal by the City Punchayat.

"Subah" of Malagarh.

The Malagurh man contemplates extending his rule to Allygurh (he is nominal Subah down to Allahabad). Ghous Mahommed, son of Noor Khan of Secundra Rao, came to Coel by Wullee Dad Khan's desire; and returned with Nuseemoollah, son of Aleemoollah. Ghous Mahommed, it is expected, will be ruler of Coel.

Ghaus Mahomed.

On the 21st July 300 Sepoys, without arms, passed through Coel from Dehli. They said that the King had fraternised with the English, and there was no longer any occasion to stay there. The disaffected Mahommedans give out that only a few hundreds of English are left.

. . . .

27*th July*, *Monday.*—Chowbey Gunsham brings a man who left Dehli on the morning of the 23rd; says that after the 20th there was no more fighting till the 23rd, when he left in the morning: large bodies of mounted troops were preparing to go out.

Reported operations of Mutineers at Delhi.

He met the Neemuch troops at Bhugorah, four miles this side of Bullubgurh: states that the enemy are projecting a move down the river, for a certain distance, then a flank movement to the right, so as to take our army in the rear in the direction of Nujufgurh.

Eta.

A man from Eta states that about four days ago 200 Sepoys, 100 Sowars, and 5 elephants came there from the east, and demanded "russud"[1] of the Rajah. He declined. They said that in the first battle they had beaten the English; but that four more European "pultuns" had come up, and, having no chance with them and the numerous reinforcements behind, they had left.

[1] Supplies.

Lucknow.—Sookha, an Aheer, left Lucknow 8 days ago. Reached this yesterday morning, which was the 7th day. Left either on Sunday or Monday. A spy reports on road from Cawnpore to Lucknow.

Sir H. Lawrence[1] had abandoned Mucheebhawun, and concentrated his force at Belcegard. There were forces beyond number (a ryot rabble) opposed to him; but he was holding his own position easily.

When Sookha reached Oonao Serai he heard for the first time that two European pultuns had reached Cawnpore. On the road to Cawnpore there were only 10 or 20 Nawabee Sepahis. Crossed the Ganges at Sirsey Ghat, Cawnpore. Boats under our officers' orders. No opposition whatever on the Oudh bank; was two days between Lucknow and Cawnpore. On Cawnpore.

Cawnpore.—Reached Cawnpore on the 21st or 22nd, Tuesday or Wednesday, about 12 o'clock. Accompanied a detachment of our troops just setting out for Bithoor. Some Sepoys caught on the road. Our troops entered before; he with them. They took the Nana's guns there—8 or 9—and gave up his houses to plunder; they were then burned. The Sikhs plundered large numbers of cows, buffaloes, etc., belonging to the Nana. Nana not found. Some say he was drowned; others that he had escaped. A gomashtah of his was caught. . . . Only a portion of the Europeans marched out to Bithoor. The rest stayed in Cawnpore. Attack on Bithoor. Nana not found.

An unconfirmed rumour that a rebel Sikh regiment had joined us at Cawnpore.

Nowgaon.—William Vermin, a drummer of the 12th N.I., arrived to-day. He used to play in the band on the cornopean. Came by Banda, Futtehpore, Cawnpore, and Mynpoorie. Came at the latter place in contact with the left wing of the 12th on its way to Dehli, and was wounded on the 1st of July by a Mahommedan shopkeeper of Nowgaon, Shah Mahomed of Mynpoorie, who was with the troops; he then returned to Bhowgaon till his wounds were healed. States that the 12th mutinied on the 10th of June. Three Sikhs commenced by murdering the Havildar-Major, who was opposing the Mutineers; they got the guns and began firing. He ran off to Major Kirke, who, with the officers, was in the mess-house. All made their way to Chutterpore, where they were hospitably entertained by the Ranee. Sixty staunch Sepoys and some non-commissioned William Vermin's story. Mutiny of the 12th N.I. Rani of Chutterpore.

[1] He had really been dead some weeks.—W. C.

officers came up with them there. Stayed at Chutterpore three days. There were the following officers:—

Officers of 12th N.I.

Major Kirke and son.	Lt. Remington.
Captain Scott.	Ensign Frank.
Capt. Ewart.	Capt. Thompson, Artillery.
Capt. Barker (?).	Bandmaster Molly (?).
Adjt. Jackson.	Sergeant-Major.
Dr. and Mrs. Maire (?).	Band Sergeant, and wife, with the men of the Band.

Mr. Cairnes.

From thence they went to Mr. Cairnes at Muhoba,—stayed three days. Then Mr. C. directed them to Kallinger. On the way they were attacked at a village called Kala Puharie. The country was up; demanded 1000 rupees: a compromise made; but next day they attacked our people, and there was a great deal of fighting. Captain Thompson, Doolaree Tewaree, Soobahdar, and a Sepoy, killed. Returned towards Muhoba; but found the country there too up, and so went on to Kobrei (a village south of our Jelalpore Pergh. and in Muhoba). On the way the heat and fatigue were so great that Major Kirke, the bandmaster's wife, and a writer, died. This was about the 18th or 19th of June. The band-boys, etc., remained at Kobrei.

Captain Thompson killed.

The officers went on to Nagode, including Dr. and Mrs. Maire (?).

Four officers—Capt. Scott, Lt. Remington, Ens. Frank, and Bandmaster Molly—were taken by the villagers to Banda and given over to the Nawab, who took care of them.

Nawab of Banda's services.

W. Vermin came on with the 60 faithful Sepoys, who went to their homes.

Native account of advance on Cawnpore.

28th July, Tuesday, Cawnpore.—Two men of Munglee Pershad, the Lieutenant-Governor's Jemadar;—they came up with the advance guard of the Cawnpore army as far as Chowbeepore. They confirm the previous accounts of the Futtehpore victory on Sunday 12th; but say we took only three guns there; but immense masses of ammunition, stores, equipage, etc. There was a little opposition at Kullianpore, where another gun was taken on Wednesday (we halted Monday and Tuesday at Futtehpore), and a fifth very large gun at the Pandoo Nuddee bridge.

Fattehpur victory.

Affairs of Kullianpore and Pandoo Nuddee Bridge.

But there was no serious fighting again after Futtehpore till we got to Joohee, a plain near Cawnpore. There the Nana set up three entrenched batteries, which we carried with immense loss to the enemy, who were utterly routed.

Fight with Nana at Joohee.

The enemy suffered most at Futtehpore, losing perhaps

1000 men; we about 12. At the Pandoo Nuddee they lost say 200; we 4. At Joohee they lost some 600; we under 40.

We arrived near Cawnpore on Friday the 17th. The fight was on Saturday 18th. All the fighting was done by the advanced detachment of 500 Europeans and 500 Sikhs. The rest of the army came on behind under command of an old officer, short, and with white hair and beard.

On Saturday the 18th we took possession of Cawnpore, and on Sunday proclamation was issued for all to reoccupy their houses in 5 days, on pain of confiscation. On Sunday afternoon, the 19th, the portion of the army forming the advance guard crossed by boats for Lucknow by a ghat below the river; it had 6 guns. *Retaking of Cawnpore.*

The rear portion marched on Monday for Chowbeepore, consisting of 500 Europeans and 500 Sikhs, 3 companies of mounted Sikhs, and 4 guns. The heavy guns were left behind. *Operations of European force at Cawnpore.*

Some 250 Europeans are left to occupy Cawnpore.

A detachment, partly from Cawnpore, partly from the Chowbeepore force, went out to attack Bithoor, and rase the Nana's houses, etc.

The Chowbeepore force was hampered by the heavy rains. It was to march next morning, and is coming up by forced marches of 11 and 12 coss a day. The Europeans, tents, etc., are conveyed in waggons. They do not walk.

The Mynpoorie Rajah has gone out to Nubbeegunge to meet the General and help with supplies. Perwanas had gone on for the collection of supplies; and they were being collected in great quantities. *Mainpúri Rajah gives help.*

The old General is with the advancing force.

29th July, Wednesday, Gwalior.—News through Gwalior of the attack on Dehli force of 23rd. The news-writer admits loss of 1000 on the Mutineer side, and states ours at 500.

Cawnpore.—Dhunput Raee (the Chowbey's brother), on the 27th July, writes from Hatrass that he has heard the Nana's brother was killed; that our army had reached Meerunkee Serai; that the Nawab was prepared to oppose them. Our army would go against him.

Thakoor Gobind Singh writes from Hatrass that a wounded Sowar passed through, and stated that the Nana had fled *wounded.* *Rumour of the Nana.*

Allygurh.—Ghous Mahomed of Secundra Rao expected at Allygurh with 100 horsemen from Wullee Dad Khan at Malagurh. *Ghaus Mahomed.*

Troops at Gwalior.

Gwalior.—A letter from Lolljee Mull Nain Sookh to Badree Doss Ram Ruttun, dated the 23rd July, Gwalior, states that the Indore troops were expected in a day or two. They were to be lodged in the Lushkur Morar. All was quiet, and no move anticipated by the Rajah on the part of the rebel troops. He was paying the Sepoys then full pay; but the officers only half pay, on account of alleged paucity of funds. The messenger stated that "the line doree"[1] of the troops had reached.

Mr. Hillersdon.

Deaths of the officers at Cawnpore.

Cawnpore, Binser.—Cawnpore Collector's Chuprassy says he accompanied Mr. Hillersdon on to the Dumduma. He died there from a shot in the groin. Mr. M'Killop was also killed. Mrs. Hillersdon and 2 children died of privation and fright at the cannonade. He left the Dumduma after that and stayed at home. On arrival of troops and reconquest of Cawnpore he left for his home here. Hoolas Singh, Cotwal, and 10 Sowars were hanged.

Postal communication in Central Provinces.

30th July, Thursday, Hoshungabad.—Kumur Pershad Kayeth brings in despatches from Hoshungabad, which he left on the 16th inst. All is right at Hoshungabad. Reached Bhilsa on night of 17th, and left it on the 18th. The post of Saugor of 17th came in; the daks in that direction (Sehore, Bhilsa, Saugor, Nursingpore, Hoshungabad) all go uninterruptedly and regularly, and so also the daks beyond Jubbulpore to Calcutta.

Saugor postmaster hanged.

30th July, Saugor.—Things went wrong at Saugor when Nubbee Buksh, Deputy Postmaster, was hung there for opening packets and communicating intelligence to Sepoys. The officers had previously gone into the Fort (the Mint) with the Artillery. No one was killed. The Sepoys remain in the Cantonments. There has been no fighting between them.

Berasia treasuries robbed.

Bhopal Begum attacks her mutinous mercenaries.

When the messenger was at Bhilsa he saw 400 Wilayaties, Kashmeerians, who had robbed the treasuries of Berasia, after killing the Assistant Political Agent, Baboo Soobh Rao. The Bhopal Begum attacked them, and, he heard, took 100 prisoners; 100 went to Serouj (?), and 200 came on in this direction. The messenger came regularly along with them.

[It seems that the Bhopal Begum had 200 of these men—probably Rohillas (or Arabs ?)—in her service. She, a short time ago, dismissed them, paying them two months' salary. They then associated 200 of the same class with them, and began depre-

[1] Literally "measuring line": the term used in North India for the advance portion of a camp.

dations as above stated. They have erected a Mahomedan flag.]

The messenger reached Gwalior the day before yesterday with them, and came on with them to Dholepore, and to a Nuddee between this and Dholepore, where he left them crossing.

(He crossed the Chumbul easily. There are from 60 to 70 large boats, both at Dholepore and the new ghat—well manned by mulláhs.)[1] They are coining rupees at Dholepore.

The Rohilla (?) party stated that they were going by a road 4 or 5 coss to the west of Agra, and thence towards Dehli. They have above a lac of rupees with them. They will probably be at Runkutta (?). There are only 30 mounted men; all the rest are on foot.

Twenty-one officers came to Hoshungabad from Bhopal; they were refugees from Indore. Pol. Agent of Sehore also came in, and others,—say 50 in all. Durand went to Bombay to come up with an army. He went by Nagpore. Mrs. D. and some officers also went with him by dak. Refugee officers from Indore. Political Agent of Sehore withdraws to Hosungabad. Colonel H. M. Durand.

The Saugor treasure has been saved in the Fort. It is believed that the treasure at Dumoh has been plundered, but there is at present no communication in that direction. Saugor treasure saved.

The Maharajah has made all preparation for the Mhow troops. The popular report is that he gives 10 Rs. to Sepahis and 60 Rs. to Cavalry.

The Cossid from Cawnpore, who brings Brigadier-General Havelock's letter of the 18th July, says he left on the 25th. Steamers coming up daily, and reinforcements going over to Lucknow. No fight there yet.

31*st July, Friday, Bareilly.*—No particular news. There is a report from Bareilly that Khan Buhadur was preparing troops and 2 guns to send to the foot of the hills to intercept supplies to Nynie Tal. The Nawab of Rampoor said to be faithful, though secretly, in order to maintain his authority, which is not strong, over his own troops. Nawab of Rampore said to be faithful.

DLXVII.

INTELLIGENCE DIARY, AUGUST 1857.

1*st August* 1857, *Saturday, Allygurh.*—Letters from Hatrass and Allygurh state that Ghous Mahomed of Secundra Rao arrived in Allygurh on the night of the 28th. He has no treasure, Ghaus Mahomed in Aligarh.

[1] Professional boatmen.

guns, or army. But he gives out that when he has raised a local force of 1000 Sowars and 200 Sepoys he will take up the management of the Tehseelies and the Thannas. Meanwhile he professes to be putting the City in order. The Mussulmans of Coel very arrogant. The Hindoos plundered and harassed. Ghous Mahomed is now engaged in laying a regular dak between Allygurh and Dehli. The Hindoos are alarmed by the report sedulously circulated by our enemies, that, wherever the Mahomedans have proved disaffected, the whole city or town, Hindoos included, will be plundered and razed by the European troops. The Chowbey recommends proclamation to disabuse the people of this idea.

Hindus plundered at Coel.

Nisar Ali Beg, Tehsildar of Debāee.

Pensioned Tehsildar appointed King's Tehsildar at Debaee.

Debaee, Bolundshuhur.—Nisar Ali Beg, Tehseeldar of Debaee, has come in to Muthra; the Malagurh man having appointed Muzhur, the previous Tehseeldar (who was pensioned), to be the King's Tehseeldar. Proclamation in and around Debaee accordingly. Therefore Nisar Ally came away. He is a relation by marriage of Vikar Ali Beg, regarding whom he asks information. He expresses his alarm at a report which is propagated, that our Government is suspicious of, and inimical to, Moslems generally.

Two men from Gwalior report the road clear between this and Gwalior. Supplies of "attah" are said to be ordered and ready at Dholepore.

2nd August, Sunday.—A messenger came *via* Etawah and Oreya; states that road to be quiet.

Rajahs join Nana.

Says that three other Rajas joined the Nana—

"Bhaoo Sahib" of Secundra.

Rasdhan Raja.

Chachendee Raja.

Calpee.—Heard at Oreya, some 5 days ago, of some Saugor troops having looted Calpee, and being about to cross into the Doab.

Nawab of Farakhabad marches troops to Cawnpore.

Rajah of Mainpúri reported ready to rebel.

Furruckabad.—Intelligence from Mynpoory that the Nawab Raees of Furruckabad had marched troops (2 Sepoy Regiments, 1 Regiment of Cavalry, and 1000 or 1500 Pathans and Meos of Shumsabad) towards Cawnpore. Says that the Raja of Mynpoory, on being called in, was prepared to join him, and had advanced money to the Cavalry, and prepared supplies.

3rd August, Monday.—Letters from Allygurh;—Debee, a Kuhar, had come in from Meerut; reports that the whole of that Zillah was in good order, and preparations were being made to attack Malagurh. Dhunouria Singh, a hurkaru[1] from Coel, brings letters from Pearee Lall, Tehseeldar of Kheir. The messenger states that there was a report in Coel that Mr. Turnbull had reached Malagurh with two companies of European troops and a great number of Jats, and killed 400 of the Malagurh Nawab, who was shut up in his fort. (This is not, however, mentioned in the letters.) **Meerut District in good order.**

Coel.—From Aftab Ray, Sheristahdar. The Coel letters state that Ghous Mahomed had enlisted 800 men, and intended to raise 5000. He gives 20 Rs. to sowars, and 4 Rs. and 5 Rs. to "peadahs."[2] The Mahomedans generally have joined him. He gives out his intention of shortly collecting the revenue. He has a perwana of appointment from the Malagurh man, signed and sealed, which he shows. Allah Buksh, a disaffected Mewattee, is made Cotwal. Hindoos are being persecuted. They fear, on the other hand, being involved in the punishment of the Mussulmans. Mahomed Ghous has issued a proclamation against batta being taken for "pahyadar" rupee (it being a royal one). He was told a Sahib was concealed by a Khakrob,[3] and writes news to Agra. Immense numbers of houses searched on this, and great excitement. Mr. Turnbull had come to Gulaotee, and was said to be going on to Malagurh. **Ghaus Mahomed in Aligarh.** **His administration.** **Mr. Turnbull, C.S.**

Ghous Mahomed had sent a perwana to Mahommed Alee Khan of Chattaree, calling on him to send on the Government guns he had with him. Several Government guns had been left at the Canal bridge of Jooan. (They were perhaps being conveyed by the Canal?) The Chattaree man had taken them (it was said by the late Collector's orders?), and had mounted and put them in order. There was also one cannon sunk at Bhumbola (by the Lall Diggee), which he had taken. It was these guns Ghous Mahomed demanded. Reply had not yet been received. [Marginal note by Mr. Colvin, Lt.-Governor: "A Secy.'s perwanah may go to Mahomed Alee Khan of Chattaree, saying that his conduct will be well remembered and rewarded hereafter if he resists all efforts to entangle him in the plots of rebels."] **Mahommed Alee Khan of Chattaree.**

Moulvee Abdool Jaleel had come in from Chattaree and joined the public prayers. It was not known what his politics were. (He is a learned Moulvee who has hitherto held aloof **Moulvee Abdool Jaleel.**

[1] Post runner. [2] Footmen. [3] Sweeper.

from politics and the society of Europeans: he is a bigoted Moslem.)

Ghous Mahomed has ordered the Fort to be dug up, in hopes of finding treasure.

There is at present no Tehseeldar of Eglass. The Chowbey says his young brother Dhunput Roy is prepared to proceed from Hatrass and take charge of it. (This might be approved.) [Mr. Colvin's marginal note—Approved.]

Mahommed Alee, Tehsildar of Coel.

Mahommed Alee, Tehseeldar of Coel, came over here with Watson. He writes to say that after the fight, not finding himself able to get into the Fort, he left Agra, and took refuge with the Moorsam Rajah, by whom he has been kindly received. He states that large parties of Sowars without horses, and Sepoys without arms, are travelling to their homes from Dehli eastwards, both by the Canal "Putree"[1] and the main road. Also on 21st and 22nd many troops making off westward (to Dehli, or home) from the Cawnpore discomfiture. [Marginal note by Mr. Colvin: "Answer Mahomed Ali, Tehseeldar of Coel, approving his having joined the Moorsam Rajah. Tell him to send constant information. A magistrate will be appointed to Allygurh at an early proper time. About Maulvi Abdool Jalil, see the note with this. 3rd."]

Moorsan Rajah.

Sowars and Sepoys travelling to their homes.

"Adulpoora" Risala.

The "Adulpoora" Risala (?) arrived in Coel on the 25th, and was breaking up and going to its home.

Little Khureef being sown. Suggests that Mr. Cocks be sent back to Coel as Magistrate, as he knows the district.

The Chowbey suggests that a notification be printed for the town giving a statement of the Futtehpore and Cawnpore victories. [Marginal note by Mr. Colvin: "This might not do good: the facts are perfectly well known already."] Sham Behari Lall, Nazir of Etawah (his brother is head writer to Dinka Rao), writes that the troops are still stopped by the Maharaja from going to Agra or Dehli, but the position of affairs becomes daily more difficult.

Troops stopped by Maharajah from going to Agra or Delhi.

4th August, Tuesday.—Jewa Ram, a Mahajunee Cossid, left Furruckabad on the 31st; says that the Nawab's younger brother left Furruckabad the day before for Mohamdabad on the Bewar road, about 15 miles from Furruckabad, with 500 new levies, with the object of arranging for the collection of the revenue. The military force was left at Furruckabad, consisting of two Seetapore "pultuns."

Refugee officers from Farakhabad.

Twelve Sahibs in one boat left Furruckabad the day the Fort was vacated, and are said to be at a village called

[1] The made road along the canal bank.

Dhurumpore. A gentleman with three ladies and two children, eight and five years old, said to have left in a smaller boat which grounded on a bank near Furruckabad and was destroyed by the Nawab's orders by guns. Refugees' boat destroyed.

Ikram Hoosain says that one hundred and five Sowars and ten Sepoys of the Saugor force passed through Phuppoond on the 26th of July, and plundered the Treasury of Rs. 3142. Saugor Sepoys plunder Treasury.

The main body of the "Saugor and Nagode" force, 700 Sepoys, expected soon, and likely to pass through Etawah.

The Coolies who brought Mohun Loll's letters of the 29th of July from Malagurh states that some ten (?) days ago an action took place between the Malagurh troops and Mr. Turnbull with some Europeans. The Malagurh entrenchment at Hauper was forced. Ten or twenty Sowars killed, and ten or twenty fled wounded to Malagurh. The entrenchments were abandoned. The Nawab was in his fort during the fight; when the fugitives arrived he fled to Khanpoor. Attack on Malagarh. Nawab flees.

5th August, Wednesday.—Teeka Ram, messenger from Allahabad says:—Two of our Sikh messengers were blown from guns by Nawab Raees because letters found on them. British Sikh messengers destroyed.

Says the Rajah (Ranee ?) of Tirooa (Chowdrain) has mounted twenty guns on her fort, and fires them off; has collected a large force in fear of the Rajah of Mynpooree. Rajah of Tirooa.

Came by Sirsa Gunge, where the Bhudooria Rajah has brought over 600 Sowars and (he hears) 4 guns. Does not know his object. Bhudooria Rajah.

. . . .

6th August, Thursday.—Jay Kishen Doss writes from Hatrass that the rebel Governor of Allygurh has issued a proclamation forbidding any Hindoo to leave the place. If they do, their property will be attached, and house confiscated. The salary of the rebel officials is to be levied from the town. Aligarh in hands of rebels.

The Chuttara Talookdar has been threatened with removal from his Talooka if he will not send his guns; another Talookdar will be appointed. Chuttaree Talookdar.

Tekum Singh has also been written to for guns, and to pay up his revenue. Tikum Singh.

When European troops come a holy war is threatened. A Thannahdar has been appointed to Akrabad, on the Cawnpore road, half-way to Secundra Rao.

The Canongoes have been desired to give up their Dufters. They say they have none. They have been threatened with having their houses plundered and burned. The Canongoes threatened.

Tehseeldars are immediately to be appointed.

No news or messenger on Meerut side.

The Tehseeldar asks what he should do if Eglass is attacked by a rebel Tehseeldar.

The Chowbey recommends two perwanas to be issued—one to Gir Pershad Singh, Talookdar of Beiswa, about five miles from Eglass, desiring him to help in maintaining the security of the road, and in preserving the Tehseelee records. [Marginal note by Mr. Muir: "Issued by Lieutenant-Governor's permission."] Another to Thakoor Bulram Singh, Talookdar of Kujroul, with similar instructions;—in both, the pleasure of the Lieutenant-Governor being promised if they exert themselves.

Rooder and Todar Singh, Talookdars.

(A report that Rooder and Todar Singh, Talookdars in that quarter, have gone to pay their respects to the Naib Sooba.)

Jay Kishen Doss of Hatrass reports an affair at Bagow, the villagers of which came to the Tehseelee to complain of the excesses of Motee Ahirya. The Tehseeldar went with a force and guns. Motee had fled from Bagow; but opposed him from a neighbouring village, Suthroulee. There was a fight: by the help of the guns he was dislodged. One Ahirya and two others killed, and the Ahirya houses burned. Motee was joined by Bhugwunt, a Rajpoot who opposed Capt. Alexander.

Motee Ahirya.

Bhugwunt, a Rajpoot.

Sahib Singh, Naib Sheristahdar of Allygurh, reports that in consequence of the excesses of the rebel Government at Allygurh he has been obliged to take refuge at Hatrass. The Naib Sooba has assessed a lac of rupees on the Hindoos and Government officials as Nuzerânah and fine.

Rebel action at Aligarh.

7th August 1857, *Friday.*—Letter from Hatrass, from Jay Kishen Doss.—Ghous Mahomed is growing in his pretensions. He has now raised 2500 followers; has established posts in the district; is taking engagements to pay from the Zemindars, and has already realised Rs. 2000 in one day. The bad characters will rally round him.

Ghaus Mahomed growing in his pretensions.

Tekum Singh got a letter from Ghous Mahomed to the following effect:—Refers to his appointment by Walee Dad Khan. States having commenced to put the district in order; take "ikrarnamehs" from the Zemindars and collect revenue; remarks on the ancient faithfulness of Tekum Singh to the royal house, etc., and desires him to arrange for putting the people of Luguswan in order who are plundering. Promises favour of King.

Attempts to seduce Tikum Singh.

Tekum Singh has asked the Tehseeldar what reply he should

give, and was advised to acknowledge receipt of the letter and say that a reply would be sent hereafter.

(The Chowbey says, with 40 Europeans and 2 guns he would engage to bring in Ghous Mahomed in 2 days. Tekum Singh and Gobind Singh would help, and the villagers generally. He says that he will daily grow in power; that Wuleedad Khan began in the same way; and being left alone, gradually gained in power. Ghous Mahomed has nothing yet to oppose us: his raw levies would fly at the first report of an attack from Agra.)

Letter from Moradabad dated 29th July. The Nawab makes good arrangements in the city, but not in the district.

Fight in Moradabad.

There had been a fight in Moradabad between the Moslems of the town and the Pathans from the Nawab. One of the former had been killed, and they, aided by the Rajpoots of Kathgurh, rose on the house of the uncle of the Nawab (the present Governor), with the intent of killing him. He sent for the Cazee Mahomed Abbas, Chowbey Girdharee Lall (brother of our Chowbey), and Ray Purdhuman Kishen—who appeased the insurgents.

Cazee Mahomed Abbas, Chowbey Girdharee Lall, and Ray Purdhuman Kishen appease the insurgents.

Our Chowbey believes Mujeedooddeen Ahmed Khan ("oorf" Majoo Khan [1]) to have been concerned in getting up the tumult. (He was the man set up when the Bareilly troops passed through.)

Mujoo Khan.

Nothing from Gwalior.

8th August, Saturday.—Still nothing from Gwalior or Dholpore. Six days ago all was still *in statu quo.* (Sherer mentions in letter of 1st a rumour that the Gwalior troops were going to Cawnpore *via* Calpee. I have never heard this report here.)

Moulvee Ikbal Alee.

Rampore.—Moulvee Ikbal Alee (brother of the late Ameer Ali Sheristahdar of Judge's court) has a letter from Rampore, 6 days old. (The Chowbey had the contents of this letter told to him. He could not vouch for the accuracy of the following till he had seen, which he hopes to do to-night, and to bring it here to-morrow.)

The account is that the Nawab of Rampore was killed; and the son of Mehndee Ali Khan, son-in-law of the previous Nawab, put on the Guddee. Calb Ali Khan (son of the present or deceased Nawab) has gone off with 500 Sowars on the pretence of going to Dehli; but probably to repair to Meerut, and there plead his cause. 500 Pathans said to have gone to Momdea (in the Bazpore Pergunah) to cut off supplies to Nynee Tal.

[1] *i.e.* commonly so called.

Allygurh.—The Taloukdar of Dutaolee (one of the two who have been charged with the care of Allygurh), in an Urzee of the 2nd (?), offers to take the charge of the Pergunah of Akberabad. He has been told to do so, and if possible to reinstate the Tehseeldar at Akberabad; if unable to do so, to keep him at Dutaolee.

Nawab of Farakhabad.

Furruckabad.—A man who has come up the Grand Trunk Road reports that the Nawab of Furruckabad has sent on his force towards Cawnpore, and that it had reached Jelalabad. (They have probably effected a junction with the Saugor force, which Sherer says had marched within 10 miles of Cawnpore, killed a Thanahdar, and broken a bridge and gone off towards Furruckabad.)

Nawab of Malagarh.

Malagurh.—A messenger from Dunlop passed by Malagurh;—says the Nawab has returned there from Khanpore; that he has now a small force again at Malagurh, where messengers are searched; also a small force and Goojurs at Bolundshuhur.

Chowdhri Puddum Singh keeps order at Khurja. Somna.

At Khoorja the Chowdhri, Puddum Singh, has organised a force of 2000 men, and keeps order for us. Also the Talookdars of Somna, at Somna.

The "Naib Sooba" has a Chowkee between Allygurh and Sassna, but nothing on this side.

Reported seizure of messengers.

A messenger of ours with despatches said to be seized at Malagurh, and two at Allygurh; they have been imprisoned, and are to be sent to Dehli.

Tirohan men loyal.

Tirohan Banda.—Mr. Reade has shown a note from the agent of the Tirohan men, which is indicative of their loyalty. It is from Radha Gobind Pundit (?) to Bheiron Pershad (Muhurrir of Man Roy, Sudder Vakeel), dated 28th. July, in reply to a letter of the 16th. By Commissioner's permission he has entertained men to keep the country quiet, in Pergunahs Budowsa, Tirohan, Mhow, and Kumasun. . . . Says most of the "Agenti"[1] Rajas against us.

Rajputana chiefs said to be mostly inimical.

(His agent promises large monetary assistance, on things getting a little quieter.)

9th August 1857, *Sunday, Moradabad.*—A letter received from Moradabad, dated 1st inst. All right there;—which throws doubt on the Rampore news of yesterday.

[1] Under the Political Agent.

Dholpore.—A man from Dholpore says there are only ten boats at the Kantra Ghat, and seven at the Raj Ghat. (Dholpore—three coss below the other.) Raj Hans, Goojur, ravages villages; the Hurkara said by the Rana's order. No intelligence of movement, Gwalior. Kharee very high;—one boat. At Jajow the Ootangun is liable to rise and fall; it is crossed by a "ghunneye" of earthen pots. Ferries on Chumbal. Raj Hans, Goojur.

Furruckabad.—Statement of Raja Ram, Sub-overseer, under Lieutenant Monckton, Engineers, Mynpoory:—On the 3rd June, on an alarm being given, a party left Furrackabad by boat, consisting of Mr. and Mrs. Monckton and child, Mr. and Mrs. Maclean and children, the Reverend J. Walsh, and two other families. In all, 25 to 30 persons. There were other boats that left and took refuge at Dhurmpore, but the above boat went on and never returned. Mutiny at Farakhabad. British refugees leave Farakhabad: Mr. and Mrs. Monckton, Mr. and Mrs. Maclean, Rev. J. Walsh. Refugees at Dhurmpore.

After the Civil Officers had left, Colonel Smith took the arrangements of the District into his own hands, gave all establishments—Military, Revenue, Judicial, Sudr, and Mofussil—two months' pay. Everything went on as usual, and the excitement passed off. Colonel Smith.

At last the Seetapore Regiments appeared on the opposite side of the river. They consisted of the "Dobaee" Pultun and a "Galla" Pultun, and five troops of Irregular Cavalry. They remained some three days, and were then invited over by the Nawab. Seetapore Regiments appear.

The 10th Native Infantry now went wrong. The guard on the jail refused to allow a Hindoo, who had been condemned, to be hung; and the Officers, distrusting the Regiment, and finding at last on the representation of the Soobahdar that it was quite mutinous and that their lives were endangered, went into the Fort. It was the next morning after this that the Seetapore troops crossed over. All the Zillah Sowars, mostly Mahomedans, went over to the Nawab with the cry of "Deen, Deen." The Nawab sent a deputation of them to call over the Seetapore troops. Two Companies of the 10th and a Soobahdar went early the next morning after the defection to the Nawab and placed him on the Guddee, firing a royal salute—22 guns. The 10th Native Infantry mutiny. Zillah Sowars mutiny. Nawab placed on the Guddee.

The Seetapore men wanted to have a share in the treasure. The 10th refused, so they fought—(that was the day after they crossed—when a few men still remained to cross over). The quarrel was on the parade: five or six men were killed. The 10th then ran off into the country villages, etc., carrying off the 10th N.I. and Seetapore troops quarrel.

treasure; but the Seetapore troops managed to get some of it also.

Bungalows burned and plundered. Then the bungalows were burned and plundered for three days.

Kaley Khan, loyal havildar, murdered, with three Sikhs. Only one Sepoy, Kaley Khan, a Havildar, accompanied them into the Fort. He was put to death by the Nawab on the 31st ultimo, with three Sikhs who were caught carrying letters for Agra at Goorsahaegunj.

Raja Ram hid himself; but was subsequently put in prison, as knowing English, from the 2nd to the 31st of July.

Fort evacuated. On the 23rd June the Fort was evacuated by the Officers, as they had no more ammunition.

Party of refugees caught. One of the boats grounded, and the party was caught and brought to the Fort. Mr. Sutherland and a grown-up son were beheaded. Mrs. Sutherland and Mrs. Jones were brought in prisoners, with two children of Mrs. Sutherland (one a girl of 12 or 14 years, and another a little child), with a child of Mrs. Jones, who was wounded by a bullet in the hand; also a child of Mrs. Hine (?)—the two last five or six years old. Eighteen days after, the Fort was evacuated (12th July). All these *Thirty-four Christian persons blown away from guns.* and some Christians, 34 persons in all, were blown away from guns. Both Mrs. Jones and Mrs. Sutherland he saw when himself in confinement in the Nawab's Fort; they were wounded in their attempts to get away from the Fort. Their boat grounded and they were taken.

The Officers fought for 11 days, till the 23rd, when, their ammunition failing, they went away in three boats;—one was *Colonel and others said to have escaped.* that above mentioned. In another boat was the Colonel and several others:—they got off. The boatmen say they took them *Hurdeo Buksh of Dhurmpore receives refugees.* down to Futtehpore, where they joined our army. The third boat was taken in by Hurdeo Buksh to Dhurmpore. It *Lieutenant Rose and Mr. Lowis.* contained Lt. Rose and Mr. Lowis. Does not know the other names. Is not aware if Mr. Thornhill was in it, but very *W. Edwards, C.S.* probably was. The Collector and Mr. Edwards of Budaon had already left on the 3rd.

Ahmed Yar Khan and Ashraf Khan of Mhow assist the Nawab with a levy of Bangash Pathans. When the Seetapore troops came over, Ahmed Yar Khan and Ashraf Khan, Zemindars of Mhow, repaired to the assistance of the Nawab with 500 or 600 Pathans, all of the Bungash connection.

Tehsildars take service with the rebel Nawab. After the Fort was evacuated, Mahomed Tukee, Tehseeldar of Chibramow, was appointed Musahib of the Nawab; and Hidayet Ali, Tehseeldar of Mohamdabad, his Dewan. Gholam Ali, Thannahdar of Mohamdabad, appointed Cotwal of the City.

Akbal Ali, our Cotwal, had fled, saying he would not assist

in procuring ammunition against his old masters. Gholam Ali, the new Cotwal, sought out ammunition throughout the City, forced labour for them, and greatly assisted the Pathans in every way, and fought with them against the Fort.

Mahomed Tukkee, Tehsildar of Chibramow. Hidayet Ali, Tehsildar of Mohamdabad. Gholam Ali, Thannahdar of Mohamdabad. Akbar Ali, Cotwal, flees. Thannahdars take service with the rebel Nawab. Nawab Ahmed Yar Khan appointed Nazim. Revenue defaulters shot from guns. Nawab's force.

The Nawab issued orders maintaining all the Tehseeldars and Thannahdars in their posts. Mahomed Syud, Thannahdar of Chibramow, was made Tehseeldar of Canou; Khoorshad Ali, Thannahdar of Canouj, made Thannahdar of Mohamdabad. Tufuzzool Hoossain Khan, Thannahdar of Kumalgunge, and the Thannahdar of Mirutpore, continued at their posts under the Nawab. On the 1st inst. Nawab Ahmed Yar Khan, Pathan of Mhow, was appointed Nazim, and deputed to Mohamdabad to make the collection of revenue. Defaulters imprisoned and shot from guns. The Nawab has about 4000 men, including say 1500 Cavalry, of which some are runaways from Cawnpore; and intend fighting.

On the 1st, hearing that there might be an attack by some Officers from Oudh, he sent a gun and 100 men to all the large ghats, and a gun and 50 men to the smaller ones. At Khodagunj bridge he posted 2 guns and 200 men.

G. Probyn, C.S. W. Edwards, C.S. Major Robertson. Mr. Lowis.

Mr. Probyn's Khansaman was sent from Dhurmpore to buy supplies for his master at Furruckabad; told him there were at Dhurmpore 16 or 17 persons well taken care of. He mentioned Mr. Probyn, Edwards, Major Robertson, who had been wounded, and Mr. Lowis.

Sheo Pershad, former Tehseeldar of Ayrwa (lately dismissed by us), appointed Tehseeldar of Mohamdabad. Mousum Ally Khan, Pathan of Shumsabad, with a body of his kin from that place, it was intended to send to Meerunkee Serai.

Rajah Ram liberated.

Mahomed Tukkee, who got Raja Ram liberated, told him this while he was in prison.

Amlah generally continued in service.

The amlah generally continued in service under the Nawab. Bisharut Ally continued Sheristahdar.

Alee Ahmed was appointed Tehseeldar of Chibramow. Does not know if he was formerly in Govt. service.

Havelock's force.

10*th August*.—The party who brought Havelock's letter of the 3rd says that he was with the camp.

Havelock's movements.

Havelock was at Mungurwar on the 28th, Wednesday. On the 29th he marched to Onao, where the first battle was fought; then to Wuzeergunge, three coss on, where a second was fought, and where he encamped the night of the 29th. Next day he marched back to Onao, and on the 31st to Mungurwar.

Mungurwar .	3 coss from Cawnpore;	21 from Lucknow.
Onao . .	5 „	19 „
Wuzeergunge .	8 „	16 „

Cawnpore road.

A messenger from Cawnpore says he met at Meerun Kee Serae 200 Cavalry (Abu Nundee ?) in white clothing, and 250 to 300 Infantry unarmed, going towards Cawnpore. They search our messengers closely.

Rebellious action of Mahmoud Khan, the Nawab of Nujeebabad.

11*th August, Bijnore.*—Letter from Bijnore dated the 13th July, from Shimboo Nath to Kunhya Lall, states that Mahmoud Khan, the Nawab of Nujeebabad, is engaging a large force of deserted Mutineers (perhaps some of the deserters from Dehli go there). He appoints Deputy Collectors, Joint Magistrates, etc., and has proclaimed that the kingdom is the King's.

The Collector on his departure cast 92,000 rupees into a well. The Nawab intends getting them out.

Rajah Tikum Singh.

Coel, Moorsan.—It is said that Nuseemoollah, formerly Sudr Vakeel, is about to be deputed by Ghous Mahomed to attend on Tekum Singh at Moorsan. (The copy of Ghous Mahomed's letter to Tekum Singh is put in this book.[1] Tekum Singh should have written to Government direct about it. He consulted with Jay Kishen Doss, but that is not enough. But we may perhaps wait a little till calling him to account.)

Proposals of Jaykishen Das.

Jay Kishen Doss desires to seize Nuseemoollah if he comes that way. (I suppose he may be told to do so.)

He says he could engage with the Jats, especially the man Luguswan, to rise on Ghous Mahomed and expel his whole tribe from Coel in a day—only, it would probably involve the sack of Coel.

Moonsiff of Hatrass asks for his pay.

The Moonsiff of Hatrass (—?), Behari Lall, is anxious to get his pay. Neither he nor establishment have been paid since April; 140 Rs. a month—560 Rs. now due. Jay Kishen Doss could help him with at least a subsistence allowance. Shall this be done?

Jay Kishen Doss says the Zemindar of Beiswan has asked back his gun which now guards Hatrass. The Tehseeldar has been told to say it must stay where it is.

Sheikh Kheiroolla, Cotwal of Hatrass, goes for two weeks on sick-leave. Lota Kunhya Lall, brother of the Moonsiff, appointed by Jay Kishen Doss to act.

Tehseeldar of Eglass applies for another.

[1] Copy of Persian letter gummed in here, to the effect noted, with the following note:—"Copy of Ghous M.'s letter to Rajah Tekum Singh," 11/8 (August). (No date.)

Dehli.—A Brahmin who left Dehli last Monday, the 2nd, says two proclamations were issued in the City. First, that two guns had been captured from the picket at the Nujjufgurh bridge; second, that 12,000 men were coming to assist the King as Crusaders from Mooltan.

Proclamations issued in city.

It is also said that bodies of the Mutineer troops had gone out in parties to stop the British supplies.

Gwalior.—Nothing new from Gwalior.

Two men came five days ago from Pirbhoo Lall, Naib Sir-Sooba there, and report all quiet and as usual.

Bolundshuhur.—Raham Ali, Khan of Khailya, Bolundshuhur (son of Muzhur Alee, Tehseeldar ?), sent 3 guns to Wullee Dad Khan. Has a Thannah in Shikarpore and Debaee. When he heard of the discomfiture he turned them back.

12*th August, Wednesday.*—A Harkara from Oojein passed through Gwalior five days ago; found all quiet. The Indore troops had come up, intending to go on; but were taken into pay by the Gwalior Maharajah.

Indore troops taken into pay by the Gwalior Maharajah.

The Bhurtpore Vakeel says his master's Vakeel at Gwalior writes that the mutinous troops were desired by the M. R. to go towards Cawnpore; if they did that he would give them a couple of pultuns, carriage, etc., to go. But they refused, and said they would go only towards Agra—which the Maharajah refused, saying he would give neither carriage nor troops nor officer to go with them; so nothing is fixed. Such communications are frequent.

13*th August.*—Phillipps' man:—Three days ago the Mutineers were all quiet at Gwalior—only 17 boats.

Reported operations against Naini Tal.

A messenger from Rampore states that Khan Buhadur has sent 3000 men and two to four guns to Huldwanee against Nynie Tal. K. B. Khan has entertained some of the Lucknow or Cawnpore Sowars.

14*th August, Etawah.*—On the 7th, 150 Sowars of the 3rd Risala from Saugor and Calpee came towards Etawah.

150 of the Nana's Sowars were going to cross the Jumna, when they were plundered by Rampershad the Dacoit; and retained by the Oreya people for their defence.

Rampershad the Dacoit plunders Nana's Sowars.

Lucknow. *15th August, Saturday.*—Letters to Muhajuns from Lucknow of the 4th inst. speak of all being right there, though surrounded by 50,000 malcontents.

Gwalior. Gwalior all right 2 days ago.

Pearee Loll, Tehseeldar of Khyr, was hurried back by the Coel people on his way here.

Rebel administration at Coel, etc. Ameer Buksh appointed by the N. Soobah to the Thannah at Jooan. Oomra Loll to Somna. Hoossain Khan, Mewattee, Cotwal of Coel. Ghous Khan, Naib ditto. Muhboob Khan of Dak establishment, to be Tehseeldar of Coel.

Hoossein Khan (tasha nawees) to be Peshkar.

The existent establishment of Chuprassies and Mirdahs generally maintained. Hindoo Zemindars called on to pay. The Mussulmans are carrying off the plundered property to Dullaolee, Julala, etc. They have generally sent their women out of the way.

Moorteza Khan, Duffadar of Nujeebs (he had been formerly imprisoned by Watson), with his brother Ghous Khan, has carried plundered property to Dullaolee.

Nawab Dooleh has been appointed Tehseeldar of Atroulee; but for the present looking after the levies.

A supply of balls, landed by the canal, is at Shekha. The Naib Sooba has sent carts for them.

Mr. Watson's carpets, etc., were in a certain village; he has sent for them.

Oomra Buhadur, son of Muzhur Ally, and adopted by the late Nawab Ashraf Khan, who had large estates in Noh Jheel, appointed to office.

Nusroollah Khan, Deputy Collector, summoned to Delhi by the King. The King has summoned Nusroollah Khan, Deputy Collector, from Khoorja to Dehli by a Firman.

KASHEE PERSHAD'S ACCOUNT OF REBELLION IN DEHLI

Statement of Kashee Pershad, formerly Vakeel of the Nawab of Jhujjur—for the last four or five years a resident trader in saltpetre, etc., here in Agra.

Left Agra early in March for his health, and went to Dehli. Lived at Huzaree-Goolzara (Cazee Houz Ka Mohulla), near the Ajmeerie Gate. Was caught at Dehli by the outbreak, and obliged to stay. When the cannonading became severe he left it for the Chawara Mohulla behind the great Mosque. Stayed there the rest of the time with Kunheya Lall.

The City was perfectly quiet and unconscious of the coming commotion till nine o'clock on Monday the 11th May. We knew that there had been discontent and burning of bungalows at Umballa, but we had no conception that any outbreak would take place at Meerut. Rode out on horseback as usual in the morning,—all was as usual. **Commencement of Mutiny.**

A little after nine there was a rush of people from the City. This I observed three times. The third rush was about ten. I had fancied it was the escape of some elephant, etc.; but the third time I enquired what it was, and they replied that there was fighting behind them. Up to that moment I had no idea anything unusual was going on.

About half-past ten a great crowd was seen moving towards the place where I lived. In front of it was a gentleman galloping rapidly along, waving a naked sword. He was going as from the Fort or Mosque in the direction of the Ajmeerie Gate, which had been shut by the Sepoys. They opened it for him and he rode out. It was said to be Sir T. Metcalfe. A little after two Sowars, one with a pistol and torn clothes, the other with a spear, rode up enquiring where the gentleman had gone; and they pursued after him. **Sir T. Metcalfe.**

Afterwards crowds upon crowds of Sowars, Sepoys, and Citizens passed by. The people were in consternation,—the shops shut. The Sepoys and Cavalry men were searching for the English as their victims.

Subsequently I heard that the Cavalry had first crossed the bridge and plundered the Toll-box there. Then they came to the Palace, and demanded admission to the King, who hastily summoned the Killadár, Captain Douglas. Captain Douglas sent to say he was undressed, but the King desired him to come quickly as he was, so he went. Meanwhile the Cavalry men were warned off from the apartment where the King was,—it being private;—but they didn't mind the remonstrance of the Guards, and forced their way in. **Occurrences at Palace.** **Captain Douglas.**

The Cavalry on their arrival opposite the Palace first killed Chimman Lall, the Christian Sub-Assistant Surgeon. Then they met four gentlemen in buggies, and shot them; one of their own number (Narain Singh) being killed. Mr. Fraser at that moment arrived at the gate, went in, tried to shut the gate, but from the crowd he could not succeed. He reached the stairs, but was killed there after defending himself with his pistol and gun. He had called on the King to bring out his guns. **Chimman Lall killed.** **Mr. Fraser killed.**

Douglas was upstairs. He called Ahsun-oolla Khan Hakeem

Captain Douglas and ladies killed.

to take care of the ladies; and he placed them in a position of safety. They were all killed.

Then the whole City was in an uproar,—shops closed, fighting, etc.

King put on throne.

About twelve the Rebels put the King on the throne, and they led Mirza Moghul, his son, through the City to restore confidence.

The King told the Rebels he was a mere Pensioner, couldn't help them in any way, or pay them. They replied that he was not to mind; they didn't want pay, etc.

When the tumult was first heard the Officers ordered out the Regiments, but when they were drawn up some of the rebel Cavalry appeared. The Regiments were desired to fire on them. They fired, but high. An Officer fired a pistol at a Cavalry man, but was killed in the scuffle. Then the Regiments told their Officers to go. All who went away got off; those who made any opposition were seized or killed.

Regiments mutiny.

The Officers at the Main Guard were said to be blown from guns by the troops.

Magazine blown up.

About 4 p.m. the Magazine was blown up. Five or six hundred men were killed or wounded. At night the bungalows were burnt.

Tuesday the 12th, the railway bungalow was burned.

On that day a "pultun" came, and was quartered at the Ajmeerie Durwaza, at the Madrassa (College) inside it. It was one of the Dehli "pultuns." Next day it was changed for another "pultun." At the Dehli Durwaza the "Alexander Pultun"[1] was quartered.

Then Companies began to come in from Coel, Mynpoorie, etc. The Bazaars were sometimes shut, sometimes open. They were sometimes plundered on the imputation of harbouring English Officers. All such Officers, Half-castes, etc., were murdered. Hoosen Bukhsh, Punjaubee Saudagur (merchant), was suspected and plundered.

English and Eurasians murdered.

It was noised abroad that an Officer was concealed in the Seeta Ram Bazaar, and search was made; he put on the clothes of a Cashmerie Brahmin and walked forth. He came in the direction where I was, and I saw him, a fine noble-looking fellow. He was suspected and challenged. The Sepoys pressed him to disclose the names of the persons who had concealed him, but he bravely refused, saying, "Kill me if you like; I am not a Company's Officer; I am in the service of Jheend,—shoot me if

[1] Probably "Sikander ka Pultun," or "Skinner's Horse."

you like,—ask Rummun." His bearing excited admiration. They shot him.

Next day they attacked Rummun (Mohun Lall), and plundered his house. He was only saved by the son of Kalu Sahib (Nizam Ooddeen) and his carter, who protested he was no traitor, but a good converted Hindoo. When Wullee Dad Khan went to Malagurh, Mohun Lall went with him. He is said to be friendly to the English. Mohun Lall plundered.

Wullee Dad Khan came to the King to get a Soobah,[1] and he returned to Malagurh with the appointment. He has been guilty of the greatest treachery of all against the British Government—having a Jagheer, etc. King appoints Wali Dad Khan to be Soobah.

When tidings came of an English force being at Ghazeeabad, troops went out from Dehli to oppose them. The second time they were accompanied by Abu Bakr, the King's son, Captain of the Cavalry. Abu Bakr.

They were completely beaten, and Dehli was then in such a fright that if the Europeans had come upon the City then, it could not have offered any resistance. Rebels defeated.

After that the Europeans came to the heights outside Dehli, and there was fighting every two or three days. Then the shells began to fall thick in the City, and the distress has been indescribable. It is the greatest mercy I escaped. Distress in city.

The Dehli troops are ordinarily pitched from the old Killa towards Bullubgurh to the City; and from the Dehli to the Ajmere Gate. The wounded were at first put in our Dispensary, then in any large house they came across;—for any such purpose they turn the occupants unceremoniously out.

The Meerut and Dehli troops are in the Fort and Palace. There is no room for any others there.

There was a guard of Sepoys over the alley in which I lived. I got off with the greatest difficulty. I saw Elahee Buksh, the present Jhujjur Vakeel, at Fureedabad. He said he had left with permission, and sick,—he is now better. He had been very ill.

At three places on the road here the Zemindars deserve credit for their good arrangements—Bunchara (2 coss beyond Hodul), Kosee (though the Zemindars there take money for their protection), and at Chatta. Loyal Zemindars at Bunchara, Kosee, and Chatta.

The Sepoys have a great jealousy of any one who is suspected of in any way assisting the English.

They plunder the Bazaars, but never without some pretext of that nature. Thus with Alopee Pershad and Ror Mull Khutrees.

[1] Territorial command.

A Cafila was going to Benares; one of the number, Bishan Pershad, an old Tehseeldar of ours, was seized in it, and certificates in English found on him. He appealed to Alopee Pershad; and without enquiry they forthwith proceeded to Alopee Pershad, and plundered him and some twenty others in the same neighbourhood.

Temper of inhabitants.

Only a small part of Dehli is actively disaffected to the English. But it is now full of bad and reckless characters who have flocked to it from without.

Bukht Khan, leader.

Bukht Khan is now the leader; he was in the Artillery. Was originally in Dehli. Transferred some time ago to Bareilly, and came back in command of the mutinous troops.

Before he came each Soobahdar managed his own Regiment. But after his arrival the King's order was to follow his command. But they disliked his interference, and used to obey him only when ordered to attack. They were subsequently, on the Nusseerabad battalion joining, divided into four divisions. First Nusseerabad, second Bareilly, and two others. The Neemuch battalion formed a fifth.

Five battalions.

Bakr-Eed Festival.

Cow-killing prohibited.

Three days before the Bacr-Eed Festival, Bukht Khan went to the King and told him it would be advisable to prohibit the Moslems from killing cows. He produced a Futwa. Proclamation was made accordingly. The Sepoys were, besides, engaged in fighting on the Eed and for two days before, and were wearied out, so the Festival passed off quietly.

Six butchers were arrested,—they were carrying a Guhwara or funeral bier to the burial-ground. It was examined, and butcher's meat found in it, which it was supposed they were taking to our camp. The Sepoys killed five, and one fled. It was after this that cow-killing was prohibited.

Two Bheesties were killed for being on the road to our camp with their mussuks filled with sugar.

King's sons appointed to command of regiments.

The King's sons were originally appointed nominally to the command of Regiments.

King's altercations with the rebels.

The King himself has several times had altercations with the Rebels, saying that he had not called them,—that he had no territory, no money, etc., for them,—and that he had told them that from the first; and has protested that they should get him out of his troubles, take him to the Kootub, take him to Agra, anywhere; upon which the Rebels cast themselves at the King's feet, declaring themselves his slaves.

I have no doubt (says Kashee Pershad) that the original real desire of the King was as generally rumoured in the City, and as he is said to have plainly told the Rebels, that he wished to have nothing to do with them. This was his feeling at first; but it is impossible to say whether ambition and desire of regaining a position of real power for his Family may not have led to a change, and a real siding with the Rebels afterwards. King's temper.

The King keeps the Shahzadas strictly in order. Abu Bakr went, in connection with some female intrigue, to a house, and plundered the adjoining residence of the Cazee's son, Abdool Huk. On this being reported to the King he directed the Cotwal to apprehend and forward to him any of his sons who committed acts of violence, and to punish himself any of the suláteen[1] similarly apprehended. He reduced Abu Bakr from his command. King keeps the Shahzadas strictly in order.

The money brought in by the Regiments and given to the King was expended three weeks ago. The King kept it separate, and devoted it solely to their use and the purchase of ammunition. The King touched none of this for his own use; he borrowed for himself from the City bankers. At first the Regiments used to give a portion of their plundered treasure to the King as "Nuzerana." The remainder was kept each by the Regiment which brought it. King's financial arrangements.

Since the Bareilly Regiments came no money has been given to the King. The Bareilly men paid themselves six months' pay, and kept the rest for themselves. Their example has been followed by all subsequent arrivals. Troops' dealings with plundered treasure.

They make up Gunpowder, having at the manufactory enough materials at a time for a single manufacture,—perhaps to last for three or four days at the works. It is probably only this amount that was lately blown up. The main stores of material are in the Fort. Gunpowder manufactured.

Besides the Sowars from Jhujjur originally in Dehli, the Nawab on being summoned sent some 150 more. They do nothing but simply attend. They do not fight. The Nawab excused himself from attending on the King. Patoudee has helped them with "russud" (supplies) on a party going there. The Bullubgurh villages help with "russud," but not the Rajah. Correspondence was intercepted between the Rajah and us, but the Rebels are not greatly incensed with him. Bahadurgurh and the other petty States are too weak to do anything. Nawab of Jhujjur sends Sowars, but excuses himself from attending. Pataudi helped with "russud." Balabgarh villages help with "russud," but uot the Rajah.

The whole country from this towards Pulwul is quite free, and might (he thinks) be occupied by us with the smallest force. Kashee Pershad says he has had frequent opportunities Country between Agra and Palwal free.

[1] The name given to the numerous scions of the Royal Family.

of conversing with the Sepoys and others. He never could get from them any other cause of discontent than the "Cartooch" (cartridges). Nor could he hear of any correspondence between the Rebels and the King. His impression is that the King and the whole City were taken by surprise.

The "Cartooch" the cause of the Mutiny.

End of Kashee Pershad's Account.

Gwalior.

17*th August, Monday, Gwalior.*———, brother of Kedarnath; left Gwalior on Thursday. He lived in the town. Was Mohurrur in the Thannah. Left because the Maharajah reduced the pay of all establishments, as fixed by Dinker Rao, one half. The reduction takes effect from Zulcada.

Indore troops at Morar.

The Indore troops are at Morar. The Maharajah and the Contingent were angry with them for their excesses on the way up. The Maharajah also regards them as rebels against Holkar. He refused therefore to supply them with russud. They have been obliged to buy their own supplies. They have received nothing from the Durbar, and are pitched outside the Cantonment. Scindia desires them to go away, and promises to supply them with carriage, etc., but gives none. They talk of going to Dehli direct, *via* Dholpore. They consist of 1½ pultuns infantry, 600 cavalry, and about 5000 or 6000 plunderers, Ghazees, etc.

Scindia's attitude to them.

Details of Indore Mutineers.

Gwalior Contingent.

The Gwalior Contingent stays in its cantonment and declares itself faithful to the Maharajah, and ready to obey his commands. It is satisfied with the pay and largesses it has received.

The troops perform no regular exercises. Only at night they post artillery round the camp for its protection. They have sold all their English articles, accoutrements, etc., by auction.

The Maharajah has issued proclamations to stop all the "melas," and all congregation of people at the Mohurrum. Only a few have been allowed to prepare Tazeas.[1]

The 4th Irregular Cavalry.

18*th August, Secundra Rao.*—Two troops of the 4th Irregular Cavalry, Oudh, passed through Secundra Rao on their way to Allygurh, in great confusion,—some on foot, some on tats,[2] some on horses. They appeared in great distress. They said that Mr. Watson, their commander, was safe in the Beleeguard at

Mr. Watson.

[1] Models (generally of bamboo and paper work) of the Tomb of Hassan and Hosein, publicly paraded in towns and villages on the great day of the Mohurrum, and buried with ceremony outside the walls of the town or village. This is the chief public religious ceremony of Islam in the Mahommedan year.—W. C.

[2] Ponies.

Lucknow; that the Oudh troops had been beaten;—that Wajid Ally's youngest son was put on the "guddee"[1] at Lucknow. They appeared to be part of the force discomfited on the 29th ult. They are Rohtuck Rangurs,—and have been since, it is said, engaged by Ghous Mahomed at Allygurh.

Sulah-ood-deen sends an Urzee saying that Ghous Mahomed has sent his brother, Ahmed Noor Khan, to oust him from the Thannahdarship of Secundra Rao. They are making up two guns at Secundra Rao. On the 12th, 100 Sowars of the 3rd Irregular Cavalry passed Secundra Rao going to their homes at Bolundshuhur (the same probably as lately appeared at Etawah). They came from Saugor, and said that their native officers and the "Lumbora" Pultun are staunch at Saugor.

The 3rd Irregular Cavalry.

Neeaz Ahmed, our Zillah (?) visitor, has been appointed by Ghous Mahomed Principal Sudder Ameen.

20th August, Thursday.—King has sent to Allygurh for the powder manufacturer.

23rd August, Sunday.—Mr. Phillipps' messenger from Gwalior reports that he left on Friday 21st, and that in the afternoon of that day the Mhow troops were packing their carriage—to go off to the Residency. They were discontented at not getting pay.

Sufder Ally, Wukeel Sudder, reports from Shekohabad on the 20th August:—The villagers assembled in Bharwul, 5000 with 6 guns. The Rajah (of Mynpoory) had 8000 men, 2 guns, and 300 cavalry, and posted himself at Ghiror, where he had set up a Thannah and Tehseel. The Aheers had no Sowars. The fight lasted from the morning of 18th to the evening of 19th. Nearly 400 Aheers and 100 of the Rajah's men killed. At night the Aheers fled, and about midnight began to arrive in Shekohabad with tremendous noise. The Rajah's force has not yet come to Shekohabad; he is not with it. They say they are going to destroy Bharwul and burn Shekohabad. Time not yet come for settling Mynpoory, for the Rajah has some 15,000 men. This is only intended to fight the Aheers with, after which they will disperse. The Mewattees threaten to plunder Shekohabad.

Mainpúri Rajah attacks Shekohabad.

[1] "Cushion" of the Ruler: equivalent to "throne."

Note of Available or Expected European Troops.

European troops.

Madras Fusiliers, up country.		32nd	. .	(Lucknow).
Wing—29th .	Calcutta.	5th	. .	(China) Mauritius, Mirzapore.
35th . .	do.	90th	. .	(China) coming to Allahabad or Benares.
74th Highlanders,	From Madras and Calcutta.	23rd, 82nd, 93rd	. .	China.
10th . .	Dinapore.	800 Marines, 600 of which come to Allahabad.		
53rd . .	Calcutta.			
37th . .	(Ceylon) wing.			
64th . .	Coming up.			
78th Highlanders,	Coming up.			
84th . .	Up.			

Details of troops before Delhi.

Before Dehli, 1*st September* 1857.—52nd, 60th, 61st, 75th H.M.'s and 7 Companies of the 8th, 1st and 2nd Ben. Fusiliers, 9th Lancers, squadron of Carabineers, some Rifles, Sirmoor Battalion, Kumaon Battalion, 1st and 2nd Punjab Infantry, 4th Sikh Regiment, Guide Corps, wings of the 1st and 2nd Punjab Cavalry; 6 troops of H.A.; 3 Reserve Companies (Europeans and Sikhs); 2nd and 3rd class siege trains.

Rajputs fight Nawab of Nujeebabad at Sherkot.

29*th August, Bijnore.*—Letter of 12th August, Moradabad:—Pertab Singh of Tajpoor, Tugga (son of Chowdree Jeeraj Singh), fought with Mahmoud Khan, Nawab of Nujeebabad. The fight was at Shercote; 1200 men said to be killed. The Rampore Nawab has now obtained jurisdiction in Bijnore.

Fight between Hindus and Musulmans.

From Kasheepore, dated 17th of August.—Ditto . . . (?) Tuggas in possession; they kill the Moslems. It is a fight between Hindoos and Musulmans.

Kasheepore Rajah loyal.

In Kasheepore the Rajah is holding the country for the English.

DLXVIII.

INTELLIGENCE DIARY, SEPTEMBER 1857.

Aligarh threatened.

3*rd Sept.*—1st Sept., Urzee of *Mohur Singh*, of Arama, Zillah Boolundshuhur: Writes to say that 2 guns, 1 pultun, 300 Sowars, and many Moslems are in Allygurh, ready to make an attack upon Allygurh. A man from Somna says he heard great firing.

Indore troops at Gwalior.

6*th Sept., Gwalior.*—*Kaley Khan*, coachman P.O. Department: On the 2nd, Wednesday, the Indore troops left Morar and marched to the Residency, taking their 7 guns with them.

They then broke open the godown, and began removing the things. The Maharajah hearing this, sent a large party of his own soldiers and stopped their proceedings.

On Thursday the 3rd, 300 Infantry and 300 Horse, with 2 guns, marched from the Residency, as an advance guard, to Cheounda, 9 coss from Dholepore. The guns and tumbrils drawn each by 6 horses. The rest of the force remained at the Residency. Yesterday 100 Sowars, in 2 parties, crossed the Chumbul, and marched to Dholepore; 50 would return with supplies, and the rest would select an encamping-ground for the force. March towards Dholpore.

It was reported at Gwalior that the 4th Regiment of the Contingent had sworn to join the Indore troops with a battery of guns, and that the Indore force would halt a short time at Dholépore to see whether any of the Gwalior men would join them or not. They themselves, and everybody else, said they were coming to Agra. The Sowars wore the uniform of the Company's Cavalry. The Sepoys wore no uniform. They consist partly of Company's partly of Holkar's infantry.

Kharee Nuddee . . .	10	miles from Fort.
Jujoo (Ootangun) . . .	9	„
Dholepore . . .	17 to 18	„

Only one boat on Kharee Nuddee carried away;—a ford a short distance above.

6th September, Sunday.—Huttee Singh, Meena: Was with the Indore troops when they left, having had no pay for 5 months. I went with them to the Residency on the 2nd. There was no plunder or disturbance there. They halted on Thursday, and intended to remain there 2 or 3 days in hopes of getting the Contingent to go with them. While encamped there, about 10 or 11 a.m., a letter was received from some one at Dholepore by the Nawab of Bhopal, saying that whoever came first, the British or the Rebels, would take Dholepore, the Fort, and Ghats,—that there would be no local resistance. The Nawab immediately called the Havildar-Major and Subahdar-Major (both Mussulmans) and ordered 2 Companies, 2 guns, and 2 troops and 100 of the new levies to go forward and seize the ghat and occupy Dholepore. So they set out about midday, and pitched at Cheounda, and started in the morning. The army said to the Nawab, "You have divided your force." So they marched on Friday and pitched at Cheounda. They have Indore troops at Gwalior. March of Indore troops to Dholpore.

Transport with rebel troops. about 20 carts, 30 or 35 camels, miscellaneous tatoos, no tents. Only 4 or 5 Shouldaries for the officers. In the hackeries are the cooking vessels. The ammunition is loaded in 4 or 5 **Details of their ordnance.** hackeries, and 7 tumbrils with the guns. They have 7 guns, 2 howitzers, and 5 cannon. They are Hindoostanee guns, say 9 or 12-pounders. They are drawn each by 4 pair of bullocks. They have no artillery horses.

The entire Army consists of—

Details of ebel troops.

1 pultun . . .	800 or 900	3 troops of Regular Cavalry . .	about 250
Nawab's, etc. . .	400 or 500	About 30 Golundazes altogether.	
Holkar . .	80 or 90 Sowars		

The Regular Sepoys have not all got muskets; perhaps 150 or 200 have none. I remained three days with them, and found out carefully all about them from their conversation.

I left Cheounda about 11, the troops being pitched there, and came on to Dholepore, reaching the Kentra Ghat about 3 p.m., where I found the advanced force above specified crossing in 12 boats. I could not get over, so I went round by Raj Ghat, where there are 34 boats. An order had reached for these boats to go to the Kentra Pass. I then came to Dholepore, and went to the Serai, where were two Sowars of the Guard, who said that the two guns and two Companies, etc., had all crossed but not yet reached the Fort. I left early next morning (Saturday), and reached Agra in the afternoon.

No Contingent Regiments are with them. Only a few here and there from the Cantonment Regiments joined the army on Thursday. They have no certain hopes now of the Contingent Regiments coming. They hope the 2nd and 5th will join. The 5th has gone to the bodyguard, but not yet got its pay. The Magazine of the Contingent has not been opened or touched. The Indore people say they have plenty of ammunition, but little grape. They hope to get some heavy guns at Dholepore. I saw two big guns (say 18-pounders) and 5 or 6 smaller ones there mounted.

The Ootangun is fordable, but the Kharee is deep. I crossed on a platform on earthen pots. The boat is taken away. He adds that the main force is probably crossing to-day; but that it will probably not cross entirely before the 3rd day, *i.e.* Tuesday. They will therefore not march probably till Wednesday.

7th September.—Gholam Mohamed: Left Dholepore at day-light, the 6th; two very small guns, and 250 Foot, and 80

Regular and 20 Irregular Horse; and 25 or 30 plunderers, horse-stealing Mewattees of Sont Ki Mundee. Coel and Hatrass Mewattees coming from behind. Rana and Soobah at Dholepore; son and ladies at Bara.

Demanded to burn the bungalow, and wanted ammunition and guns. Surrounded his guns—10 or 12; but let them go on the Soobah's giving them 200 Rupees and a meal to each. They are pitched at the bungalow.

Advance of mixed force on Dholpore from Gwalior.

A Jungee Sowar,—"We are going to D[ehli]." An Irregular, —"We are going to Agra." At Munniah was an Irregular horseman with 4 or 5 foot ordering supplies.

The Regular Cavalry man said, "The Morar people gave us neither guns, powder, nor shells. Scindia angry with us. We go to Dehli lest he should attack us from behind." The Morar people said, "We are going to Poorub."[1] We said, "You are Poorbeas; we are Pachanias, and will go to Pachham."[2]

. . . .

A man belonging to the Vakeel of Dholepore states that the advance guard, principally of horse, have crossed the Chumbul. The Infantry had not arrived, but were coming with small guns. The 6th Contingent will certainly accompany Holkar's Mutineers.

Mohamed Waris Khan, said to be a Shahzada from Dehli, is in command of the force. But other names also are mentioned.

They give out decidedly that they are coming to Agra. They had no opposition to their crossing the Chumbul.

The Kharee not fordable: crossed on Ghunneys.

Danee Kuhar, servant of the Chowbey's: Left this on Saturday at midday: reached Dholepore yesterday evening: left this morning very early.

Found the force (half troop and 2 companies) on this side as described by others. Stayed in the Serai. Saw the troops in the new Chownee to the west of the town.

The rest of the force is on the other side; they said there were two Regiments and two Risalas.

The Chumbul has been very high for two or three days, and they cannot cross. They will cross when the river decreases.

No Contingent troops have come, nor are they expected. The M. R. keeps them back.

The Maharajah restrains the Gwalior Contingent.

The men at Dholepore say that if the Morar troops join them they will come on to Agra, otherwise they will not come this way,—they will go elsewhere.

[1] The east. [2] The west.

Cannot say whether they may not have crossed to-day.

The Chowbey says the passage of Cossids by Dholepore is entirely cut off. Suggests a dak being opened up by Futtehabad.

8th September, 9 *a.m.*—*Ram Chunder*, of Butesur:—Left this on Saturday; reached Dholepore on Sunday evening. Left it again on Monday about 8 a.m. A number of Ghazees, etc., crossed on Saturday, besides the advance guard—four guns, 2 very small, and 2 large, have been crossed over; the two large ones are at the Chaonee, the two small ones are at the Fort:—the Sepoys said the big ones are dragged by horses, but I did not see any horses.

Details of guns with rebel troops advancing *via* Dholpore.

. . . .

They said the Contingent troops would not come till the Dussehra. They abused the Morar troops for keeping them; and the Maharajah, who, they said, had become a Christian. Some said they were going to Dehli,—some, to Agra.

On the road at Munniah I met five ekkas[1] with Mussulmans on them. They said they were going to Muthra (probably to spy out the [land]).

A Sowar with 10 or 20 "lifafas"[2] I met on the road between the Ootanghan and Kharee; he examined everybody he met, and seized papers from them. He was going to Dholepore with the envelopes.

3 *p.m.*—*Buldeo Sahae*, Randheer Patuck of the Agra Police:—Left Dholepore at gun-fire morning of 6th; saw the advance guard and 4 guns all together. Two pultuns on the other side are waiting for the bridge to be set up. They say they will not come on from Dholepore till the Morar troops come. The Indore men say they will have their Dussehra at Dholepore.

At Munniah saw 10 Sowars and a guard in a fort of the Zemindar's making preparations for supplies, etc. Also a Sowar patrolling the road, and with a lot of letters in his hands.

26*th August*,[3] *Furruckabad.*—Plenty of ammunition, but little money. Collecting a 6-anna kist.

Banda.—Narain Rao and Madho Rao, 26th August, [send letter] expressive of their fidelity. Sending elephants, etc. Refers to his Company's paper, 31 lacs.

[1] Cars. [2] Envelopes.

[3] The position of this entry (which evidently refers to the rebels in occupation), dated 26th August, between entries of 8th and 9th Sept., indicates the difficulty of communication between Agra and Furruckabad. See pp. 28–31, *ante*.—W. C.

Dholepore.—Major Macpherson's note for the 7th:—Guns possessed by Rana of Dholepore. At Dholepore, 4 or 5 small guns,—say 6-pounders. Sheregurh, do. do. Poorani Chouni, 4 miles off, 3 or 4 do. At Baree, 10 coss off, a 24-pounder, and 4 or 5 smaller, but still big guns. At Rajghat, 12 boats; at Khentri, 13.

Agra.—Kharee, 10 miles. Moonia, 8 miles.
Jajow, 9 „ Dholepore, 9 „

9th September, Midday.—Vakeel of Dholepore crossed on Saturday.

300 Sowars with 2 guns pitched in Dholepore.

400 of the Bhopal men on the Chumbul.

No one crossed on Sunday. On Monday there crossed 4 Companies, 2 guns, 1 Ghol of Vilayates, and some Sowars. These crossed notwithstanding the river was very high. Yesterday probably more crossed. On Sunday they wanted to burn the bungalow.

The messengers are obliged to go round 24 coss instead of 18, as everybody is stopped on the road.

10th September, Shekohabad.—There are only about 150 men now at Shekohabad, employed in Thannah, Tehseel, etc. The Rajah of Mynpooree left the charge of the Tehseel and Thannah in the hands of the Zemindars of Khyragurh (a set of disaffected men).

Somna.—Letter from Moonshee Salamat Raee, Deputy Collector at Somna: reports arrival of Govt. army at Haupper—2000 Jats, etc.

Khyragurh.—A perwanah was received from the Indore force appointing the Tehseeldar and Thannadar King's servants, and ordering them to appear at Jajow. **Indore force acts in the name of the King of Delhi.**

11th September, Friday.—A man of the Vakeel of Dholepore left Dholepore about 6 yesterday morning. Says all the force is now across the Chumbul—encamped on the other side of Dholepore, between Dholepore and the ghat.

They were still encamped when he left, and had made no preparations for a march. Some talked of Dehli, some of Agra. There is no officer or leader whose order is followed. Their Sowars come on to the Kharee, and prevent all comers. This **Rebel force without a leader.**

messenger got along with great difficulty. Cannot say whether any disturbance or fight may not have arisen after the messenger left. The troops commit great oppression—seizing bullocks, horses, etc., without payment. And they demand guns from the Rana. They have 7 guns,—4 are very small: one is larger, and two still larger. He says the 4 small ones are pulled by horses, the large by bullocks. They have very little ammunition. Only three tumbrils have come in.

The Rana is in his Poorani Chaoni,—2 coss off.

There are—

Details of force.

2 Pultuns.	1 Risala of Mewattees.
1000 to 1200 Cavalry.	1 „ Vilayatis.

3750 to 4000 men.

They entertain new levies.

Contingent still at Gwalior.

The Contingent still at Gwalior. 600 Sowars are at Jhara, on the other side the river, belonging to Scindia. Their object not known.

8 *a.m.*—Luchman Singh came back last night from his attempted journey to Dholepore; he got within 5 or 6 miles of Dholepore, but was obliged to turn back about 7 a.m. yesterday. I have desired him to record here a brief statement of what he saw and heard.

Luchman Singh's Statement.

[The following written in the MS. volume by Luchman Singh, Moonshee, himself]—

"On reaching Jajou I was questioned by a party of about 50 armed men, who said they were the King's policemen, and who had a Moonshee as their superior officer. They seemed to be very careful in searching for English letters; which when they did not find with me they allowed me to pass, but gave me two men to take me to a Chokey at Munia, which is stationed there for detecting spies. When I reached half the distance between Jajou and Munia I did not think it safe to go to the Chokey, and told my guides that I would first go to Khyragurh and then to Munia. I took a circuitous route and reached to about 5 or 6 miles distance from Dholepore. From all the enquiries I made there it appears that about 800 men of the Regiment called 'Kirafut ka Pultun,' about 400 Sowars, have crossed the Chumbul with 4 guns of a small size, probably none larger than a 12-pounder. These men have advanced on Dholepore for the purpose of keeping the boats in their possession, and for making a bridge of boats for the rest of the army when they come towards Agra,—after the Dussehra, of course. They have left all the treasure they brought from Mhow at Gwalior in charge of the Gwalior Contingent people. There was an alarm at Dholepore the day before yesterday, on account of a rumour that some European soldiers were on their way to that place. The Rana has promised to lend his larger guns to the Mutineers, should they want any, and has held himself responsible for supplying "russud" to the whole army. The Kharee Nuddee is too deep for guns or ammunition tumbrils to cross it without a boat, 16 cubits. Spies of the Mutineers are in almost every village near the road, and mounted parties come as far as Jajou.

Rana of Dholpore promises support to the Mutineers.

"LUCHMAN SINGH.

"*P.S.*—Perwanas have been written to all the Government officials and respectable Zemindars, informing them that hereafter they are servants and subjects to the King, and that the Zemindars who are disposed to be the King's ryots should assemble at Jajou with all the force they can bring with them. In carrying out this order a Zemindar, named Sonpal of Mowza Secunderpoor of Perg. Iradutnuggur, has gone to Jajou with a strong armed body of 25 men, and has advised his neighbours to do the same.—L. S."

. . . .

Dated 12*th.*—*Moolchund*, servant of Major Raikes: Left this on the 2nd. Reached Gwalior on the 5th; stayed three days there in Jumna Gunge. Did not go to Morar; left on the 8th, *i.e.* on Tuesday; reached the Kentra Ghat on the 9th. Left Dholpore on the left about half a mile; reached Muniah on the night of the 9th, and this yesterday.

The whole of the Contingent is at Morar. They wait the Maharaja's orders. They have as yet got no carriage. They gave no ammunition to the Indore men. The latter asked it, but it was refused. And the Indore men left vexed.

Contingent is at Morar. Wait the Maharajah's orders.

A number of the Maharaja's own horse, Poorbea Mewattees, etc.—say 100 or 200—fell out with the Maharaja, and were allowed by him to leave;—they are with the Indore [men].

Description of Indore force.

I saw no cavalry of the Maharaja's on the road; there are some of his Thannahs. Of the Indore force 3 companies are on this side, 4 guns, and 100 cavalry, and a great rabble of camp-followers. On the other side are about 2000 men.

100 to 125 of the Pultun 23rd have run away. 800 to 900 Cavalry are on the other side, and 3 guns. I saw only 2; they said there were 4. They are *all* dragged by bullocks. I was stopped and examined at three places. I saw nobody at Munnia, and nobody at all on the road, excepting one of our own Sowars. The Indore force say that they will go to Agra—and then go to Dehli. "The British Government will not let us go; therefore we are prepared to die."

Excesses of Sepoys.

[1] *5th, Saturday, Dehli.*—Dadree men asked (for guns ?). . . . Sahoocars complain of excesses of Sepoys (one Company and one gun ?) sent to Sadroorsee, 1 coss off. Each Sepoy a Shahzada, squeeze Bankers.

[1] *6th, Sunday.*—Men fly—city in distress.—Army masters. King said he can't do anything (?).

[1] . . . (?) recommended to catch and kill the Bankers' guards. We then "bisiár tang and hairán."[2]

Twenty (?) men fled, caught. Mirza Moghul asked them; said they had no pay for two months. Labourers not to be had for powder, . . .

12*th September* '57, *Saturday, Mynpoory.*—The Canoongoe reports that on the 9th 2 guns and 800 men arrived; and tidings that the Rajah with a great concourse is coming. South of Shekohabad there are some 4000 Aheers. They have probably come to oppose these Aheers.

An Urzee of the Khyragurh Tehseeldar: he says that 3 pultuns of Indore and one Risala and 2 Morar pultuns started. 2 pultuns, 300 Cavalry, and 4 guns have crossed; one fell into the river.

Hunuman Kuhar: Left Dholepore yesterday at 12,—saw some 1000 Infantry, 500 Sowars; they have their families, 5 guns, 2 brass ones,—the other three were covered. They will wait for the Contingent troops.

8*th, Tuesday, Dehli.*—

. . . .

Four Companies of Sappers and Miners going to sink a mine on the Fort of Akberabad.[3]

[1] These paragraphs indistinctly written in pencil.—W. C.

[2] Much straitened and perplexed.

[3] *i.e.* Agra.

14*th September, afternoon.—Huttee Singh:* Went to Hingowria, 6 coss other side Chumbul.

. . . .

There are 150 to 175 Sowars at Hingowria of the Contingent who have taken away their horses. The Shahzada was at the ghat last night, and the Nawab had come on this side.

All the Indore and Mhow troops are now on this side,—the 23rd, 400 or 500 Ghazies, 200 or 300 Vilayaties, 3 troops, 250 irregulars, and about 250 —— (?) They are coming to Agra, but they have to settle with Dholepore. 100 Sepoys came to Jajow, and have gone on to Jugneyr.

15*th September, morning, Gwalior.—Asa Doss,* Byragee of Eglass, a Gwalior spy: Left this on Wednesday, and reached Gwalior on Friday, 11 a.m. Left early on Saturday morning; reached Dholepore on Monday. Left it yesterday morning.

On Wednesday the Morar pultuns demanded 1¼ lakhs from the Maharaja. He refused, saying, . . . (?) "Go where you like." Then the Morar troops brought out their guns. Then the Maharaja also brought out his; and stopped access to the city, so that no supplies reached. **Gwalior-Morar regiments demand money,**

In the evening 2 Soobahdars came and begged pardon. They said they were his servants, and would go if he got them carriage. So the Maharaja sent out chuprassies to get carts and bullocks. Saw a great number; so they will set out on Friday next, 18th; they will join the Indore troops, and then march this way. **and transport.**

Seven hundred Sowars have left Morar, and come with Indore troops.

18*th September,* 6 *a.m.—Hunoman Kuhar:* Left this on 4th; reached Dholepore at night; stayed there till yesterday morning,—visited the places and stayed in a Mosque with a Brahmin.

There are now 3 more guns,—in all 10 guns. They say they are the Soobah's guns which have been seized, *i.e.* Deo Huns'. He has been seized, his cantonment looted, and nine of his Goojur followers killed. One of the gunners with the Indore force killed by a gunshot. They intended to take more of the Dholepore guns, and also demand treasure. Deo Huns does not tell where his treasure is. **Deo Huns, Subah at Dholpore, seized.**

The report was that the Contingent was to march last night. They expected them to reach in three days. Chumbul is very high.

The Indore army is waiting for the Gwalior troops. When

they arrive they will all march in to Jajow together. They all talk of coming to Agra.

There were 16 elephants. No hackeries. Some camels, say 50 or 100.

18th September, 9 a.m.—Moolchund: Left this on the 12th; reached Dholepore on the 13th. Went to the Chaonie. Left it at 4 p.m. of the 16th, and returned yesterday. 23rd is there; 700 Sepoys. They say they are neither going to Agra nor Dehli till they get magazine from Gwalior men. They have seized 12 guns from the Dholepore men; one big, the rest small. They have seized Deo Huns and put irons on him, for he opposed them; 5 to 7 Sepoys killed, and 10 or 12 of his men. They ask treasure. There are 16 Sowars at Munniah. At Jajow 20 to 25 Zemindaree bandookchies.[1] It began to rain at Dholepore the evening of the 16th.

Deo Huns, Dholpore official, seized by Mutineers.

21st September.—Hunoman Kuhar: Left Dholepore on evening of the 19th. The Rana had given a lakh of rupees, and got back all his arms which were plundered from the city. But they refuse to give back the guns and ammunition, and have seized 4 tumbrils of Dholepore ammunition.

Rana of Dholpore pays the Mutineers a lac of rupees.

A Kayeth, who had left Gwalior 8 days before, said that the Contingent were not now about to march. They would stay and get this month's pay. Possibly they might wait over the Dussehra. He said he met 20 Sowars who brought a perwana from the King asking why they did not come to Agra. They had gone by Bhurtpore (this would be about the 15th or 16th).

The Indore fellows said they had plenty of ammunition for 2 days. They said they knew a private way to the Fort of Agra from the city. What need of taking more ammunition?

22nd September, Lucknow.—A letter from Shah Behari Lal's house, dated 13th, from Lucknow, written under fear and apprehension of approach of troops—in a few days. (All apparently well.)

13th September (23 Mohurrim), Gwalior.—Letter from Gwalior. Jummun Lall, Officer of Morar, went to Maharajah and asked 22 lacs and carriage; both were refused, and pay stopped; on this the Morar troops with artillery turned out at Phoolbagh. They seized carriage.

Differences between Scindia and Mutineers.

[1] Native musketeers.

5th Regt. and 465 new Cavalry are subservient to Maharajah. Gohud, etc., looted. In Munsour, a Shahzada with Mewattees raised green flag.

The Maharajah has now given pay and promised carriage, and desired them to go. So they will be going soon. Many have fled, and the camp is in confusion.

22*nd September, Gwalior.—Pirthee:* Left Gwalior on 18th, morning—(left this 16th). Many of the Sepoys have left the Regiments, and taken service with Maharajah. Fifth have joined the Maharajah. There are no Sowars at Morar,—all at Phoolbagh. At Morar there are 400 or 500 bullocks, but no carts. A man called Loll Khan had arrived in Gwalior on 16th with orders from Dehli—to go direct to Dehli, not to Agra. The Thakoors pour in from all sides to protect Maharajah, who had out his guns. **Orders from Delhi reach the Mutineers at Gwalior.**

At Dholepore all there; but Sowars drop off towards Gwalior, as they do not get enough for themselves and horses.

26*th September.*—Jyekishindoss, 8 a.m. (letter dated Muthra), 25th. 1000 said to be already in Muthra; no guns yet come, but it is said they will arrive by 12 o'clock. It is said that half will go to Agra; half to Hattrass. Boats in the hands of the rebels. Jyekishindoss trying to detain them on the other side. **Rebels at Muttra.**

P.S.—Kulyan Doss went over in a dinghee to Muthra. About 400 or 500 Sepoys reached Muthra on the night of the 24th, and are still there. Altogether there are 4000 or 5000. Some say there are 10, others 20 guns; no certainty. There are also 4000 or 5000 villagers with them. All the boats on left side are in hands of rebels. Nobody gets across this side. The Chowbee was obliged to swim back. The Sepoys were greatly alarmed. When the Chowbee went over 3 or 4 "telingas" came and asked him if any Goras[1] were coming, and any Cavalry. He said he did not know,—he was a traveller. They greatly distressed the Jemadar of Cotwali yesterday, and burned his duftur. 5000 or 6000 Mahomedans with the rebels. City shut up, and there will be plunder.

Some Sowars were crossing in a boat; when they saw our Sowars they went back. I think they are alarmed at Hatrass. They have got 100 to 125 boats.

Other Urzee.—Great firing of muskets at Bindrabun.

Rebels from Besran Ghat to Rawul Ghat—thousands bathing; but "pureshan."[2]

[1] Europeans.

[2] Alarmed.

They fire across, 30 or 40 balls.

10 *a.m.*—A body said to have crossed at Rawul Ghat—to be going towards Buldeojee—and onwards either to Saidabàd or Khundowlee.

27th September, Sunday, Muthra.—Choonnee brought by the young Chowbee. Left this on Thursday night. Spent Friday at

Fugitives from Delhi.

Muthra—left Muthra yesterday about 9 a.m. On Thursday evening about 50 Sowars came at the Chaonie—they took off the tiles of the Chaonie to use the bamboos for firewood. They let off their guns. Half an hour afterwards the fugitives began

Distressed condition of fugitive Mutineers.

to appear in all parts of the town. They are wounded and ill off. Selling carbines for 17 and 18 annas. They have 23 guns—13 on the road this side, and 10 turned the other way. Very ill off for supplies. They are going to Lucknow. They demanded of the Manjhee to construct the bridge. He required first the necessary expenses. They had commenced to make the bridge when I left.[1] There are 700 or 800 Punjabees who are tolerably well off; the rest wretched. Altogether there must be some 9000 men.

Fifty or sixty Mussulmans came along with me. They had gone to Dehli, and came back with these people. They said they would stay at Agra to-day and go on to-morrow. They came on with me to Sont Kee Mundee,—some said they would

Disorganised condition of the fugitives from Delhi.

stay in Lohe Kee Mundee. All go in a crowd (phail phool), in no military order. There are a few Artillery men only. Very many of them wounded—some without arms, some without legs. No ammunition; only 4 carts of supplies probably. The tumbrils are open. 50 or 60 Sowars and 1 camel (with a woman on it) were on their way (*via* Furrah) to Bhurtpore. They are in desperate fright of being pursued or attacked by Europeans—always on the look-out, and alarmed at the least appearance of

State of things at Delhi.

men. They said they had left 1000 or 1500 in the Palace. And 50 or 60 "Goras" are outside in the Kala Mehal. They don't know what happened. Had been 8 days without food or water in Dehli, and had come 20 coss a day. They had sent a man to the Gwalior force to see what they were going to do. If called there they would go there—but not likely to go as their bridge was not ready. They had got their women (common ?) with them.

27th September, Gwalior.—Left this on Tuesday 22nd; reached Dholpore on Wednesday 23rd. Gwalior, Thursday

[1] Crossing at Muthra for Doab or Lucknow.—W. M.

24th; went on to Morar; came back that night to Jinsee in Gwalior. Friday morning, left Gwalior; reached Dholpore that day; and this, last night.

At Morar there are some 250 or 300 earts and bulloeks. The Maharajah had told them he would not let them take away their magazine; and at his and the Baee's instanee they had consented to wait over the full moon. The Maharajah had sent 500 Cavalry and 15 guns to Cheounda, 9 coss on this side Gwalior, saying that they should not advance this way. The Maharajah has taken away all the boats; there is only one light one, in which I crossed. 8 men with muskets are there, who prevent any one coming over. The Morar people say that as they have mutinied they can't help themselves. The Maharajah exhorts them to be quiet, and he will do what he can for them. The 5th Regiment has joined the Maharajah at the Barah Ghat, with the Maharajah's other pultuns. The four that are left are of the same mind with the 20th (?) Regiment. There are 200 Cavalry at Morar; they have joined the Maharajah. There are about 30 good-sized guns at Morar. They are all in park. There had been a contention before; but I never heard of there being any entrenchments. They had their guns out on both sides, but at last they gave in to the Baee's adviee to be quiet. The magazine is all shut up in Godowns. A good many are going off secretly to their homes. There are, say, 3000 men in the four Regiments. No troops on road to Khentrie Ghat, except the foree posted by the Maharajah.

Condition of troops at Gwalior.

At Dholpore the troops are as before; 100 Sowars at Munnia.

21*st*, *Meerut*.—Said to be fallen at 12 m. on that day. [Some detail of troops at Dholpore (?) here follows.]

Delhi falls.

. . . .

In Gwalior are four Contingent Regiments and two Companies from Cawnpore. At Dholpore some say "we shall go to Agra," some "to Dehli."

In the Crauford Pultun Sikhs say they will go to Dehli. Mussulmans want to go to Agra. Making ladders 30 and 40 feet high.[1] Scindia has taken away all the boats; no passage. Two Companies posted to prevent it. The Sepoys have taken $1\frac{1}{4}$ lakhs from Rajah, and paid 12 rupees to Sepoys and 15 rupees to Golundazes, 30 rupees to Sowars, and the rest 8 rupees.

Scindia opposes rebel force.

[1] Ladders for scaling Agra Fort!—W. M.

26th September, Muthra.—*Sewa Ram:* Left Muthra 26th, at 11 a.m.; 30 guns—28 small and two big ones. Met no men this side Muthra.

26th September, Gwalior.—The Morar people wish to sell the magazine (stupid fellows).

Tantia Sahib.

Of the 5th Regiment, which came to the Maharajah's side, some have gone back to the rebels. Tantia Sahib, uncle of Peshwa, has arrived with a perwana summoning the Morar force and Jeheenger Khan. The men from the Eastward wish to go thither; a few take the name of Agra. No movement till after Dussehra. At Dholpore they have got 1½ lacs.

Flight from Delhi of rebel soldiery. Composition of fugitive force.

Demurria of Oreya, a camp-follower of 44th: Left Dehli on Tuesday 22nd, at 4 p.m., in company with men of 44th and 67th Regiments, and mutinous corps from Meerut, Neemuch, Bareilly, Nusseerabad, and Oudh;—in all, remnants of 20 Regiments of Infantry, besides Cavalry. Cavalry have horses,—feed them on "churra" (?).

Sikh rebels return to their own country.

The numbers of each remainder in Corps is from 100 to 500 men. Say 5000 men, of whom 2000 sick and wounded; 20 guns H.A., 6 horses to a gun; 20 tumbrils and 3 keranchies[1] of powder in barrels; 20 elephants, which went from this after battle of 5th; and some have wives and children. The Sikhs left Dehli for their own country in boats across river. The force at Muthra intend leaving for Lucknow in 2 or 3 days.

Troops flying from Delhi down country (cross at Muttra). Distressed condition of rebel soldiery at Muttra.

Two men of M. Thornhill's left Muthra on Saturday 20th, at night. The force lies from Holee Darwaza to the "Nyee Line" in the Sudder Bazaar. They have 22 guns, of which 6 are disabled; all small. They are drawn by horses. There are 14 tumbrils, covered over with a covering. 5000 or 6000 Sepoys and 3000 horse, many wounded and sick; 200 with their noses cut off. The bridge was to be ready yesterday. Fatigued, foot-swollen, and humbly ask for provisions, etc.

The guns are arranged in no order.

28th September 1857.—*Toolai:* Left Dholpore yesterday morning with a party of Sowars, who came on to Munnia. Two bunnias were killed in a village beyond Munnia, and it was on this account the Sowars (500) with 2 guns came to Munnia.

Two men from Taee Bhaie, from Jaloun, passed through Gwalior 5 days ago. He says they are all at Morar; only ½ the 5th, say 500 men and 2 guns, with the Maharajah.

[1] Bullock carts.

The Nana has sent Tantia Topey with a lac of rupees to the people and called them to Cawnpore. Their great day is to-day. They say they will start on the 11th (to-morrow). They want Maharajah to go to Agra or to Cawnpore; Maharajah keeps them back.[1] 7000 Thakoors came; 3000 or 4000 in Fort. **Indore troops prepare for Agra.**

29th September (*Muthra, 28th*)—*Deputy Postmaster:* Army proclaims that no Sepoy is to remain in the city, nor any to sell his arms. They say Sikhs are coming behind. Some are running away. Bholoo Chowdhry has absconded. They are urging and beating the Mulláhs to finish the bridge. All our Officers' houses being plundered. To-day a few boats are wanting to complete the bridge. To-morrow it will be finished, but more "takhtas"[2] and "kurries"[3] and ropes will be required. **Fugitive army at Muttra.**

29th September.—Rambuksh: Left Muthra yesterday morning. The bridge would not be ready yesterday; 25 boats were wanting, and it has to be floored. It may be ready to-day or to-morrow. Saw 28 guns. There are some 20 tumbrils, but ammunition only in 5; rest empty. They intend to go *via* Hatrass to Lucknow. **Delhi force crossing at Muttra into Doab.**

Dyaram, Postmaster's man, writes:—20 guns, going to Lucknow, some say Bareilly. Boats all in position, but not yet floored. 1000 men must have run away. Rumour that the Government army is coming, and that it is near Pulwul. **Fugitives escape.**

. . . .

Futtehpore Sicri quiet on 28th. Road secure; but expected that Mutineers from Dholpore would pass that way.

Rambuksh, 28th.—Went to Muthra. *29th*, saw all the army. Saw 18 guns in one place, and 3 in another place; 4000 or 5000 infantry and 2000 cavalry. Many wounded. About 30 elephants. 50 to 100 run away every day. 50 Sowars went to Bhurtpore for ammunition. The Rana would not give it. They returned yesterday at 12 a.m. They intended to go to Lucknow. The bridge was finished by yesterday evening, a little before sunset. Men could go across, and "tats." The army had not gone. They have heard that an army is coming from Dehli, but don't know when. It is alarmed and dispirited. Some speak of Lucknow, others of Bareilly. They intend to loot Hatrass. They told the Moorsan Vakeel that they would loot Moorsan if the Rajah did not give them "russud." **Details of rebel force at Muttra. Their intention.**

[1] All owing to Dinker Rao.—W. M. [2] Planks. [3] Beams.

DLXVIIIA.

INTELLIGENCE DIARY, OCTOBER 1857.

1*st October.*—*Hunoman:* Left this 29th September; reached that night. Left Dholpore yesterday morning, 30th Sept., early after sunrise. They have seized 4 other guns of the Rana—great big ones. They brought them from Shergunj Killa. They have made arrangements for their being drawn by bullocks and propelled by elephants. They are 24-pounders.

The rebels at Muttra summon the force at Dholpore to accompany them to Lucknow.

The Muthra man sent Sowars to say that they had come from Dehli beaten. The Sahiblogue were victorious, and bid them come along with them. We got no food at Dehli, etc. They asked them to come to Lucknow *via* Futtehpore. Accordingly they intended to march last night, and would be at Jajow this morning, if they marched; to-morrow at Futtehpore Sicri, and say, by 2 days after, the 4th, at Muthra. They expect the Muthra people to wait there for them.

Scindia restrains the Gwalior Contingent.

Gwalior.—The Maharajah is said to have had another altercation with the Contingent.[1] They complained of not getting "russud." He declared he would give none; and would not allow them to cross the Chumbul nor take away their magazine. On this the Contingent set fire to their cantonment. The Maharajah's force has reached Cheonda to prevent their going farther this way. They are thus helpless. The Maharajah is prepared to fight them. The Kharee is still deep, unfordable,—but it is said to be fordable near Futtehpore Sicri.

Malagurh. — *Tota, Bunya of Khoorja:* I was sent to Secundrabad; on Sunday 27th I arrived there; on that day after midnight, 2 o'clock of morning of 28th, the army marched to Bolundshuhur. About six o'clock it reached the bungalow near Bolundshuhur, where the road bifurcates.

Action of Bulandshahr. Wali Dad Khan fights and flees. Delhi victors coming down country. Advance on Malagarh.

First, 3 guns opened fire on the part of Wullee Dad Khan, after that 5 of our guns opened fire, and 300 of the enemy were killed. They fled, and we seized their three guns and pursued them. Many rebels were slain in Deputy Gunge in Bolundshuhur, and multitudes fled. Two more guns seized at Deputy Gunge; thence an expedition was started for Malagurh. Wullee Dad fled, some say to Neemachana,—others, over the Ganges.

Details of British force.

One European Regiment, 3 Sikhs, 2 Goorkhas, and 2 Guides. Multitudes of Jats with the army.

[1] Dinker Rao keeps the Contingent behind.—W. M.

1st October.—Dyaram: Left [Muthra] at 8 a.m. this morning. The Bareilly Brigade began to cross over about 5 p.m., and crossed over all night, and by the time I left they had all crossed over with 5 guns. I don't know whether all their guns were taken over or not. All the Sowars and 34 elephants had crossed over. There were 24 guns; all but the 5 were still on this side. There was a contention between the Bareilly Brigade and the rest. The Bareilly men wishing to go to Bareilly, the rest wishing to remain. Messenger thinks that all will go. They were going on crossing when I left. They spoke of going by Hatrass. **Delhi fugitives crossing at Muttra.**

2nd October.—Goojur Mull, from Muthra: 8/25ths or 10/25ths (2/5ths) gone over river. . . .

Kasheenath says 20,000 or 25,000 crossed. Ten thousand Telingas and 3000 Sowars; 16 larger guns—8 very small, only half "háths" long. With each large gun are two tumbrils,— . . . little ammunition. 80 elephants with them.

Heera Singh wanted to go to Agra. With the Bareilly Brigade is a Mussulman head. He said, "We will not go to Agra, but to Lucknow." Three days the Punchayet lasted. Yesterday (30th) there was violent dispute. Heera Singh wanted to break the bridge. The Bareilly men said, "If you try to break the bridge we will die fighting." The Bareilly men took their stand on the bridge and prevented them breaking it. From 5 yesterday the Bareilly Brigade began to cross. In the morning they were still crossing,—a great crowd. Four bullock-drawn guns had crossed, and 3000 Telingas, of whom 2000 are disabled, and 1000 able-bodied and 500 Sowars; and there are many small horses on which the sick are carried, and 500 Moslems, and 5000 or 6000 other crowd; and 8 tumbrils are with the guns. The old respectable Sepoys say they have not the power to fight against Europeans. "Our fortune is broken." The bad characters say, "We are about to conquer; Agra is not far off." Two of the Bareilly guns not yet crossed. The Bareilly men have much silver and gold. The rest have not even food, and many Sepoys have gone off as Faqueers. They have shaved off their hair. Heera Singh's force went yesterday to Bundrabun. Otherwise there would have been a fight about the bridge. Two guns and 1200 men reached near Raie. They are coming. Three guns yet on other side. Heera Singh stops them.

Delhi fugitives: some wanted to attack Agra, others to go to Lucknow; all crossed at Muttra.

Details of Delhi fugitive force.

Bareilly rebels.

Sepoys going off as Faqeers.

2nd October.—Nuthoo (Clark's man): Left Muthra yesterday, at 12. 1½ "kumpoo" had crossed over; 34 elephants, 13 guns, left on this side.

3rd October, Dholepore.—Ram Buksh (*Chowbey*) left this on the 1st. Reached that evening. Remained there all the 2nd; and left yesterday morning about 7 a.m. The army had not then left; but it had been preparing to move for two or three days. They had taken 7 guns from the Raja; they gave back three small ones, and kept four large ones. They are to be drawn by bullocks. The Rana has not, that I know of, given them any Magazine. They have got 50 carts or so for their things,—seized five or six days ago. They have also 80 or 90 camels. They were preparing to leave day before yesterday, but did not go; 25 Sowars came from Muthra four or five days ago. There is daily communication between Muthra and Dholepore; and they will go that way. Nobody speaks of any other direction. They have altogether 12 or 13 guns in all. They will go by Khyragurh. They have some 25 Cavalry in Munnia. They will reach Muthra in three or four days. A man from Gwalior says that the Morar troops invited the Indore men back again, but they were hindered by the Maharajah, who took away all the boats.

Dholpore force going to Muttra.

Scindia's loyal action.

Gwalior.—Ram Buksh: Left Gwalior on the 30th about three p.m.; came *via* Punahut. The 5th Regiment and Cavalry, and 50 or 60 men of the 4th, have joined the Maharajah. Four pultuns and 200 or 250 Sowars are at Morar and 40 guns, of which three are 24-pounders, one 18-, and the rest 9- and 12-pounders. The Maharajah's entrenchment is at the Lushkur by the river. The Morar Morcha is at the river. The Poorbeahs say, "Let us go to Cawnpore"; the Upper Doab men say, "Let us go to Agra." They are equally divided. The Poorbeahs are the strongest. They have laden the Magazine on 1200 bullocks, 1000 camels, and 800 carts, and want more carriage. The Maharajah has not given them this month's pay. The Morar men called the Indore men because they wanted Cavalry, but they were hindered by the Maharajah, who took away all the boats.

Gwalior Contingent divided as to Agra or Cawnpore. Poorbeahs strongest for east.

The Maharajah tells them he won't let them go to Agra: they may go to Cawnpore.

They cut off the nose of a man who attempted to desert, and paraded him about the camp.

Evening.—Jewa Ram: Left Muthra at 8 a.m. Day before yesterday Bareilly pultuns went across. Yesterday, from 4 p.m., the Nusseerabad pultuns began to cross. By morning all had gone across. The Neemuch Brigade only left; it is much reduced in numbers. The Bareilly Brigade is the biggest. The Nusseerabad the next. The Neemuch the smallest. It has in all only 5000 or 6000 men; 500 or 600 Sowars; 8 guns H.A., small ones. Heera Singh is with them. They sent on their "line-doree"[1] with 100 Sowars or so to Furrah. They would have marched this afternoon, and be at Furrah to-night. They will go by Futtehpore Sicri to Dholepore.

The rebel brigades at Muttra: the Bareilly Brigade, the Nusseerabad Brigade, the Neemuch Brigade. Proceeding to Dholpore.

The day before yesterday the Bareilly people came back from the other side, 2 Companies and 100 Sowars, to plunder Seth Luchmee Chund's house. Then Heera Singh came with 2 guns to save the house. Then Heera Singh said he would not go with them. The Nusseerabad people then left. 17 or 18 guns have gone on the opposite side. The troops will have gone on to Hatrass.

Attempt to plunder the Seth. Quarrels between the brigades.

3rd October, 8 p.m.—Chowbey's man, Hunoman: Left about 7 a.m. 3 Brigades, Bareilly, Nusseerabad, and Dehli, have gone across. The Neemuch corps, with Heera Singh, was on the road to Furrah.

Muthra.—Eesree Pershad: Went to Furrah and left at about 11. No guns had come on then,—some 500 or 600 Sowars; they said they were going by Uchneyra to Dholepore. There are six guns with them at Muthra. He does not know whether any of them even may not have gone over the river.

Mohuna left Muthra about 6. Two Brigades went across. One Kumpoo[2] remained, only 3 or 4 guns; they said the remaining brigade was going to Dholepore.

Dholepore.—Ramjeet: Left Dholepore at gun-fire. About 4000 or 5000. The soldiers talked of going to Munnia. There are only 6 Sowars at Kukowa to examine travellers. It is 4 coss on this side the Kharee. There is no Govt. Choukee at the Kharee (?). At Jajow there are 100 Sowars. Their "line-doree" had gone to Munnia with 25 Sowars. They say that, having congregated at Munnia, they will come on to Agra. 10 guns they had before, and they got 3 from the Rana—large ones.

5th October, Monday morning.—Asa Doss: Left the day before yesterday; arrived at Furrah about midday; left it yesterday

[1] Advance tents. [2] Camp.

Neemuch Brigade arrives at Furrah. Going to Dholpore and join Dholpore attack on Agra.

morning about 7 a.m. When I reached Furrah some of Heera Singh's people had begun to arrive. They had all reached by 4 p.m. They stayed there all night. They began to move again about 4 in the morning; when I left they had all left except a few camp-followers. They bought their supplies in the bazaar. They fed the horses in the fields. They committed no other injury. They would encamp at Uchneyra or Khyragurh.

Details of Hira Singh's (Neemuch) force.

They said they had had a letter from Dholepore, and were going there. And, after forming a junction there, would attack Agra. Of the whole force 2/3rds have gone to the Doab; only 1/3rd follows Heera Singh. There are 500 or 600 Cavalry and about 600 Sepoys. They are all armed. Of these some 200 are wounded. Some 400 or 500 are fit for fight. The Sowars are armed with pistols and swords. There are six guns. They arrived near sunset. They are drawn by horses. They are light guns, not above 6- or 9-pounders.

The people say that it is the same "Cumpoo" that formerly attacked Agra. The whole remaining Neemuch force has gone this way. Heera Singh marches with the advance guard.

Delhi, Nana's, and Jhansi vakils bid for the Contingent. Gwalior Contingent go east.

Gwalior.—Macpherson: Three (vakils ?) have been bidding. Jehangeer, Dehli (Vakeel); nobody listens to him: Nana Sahib's Vakeel, who promised them money but gave only bills: Third, Jhansi Vakeel promises money without limit, and 2 lacs on arrival, to include Magazine which is to be bought. Rs. 1,50,000 for Magazine, and Rs. 50,000. First to Jhansi, afterwards to Calpee and Nana. Made arrangements with the Vakeels, and likelier to go that way than any other. (Maharajah fired salute.) Also to Jaloun, . . . also Duttia.

Ram Rukk Mina: Was yesterday at Ukholey at midday. Half the force was there and half at Uchneyra; then I went on to Uchneyra, and found nobody. The army will have arrived at Khyragurh to-day. There are no guns—chiefly Sowars.

Neemuch Brigade.

5th October.—Dhokul: Left Muthra yesterday at midday. The Neemuch Brigade left on Saturday, and part of it yesterday morning. I left after it all went. There are about 1500 or 1600 people. There are 5 guns with horses; in some 6, in some 4. The guns started on Saturday. There are 700 or 800 Sepoys; 100 to 125 Sowars; and 700 or 800 Mussulmans, etc.;—they have no ammunition.

Jeewa Ram: Left the force at Jingaroo, about 10 coss. Left it this morning. Great rain. The troops came there at night. There are only 700 or 800 men altogether; 500 or 600 Sowars; 100 or 50 Sepoys; 200 to 250 peadahs[1] altogether. No guns,—they will nearly reach Dholepore to-day. There are wounded Sepoys among them. It is the Neemuch Brigade. Great numbers have deserted. If these get food and pay anywhere they will stay; otherwise disperse to their homes.

Dholpore pays money to the Sepoys at Dholpore.

6th.—Rambuksh: Left day before yesterday at midday. On the 3rd they got a lac of rupees out of Deo Huns, and divided it among themselves. On the morning of the 4th they got out an immensely large gun, and made arrangements for drawing it by 20 bullocks to their camp. When they brought it out and the elephants pushed it behind, the carriage broke and the gun rolled, and crushed one man. Four or five days back the Nawab went to Gwalior. The Sepoys talk of taking money from Bhurtpore as they have done from Dholepore. They don't at all speak of Agra. On the 4th it was expected the Sowars from Muthra would reach: on that day 100 Sowars from Dholepore went to Khyragurh. On the 3rd a man left Gwalior who says the Contingent is still there. There are no Sowars at Munnia or Jajow—only one long ladder, 32 steps and 2 yards broad. They made it at Jajow.

Contingent still at Gwalior.

Controversy with Scindia.

Gwalior.—Amanut Khan, sent by Shimboo Mull. . . .: Left on the 30th Sept., Wednesday evening; reached this on 3rd Oct. The Cavalry 550, and 5 Companies of the 5th Cavalry, and 2 guns from Mehidpore, have joined Scindia. On the 21st the army (4 pultuns) asked carriage,—they (were) refused. When they put forward entrenchments. Also Scindia. Four days it remained so. Then Maharajah gave 5000 bullocks, 150 hackeries, 150 camels, and 9 elephants. These would not suffice for Magazine, and they wanted more. Maharajah said no, and threatened to stay Magazine and tumbrils. Then intended to fight again. The Maharajah raised more entrenchments, and urged his army to destroy Mutineers if they made any row. No agreement yet.

Poorbeahs say, "Go to Cawnpore"; those on this side, "Agra." The Maharajah wants to send off the force towards Tehree and Jhansi. The Nana's Vakeel wants to take them to

[1] Foot men.

Cawnpore. They don't talk of Agra. The 4th troop is said to wish to join Maharajah.

Muthra, 6 p.m., 4th.—Imdad Ally: Returned to Muthra;—post office opened on all sides.

Gwalior.—Dobie, Dak-master, Pinahut;—5th: Dak stopped. Here and elsewhere boats seized—no one let pass—not even Government servants. The news is only that some of the Morar army are slaughtered.

Gwalior Contingent attacked by Scindia.

Nund Kishore, Brahman, . . . a man disguised as "bairagee," with a false red stick of the Maharajah's Household, who had fled from Morar, told him that on Saturday, 3rd, 3 pultuns of (Nagees?) came, and, being joined with Maharajah's army and Goojurs, etc., entirely surrounded the rebels, and Maharajah poured grape on them, so that no man can escape.

. . . .

7th October.

Movement of rebel force from Dholpore on Agra.

Macpherson (messenger?): Left on 5th. On 6th, at Jajow; outside Serae, bunniahs, bullocks, and grain, for Pultun;—beyond them, Sowars catching bullocks. Near Munnia, Palankin (?) and 2 carriages, with 50 Sowars, red jackets and high boots. . . .

In Munnia saw four small guns: on road with gunners.

At Suttee Macam 2 large guns, 4 pairs of bullocks.

Nawab in Munnia with Wilaiatees.

Advance on Agra.

A Pultun with Sowars—2000. "A pultun and Sowars came yesterday from Muthra, and they and Dholepories (?) going to Agra."

Ladders to scale Agra Fort.

At Jajow—33 ladders, 2 yards broad and 20 yards long, made there from boats—to take fort.[1] Munnia people said all force coming from Gwalior.

Neemuch people join the Sepoys at Dholpore for attack on Agra.

Vakeel of Dholepore says that the Dholepore army left Dholepore yesterday morning—11 guns, some horsed; some bullocked—2000 to 2500 horse; 1½ pultuns Sepoys:—1200 or 1300 miscellaneous men with muskets. They are encamped from Munnia to one coss on the other side. Heera Singh has reached Dholepore with 700 or 800 Sowars. They are to come to Jajow and form a junction there, and then march on Agra.

Things as before at Gwalior.

[1] *i.e.* of Agra.

8th October 1857.—*Juggur:* Went to Khyragurh; left it about 5 last night. Heera Singh's force arrived there on the 5th, and marched on the morning of the 6th about midnight. It has about 500 or 600 Sowars, and about 800 or 900 Sepoys. I heard of no guns. They went to Dholepore direct, and yesterday came all on to Munnia. 100 Sowars are at Khyragurh for "russud" under Captain Idiad Khan. I didn't go to Munnia, but they said that besides the Neemuch force there are a few of the Dholepore troops there. The village people said they would go to Bhurtpore.

A Doby of the Cavalry from L—— said on Saturday or Sunday they would all go to Agra.

8th.—*Dhusoolah* (Vakeel's man), on 6th, went to Dholepore in evening. No fauj (army) there. On the morning all had gone to Munnia. Left early yesterday and came to Munnia; saw there 14 guns (12 small and 2 large), 100 maunds powder taken from Rana; 11 or 12 tumbrils and carts. They had brought a number of balls from Rana's fort. This is all their magazine. The Muthra "fauj" has joined them, 2000 cavalry and 4000 foot of the Dehli Telungas; 50 to 100 are wounded. **Advance on Agra.** **Muttra forces join Dholpore force to attack Agra.**

Their intention is to come to Agra. They are to come to Jajow to-day. Russud (supplies) was there with 30 or 40 Sowars. They have brought Deo Huns. Kharee swimmable. At Bissehra, 1½ west, it is below waist; but bad road. Eastward it is all swimmable. **Dholpore minister with them.**

Neemuch force, 500 Sowars and 500 Infantry (some wounded).

4 *p.m.*—*Huttee Singh:* Left this yesterday, midday; reached Munnia, 7 p.m.; saw nothing on road. Saw the whole army at Munnia. Neemuch force there,—some 500 or 600 Sowars, and 300 or 400 Infantry. There is the 23rd, 3 troops Regulars, many Ghazees, 2000 or 3000. They marched at 4 this morning, crossed the Ootangan, and encamped at a bridge between Jajow and Sajan. They reached it about 7 o'clock. **Advance of Mutineers on Agra.**

They said they would then go to the Nuddee. They will cross it by the two big ladders which will be thrown across. They have got planks to plank it with. To-morrow morning, if they march, they will be at the Kharee. They are going to arrange for supplies at Tehree, on the other side of the Kharee;—they will have godowns there, and supply themselves from behind. They all talk of coming on to Agra, and say, "We can take the Fort in three hours."

They have 11 guns, 7 of them old ones; 4 Dholepore ones, of which 2 small and 2 big, say 15- or 18-pounders. *All* drawn by bullocks,—6 pairs for the big guns, 4 pairs for the little ones. One tumbril is behind each gun. They have very many carts; can't say if they contain ammunition. The force all goes in disorder; neither Cavalry nor Infantry march in order. The Badshazadah not now among them. There is a Nawab Soobahdar-Major, and Hawaldar-Major, and Heera Singh. They most mind Heera Singh, whom they have made a Colonel.

The leaders of the force.

They have no golandazes that I know of, unless they have got them with the Dehli force, or from Dholepore.

The Neemuch force was dispirited and indisposed to fight, till it joined the Indore people, and they persuaded it.

On 10th October the Rebels coming from Gwalior and Dholepore, of whom account is given above, attacked Agra; but were driven back and scattered by a Column opportunely marching down from Dehli, as described elsewhere.[1] *The notes now go on as before.*

11*th October* 1857.—*Sri Ram of Lucknow Zillah, sent by Chowbee.*

. . . .

Maharajah restrains troops from marching towards Agra.

On 8th, left Gwalior. Morar army still there. They wish to come this way, but the Maharajah won't let them.

1 *p.m.*—Last night the fugitive Sowars were observed in parties of twos and fours returning from the direction of Futteh-abad towards Syan. 16 Sowars seen leaving Syan for Munnia; no foot men seen.

Sunday, at 8 *p.m.*—*Hetram of Pamahut of Kemtera:* Left house on Saturday morning; reached Futtehabad evening. Saw 20 Sowars there, and 20 at night going towards Butesur. They did not stay there; they ate their dinner hastily and went, and said, "We are going to Nowgaon, to the Raja of Bhudawar." 4 Sowars met me at the Ootangun. They said the same—they had no Sirdar.

[1] See p. 186, vol. i.

Sheopershad Chuprassy: Went to Iradutnugger on the night of the 10th. Returned Sunday night; reached Iradutnugger at 11½—saw 20 new levies; and 20 Sepoys are at the Thannah, and 50 Sowars at the Tehseel. They heard that they were about to be attacked, and were ready to run away. I heard that the force that fled on Saturday had fled across the Ootangun and taken refuge in the ravines,—afraid of Government army, and about to run away, and some 50 or 60 at Shumsabad. At Lohetta (east of the road) water is up to waist. **Iradutnugger.**

Gunnesh (*Chowbey*) on 3rd Sept. (Oct. 2) reached Lushker. Left on morning of 5th. Scindia has 150 guns in position to destroy army if it goes towards Agra. The Morar people gave up idea of plundering Maharajah's army when they saw his many soldiers. On 4th went to Morar. 3½ Pultuns and 800 or 900 Sowars. At first they went over to Maharajah. 8 or 10 days ago they returned to their camp. 5 Companies of the 4th went over to Maharajah and are encamped. Morar wanted treasure. Two Pultuns will go, it is said, towards Jhansi on the 11th; and 1½ Pultuns to Cawnpore. Nana's Vakeel came to call them: 2 lakhs (?), 200 garis, and 200 bullocks given by Maharajah. They wanted more, but he would not give them. **Scindia's loyal attitude.**

A Cawnpore messenger met a great number of men and Sowars between Etawah and Oreya on Saturday: a few beyond Futtehabad.

. . . .

14*th October.*

11*th October, Bhurtpore.*—100 Sowars arrived and encamped on Muthra road. Rajah's troops in readiness.

35 caught. To be sent into Agra. **Bhurtpore catches rebels.**

12*th October, Bhurtpore.*—*Mogul Kishore:* 35 Sowars taken prisoners on morning of 11th were ordered by the Mookhtar Raj to be disarmed. They refused, mounted their horses and drew their swords. At 6 p.m. shot was fired at them from the 4 guns and killed 9 of them. Others made off to Goberdhun. Pursued by Faujdar Mookund Singh. Another cut down in a village. **Occurrences at Bhurtpore.**

Another party of 12 taken up and sent to Bhurtpore. One escaped—arrived evening—disarmed and unhorsed. Now in a serai imprisoned.

600 or 700 at Roopbas; demand the 2 (1?) guns from B. Sepoys there.

13*th*, 3 *p.m.*, *Hatrass.*—About 500 horse and 500 foot arrived at Jooar (which is 7 or 8 miles from Hatrass on the Muthra road, and near Moorsan): they sought for Durya Singh, and wanted russud. They say they will go to Hatrass. No gun had reached then. They reached at 2, and were still arriving when the reporter left. No guns had come up.

13*th*, *Dholepore.*—No fugitives at Dholepore. Rana had slain seven fugitives on horseback. Road to Dholepore open.

Many of the rebels gone towards Kheragurh (and Bhurtpore?). No move from Gwalior.

14*th*, *Gwalior.*—Macpherson has a letter from Scindia of the 10th, saying he will be obliged to allow the Contingent to march on the 15th *via* Jhansi to Cawnpore.

13*th*, *afternoon.*—*Gokul:* Left Furra in the morning. On 12th, afternoon, about 500 Infantry and 4 or 5 Cavalry arrived at Furra, and stayed at the Neroulee Ghat. Some had guns, some had none.

13*th*, *Jhunda.*—Left Dholepore on 12th; in the morning about 1200 Infantry and 70 Sowars went towards Keraolee. Nobody now left in Dholepore.

13*th*, *Chedda.*—On 11th left Mynpoory in afternoon and stayed in Bugry. On 12th reached Shekoabed; saw there 50 Sowars and 300 Sepoys: they said they were going to Lucknow.

The Bareilly, etc., Mutineers 7 days ago (8th) were pitched from Bhurgaon (?) to Bewar.

14*th.*—*Luchmun Singh of Soojrey*, Urzee dated 9th: Of the above force—about 1000, 1200 men on 6th; and 15,000 to 16,000 men with 22 guns on 7th October; and 4000 or 5000 on 8th with 11 guns; on the 8th at Keraolee, left for the East. The Nawab's sepahees got them russud. The chief people got out of the way. Those that were left gave up their food; some paid, some did not. On the 9th returned home. The fugitives are in a sorry condition, and have no ammunition.

Fugitives at Keraolee

in distressed condition.

14*th*, *Ramnarain.*—From Kurra, my home, a messenger came; says the Muthra fugitives met him at Chubramow;—extended 2 coss: ill off for food; plunder villages; going to Lucknow. Don't know number. Left it 4 or 5 days ago. Muttra fugitives ill off for food.

13*th*, *Muthra.*—*Imdad Ali:*[1] (On the) 12th, 800 fugitives arrived and opposed; repulsed at 9 p.m. At 3 and 4 in the afternoon of 12th they came to cross at Muthra. All the boats were away; they surrounded me and the Cotwal. Some Sowars entered the City.

500 came to the Seth's place, and made entrenchment near Seth's place. I also attacked with my men and followed those who entered the City. They fled and joined the rest. They continued to attack me. Choosing to die, I attacked them for several hours. 300 Sowars and 200 Cavalry attacked me, but could not succeed and would not come within reach of our shot. We prepared to defend at night—they and we. After 12 at night the fugitives, who got no russud or food from the City and no help, went off towards Shergurh. They will go by these villages. Imdad Ali describes engagement with a fugitive body.

Bindraban.—200 Cavalry and 300 Foot at Sikragan near B., with 2 very small guns.

13*th*, *Dholepore.*—Macpherson's man, *Ghoolam Mahomed:* Says no one at Dholepore,—the Nana's people disarm them and kill them (?).

. . . .

14*th.*—Clark's man, *Jowahir*, 2 *p.m.:* Deo Huns at Dholepore. Rana did not let the fugitives go his way. The Rana's Sowars are at the Ootangun, and don't let any go. A few men have gone by Futtehabad. Most towards Futtehpore. Dholpore minister at Dholpore. Rana opposes fugitives.

Do., *Nowla.*—13th, reached Futtehpore 10 or 15 foot soldiers in Serai; the day before (12th) 200 Sowars, and 200 to 250 foot fled towards Muthra, Bhurtpore, and Roopbas. Those who were in the Serai also went towards Roopbas. Nobody now in Futtehpore Sicri. Met nobody on my way back on morning of 14th. Fugitive troops.

14*th October.*—*Bullubgurh Messenger:* Left on 10th; reached 13th. On 12th met 15 Cavalry flying at Goburdhun:—came from Dholepore: going to Puttiala. The Bhurtpore troops the same day opposed 20 or 30 Sowars: 12 were killed;—I met Bhurtpore opposes rebels.

[1] In charge at Muttra.

some running. No others went to Bhurtpore, and I met no others. The day I left Bullubgurh the Rajah had gone to see the General at Dehli.

14*th October, Munsaram.*—Futtehpore, 12th. 300 Cavalry and other camp-followers arrived there; and asking the road to Bhurtpore, went off in that direction. (Passed through Chukrana.) 20 Cavalry arrived there on morning of the 13th, from Dholepore. They said if the Morar force will come to Dholepore we will join it. It is coming from Morar. If it does not come, we will see what we will do. They were still there on the morning of the 14th.

Hunoman and Pirthie (Chowbeys) went to Dholepore on 13th; met 30 or 40 Sowars at Munnia. On the same day, at night, I saw 300 to 350 cavalry and about the same number of camp-followers, and some Sepoys, who had come together there from various quarters. They said among themselves, "We must go somewhere; there is no certainty here." They were still there yesterday morning. Some Sepoys are also, they say, at Raja Khera.

The fugitives puzzled what to do.

I didn't hear anything at Dholepore of the Contingent being likely to come.

14*th October, Eglass.*—Tehseeldar of Eglass. At midday of 13th, 300 Sepoys at Jowar. At midnight intelligence was received that they were going towards Sassnee, and will go to Secundra Rao. 600 Cavalry and Foot with families came to Eglass unexpectedly; they did not stay, but went on by Byohra towards Sassnee; will go to Secundra Rao and Khangunge;—some armed, others not,—women with them.

Troops come to Eglass.

14*th October, Hatrass.*—250 Sepoys crossed the Grand Trunk Road at Keohree with 50 or 60 bullocks,—pursued, but not overtaken; gone towards Secundra Rao.

Rebel administration at Khassgunje broken up.

10*th October, Khassgunge, Peshkar.* — Nawab's Tehseeldar and Thannahdar for 1½ months there, fled on the 9th instant. Peshkar Wasilbakee navees, and others with Tehseeldar, is at his post.

11*th October, Dewan Ally.*—Tehseeldar writes, according to perwana of 2nd, ordered Dheer Singh and Gobind and Bija to catch the Nawab's Tehseeldar and Thannahdar. They collected men, and then officials fled.

A Dak Moonshee, Madho Chunder Baboo, sought to exercise authority as Hakim.

16*th October, Bindrabun.*—Deputy Postmaster at Bindrabun on the 13th;—writes that 300 Mutineers with families passed through Bindrabun on the 12th, some without arms. "The city men of this place" killed 5 of them and took their muskets, swords, etc. The rest crossed the Jumna. More expected.

Gwalior, Sohna.—Left this, 12th, by Dholepore: reached Gwalior 13th, at night. 14th, left in afternoon. Heard that the Morar force left on Saturday for Cawnpore—4 pultuns; and carried some guns with them, number not known. Heard that they had 7 or 8 guns. Maharajah's army is at Phoolbagh. He is there. The Baiee is at Bara. Heard of no fight or dispute between Maharajah and Contingent.

Morar force left for Cawnpore.

15*th October.*—Reached Dholepore; saw no trace of Mutineers. The Rana's soldiers go along the banks of the Ootangan with orders to kill any Mutineers they may meet. At Jajow there is a very big ladder. Saw nobody at the Kharee. The Rana has ordered the nose and ears of all Mutineers to be cut off. 4 or 5 so treated.

Rana openly opposed to Mutineers.

3 *men.*—We are at Khentra Ghat on part of Sookha Ram Baboo. On the 14th October, at 9 p.m., Harkaras came to say that on the 13th the Regiments came out of their cantonments, and encamped till evening on the parade. Their intention was to come towards Agra, but the Maharajah would not let them go that way; he ordered them to go to Calpee Ghat. They cannot by any device get this way, as the Maharajah has raised entrenchments. They will go towards Cawnpore. They have laden their magazine on 1000 bullocks and 1000 carts. The Maharajah wanted to seize the magazine. But his army said, "Let them go: if they go towards Agra we will attack them." The Hurkaru had left Gwalior on the 14th at 3 p.m. They said that till he left they had not then moved any way.

Maharajah prevents Gwalior troops coming to Agra.

Dholepore.—There is nobody in Dholepore, or anybody on the road.

14*th October, Muthra.*—Sehan (Cosee direction). On the 12th, at evening, 100 red-dressed Cavalry came from Muthra and wanted the Purao.[1] They went on to Cosee. Same night 150 Cavalry came from Muthra and went on towards Cosee. And on the 13th, 250 Cavalry went the same way. The same night the Zemindars opposed them for trespassing in their fields. Two were wounded, of whom one died. On the 13th, 100 Cavalry and 2 elephants, and on the same day 250 Cavalry and Foot, went towards Sheregurh.

Syud-ood-Deen of Dullana (Cosee) kept some of them in his village.

Fugitive soldiery pass Hatrass.

15*th, night, Hatrass.*—At night on the 14th, or rather morning of the 15th, early, the military began to arrive, and they went on passing for 2 hours till 5. They came from Moorsan, and are going towards Secundra. Seen as far as canal,—not traced after that.

Secundra Rao.—Report that Mynpory Rajah seized 5 guns from Bareilly force (?).

200 Sikhs at Furruckabad. A Sikh came to say they were anxious to get out and be pardoned.

Gwalior.—Letter to Macpherson. Contingent to march to Sonee Puchowlee, by Antra Pass, on evening of 14th. "Linedooree" had gone on on 13th.

Amanat Ally, Soobahdar-Major, 1st Grenadiers; and Muhadeo Singh, Adjutant, had gone over to the Maharajah.

(Alexander tells me) 10 horses left behind at Bindrabun. Alexander asked to write to Mr. Thornhill about it.

14*th October.—Letter from Dholcpore.* One Regiment gone to Sehore; 2 or 3 Pultuns now encamped on the Parade, but not known which way they will go.

19*th October.*—(Alexander mentioned yesterday that 10 horses were left at Bundrabun by the retreating Cavalry.)

Rebel soldiery puzzled where to go to escape.

16*th.—Eessree Singh.*—At 6 p.m. on the 15th, midday, 200 Cavalry, with muskets, etc., came to the Tehseeldar at Futtehpore Sicri, and were there yesterday morning at 6 a.m. They say, "If we go towards Bhurtpore, the Rajah attacks; if other places, the Europeans;"—therefore they hold on. It isn't apparent what they will do—stay or go.

[1] Encamping-ground.

20th, Futtehpore Sicri.—Saligram on 17th went to Futtehpore Sicri; reached it in the evening. On that day there were 150 to 200 men in the Tehseel. In the evening they came out, and some went to Adheen Shah's Tukia,[1] and some to the Tehseeldaree Durwaza, and some to the Serai.

I stayed all the 18th there. I left in the morning of 19th. During the day they wander about the bazaar armed. At night they go to their several places. 5 or 6 large horses for Sowars; and about 20 tattoos for burdens.

They say they have no road, and will die there. The Mewattees on the hill collude with them—some 40 men, 20 like Telingas. None have on uniform. They have matchlocks and carbines, and some 10 or 12 flint guns. Some have sold their arms.

Rebel soldiery puzzled where to go.

Rampore, Aonli, Dhurrum: Left Rampore on the 11th. On 13th, at Bhilsa, heard that 3000 to 4000 Sepoys went towards Bareilly by the Kuchla Ghat, for Lucknow. All was well at Rampore and Moradabad. 300 or 400 men of Khan Buhadur went to Huldwanee. The Sahibs attacked them; 200 or 300 killed, and the rest fled. Sahibs pursued them, and returned towards the hills; the Sahibs lost their way. Then the men of Khan Buhadur made a *Chapao*[2] (14 Goorkas and 3 Sahibs killed) about 20 days ago. Only heard this. The Nawab is a well-wisher, but his servants sometimes go wrong, and desire to go to Bareilly for the larger pay. The Nawab has raised his servants' pay, and has entertained numerous Hindoos, 3000 or 4000 men.

Affair at Haldwani.

Khan Buhadur reported to have made a successful ambuscade.

The Nawab a well-wisher.

20th October.—Kesra (Clarke's ?) went to Futtehpore; reached it at night. On enquiry found that 10 or 11 days ago 300 or 400 Sowars came from the west, and rested in the buildings of Futtehpore, and some below hill,—no foot. "We have 2 Campoos coming from Biana." This morning saw 400 Sowars in puhar,—no gun. No intention of going anywhere.

In Mouza Bheirawatee, 3 coss north of Futtehpore Sicri, are said to be 300 or 400 Sowars.

Furruckabad.—Hookma Ahir: Left Furruckabad on the 16th October. The fugitive force that went by Eta, one-third with seven guns, and five guns went to Furruckabad; before that 2 pultuns and 1 Rissala of Seetapore were there; and some 10,000 new

[1] Abode of a Mahommedan devotee. [2] Attack from ambuscade.

Rebel force in Farakhabad.

levies and 12 guns were before in Furruckabad. In all 19 guns are in Furruckabad, and the entire army of Mutineers is 6000 or 7000; the rest are villagers. But the Mutineers have no heart either to remain or to stay. 2/3 went by Canouj to Lucknow; they never meant to go to Cawnpore. The force heard that an army was going from Agra to Cawnpore. No Mutineer has the heart to fight. Those who have gone with 15 guns to Lucknow have no magazine. They are the Neemuch and Nusseerabad Brigades.

Mutineers disheartened. Neemuch and Nusseerabad Brigades gone to Lucknow.

The Nawab's servants say, "When all this army fled from Dehli, how can we face the English?" They want to flee, but will certainly fight once.

Bewar.

At Bewar, 2 pultuns and one newly raised pultun with 5 guns, the Nawab has placed as an entrenchment. Gooldad Khan as its officer. They have seized Baboo Chobey Lall and three other Muhajuns, asking money.

Extortion from bankers.

Despair of Sooba of Nusseerabad Brigade.

Debeedeen Soobadar of Nusseerabad pultun said, "I am lachar;[1] it is Bhagwan's will.[2] On earth and heaven there is no place to rest. The English will seek me out and kill me." This man went with the Mutineers from Hatrass to Furruckabad. Gungabishan's wife was carried off by the Telingas from Hatrass. He went to fetch her; he brought her back from Furruckabad.

They burned Ranjee's house and carried off Gungabishan's wife.

Jyepore.—Mahommed Alee Khan (relative of Chattareewala), 16th October:—He went to his home. On 15th many fugitives came to cross the ghat at Puhasoo,—at evening I heard. Sent Jyepore Sowars and foot to catch them. Caught 45 men and women with 23 English muskets; and 9 horses, big and small, were caught. Sent all to Bulundshuhur.

Bhudawur Rajah helps.

Etawah, 21*st*.—On the 18th saw nobody towards Futtehabad. Ghats stopped by Bhudawur Raja.

Fattehpur.

Futtehpore.—Wuzeer Khan Chuprassee:—20th, reached Futtehpore Sicri. 150 to 200 are there. No Sowars, but 7 or 8 tats, and 2 camels; 25 or 30 at Tehra Durwaza. And 30 or 40 at Kalee Khet below Mehal; 30 or 40 behind Mehal. Some in bazaar; matchlocks and carbines. No intention anywhere. The Mewatties collude with them.

Mewattis collude with rebels.

22*nd*.—*Radhey* (Clarke's), 21st, was there. 60 Sowars at the Gate towards Biana. Their horses are there in a bagh. On

[1] Helpless. [2] *i.e.* God's will.

the hill the horses are in parties here and there, say 500. No foot or guns. We won't allow a Thannah to be set up. There are some Sowars in Santin (?). And at Hindown and Biana a "fauj" is coming from Indore,—some say 23, some 24 pultuns.

22nd, Refugees in Rohilkhund.—One with Raja of Powain (agent for purchase of railway sleepers); three with Metoulee Raja (between Mohumdee and Shahjehenpore); and 2 in Sota Mujla, Khera Bujhera, near where Gowan is.

European refugees with Rajah of Powain and Rajah of Metoulee.

Futtehpore Sicri.—A report from Naib Thannahdar of Futtehpore Sicri, 11 o'clock. The Mutineers left for Biana; left 21st, in the morning. Only some 20 Mewatties of Gwalior remained. In the afternoon 40 or 50 Sowars of Beree came and put up in the Tehseel. They said, "We and 500 men are in Beree. We have come to see; and when we report, all will come."

23rd October, Friday.—22nd, Taj Khan of Futtehpore Sicri very ill. Saw yesterday morning the Mutineers who left at the instance of the Mewattees. 50 Cavalry and 200 or 300 Infantry (?) came from Behra and took up residence in Tehseelee; and those who left in the morning, they too came and put up again in the Tehseelee. They said, to-morrow, on the 22nd, of the 900 Cavalry at Behra some will come. To-day (22nd) I waited till 12 o'clock; nobody came. They are coming, though.

Fattehpur Sikri.

16th October, Bareilly.—5th October, Wullee Dad, with 500 followers, reached Bareilly, and went to see Khan Buhadur. The latter has given him four pultuns, 1100 Cavalry, and 2 guns to go to Malagurh again. The soldiers have not yet consented to go, and want their pay. It seems the Nawab himself is not very anxious to go. To-day the Nawab's brother (nephew), who fled with him, is taking the troops and guns towards Malagurh, and the Naib is going to Furruckabad, and intends to get troops there.

Wali Dad Khan visits Khan Buhadur.

Rebel movement on Malagarh.

Wullee Dad is still at Bareilly.

To-day a Nawab with 500 Sowars has come from Kumona.

Bukht Khan, with the Nana's brother and some troops, has gone by Budaon to Furruckabad. The Nana is in Oudh. He keeps 400 followers by him.

Bukht Khan. Nana's brother. The Nana.

Khan Buhadur is collecting 1½ anas[1] from Malgoozars[2] (?). He sends troops to collect it.

Thakurs resist Khan Buhadur.

Five days ago he sent troops to Khundia. The Thakoors disputed, and killed 100 to 125 of the troops.

Ahirs in Budaon resist Khan Buhadur.

The Aheers of Gonour, in Budaon, also refused to pay. Khan Buhadur sent troops, but they did not dare to fight, and slunk back.

English property disposed of by rebels.

The villages of Englishmen are given in "theeka" to others.

Naini Tal attacked.

Eight days ago, of the Force sent to Nynee Tal, some were killed and the rest returned. K(han) B(uhadur) was displeased, and desired them at once to depart. They demanded their pay. He didn't give it.

The Rampoor Sepoys who have taken service with the Nawab have gone to Nynee Tal. Ten days ago my man came from Nynee Tal; the gentlemen are all well there. Nepaul troops are coming.

Nepal assisting Naini Tal.

The troops wanted pay from Sobha Ram, Dewan of the Moofsids.[3] He said, "I have none." Many resigned; and all say that when troops come they won't be able to fight. The Mahomedans say, "We will fight." Thousands of fugitive Cavalry come and leave. The Nawab has entertained some.

Fugitive Cavalry come and leave.

Lucknow news of British troops having entered,—multitudes fled.

Thousands of Hindoos and Mahomedan families have left B.[4] and gone to live in the villages.

Naini Tal attacked. Troops in Bareilly.

Khan Buhadur's army, 6000 Sepoys with 4 guns, gone to Nynee Tal. In Bareilly are 10 pultuns and some Cavalry, and 2 guns. Rent collecting in villages. In all he has 30 pultuns and 21 guns. But none are well armed. Some have guns, some swords, some clubs, and many don't know how to use a gun. There are no skilful gunners. Great distress among inhabitants. (Reported to Colonel Fraser.)

Mewattis and other rebels at Fattehpur Sikri.

Futtehpore Sicri, Subsookha.—Went to Futtehpore Sicri on the 20th; reached on 21st. 50 or 60 horses at Tehra D., not Sowars. 300 or 350 Infantry, Mewatties and Musulmans, concealed in Tehsuldaree. Some have lathis, etc., and native arms; no English muskets. The Mewatties have kept these people, and give them food. 200 to 250 Sowars fled to Behree: 50 or 60 to Biana. On 22nd I stayed at Chundowsee. There is nobody at Futtehpore but the Infantry above noted. The 60 Sowars went off to Biana. I left 4 a.m. this morning.

[1] Apparently per head.
[2] Payers of land revenue.
[3] Insurgents.
[4] Bareilly?

24th October, Buljecta.—Reached Cawnpore on 16th; stayed 17th and 18th. On 18th, 250 to 300 Europeans, with 5 or 6 guns, went to Bithoor. Next morning there was a fight. I was coming on the road when I heard report of guns. There were 400 or 500 men at Bithoor. Three hundred Sepoys with 4 carts of things met me at Akberpore, fleeing; going to Calpee. The European troops were pursuing the Nana towards Furruckabad.

Fight at Bithoor.

Nana in flight.

Dhowkla. — Saw nobody at Biana. 150 to 200 men in Futtehpore Sicri.

27th October.—Several witnesses regarding Hindown and Beree. Nobody there.

24th October. — Syfoolla (Keraolee), hearing that 1500 Mutineers had fled towards Biana, after battle of Agra, represented it to the Maharajah, who, earnestly desiring well to country, immediately, at my request, sent 1200 horse and foot at 10 p.m., ordering them to march rapidly and surprise them: and placed men at all the Nakas;[1] and I (though I have now no troops) was ready. They went accordingly and reported that no fugitives had come. At the same time intelligence came that the Mutineers had gone, some towards Pisawur, in Bhurtpore; and others dispersed; and 50 or 60 in Baroda zilla (Hindown ?), and had given money to Minas to guide and take them across the Chumbul,—towards Kyla Debee, in Keroalee.

Keraolee.

So I made arrangements, and got more soldiers to be sent to catch them. So the Durbar Cavalry surrounded the rebels, and caught them in the hilly country and fought with them. Of the rebels some were killed and some caught. Those who fled, in consequence of the hills and difficult country, were caught at the Nakas and killed; and those who tried to swim on horseback across the Chumbul were mostly drowned and their horses caught.

Rebels attacked in Keraolee.

The details will be in Khureeta.[2]

[1] Outlets or passes. [2] Letter.

INTELLIGENCE DEPARTMENT, AGRA.

MSS. VOL. VII.

TENTH SERIES.

CORRESPONDENCE WITH DEHLI, ETC.

October to December 1857.

INTELLIGENCE DEPARTMENT, AGRA.

MSS. VOL. VII.

TENTH SERIES.

CORRESPONDENCE WITH DEHLI, ETC.

October to December 1857.

DLXIX.

AGRA, *2nd October* 1857.

MY DEAR SIR,—We have still nothing later from you than the 23rd ult. A letter from Mr. Sapte to our Hattrass Detachment tells us that another pursuing column is coming down the right bank under Captain Showers. We conclude that some of your Cossids to us must have been intercepted, as we have heard nothing of this column yet. The Muthra Mutineers are crossing, but there does not exist unanimity as to the course they should take. The Bareilly Brigade has actually crossed, and part of the Neemuch one is said to have followed—so the rest may also go.

Rebels crossing at Muttra.

Indore Mutineers' movements still not certain: some say they are looking to Bhurtpore, but the general impression is that they will still go *via* Muthra.

Indore Mutineers.

There is nothing new to tell you from here.

Lucknow news still not received.

W. MUIR.

C. B. SAUNDERS, ESQ.,
Commissioner, Dehli.

We have had a letter from Sapte giving an account of the Malagurh action.

DLXX.

AGRA, *3rd October* 1857.

MY DEAR SIR,—Yesterday Captain Nixon got a letter from Colonel Becher dated the 28th. We cannot make out what has become of the intervening correspondence. In case it has not been regularly kept up, an official letter is being sent to remind you that the Government of India expected for the present that daily semi-official communications should be kept up by cossid between the Agent and Agra.

. . . .

The Bareilly Brigade has all crossed at Muthra, and their advanced guard this morning reached Moorsan, and occupied Thekum Singh's fort, burning Mr. Saunders' factory at Chittore. Some from the other brigades have crossed also, and the likelihood is that all will go the same way. Indore troops not yet moved from Dholpore, but daily expected to do so; Gwalior Mutineers now talk of marching *via* Duttia, and others Bundlekund States, to Calpee.

Bareilly Brigade.

Indore troops.

W. MUIR.

C. B. SAUNDERS, ESQ.,
Official Agent, Lt.-Governor.

P.S.—Native report has it that General Havelock dined in state at Lucknow on the 25th or 26th. But we have as yet had no letters from Cawnpore of later date than the 24th.

DLXXI.

AGRA, *4th October* 1857.

(*Enclosing Extra of Relief of Lucknow.*)

MY DEAR SIR,—This is glad news.[1] Please send it on to Sir J. Lawrence. I send also yesterday's extra. Nothing has come from you since the 22nd date.

Communicates news of the relief of Lucknow.

The Bareilly, Nusseerabad, and Dehli fugitive regiments, after plundering Hatrass, have gone north-eastwards; and I fear have escaped Greathed's Column.

Rebel movements.

Heera Singh with the Neemuch Brigade is half-way to Dholepore, there to join the Indore Mutineers. They may either go on towards Oudh *via* Etawah, or endeavour to effect a junction

Neemuch Brigade.

[1] Victory at Lucknow.

with the Gwalior troops, or combine to annoy us here. The latter is what they most talk of.

The officers killed before Lucknow are as follows.

[Names.]

W. M.

C. B. SAUNDERS, ESQ.

DLXXII.

AGRA, *5th October* 1857.

Muttra fugitives escape Greathed's Column.

MY DEAR SIR,—Yours of the 28th has been received. Many thanks for it. The Muthra fugitives by their stay at that place might have been intercepted by Colonel Greathed had his movements been more rapid. He was detained, Mr. Sapte writes, two days at Boolundshuhur, and was at Khoorja only on the 3rd. To-day he will probably be at Allygurh, but the main body of the fugitives with all their guns and elephants are to-day at Secundra Rao, some 25 to 30 miles eastward of Allygurh, so I fear Greathed has no chance of overtaking them. In that case he has been requested to march direct on Agra, in order that an immediate attack may be made on Dholepore.

Neemuch Brigade.

Heera Singh with the remnants of the Neemuch Brigade—a wretched fragment—will probably be at Dholepore to-morrow.

W. MUIR.

C. B. SAUNDERS, ESQ.

DLXXIII.

6th October.

SENDING extra of 5th October, and mentioning movements of Greathed's Column.

DLXXIV.

AGRA, *7th October* 1857.

Doubtful intelligence as to march of troops from Dholpore on Agra.

MY DEAR SIR,—We have intelligence, though of a considerably conflicting and uncertain character, that the Indore troops marched yesterday from Dholepore, and, joined by the remnant of the Neemuch Brigade, chiefly horse, were yesterday one stage this side of Dholepore. They have from 11 to 13 guns, of which 3 or 4 taken from the Dholepore Rana are heavy ones; 24- or 18-pounders. Their object is said to be to attack Agra; at least that is what they talk of.

If it be really their intention, it is not impossible that they may be expecting the Gwalior Contingent to follow them. This is at present only speculation, but we must be prepared for it. Agra cannot be allowed to be menaced by these troops, and they must not be permitted to settle in the neighbourhood with the power of entrenching themselves too strongly to be dislodged without heavy loss to us.

Colonel Greathed has therefore been written to to march this way with all despatch, and if anything prevents his marching quickly, to send 500 Cavalry and 1 troop H.A. by forced marches;—with this reinforcement we shall be able to hold our own, at any rate outside the Fort. **Colonel Greathed hurried on to Agra.**

A letter from Cawnpore mentions that, out of the force of 2000, 500 had been killed and wounded. No other names given than those already published.

We have no fresh news from that direction, and nothing local, save what I have given above. In reference to it, however, I have the Chief Commissioner's authority to urge that if possible a force be sent down the right bank of the Jumna without delay. "The best policy," Colonel Fraser holds, "is to clear as we go, and any body of troops which General Wilson may be able to send down this bank now will give confidence, tend to restore order, and can, it is hoped, soon join Greathed's Column and make it a commanding force." **Asks General Wilson to send a force down the right bank of the Jumna.**

Pray show this to General Wilson, and urge this view if it be not opposed by imperative military considerations.

W. MUIR.

C. B. SAUNDERS, ESQ.

DLXXV.

AGRA, *8th October* 1857.

MY DEAR SIR,—A letter was yesterday received from Capt. Halsted from Capt. Nixon. I have not had any others from you besides that of the 28th. Colonel Fraser desires me to say that you are expected to correspond with me daily for the present.

Although the immediate direction of affairs may be from the Punjaub, yet that does not diminish the necessity of your reporting daily your proceedings to Agra; and, even if there were not this necessity, it would still be proper for you to do so, in order that such intelligence as may be thought advisable may be sent on at once to Calcutta.

Notes points on which Agra Government requires information.

The principles upon which the reoccupation of the City by its old inhabitants is guided, and under what restrictions; any revelations brought to light as to the origin and causes of the Mutiny; the share taken in the rebel proceedings by the Chieftains and Jagheerdars of Dehli; the number of offenders tried and executed, etc., are some of the various points which should be fully explained. We gain some information, but vague and uncertain, from the Gwalior news-writer at Dehli, in whose pages General Wilson now occupies the place of the old King. Both from his statements and Capt. H.'s letter it would seem that the population of Dehli is still wandering at a distance, and not allowed to return. Is this the case, and is it intended to continue this line of policy? May it not drive many into lawless habits? And after exemplary punishment inflicted, would it not be advisable to allow all peaceably inclined persons to return? I ask these questions in ignorance of the reasons that may have dictated an opposite course. I am glad to see in the Gwalior news that the P. S. Ameen[1] was at work again, from which I gather his innocence and rejoice at it.

Principal Sudder Amin of Delhi at work.

W. MUIR.

C. B. SAUNDERS, ESQ.

DLXXVI.

AGRA, *9th October* 1857.

Mutineers, 10 miles off, threaten Agra.

MY DEAR SIR,—The Indore Mutineers are crossing the Kharee 10 miles off, and insolently threaten Agra. Their Cavalry are prowling about, and fired on our reconnoitring party this morning. Providentially, just as we should have been reduced to straits from the smallness of our force and want of horse, the moveable column arrives. Capt. E. Anson has just ridden in from the camp, 500 Horse; and 2 Troops of Cavalry are within a few miles of us. To-morrow the rest of the column will come in. So, if the Indore men will only wait a little, we hope to read them a lesson for their impudence. Nothing further from Lucknow than what you find here. The reinforcements were just in time, as the main defences of the Baillee guard had been mined and were ready to be blown up!

Captain E. Anson rides into Agra.

Lucknow relieved just in time.

Hoping to hear from you soon.—I am, W. MUIR.

. . . .

C. B. SAUNDERS, ESQ.

[1] Sir Sayad Ahmed?

DLXXVII.

AGRA, *10th October* 1857.

MY DEAR SIR,—Many thanks for your interesting letter of the 4th about the Palace papers, etc., extracts of which I have sent on to Mr. Edmonstone.

I now enclose in original a letter from Capt. Bruce at Cawnpore, to the General commanding at Dehli,—urgently calling for reinforcements. This letter of course shows the black points of the picture. I give the particulars of another to Lady Outram, which reads rather more lightly. "There had been a good deal of fighting at Lucknow, but I suspect the rebels have suffered enormously. The City is so very extensive, otherwise all would have been over in one day, and the rebels ran about like rabbits out of one house into another. The place is, for all the world, like a huge warren! **Captain Bruce at Cawnpore calling for reinforcements.** **Taking of Lucknow by Havelock's force.**

"But our Enfields are working great mischief, and I expect that part of the force which is not destined to remain there, as well as the women and children, will return in a few days."

After all, the arrangement which has been determined on is the best for the prestige of the Empire. Had we altogether abandoned Lucknow, the people throughout the country would have believed that we were in a far worse way than we really are.

And now for our own exciting intelligence. Our whole reinforcements—Greathed's entire Column—came in upon our urgent summons, by forced marches, this morning. Fortunate that they did! Our insolent enemy—not calculating that help was so near—attempted a surprise of the City. The troops were refreshing themselves on the Parade Ground, between the Metcalfe Testimonial and the Burying Ground, when, from the high crops around, our concealed enemy opened on them from three sides. All was confusion at first, and a few of our poor fellows were cut up. But order was soon restored, and the enemy's fifth shot, it is said, was replied to. The Cannonade at first was very sharp, but we could soon perceive that the reports became more and more distant. By midday we were in full pursuit; by 1 p.m. the intervals between the discharges of Artillery showed that we were rapidly proceeding onwards, unlimbering occasionally. We have had no direct report of the result yet, excepting that great numbers of dead bodies of the enemy are left beyond our encampments, and several guns—some say 8—have been taken. You shall have particulars hereafter. **Attempt at surprise of troops at Agra by rebel troops from Dholpore.** **Pursuit of enemy.** **Guns taken.**

Wonders how surprise occurred.

I do not know how the surprise occurred. There was full intimation that the enemy were crossing yesterday, and that our reconnoitring party were fired upon. What Military precautions were taken this morning I do not know.[1] French of the Lancers has been killed; Jones badly wounded by a sword-cut over the head, I think; and a 3rd Cavalry officer slightly wounded.

Casualties: French, Jones, and another officer.

In regard to the call for reinforcements, could not Brigadier Showers' Column come down here? We shall require certainly reinforcements to remain with us. The matter has not been fully discussed yet. Allygurh must be occupied by a small detachment; say, 150 Europeans and a couple of hundred Sikhs and 3 guns. We have also the Gwalior Contingent yet within 80 miles of us with a siege train. We shall see what the effect will be of the beating of the Indore troops on them. Thanks for all that you say about the MSS. Do try and save Hishâmi. I will mention your enquiry about employment of military officers to Colonel Fraser and also to the Government of India and get their orders.

Asks for reinforcements.

Gwalior Contingent has siege train, and within 80 miles of Agra.

Arabic and Persian MSS.

W. Muir.

C. B. Saunders, Esq., Dehli.

Letters from Calcutta speak of large reinforcements arriving quicker almost than they have the means of sending them up.

Reinforcements arriving at Calcutta.

DLXXVIII.

Agra, 11*th October* 1857.

My Dear Saunders,—Thanks for yours of the 6th. My yesterday's account of the action requires little to be added to it. The pursuit and defeat of the enemy were complete—11 guns;—some immense fellows were taken. Very many of the enemy killed; and on our side very few indeed,—only 3 or 4, I believe, with a number wounded in the first surprise. The enemy's camp, ammunition, plunder, everything taken from them.

Eleven guns taken.

The call for assistance from Cawnpore is, as I already stated, urgent. We may have some ulterior operations against Dholepore. But that will depend upon the information we get. Meanwhile, if Greathed's Column goes, as it must go sooner or later, towards Mynpoory and Cawnpore, we shall urgently need the presence of something more here than our very weak

Urgent call for assistance from Cawnpore.

Troops required for Agra.

[1] As in charge of the Intelligence I had given full intimation of the Mutineers' approach, and reconnoitring parties had consequently gone out. How the surprise overtook them was never explained.—W. M.

European Regiment, which is sufficient for little more than garrisoning the Fort. Col. Fraser is very anxious indeed that Brigadier Showers' Column should move downward and occupy Muthra, which at present is quite defenceless. He desires me strongly to suggest to General Penny that Rewaree can be readily occupied by Jyepore troops, and that if Brigadier Showers' Column is at once pushed on to Muthra it will render our position here secure, and make Greathed's Column available for service in the direction of Cawnpore. Jyepore could send troops to Rewaree with perfect ease.

Suggests that Brigadier Showers Column should occupy Muttra, and Jyepore garrison Rewaree.

Please to secure early attention to this point, and let me know the General's views for the Chief Commissioner's information.

W. Muir.

C. B. Saunders, Esq.,
Officiating Agent, Lt.-Gov., Dehli.

. . . .

DLXXX.

Agra, 13*th October* 1857.

My Dear Sir,—

. . . .

Our Indore Mutineers have, as far as we can see, dispersed. There is a gathering of 700 to 800 at Roopbas, but we hope they too will break up. The Durbar at Bhurtpore seized and attempted to disarm a number; they resisted, and several were killed, the rest escaping.

Indore Mutineers dispersed. Durbar at Bhurtpore actively loyal.

Col. Greathed's Column[1] crosses the bridge to-morrow, and the next day will probably move on towards Mynpoorie and (if not directed to Furruckabad) to Cawnpore. Campbell goes with it, and Cocks as far as Mynpoorie to adjust matters there. How providentially the Indore attack was timed, just to happen during the short visit of Greathed's Column.

Greathed's Column moves towards Mainpúri and Cawnpore. Campbell and Cocks with Greathed's Column.

W. Muir.

C. Saunders, Esq. (?)

DLXXXI.

Agra, 14*th October* 1857.

My Dear Sir,—Many thanks for yours of the 10th. The project of Military Police Battalions for preventive purposes will no doubt be generally introduced. More of this hereafter. Let

Project of Military Police Battalions.

[1] Lord Roberts was with Greathed's Column.—W. M.

us have news of the concentrated force at Jujjur. The Indore rebels have dispersed. They were beaten off from Muthra, a small body of them—and another from Bhurtpore, which will, I hope, give the people returning confidence.

W. MUIR.

To C. SAUNDERS, ESQ. (?)

Tribute to the services of Sir John Lawrence.

Send on the enclosed admirable order and well-merited tribute to the services of Sir John Lawrence to him. It expresses the feeling of all India towards him.

DLXXXII.

AGRA, *15th October* 1857.

Road between Agra and Delhi open.

MY DEAR SIR,—To-day yours of the 11th by cossid, and Colonel Burns' of the 12th by post, to Colonel Cotton, both arrived. So there will be no use in sending communications by cossid so long as the road remains thus freely open.

Change of headquarters in Goorgaon District.

As regards the alterations of the headquarters of Goorgaon, you are of course aware of the long correspondence that has already passed on the subject. Care must be taken, if the change is made (and the present position is decidedly objectionable), to select a salubrious spot. Is there any chance of additions to the district from resumptions in any quarter?

The instructions for daily reports were issued at a time when stirring events were daily occurring. There is now, I believe, no longer any necessity for a daily letter when nothing new is occurring. But we look to you to give us a few words every two or three days at any rate. You are in a position from the telegraph to give us also the earliest intimation of events in the Punjaub.

W. MUIR.

To C. SAUNDERS, ESQ. (?)

DLXXXIII.

AGRA, *16th October* 1857.

MY DEAR SAUNDERS,—Many thanks for yours. The progress of the King's trial, of the trial of the other parties for political offences, and of the unravelment of the proof of complicity in the rebellion against the native States and Chief men, are all points on which we gladly receive information, and promptly communicate it to Calcutta.

We have the reports of messengers that the Gwalior Contingent left Gwalior some days ago (10th or 11th) *en route* to Cawnpore. The interest of the drama will now centre there, and I trust Greathed's Column will get down in time. The report comes with every appearance of truthfulness; though it as yet wants the confirmation of letters hourly expected from the Durbar. Gwalior Contingent left for Cawnpore.

A Lahore letter of 9th speaks of the country on the Mooltan side as being still unquiet. Any information you can communicate to us on the subject, and any important movements in the Punjaub, will always be welcome.

Greathed's Column marched 13 miles this morning. It ought to be in Cawnpore in some 12 days.

W MUIR.

C. B. SAUNDERS, ESQ., Dehli.

P.S.—To the effect that the actual move was to take place in the evening of the 14th, that they would probably go by Calpee, and that Scindia was going to send his Vakeel. Move of Gwalior Contingent.

DLXXXIV.

TO SAUNDERS.

17th October.

SENDS cossid message for General Wilson, and advises of Grant's arrival and movements of Contingent and Column. Sir Hope Grant arrives at Agra.

DLXXXV.

AGRA, *19th October* 1857.

MY DEAR SAUNDERS,—Colonel Fraser has desired me to send this through you. After perusal you are to forward it to Sir J. Lawrence. The departure of the 2nd Detachment of the Gwalior Contingent (the first left on the 15th) was delayed by the desertion of 130 pairs of bullocks. The Maharajah, however, too glad to get rid of his unwelcome neighbours, supplied the want, and they marched on the 17th, taking their siege train and magazine with them. It will be all the more for Grant to capture, I trust, in the vicinity of Cawnpore. Departure of the second detachment of the Gwalior Contingent.

At Cawnpore there were, a week or ten days ago, 800 Europeans, and 500 were on their way from Allahabad. The 93rd, you see from the extra, were to be at Allahabad on the 21st. European reinforcements at Cawnpore.

Do you get copies of my bulletins regularly? I have been

arranging with the press to send you our vernacular issues also, and regularly to all districts.

Let Sir John know the few details in this letter.

W. MUIR.

C. B. SAUNDERS, ESQ.,
Dehli.

DLXXXVI.

AGRA, 20*th October* 1857.

MY DEAR WILLIAMS,—Many thanks for yours of the 15th. Colonel Fraser authorises any measures which the Military or Civil authorities may deem most expedient for the relief of Nainee Tal. This refers to your proposal to send the Goorkhas from Saharunpore. But such succour would be long in reaching. Would not the occasion have passed away by that time?

Relief of Naini Tal.

Also in regard to sending provisions. In respect of the latter point, Colonel Fraser suggests that the export of grain towards Thibet should be stopped, which will check the diminution of the supply in the Kemaon Province.

Export of grain towards Thibet stopped.

All well here.

Grant's Column at Shekoabad, and being pressed on towards Cawnpore.

W. MUIR.

F. WILLIAMS, ESQ.,
Commissioner, Meerut.

DLXXXVII.

AGRA, 20*th October* 1857.

MY DEAR SAUNDERS,—Your letter of the 15th was received only yesterday.

Will you kindly tell Sir John Lawrence that we have received no list of the Lucknow garrison. It is what we have been eagerly asking and looking for from Cawnpore; but they have as yet none there. The only names in addition to those first published are of Brigadier Gray and party and the Atkinsons, which were incidentally mentioned by a Lucknow correspondent. Additional troops will now soon be going over to Lucknow, and we shall have freer and fuller communications. Grant's Column is being urged forward, and is almost certain to anticipate the Gwalior Contingent.

General Penny sends Muzbees to Agra.

We are heartily obliged to General Penny for the Muzbees. We shall be now fully set up.

J. C. Wilson, who has run over here, tells us that there is a superabundance of Horse Artillery at Meerut. If any could be spared for us it would be a material assistance. We have but one battery; and 2 guns and 2 mortars are detached with the Europeans holding Allygurh. If all goes well we hope now, with the aid of the Muzbees, to reoccupy Muthra and Etawah; but to do this satisfactorily each party should have a couple of guns with them. A troop or battery would enable us fully to do this. Please represent the case to the General. We have plenty of guns: it is the Artillery men and horses we want.

Want of Horse Artillery at Agra.

We are uneasy at the policy regarding Dehli, and at the general tenor of conversation held regarding it by the officers of the Column who have just passed down. I have no doubt that there has been much exaggeration and misunderstanding. But *that* unless checked is likely to go forth as the unchallenged views of Government. It would be very satisfactory to have from you a statement of the facts, as well as of the principles, which have guided the Military authorities. We ought to be able to contradict misstatements, and we should be in a position, in the present imperfect state of communication, to give, in our despatches of information to the Governor-General of India, correct impressions when we touch on the subject.

Treatment of Delhi.

The visit of the Column was very hurried, but in brief conversation with the officers three grounds appeared to be taken up. First, the inability to guard the City if the population were at once readmitted. Second, the difficulty of distinguishing the evil from the well-affected citizens. Third, that a ransom was required before any inhabitant could claim to return.

Questions relating to re-admission of inhabitants to Delhi.

I conclude that the first was the real cause for the course pursued,—and indeed the terms of all your letters lead to this conclusion. But would it not have been possible to have demolished portions of the wall on each side of the several gates; to have left the outer wall and gates without any guards; and to have taken up a strong military position, as the whole available force should have been concentrated? There may have been objections to this. I only ask, in order that we may be able satisfactorily to explain the course which has been followed.

The second ground could only have a partial application. There must be large classes of the population who never took any part in the rebel cause, and many who, from first to last, were unoffending and grievous sufferers. For example, the

Treatment of Mahajuns and Bunyas by rebel soldiery.

Mahajuns and better class of Bunyas. They were the first victims of the cupidity of the lawless soldiery. When the King wanted money they were again coerced, and from the Gwalior news-writer we learned that some 50 or 60 had been for a considerable period in confinement, until the progress of our advance into the City compelled the King to relinquish his grasp. Money was wrung from them at every stage; it was given not willingly, but under the severest pressure. If this be admitted, then these men have not only nothing against them, but apparently the strongest claims upon our sympathy. And similarly, among the Hindoo portion, at any rate of the one hundred and fifty-three thousand inhabitants, there must be numerous and large classes which one would have thought might have been easily distinguishable as not disaffected and as safely to be readmitted.

Large classes of Hindus probably distinguishable as not disaffected.

Ideas common among Military as to private property in Delhi.

The third ground it is difficult to understand. The officers speak as if, having conquered Dehli, it had become their own property, not the State's; and that the State and private individuals must repurchase it from them, and that no inhabitant can return to his house till he has given a full consideration for it, and that, meanwhile, everything valuable about, the treasure which the fugitive people secreted, etc., is being gathered together for the conquerors. An officer of high rank suggested that the difficulty might be got over if the population could get the services of some millionaire, the Seth or Joteé Pershaud, to compound for the ransom, and guarantee the payment of an adequate sum—say two lakhs.

Suggestion as to a general ransom.

The understood idea of ransom.

But the understood idea of ransom is a sum paid by a city to troops who have assaulted it, in order to save it from plunder; if no ransom is paid, the city is ordinarily given up for one, two, or three days to plunder. The idea is novel of subjecting a city for above a month to plunder, and its inhabitants to temporary exile, and then requiring them to pay down the value of their property. For people or classes of people who have connected themselves with the rebellion, confiscation of property *to the State* is of course a just and reasonable punishment. But the property would be the State's, not that of the Army.

It is presumable that these statements are not warranted by any acts or express orders of the authorities; and I again repeat that I mention all this, simply that we may be able to give a satisfactory account of the policy which is being pursued.

There are other loose stories afloat which it may be well

just to mention. For example, that certain Mahajuns who were not prepared to pay the sum assessed upon them were threatened with execution, and blank cartridges fired, or threatened to be fired, upon them. It is painful to hear such stories circulated, and one is naturally anxious for authority to contradict them. Reported acts of extortion.

Colonel Fraser is, I believe, writing to Sir John Lawrence on the policy which has been observed towards the City. Will you kindly show this letter to General Penny, assuring him at the same time that what we want is information, as before explained, and I trust that the friendly spirit in which it is asked for will be understood. It will be a concession on the part of the General to allow the information to be given—a concession which we shall highly appreciate.

W. MUIR.

C. B. SAUNDERS, ESQ.,
Dehli.

P.S.—I have shown this letter to Colonel Fraser. He says that he is writing to Sir John on the subject, but that he would be obliged by your conveying the gist or a copy of my letter to him, stating that "he quite concurs in the views I have taken."

DLXXXVIII.

21*st October* 1857.

LIST of Lucknow survivors sent in; and one for Sir J. Lawrence.

Occupation of Mynpoory announced. Mainpúri occupied.

DLXXXIX.

AGRA, 22*nd October* 1857.

MY DEAR SAUNDERS,—Grant's matter has been managed very satisfactorily. You will receive the Memorandum.

Rajpootana is looking a little awkward. Difficulties in Rajputana.

Of poor Burton's foul murder and the rise of the Kota Raj troops you will have heard. Also of the Jyepore Dewan's intrigue with the Mahommedans. Are the Mewattees of Goorgaon at all in league with them?—or Wullee Dad? He speaks of avoiding the Doab. Burton's murder. Rise of the Kota troops. Jyepore Dewan's intrigue.

Some of our Indore fugitives are tending towards Biana and Tonk. Indore fugitives.

A sharp look-out must be kept in that direction.

W. MUIR.

DXC.

AGRA, *29th October* 1857.

MY DEAR SAUNDERS,—Yours of the 21st received, and General Penny's letter to Capt. Bruce despatched by to-day's despatch. We run the mail-cart to Mynpoorie, thence a cossid, and by and by a runner dak.

Postal arrangements.

Muzbees.

Captain Taylor reports the Muzbees to be raw and ill drilled. They will not be so useful as fully trained troops.

Defence of Aligarh.

Now we are sending out a couple of heavy guns and mortars to Allygurh where the Fort is to be occupied, and the force there could not fall back on us in light marching order in case of surprise (and Rohilkhund and Furruckabad threaten, though maybe they are not likely to put their threats in execution). Could not a couple of hundred Carabineers be spared from Meerut for Allygurh? We hear that they are not urgently needed there, and they would be of the most material service to us. Pray see if they cannot be obtained.

I have communicated to Calcutta your remarks about the guarantee of his life to the King.

W. MUIR.

C. B. SAUNDERS, ESQ.

DXCI.

TO SAUNDERS.

25th October 1857.

(*Encloses slips.*)

Aligarh menaced.

THE only new point to-day is that at Allygurh they are receiving very threatening reports of heavy gatherings on the north bank of the Ganges, menacing Allygurh. If it come to anything, we look to General Penny to repel the attack. This adds force to all I said yesterday about the two hundred Carabineers.

Might not the force which went to Thannah Bhower with good effect make a second circuit down by Allygurh? These demonstrations have a wonderful effect in overawing the enemy.

Anything done about the rare books and MSS.?

DXCII.

AGRA, *26th October* 1857.

Fall of Delhi now known at Bombay.

MY DEAR SAUNDERS,—By a letter from Lord Elphinstone I see that the first news he had of the fall of Dehli was from a

Jyepore letter, and one from the Nawab of Jhujjur. It is worth mentioning this with reference to the coming trial. It enabled Lord Elphinstone to transmit by the mail, then under despatch, tidings of the fall of Dehli to England.

Thanks for yours of the 23rd. Brigadier Showers' proceedings at Jhujjur and Kunound appear to have been very successful and complete.

Thanks for Sir John Lawrence's opinion about keeping troops in the Upper Doab. He was not then aware, I presume, of the extreme urgency of the demand from Lucknow. The Gwalior Contingent too has since gone off towards Cawnpore. Still, the position of the Upper Doab demands serious consideration. I have been urging this both on you and on Cawnpore; the latter are daily told that the moment any surplus men are available, or any men are set free by success at Lucknow, they are greatly needed up the country. Rajpootana too is in need of troops. Every day brings them nearer.

Demand for troops at Lucknow, in Upper Doab, and in Rajputana.

W. MUIR.

C. B. SAUNDERS, ESQ.

DXCIII.

TO SAUNDERS (with News).

27th October.

THERE is an outcry by some against Colonel Hogge, for taking J. B. on his elephant. What are the merits of the matter? It requires much courage and discretion to stem the indiscriminate flood of feeling against all natives.

DXCIV.

AGRA, *28th October* 1857.

MY DEAR SAUNDERS,—Many thanks for yours of the 26th.

It is satisfactory to learn that Showers' Brigade will be available for the Upper Doab in case of actual attack.

Movements of troops.

Our party is to-day at Futtehpore Sicri, and will probably move round by Muthra.

The approximation of the two forces in that direction will have a beneficial effect, not only locally but on the adjacent parts of Rajpootana.

W. MUIR.

C. B. SAUNDERS, ESQ.

DXCVI.

AGRA, 31*st October* 1857.

MY DEAR SAUNDERS,—Sir J. Lawrence, writing from Lahore on the 28th, two days after the receipt of a letter from Colonel Fraser, dated the 20th, says that he has not received from you any information regarding my letter of the 20th regarding the treatment of Dehli. As you yourself have not noticed the receipt of that letter, I think it as well to enclose a copy, though it is now rather out of date, the Governor-General's message having, in part at least, disposed of the question. However, it would at any rate be satisfactory to Colonel Fraser to be in possession of the views and principles which have guided the authorities at Dehli in the course which has been pursued.

In a letter just received from Cawnpore, dated the 26th, reporting the arrival there of Grant's Column, Capt. Bruce sends a message from the Governor-General, of which the following is an extract:—

Governor-General urges despatch of remount horses to Cawnpore.

"I also beg you to send to Dehli and Meerut and to press General Penny to despatch as many remount horses to Cawnpore as he can spare, and to send with them as many of the Carabineers as he can spare. Tell him Cavalry is urgently wanted." In reply I have given extract of General Penny's letter to you of the 26th, in reply to our application for Carabineers, showing that none can be spared from Meerut. I have also told Sherer that between this and Cawnpore, in the present state of the country, they would need to help us with an escort at least half-way.

The prize agents have advertised the sale of *arms*, among other things. Is this politic? The views of Government are all for *disarming* now, and this would be merely to throw more arms into the country. Would it not be well to take Sir John Lawrence's orders on the subject?

W. MUIR.

C. B. SAUNDERS, ESQ.

DXCVII.

AGRA, 3*rd November* 1857.

Colonel Cotton's Column.

MY DEAR SAUNDERS,—Colonel Cotton's Column has shot away from us in your direction. He has gone up beyond Cosee to the confines of Goorgaon, and must be not far from Showers' Column.

By the way, I am glad to see from the P.S. of your letter of the 31st that there is a prospect, on Showers' Column being reconstituted, of its being sent across the Jumna. Fraser thinks it possible that Cotton's force might effect a junction with Showers' reconstituted brigade, and then, if nothing were threatening in other directions, a movement might be possible on Furruckabad or Rohilkhund.

From Sir J. Lawrence's letters he appears to be sending down more horse to you, which should give the power of effecting something more than is doing at present.

There must, I should suppose, be very shortly an upward movement from Cawnpore. But every day anticipated in dislodging the enemy from Furruckabad, and hemming them in towards Bareilly, will be an advantage in shortening the campaign; and there is plenty to do and to spare for the coming cold weather.

W. MUIR.

C. B. SAUNDERS, ESQ.

DCI.

AGRA, *20th November* 1857.

MY DEAR SAUNDERS,—Yours of the 18th only reached me to-day. Other private letters, however, of the same date, reached yesterday, and I was able to manufacture a bulletin out of them, which I have in one or two points corrected by yours of to-day.

A private letter mentions Wallace as *killed*, which I trust is not the case. I also hope to hear soon of the actual loss of officers;—I trust with you that the *24* is a mistake. It was a hard contested and noble victory.

I am much obliged to you for your interesting explanatory letter of the 16th. I greatly admire the spirit and tenor of Sir J. Lawrence's despatch of the 20th ultimo. It is satisfactory to see that so much has been done by the Civil authority to stay harsh proceedings towards the guiltless. Treatment of Delhi.

I enclose a note from Mr. Lowe in favour of the family of the revenue Serishtahdar here, Sham Pershaud. They are described as being at Shahdera in great distress at being exiled from their homes, having neither shelter nor change of clothes. I shall be much obliged if you can get them reinstated. Sham Pershaud has behaved well. Sham Pershaud, Revenue Sheristahdar of Agra.

W. MUIR.

C. B. SAUNDERS, ESQ., Dehli.

DCII.

AGRA, *26th November* 1857.

MY DEAR SAUNDERS,—Your public letter of the 23rd, reporting the Roopraka business, has come to hand. Colonel Fraser wishes me to call attention to the undesirableness of burning the stacks and corn of the villages which are attacked.

Punitive measures on villages.

The best policy is to seize their *cattle*, which has ordinarily the effect of inducing prompt submission.

To leave the cattle and burn the stacks and corn is sure to drive the people to plunder for subsistence.

The policy now suggested is believed to be that followed with success in the Punjaub.

As Ram Chunder is so usefully employed at present, he had better stay where he is.

Books and MSS. in Palace.

Dr. Anderson, who has arrived here, speaks of another stock of books and MSS. *in the Palace*;—have these been examined?

Wali Dad. Riddel's Column.

I am glad General Penny has resolved to detain the moveable column for a time. The insurgents over the Ganges are showing signs of activity here and there, and Wullee Dad is said to have advanced on Puttialee, and by threatening that side of the Allygurh district is keeping the people in alarm. Riddel's Column has halted on that account at Hatrass; but we are very weak here, even in the matter of regular guards for the Fort Gates, and it will probably be recalled.

Communications with Cawnpore very difficult.

Colonel Fraser is unwilling to attempt any distant expedition, so Mynpoorie must lie over for the present; and till it is occupied all the Central Doab will be in confusion. All the Cossids despatched to Cawnpore on the 17th, 18th, and 19th were seized on the road. Our communications with Cawnpore are becoming very difficult.

W. MUIR.

C. B. SAUNDERS, ESQ., Dehli.

H. S. Reid, C.S. Patiáli force.

P.S.—H. S. Reid is about to leave for the purpose of escorting the Putiala force on its way to Dholepore. If that force could march *via* Goorgaon and Muthra the effect would be excellent. As it belongs to an independent State, and is coming down for its own objects, Colonel Fraser does not like to make any recommendation on the subject; but if it is all the same to them, it will be well if you can arrange for its coming the routes I mention.

W. M.

DCIII.

AGRA, *2nd December* 1875.

MY DEAR SAUNDERS,—Herewith the message. Return it, please, with your reply, and kindly send the reply as early as you can.

I also enclose copies of letters received by Cocks from Wilson regarding Wullee Dad's movements.

The Furruckabad troops have long been threatening the eastern half of Allygurh, and their movements have been stimulated by the advent of Wullee Dad. I fear Kassgunge will go, and it will be well if the Mahommedans of the district generally are not unsettled and Allygurh menaced. Farakhabad rebels.

In reference to this, Colonel Fraser would be glad if General Penny would hasten the departure of the convoy as rapidly as possible. The carriage and stores will be safe in the Fort or under it, while the escort will be of the most essential service to Allygurh. Its very presence will check any insolent advances from Wullee Dad, and will repress any risings of Mahommedan disaffection.

And if it were necessary to fight, Colonel Fraser says he would send out reinforcements from here, so that, what with the Allygurh troops, your escort, and our aid, a strong brigade would in case of emergency be available.

(Signed) W. MUIR.

C. B. SAUNDERS, ESQ., Dehli.

DCIV.

AGRA, *2nd December* 1857.

MY DEAR SAUNDERS,—Lord Canning's Private Secretary has written to enquire of me as to the evidence of violation having been (except in rare and exceptional cases) added to the atrocities with which English women and girls were visited. Enquiry as to violation of English women.

The evidence will be negative; and negative evidence, unless universal, does not prove a positive. Still it will be satisfactory to have evidence from all quarters.

I beg you will favour me with your own impressions both as to the proceedings in this respect at Dehli and elsewhere. You will have had special opportunities of hearing the truth as to Dehli, and perhaps as to Meerut.

The conviction of the people themselves on this subject is an important point: what is their belief? Ram Chunder may help you. The subject is of so delicate a nature that I do not like to write about it to any native.

So far as my enquiries extend, my impression is that the tales of violation are not sustained by any evidence (possibly sustained in one or two *exceptional* cases), and that the belief of the people is against it.[1]

W. MUIR.

C. B. SAUNDERS.

DCV.

AGRA, *4th December* 1857.

Farakhabad rebels advance on Etah.

MY DEAR SAUNDERS,—The Furruckabad rebels are advancing on Etah and threatening Awa about fifteen miles on this side, and the country generally towards this and Allygurh. The people in that direction are becoming unsettled.

Action of the Nawab (?) of Farakhabad.

The Furruckabad man has also sent two Pultuns, a Rissala, and six guns (it is said) to Mynpoorie, and is threatening Shekoabad. These movements are not unlikely in combination with the Nana, and his retainers of the Contingent, and other rebels, who advanced on Cawnpore on the 28th ult. It is very necessary that we should repress the rebels, who are creeping in again gradually upon our borders. Could not the General send on at once the escort that was intended for the convoy at Allygurh? The carts I cannot get through just now, and might wait a bit at Dehli (like ours here) till the Cawnpore people seem likely to send up for them.

Agra urgently in need of aid.

We have not even a troop of H.M. here, as two of the guns are at Allygurh. We therefore are in a position, I think, to warrant an urgent application for aid.

W. MUIR.

It will never do to let Allygurh be seriously menaced, as all our communications depend on it. The right bank of the Jumna, on the other hand, is by your report quieting down, and the Putiala Column will make the tranquillisation more rapid.

DCVI.

AGRA, *4th December* 1857.

Explanations by Mr. Saunders accepted as entirely satisfactory.

MY DEAR SAUNDERS,—I have had great pleasure in receiving your letter of yesterday, and in showing your refutation of the imputation cast upon your proceedings at Dehli to Col. Fraser.

[1] For result, see pp. 367–379, vol. i.—W. M.

Both he and I regard it as highly satisfactory. The explanation will, I doubt not, be received (excepting perhaps in respect of the part taken by Col. Hogge regarding Jewan Bukht, and that is a very light and secondary matter) as a complete justification.

Our Cossid communication with Cawnpore is at this moment entirely uncertain, and I could not trust your valuable despatch to so insecure a passage. It will go *via* Bombay, and the moment we are secure of some degree of safety in the transit of our packets to Cawnpore I will send a copy that way. As I am sending away the original, we look to you to give us an early and complete copy from which a transcript may be made for Cossid despatch.

Meanwhile a message goes by Cossid to say that your report goes by Bombay, and that Col. Fraser regards the justification complete in respect to the chief allegation against you.

The road to Cawnpore is very difficult at present. We have nothing later than the 25th from there. **Road to Cawnpore difficult.**

W. Muir.

C. B. Saunders.

DCVII.

Agra, 11*th December* 1857.

My Lord,—We have still no direct communication from Cawnpore. But the tidings of a glorious victory achieved by our troops over the Contingent and other rebels have reached us through the Gwalior Durbar. The statement is communicated by the news-writer at Calpee, who received the intelligence from Gwalior messengers with the enemy's camp on the 8th. I conclude the action was fought on the 7th. **Gwalior Contingent beaten.**

The Commander-in-Chief with the whole of the Lucknow force apparently crossed the Ganges on Monday and Tuesday, the 30th November and 1st December. Between that date and the date of the battle it is presumed that the enemy were obliged to fall back towards the position they occupied on the first or second engagement.

On the 7th it was resolved by the enemy to make a general attack, and at midnight assault the entrenchments. **Description of the fight.**

The account is that they attacked us with great vigour; that we retired; and that the enemy followed us two coss from their own camp;—that then a detachment of our army by a flank movement attacked and captured their camp, and took the enemy in the rear. The insurgent force soon gave way, and fled in confusion towards Luckeindee (?), abandoning all their guns, their ammunition, their baggage, and everything. Two large guns coming over to them from Calpee were also captured.

Koer Dowlat Singh.

The flying Sepoys were rejected by the whole population. No one found refuge anywhere. Koer Dowlat Singh met with the same treatment in his flight.

Balla Sahib.

The gallantry of our troops is described as something beyond all conception; our Officers cutting down the Artillery men at their guns. The slaughter amongst the enemy said to be very great. The Balla Sahib was wounded in the shoulder and fled to Calpee. He has there removed the remaining artillery ammunition, etc., into the fort.

God grant that this splendid victory may speedily be confirmed by our own despatches.

I remain,

Your Lordship's obedt. servant,

W. MUIR.

TO THE RT. HONBLE. THE GOVERNOR OF BOMBAY.

P.S.—Since writing the above a despatch has come in from Gen. Mansfield, dated the 3rd inst. He states in it that so soon as the women, sick, etc., are well on the rear, *en route* to Allahabad, the Commander-in-Chief expected that one day would suffice to drive off the rebels. He complains greatly of the want of Cavalry.

It will be as well not to make public the details of the victory till some further corroboration is received.

W. MUIR.

DCVIII.

CITY CAWNPORE, *3rd December.*

General Mansfield's letter. Commander-in-Chief applies to Sir John Lawrence for Cavalry.

MY DEAR SIR JOHN,—I am desired by the Commander-in-Chief to write and let you know that we are very badly off indeed for Cavalry,—so much so that advantages gained cannot be followed up for want of horsemen.

His Excellency is very desirous that you should send him as many Sikh Sowars as you can spare. He is aware that you promised to send some five or six hundred to Dehli, and has desired me to write and request of you to press on Cavalry as fast as you can. We are now in the presence of the rebels; and as soon as all the families, sick, wounded, and other enormous encumbrances from Lucknow, which now hamper the camp, are well on their way to the rear, *en route* to Prag,[1] His Excellency hopes that one day will suffice to drive them out of Cawnpore, a portion of which place they at present hold possession of.

The frontier towards Jounpore is heavily threatened, and troops are being stopped at Benares to reinforce Col. Longden and the Goorkas. Col. Franks has been directed to assume command of the field force in the Jounpore and Azimgurh districts. Col. Longden (?) had been obliged to fall back. Colonel Longden. Colonel Franks.

W. MANSFIELD, MAJOR-GENL. (?)

SIR J. LAWRENCE.

[1] Allahabad.

MSS. VOL. VIII.

ELEVENTH SERIES

LETTERS FROM W. MUIR, C.S.

PRINCIPALLY TO

GENERAL HAVELOCK:

A FEW TO SIR JOHN LAWRENCE, MESSRS. TUCKER, GREATHED, BEADON, SHERER, AND WILLIAMS.

COPIED IN GREAT PART

BY

E. H. MUIR.[1]

[1] Lady Muir.

DCIX.

From W. Muir, C.S., to General Havelock, Cawnpore.[1]

Agra, *6th August* 1857.

My Dear Havelock,—I send you the news of the day. Letters from Dehli up to the 2nd. That was Sunday, the Eed ooz Zoha or Bakr Eed, on which dissensions were reported, but Greathed mentions nothing on the subject. He may have written early in the day, and so something may yet be heard of the bad feeling in the City excited by the Mussulman proceedings of the day. There is no ground either for the native report mentioned yesterday of the desertion of Sepoys from the rebel cause. They desert, but in small parties, and go to their homes. The Palace overtures have come to nothing, and will not be renewed. On the 31st July the Pandies moved out in great strength, and, skirting the distant hills, made a circuit to reach the bridges on the Nujuffgurh Jheel cut. We had destroyed, as you may recollect, those bridges by blowing them up, and the enemy now sought to replace them by wooden structures. By this movement they crossed our rear and menaced our camp, while the force left in the City simultaneously attacked our front. Whatever the enemy managed to do while we were engaged before and behind was undone by the floods during the night. What with the heavy rain of the 31st July and 1st August (and, the natives add, the opening of our Canal escapes), the bridges were washed away, and swept by the Jheel cut to our Camp. After this bootless expedition the enemy returned to the City, and it was then resolved to attack our right throughout the night. They opened a cannonade and discharge of musketry in that direction at 5 p.m., and the firing was kept up without intermission till 6 a.m. But they made no impression: every advance was repelled, and our loss was very slight—so slight that Greathed gives no details of it. They had recommended, Greathed adds, an attack on the Subzee Mundie Pickets, but it had not assumed sufficient importance to call up the supports. Though the Jumna was high, the bridge below Dehli stood.

Position of affairs at Delhi.

Attack via Nujjufgurh.

[1] These pages copied out in great part by Lady Muir.

Constant communication was held with Meerut *via* Baghput. The Kemaon battalion, with treasure, ammunition, and stores, had arrived on the 1st. All was quiet in the Punjaub, which is a great comfort.

Mr. F. Williams, Commissioner, writing from Meerut on the 2nd, gives an account of the affair with the Malagurh rebel troops. Many of our Meerut communications seem to have been interrupted by this rebel and his emissaries, who are now in possession of Allygurh. Wulidad Khan had advanced post with guns to Gulaothee between Malagurh and Meerut. They were attacked by our force of 50 Carabineers and Rifles, who killed 920 of them, [and the rest fled in such ?][1] a fright and haste that it is said they even left Boolundshuhur. I fear, however, that Malagurh is not evacuated, though the Nawab fled from it at the first tidings of defeat. Mr. Williams says we cannot attack Malagurh safely until either the Hindun or the (Jumna ?) bridge is broken, and attack thus intercepted from Dehli. He thinks we could not hold it, and that the effect of abandoning it would be worse than not attacking it. He has pressed on the Brigr.-General at Dehli the necessity of breaking the Hindun bridge. It was supposed to be broken by an Engineer from his force, but the rebels had it repaired for the Bareilly Brigade. "As soon as it is broken and the Sikh reinforcements arrive at Meerut," Williams writes, "Wullee Dad Khan's short reign will, *D.V.*, be over, and you will hear of us at Allygurh." I hope this will soon be the case, as we cannot afford to let the Malagurh Sooba collect the revenue within 50 miles of this and be remitted to the King.

Attack on Malagarh rebels at Gulaothee.

Wali Dad Khan.

Hindun Bridge.

Williams writes: "2 wonderful guns made of cast-iron screw piles of the Electric Telegraph posts, with grape made of the wire," were brought away from Gulaothee, and are now at Meerut as curiosities.

Districts of Meerut Division.

Guns made of telegraph posts.

Seharunpore and Muzuffernugger quiet and in order. Two guns were being sent to Seharunpore. The passage of the party had a wonderful effect on the surrounding country. The following from him regarding Dehli, though not the latest, may be of interest.

"From the 23rd (July) to the 1st (August) nothing had been done. We were occupied in strengthening our position by breastworks. 600 labourers were allowed by the enemy to be on this work without even a shot fired at them. The walls and garden in Teleewara and Subzeemundee have been cleared away,

Position at Delhi.

[1] Writing worn away.

and a sortie is no fun now to Pandey, for he does not like the open."

After referring to the strong reinforcements expected on 10th instant, he says: "But I question whether they will go at Dehli even then. I believe that, till they get the European reinforcements from below, they will rest. It is highly desirable to push them up and settle Dehli. The people everywhere are looking for that; and partly believe the utterly false accounts which issue from the rebels, and are most industriously spread by those who have already committed themselves, to induce the people to side with them." He adds, that without these reinforcements the destruction of the rebel force could not be complete, however successful the result, but I believe it is quite a work of supererogation now to press the urgency of a rapid advance.

The accounts from Gwalior remain as before. Major Macpherson has letters from the Durbar, which gave the

Strength of Gwalior Mutineer force.

Mutineer force there as follows.[1] The numbers are greatly inferior to those formerly stated, as some thought the force was not less than 10,000, others 14,000, some 18,000 strong. The Artillery, however, is powerful, and they have besides a siege train and 3rd class Magazine. The Indore guns are believed to have come up without Artillery men.

(*Printed note enclosed* (?).)

Agra.

I MENTIONED before that the want of tents was felt at Dehli. They could be made up either at Cawnpore or here, and be taken up by your advancing Column.

We have a few camels to send down, but no other convoy than the retainers of Zemindars, who are not much to be trusted. Besides, those "Saugor-Nagode" troops are, I fear, not out of our vicinity yet. I have heard nothing of them these two days.

Panic on Grand Trunk Road.

There is a great terror spread up the Grand Trunk Road, that the European troops destroy all villages in their line, killing the inhabitants and burning the houses. The ill-disposed take advantage of this to persuade the others to join with them, as they will, under any circumstances, share their fall if we triumph. Of course, severe example must be made wherever treachery and disloyalty have appeared, and we cannot help our acts being misinterpreted by our enemies. But it will be well to bear

[1] A blank space is left for the statement, which, however, is not given in the MSS. volume.—W. C.

the rumour I have mentioned in mind, in order that any opportunity may be taken for impressing upon the people the conviction that we seek to punish only the guilty, and that the faithful, instead of being involved in their fall, will be treated with favour.

No messenger either yesterday or to-day from Cawnpore. These Saugor fellows may have intercepted your letter.

Two Sikh men, sent by us with letters, are said to have been blown from guns by order of the Furruckabad Nawab on the way to Cawnpore. **Cossids blown from guns.**

[W. M.]

DCX.

W. Muir, C.S., to H. C. Tucker, C.S. Commr., Benares.

Agra, *7th August* 1857.

My Dear Tucker,—As a messenger is going back to Benares, I send you a few lines. Though it is some time since you have heard from us direct, yet I doubt not you are familiar with our position. Besides the official and demi-official despatches from Mr. Colvin, I have taken pains to send almost daily letters to Havelock (a personal friend and connection) containing all the news of any importance relating to us, Dehli, etc., and he probably sends on such portions of the intelligence as he thinks expedient. Our position at Agra remains pretty much what it was ten or fifteen days after the fight of the 5th. The Neemuch Mutineers left Muthra for Dehli on the 18th, and since that time we have not been directly threatened from any quarter. Gwalior we have all along felt to be our weak point. The Mutineer troops menace us with a siege on their way to Dehli. Their numbers are greatly exaggerated. Persons who ought to have known represented them at 10,000, 15,000, or even 18,000. By a late statement received by Major Macpherson from Gwalior, it is shown that, including Indore Mutineers, the Cavalry is under 1000, the Infantry only 4000, and 1000 Ghazees. But they are strong in Artillery. They have four batteries of six guns each, and seven guns from Indore; but the latter without gunners. They have also a well-stocked 3rd class Magazine. Scindia, however, has talked them over to stay till after the rains,—and after the rains, please God, we shall be able to turn the scales against them. Meanwhile a regular siege of Agra, endangering *θε μοστ ιμπορταντ αρσεναλ* in these parts, would have created a serious *διυερσιον ιν favoup οφ θε Δελι μυτινεερς*. The possibility of this *δανgερ* is, I trust, passing

Position at Agra. **Neemuch Mutineers.** **Strength of Gwalior force.**

Indore Mutineer troops at Gwalior.

away. The Indore Mutineer troops have arrived at Gwalior. We have not heard particularly what has transpired since. The Gwalior and Mhow Mutineers were not reputed to pull well together. Scindia might possibly be unable to restrain them. He was certainly every day finding his position more difficult. But we must trust he will succeed in holding the Gwalior force in hand. He has paid them large advances, but there is no reason to question the friendliness, I think, of Scindia's present conduct. There are frequent communications, but of an informal nature, between him and Macpherson. As to Dehli, our position is improving. There was a lull on the enemy's attacks during the last nine or ten days of the month. And this was taken advantage of by us in strengthening our outworks. The Kumaon (Goorkha) Battalion joined on the 1st. Regular trains are established for the conveyance of stores, etc., from Umballa. The road is free to Meerut *via* Baghput. But the country south and east of Dehli is utterly disorganised; our cossids from Dehli and Meerut encounter much risk, and several are reported to have lost their lives. Large premiums are paid for rapidly delivered communications, yet we receive our letters most irregularly and insecurely. It had been remarked last month that the attacks of the Pandies (as they are now usually styled at Dehli and Meerut) have become feebler and feebler. They have lost heart. The reproaches of the King, etc., drive them out into the field with vaunting speeches as to dislodging us from the heights, but the moment we turn on them they fly, as Greathed says, "like the wind." The affairs of the 31st and 1st instant are quite in accordance with this. A long-concocted plan of attacking us in front and rear utterly failed, and a night attack protracted from 5 p.m. to 6 a.m., during which the cannonading and musketry were kept up without interruption, was resisted by us with very slight loss. On the 2nd an attack had been made on our picket at Subzeemundee, but was so feeble as not to require us to call up the supports. Unable thus to succeed in offensive operations, the Mutineers will find their position entirely altered by the arrival of the reinforcements. On the 10th, 1600 Europeans and 300 Punjaubies will enable us, there can be little doubt, to resume active attacks. But even with this addition the enemy are so numerous and have such a weight of Artillery that it seems more than doubtful whether anything will be attempted at a general assault till your reinforcements join the Dehli (?) camp. If Havelock is able to dispose of the Oudh Mutineers without much delay, we

Scindia's loyal action.

Kumaon (Goorkha) Battalion.

Cossids run risks.

The term "*Pandy.*"

Delhi Mutineers losing heart.

are looking for an early (?) advance this way, and we can send any amount of ammunition and heavy guns and mortars with the Column. Dehli once settled, the country will for the most part be settled also—though a campaign in Bundelkhund and probably in Rohilkhund may be anticipated in the cold weather. You know, of course, that from Meerut to Cawnpore, and from Nynee Tal to Etawah, we have not a single post or officer exercising an authority for us. This encourages the enemy to throw out offshoots from Dehli. He can do little in Rohilkhund, where the Nawab of Rampore is holding Mooradabad (it is believed *bonâ fide*) for us; but between this and Meerut a petty Nawab, Wullee Dad Khan, professing to have a patent from the King, set up at a Fort called Malagurh, and from small beginnings raised a numerous troop of followers, and assumed the "Sooba" from Dehli to Allahabad. He has had the arrogance to send a Naib Sooba to Allygurh, who within a week has, with the countenance of a part of the Mahommedan population, set up an administration, raised levies, and commenced collecting the revenue. I hope it may be possible for us to organise an expedition for chasing the fellows away, and put two faithful Talookdars, who have already received a warrant for the purpose, in charge of the city. The Malagurh rebel has received a serious check in attempts to extend his rule towards Meerut. He was charged by the Militia and a small party of the Carabineers and Rifles, who carried his entrenchments to Guloutie, killed 92 of his Cavalry, and carried off his guns, some of which are manufactured out of Telegraph Post piles, with bits of the wire for grape! It is likely we may make some dashing attempts of this sort now, under the vigorous auspices of Col. Cotton. But we have no Cavalry except a small body of Militia, and only some 700 European soldiers. We have plenty of guns, but are not well off for gunners, either officers or men, and our Artillery . . . was fearfully crippled at the battle. The Nana extended his attempt at rule up to our doors, sending perwanahs and roobekurs to Etawah; but as he has gone, Etawah is now ready to receive us. But no European officer could go without some troops. At Furruckabad our pensioner, the Nawab Races, has entertained the mutinous Seetapore force, and threatens to march on Cawnpore. Havelock or Neill will, no doubt, give a good account of him. We are delighted to see by Beadon's letter the activity in preparing reinforcements both by land and water. The armed boats will be of great use, both on the Ganges and the Jumna. If we only

Condition of country very unsettled.

Nawab of Rampore believed to be loyal.

Wali Dad Khan at Malagarh assumes rule from Delhi to Allahabad.

Pretensions of Wali Dad Khan, Malagarh.

The Nana.

Nawab Races at Farakhabad.

had 1 or 2 as a guard, we might send down a fleet of boats with women and children. The prospect of 25,000 men by the cold weather is glorious.

Lord Ellenborough and the Mutiny.

It is very painful to read Lord Ellenborough's debate on the Barrackpoor Mutiny. Certainly no one in the country could say the Government at all interferes in favour of Christianity. One can hardly conceive any line of conduct more rigidly neutral. The only apparent exception is one which has been decidedly lauded, and which is in reality the carrying out of an equitable principle, namely, grants in aid to existing schools. But neither this, nor private subscriptions on the part of the men in authority, have been in the slightest degree felt in the country practically as symptoms of a proselytising spirit. It is also remarkable that, in all the wild outrages that have taken place, I have observed no mark of antipathy or exhibition of revenge against our Magistracy or the Establishments. The C. M. College here has fared better than the Government College. The truth is that the movement is a political one, led on by designing men, who seized on any convenient handle which they could twist against us. The Sepoys thought, and (considering the rare appearance of a European Regiment) not unnaturally, that they formed the sole pillar of the Empire. Their pride and conceit were easily wrought upon by that idea. The ringleaders took the opportunity for a grand revolution, in which ambition and avarice would be gratified. The better class were frightened into joining them, by adroitly converted lies, to which the cartridge myth was regarded as giving a stamp of truth, and when 1 or 2 bad men had fired a shot the whole Regiment held themselves compromised, and mutinied. The tale that the Sepoys were to be Christianised was no doubt a common and popular one in the hands of the ringleaders, but its mould and colour were all political;—at no point that I have seen was the tale grafted on the alleged existence of a grievance from our missionary institutions or their support by officers of Government. I think Lord Ellenborough's assertion singularly unhappy, and believe from observation that the natives do most thoroughly distinguish between a public and a private act in favour of Christianity, and I believe that it adds, in the opinion of the natives, essentially to their esteem and confidence, when they see a man follow his convictions in privately supporting his religion. It will be a sadly backward step if the Court of Directors think of shackling their officers in this respect. If, with the Divine favour helping us, we get well through these difficulties, our Government will be

Attitude of Government towards Christianity.

Agra Church Mission College.

The Mutiny a political and military one.

No grievance from our Missionary Institutions.

Public and private acts of officers clearly distinguished in religious matters.

infinitely stronger than before for all that is beneficial to the country, both physical and moral. I wish we could have looked forward to Mr. Colvin's hand in the remodelling of our institutions to suit our altered circumstances: though much recovered, he is still far from being in the buoyant health he had three or four months ago, and the medical men *may* advise a retreat. This is unfortunate, as there is no one so well fitted, from experience, ability, and now from local knowledge, for reorganising our system.

What a host of interesting questions will now be raised!

I have drawn up a draft of rules for the first reintroduction of our revenue system into a disturbed district. They are now with Reade. But as far as regards us here, the thing is almost premature. However, districts in rear of our advancing column should soon be ready for something of the kind. Let us hear frequently from you. If you write on thin paper and fold small, it can easily be forwarded from Cawnpore.[1]

W: M.

DCXI.

W. Muir, C.S., to Genl. Havelock, Cawnpore.

7th October.

My Dear Havelock,—Congratulations on success of 29th. Brigadier Neill regrets your retrograde movement on the 1st for artillery reinforcement; but you, no doubt, had good grounds for it: and, *D.V.*, you will march triumphantly on Lucknow.

Malagurh and expected expedition.

Affair at Gulouthee.

Nothing from Gwalior.

W. M.

DCXII.

W. Muir, C.S., to Genl. Havelock, Cawnpore.

Agra, *8th August* 1857.

My Dear Havelock,—We have another letter of the 1st from Cawnpore, from Sherer, but it does not give any further information as to the cause of your movement in falling back on Cawnpore. Meanwhile we know that in three actions in one day you beat a force enormously superior in numbers, and took

Havelock's successful fights.

[1] It will be remembered that all our communications down country were on thin paper crushed into the smallest space, and so secreted by the Cossid. —W. M.

all their guns, and that is enough for us. Your admirable order of the 13th July, after the Futtehpore fight, has just reached us through the *Poona Observer*; that is the spirit for the occasion. With it, all will go well by the blessing of God. A letter has been received from Moradabad, stating that the Nawab of Rampoor has been killed by a faction amongst his people; that the son of a son-in-law of the former Nawab (now at home) has been placed on the Guddee; and that the son of the deceased Nawab has escaped with 500 Pathan horsemen on pretence of going to Dehli, but probably with the view of casting himself on our protection at Meerut. I cannot yet vouch for the truth of this, but shall probably know more as to its certainty to-morrow.

Nothing from Gwalior.

The Nawab Raees (of Farakhabad). We hear that the Nawab Raees has sent forward his troops to Jelalabad; and they would probably form a junction in that quarter with the Saugor and Nagode troops. General Neill may possibly see something of them before your return.

We do not know where the entrenched camp at Cawnpore is. General Neill only mentioned its being strongly situated on the river, but the Cawnpore bank has a run of 4 or 5 miles. It would be interesting to us to know the exact locality. Sherer mentions that the Saugor troops killed a Thannahdar and broke down a bridge, but he did not specify the name of the Thannahdar or the bridge. All details of the sort are useful. This goes with a reply from Mr. Colvin to General Neill. You will see that we can get you plenty of camels, 250 now, and 1000 more perhaps in a week. But it would be very unsafe to send them without a regular military Guard; the drivers (?) in fact decline to go without such an escort. It was great good fortune your finding such a supply of gun-caps at Cawnpore. I wrote before that we are well supplied with them here for our own use, but could not probably meet large indents from below, and that it would be advisable to have the stores replenished from below. We have no *Enfield* rifles or ammunition. I have suggested to Colonel Cotton to send down an abstracted statement of our ordnance and ammunition as it now stands in this Magazine, and he agrees that it will be a good plan. So you will probably receive it soon.

Sending transport down country unsafe.

Deficient military equipment at Agra.

W. M.

Country quieting down near Agra. *P.S.*—The country in this immediate vicinity is getting quieter and more amenable to our authority—thanks to your victories, though their effect on us locally is as yet somewhat counteracted by the Allygurh and Furruckabad movements. I have written to you every day, I think, of late. Are you receiving my letters?

DCXIII.

W. Muir, C.S., to General Havelock, Cawnpore.

Agra, *9th August* 1857.

My Dear Havelock,—Many thanks for yours of the 1st, kind and hearty, though short. Your note of the 3rd, in Greek, has also come to hand. The Supreme Government have now all the facts before them. The Governor-General will no doubt do what is possible and the most expedient under all the circumstances for an upward movement. So, being unthreatened ourselves for the present, and Dehli being about to be greatly strengthened by the P[unjab] reinforcements, we may trust the matter to higher hands.

. . . .

We know that the Nana's jewels were of vast value. Did Nana's jewels.
you take them all? I have sent on your note to Dehli to be passed on to Mussourie,[1] where they will be delighted to see your handwriting.—Yours affectionately,

W. M.

DCXIV.

W. Muir, C.S., to Genl. Havelock.

Agra, *10th August* 1857.

My Dear Havelock,—We have news from Dehli up to the 4th. I propose enclosing Greathed's last in this, but it is now with Colonel Cotton, and in case it should not return in time I give you the following details of its contents.

"Position in camp stronger than it has ever been. The Affairs at Delhi.
failure of the entire weight of the enemy, backed by the last of their reinforcements, and attempting to take us in rear and front at the same time, has really broken their spirit. They have abandoned the hope of dislodging our army, which is a most significant fact. 900 of the Neemuch force never returned into Dehli from that night's long fight between 1st and 2nd instant. The Dehli people estimate their own loss at 3000, inclusive, no doubt, of the runaways."

"*Dispersion*," Greathed says, "*may now really be looked for.*" Sepoys beginning to disperse.
The Sepoys are asking for leave to go to their homes; the tidings

[1] *i.e.* to members of our family there.—W. M.

Killing of butchers.

of your victories making them uneasy as to their homes in Oudh Your success, you see, besides its immediate effects, has a wide-spread indirect influence, already telling on the Sepoys in Dehli and influencing the fate of the rebels there. The news, I think, is highly encouraging. I enclose also a letter of Greathed's of the 2nd; the closing item about the killing of 5 butchers for slaughtering cows is evidence of the power of the Hindoo faction.

Eed at Delhi.

Mutiny of 26th N.I. at Meean Meer.

You will see also that they managed so that the bulk of the troops were out of the City at the time of the Eed, which was thus so managed by the leaders of the King's party as to pass off quietly. To balance this good news there is the account of the mutiny *οφ θε* 26th at Meean Meer. I copy the statement, which is going on in a printed form to Mr. Sherer to be forwarded down the country.

Punjab reinforcements.

Position at Delhi vastly improved.

Another letter says, D.,[1] or nearly the entire number, have been cut up in crossing the *Pavee*. So that these fellows are not likely to give us more trouble. *Βυτ θις ἁς ρεταρδεδ θε αδυανς οφ ουρ Πυνjαβ ρειυφορσεμεντς.* Some letters speak of their being expected to reach on the 18th our camp at Dehli. And besides these the *πρεσεδεντ ις αν υνεασι ονε. Ιφ οθερ δισαρμεδ Ρεγιμεντς φολλοω θειρ εκσαμπλε ιτ νιλλ εμβαρρασς θε Πυνjαβ λοκαλ φορσες.* So you see there is still the same *υρjεντ νεεδ οφ ραπιδ αδυανς φρομ θε Εαστ.* At the same time our vastly improved position at *Δεχλι*, with the evident discontent and defection of the Sepoys, may lead to something down there earlier than we have been expecting. If D. were to *φαλλ αλλ* would soon come straight. I enclose two letters from Anson, which you may read with some interest. You can tear them up. Nothing new from any quarter. No corroboration of the Rampore report throws extreme doubt upon it.

W. MUIR.

P.S.—May the same divine blessing attend your onward movement. We do trust you will find dear Mary and B. Thornhill[2] well. One hardly dares send a message for them till one hears that they are all right.

[1] *i.e.* 500.

[2] *Note.*—John Bensley Thornhill, of the Bengal Civil Service, was married to a niece of General Sir H. Havelock. They were in Lucknow during the siege; and Mr. Thornhill died of wounds received, it is believed, when he had left the Residency to show the relieving force the way through the city.—W. C.

DCXV.

W. MUIR, C.S., TO H. H. GREATHED, C.S., DEHLI.

AGRA, *11th August.*

MY DEAR GREATHED,—Your reply by the Cosee Tehsildar's man came pretty quickly, so we are trying them again. I send two notes: one your answer, and the other for Hodson Commanding the Guides. There is little new here. Bazaar reports of the reoccupation of Lucknow, but premature, I think, as there is hardly time for the news yet to have reached us. All quiet at Gwalior, and between this and Cawnpore *βι θε Ετawα ρουτε, βυτ βι θε Τοορσαχαγυνγ ανδ Κανουγ ρουτε θε τροοπς οφ θε Ναωαβ Ραεες άνε οκκυπιεδ θε ροαδ & σειζε ουρ μεσσενγερς. νιθ* what *οβγεκτ άνε θε γυνς & τροοπς κροσσεδ φρομ Δελι το θε οθερ σιδε θε ρινερ? άνε ανι γονε ουερ το έλπ Μαλαγυρχ ορ φλεδ ουερ θε Γανγες το θε Βυγνορε Ναναβ?*

Nawab Raees interrupting communications.

W. Edwards was at Futtehgurh, and is safe with a Zemindar on Oudh side along with some other Futtehgurh people. Major Blake was *κιλλεδ ατ Γυαλιορ*: she is here. The accounts of the rebels in Dehli being dispersed and ready to forsake their cause correspond with what we hear here.

W. Edwards, C.S.

Major Blake killed.

When the *ρεινφορσεμεντς* reach we trust *θατ οφενσινε* measures will be renewed.

W. MUIR.

DCXVI.

W. MUIR, C.S., TO GENL. HAVELOCK.

AGRA, *11th August.*

MY DEAR HAVELOCK,—I enclose two letters: one from Greathed and another from Anson;—you will like the cheerful spirit of the latter. I don't know what the rebels are after on the other side the river, but their cause seems failing evidently. You will observe the letter of the King to General Metcalfe. He was very fond of his father, old Sir Thomas Metcalfe. It is highly satisfactory to see that the progress of reinforcements continues unimpeded *Βι θε μυτινι* of the 26th. The column should be reaching Dehli by this time. You will see also that attempts are not omitted to destroy the bridge of boats, and they may yet prove successful.

King writes to Sir Thomas Metcalfe.

There have been Bazaar reports rife here for a day or two that you have reached Lucknow and accepted "Man Şingh's terms." But the tidings could not have reached so soon. We are, however, expecting, please God, some early news of further victorious proceedings. Mr. Colvin is anxious to get a copy of one of the Nana's proclamations, which General Neill said were skilfully drawn up. If possible send us copies of all. I am anxious to see if he refers to Missionary efforts. The ordnance and ammunition statement will follow to-morrow. We have already six 24-pounders and three 8-inch howitzers with 500 rounds each, and two 32-pounders, ready to start.—Yours affectionately,

Nana's proclamations.

W. MUIR.

DCXVII.

W. MUIR, C.S., TO GENL. HAVELOCK.

AGRA, *12th August* 1857.

MY DEAR HAVELOCK,—We have again rapid intelligence from Delhi up to the 7th and 8th. Mr. Colvin is sending extracts of these to Brigadier Neill, which you will see, but I may recapitulate the intelligence here.

Rebels' efforts to raise money at Delhi.

In the letter of the 7th Mr. Greathed says that the rebels have sent a force from Delhi to Jhujjur to enforce a demand of 5 lacs. Another body of 800 foot and 150 horse and 2 guns have been sent into the Doab to Dasneh or Malagurh to raise money. Marwaris, etc., called in for forced loans. The Ghazies are going home, *for they get nothing to eat!*

Marwaris. Ghazis.

The attack of the 6th had died out by 2 p.m. An attack on the Metcalfe Picket was abandoned on the first show of resistance by us.

Nicholson arrived at Delhi.

Nicholson had arrived, and the reinforcements were expected on the 13th to the 15th. They must have been about Kurnaul. They had heard through Lahore of the message from the Ministry of 27th June, regarding reinforcements from home. The first rumours of your victories between Cawnpore and Lucknow had reached the city, with the addition that your troops had sacked Lucknow for three days.

Explosion in Delhi powder factory. Hakim Ahsunoolla Khan.

The letter of the 8th relates that a great conflagration (?) had been caused the day before in the city, whereby 500 artificers, and the stock in hand of sulphur and saltpetre, were blown into the air; the place continued to burn. The Sepoys suspected Hakeem Ahsunoolla Khan being at the bottom of it, and plundered his house. There had been no attack to speak of since the 2nd. Besides the Doab force, one had been sent towards Nujjufgurh to levy contributions, the same perhaps as before mentioned as having gone to Jhujjur.

They have taken now to attacking our position with field-pieces behind the cover of trees and buildings, but their fire is in-effectual. They tried a heavy fire on the 7th, but it was soon silenced. On the 8th all was quiet. Health good. Cholera ceased. *All are looking forward to the day when the approaches will be made.*

You will see from Mr. Colvin's to Brigadier-General Neill that he regards as an unfavourable symptom the ability of the enemy to be detaching bodies of troops to beat up for money. No doubt it shows that they have still plenty of men. But besides that, their heart is broken for fighting at Dehli. I think the last words I have underlined are so full of promise and hope as quite to outweigh that consideration. In another letter of the 5th, when speaking of the expectation held out by Colonel Tytler in his letter *via* Meerut dated the 25th ult., of your marching towards Dehli from Lucknow on the 29th, he adds, "I do not think the capture of Dehli depends now upon his coming." This point is so important that I send the letter in original to you.

Position of affairs at Delhi.

From all which I gather that when the reinforcements arrive active offensive measures will be recommenced, regular approaches made, and, please God, a successful assault. When matters begin to go hard at Dehli we shall afford to laugh at the detachments sent east and west for money. Otherwise, of course, these out-ward movements were not to be despised.

F. Williams, Commissioner at Meerut, writes, 4th, that spies had been discovered taking plans of the entrenchments there. Two were hung. And he thinks an attack there in force not at all improbable, especially as it is his opinion that the rebels are likely on evacuating Dehli to pass over into Rohilkhund. As our siege train closes in upon Dehli I should think that all thought of attacking Meerut would be abandoned. They appear to be strengthening on the left bank, and are "throwing up entrench-ments on the eastern side of the bridge of boats," and Williams adds he cannot send out a party strong enough to δεφι even two regiments with guns, in addition to Wullee Dad Khan and his Goojurs. The latter since his defeat at Golowtie has got an addition of 500 men to his force.

Wali Dad Khan.

Fancy the arrogance of the King and his adherents. If they had succeeded in their night attack, the King was to have held his Eed in our camp, and the termination of our reign was to have been proclaimed. But as Greathed adds: "It is one thing to make projects and another to carry them out; and with the country so much under water, Pandey will find himself in a fix if he tries to work in our rear."

Ambitious plans of the King.

As regards the origin of the disaffection, Greathed was asked to make all the enquiry he could from deserters, etc. He writes in reply:—"The result of all questionings of Sepoys who have fallen into our hands regarding the cause of the Mutiny is the same. They invariably cite the *Cartooch* as the origin. No other cause of complaint was ever alluded to. His Majesty of Dehli has composed a couplet to the effect that the mighty English who boast of having vanquished Roos and Iran have been overthrown in Hindoostan by a single Cartridge. A consciousness of power had grown up in the Army which could only be exercised by Mutiny. The cry of the Cartridges brought the latent spirit of revolt into action."

The Cartridge the origin of the Mutiny.

I fully believe this to have been the case with the main body of the Sepoys. There were ringleaders no doubt who had deeper views, and possibly held correspondence with the Dehli family, etc.; but they made use of the Cartridge as their argument to gain over the mass of the Army to the belief that their caste was dishonoured. Nothing new from Greathed. 4 or 5 days ago a messenger passed through and found all quiet.

W. MUIR.

P.S.—Sending some of the enclosures of Mr. Colvin's letter.

DCXVIII.

W. MUIR, C.S., TO GENL. HAVELOCK.

AGRA, 13*th August* 1857.

MY DEAR HAVELOCK,—I yesterday sent you an abstract of the Dehli intelligence of the 7th and 8th, observing how much all unfavourable points were counterbalanced by the cheering prospect of early active measures against the City. Besides the messages from Greathed little bearing on that point, the following (taken from a private letter to a friend dated the 5th instant, from an official on the Staff who has every opportunity of knowing the state of affairs) bears out the expectation. "We could take a portion of Dehli any day, but to do so we should have to leave our camp empty, and the risk of failing in our ability to keep the town after our assault has, I suspect, deterred us from making the attempt till reinforcements arrived. Brigadier-General Nicholson with his moveable column is expected here about the 14th or 15th instant. He has 1100 European infantry with him. After his arrival you may expect to hear of

Position at Delhi.

our walking into Dehli, for it is not likely that we shall wait for Havelock." This is very encouraging, but it does not, of course, render the necessity of your coming up much the less urgent; for besides the expediency of a reserve for contingencies, there will be abundance to do after Dehli falls. The same writer adds: "The troops of all arms, except the European cavalry, are worked to death. They are, however, in first-rate spirits, and barring the 75th none have suffered from sickness." As to the numbers of the force, he says: "We have only MM effective European Infantry, about D European Cavalry (part of which, the Carabineers, are υσελεσς because they καννοτ ride), and D European Artillery, CC Guide Infantry, DC of Coke's men, CCC Sirmoor Battalion, CCC4 [1] Kemaon Brigade, CC Punjaub Cavalry." Nothing from Gwalior. Three days ago all was well there. The Maharajah telling them if they want to move they had better go to Cawnpore. Good accounts from Meerut till the 4th and 5th. We long to hear tidings of Bensley and Mary.

Troops at Delhi healthy.

Details of Delhi force.

W. MUIR.

DCXIX.

W. MUIR, C.S., TO H. C. TUCKER, C.S., BENARES.

AGRA, *13th August*.

MY DEAR TUCKER,—A messenger going to Allahabad, I enclose a few lines for you, as you may like to hear details. Locally, our position remains pretty much the same as when I last wrote. The present aspect of affairs you may perhaps have from the enclosed copy of a note to Havelock yesterday. In addition, I may subjoin the following from an earlier letter (5th) of an official on the Staff, which shows that, on the reinforcements reaching it, almost immediately offensive measures will be resumed. "We could take a portion of Dehli, etc. (see last letter to Havelock)," etc., etc. Nicholson himself reached camp on the 7th or 8th, and is a host in himself. Please God, we may now look forward to something. It will be grand if the N.-W. troops can finish the business themselves. How admirably Sir J. Lawrence has managed in keeping the Punjaub quiet, and in detaching so large a force for Dehli.

Allahabad.

Sir J. Lawrence.

Gwalior keeps quiet—the Maharajah managing somehow to restrain for the present the unruly Mutineers in the Lushkur. The Nawab Raees of Furruckabad is levying forces against us, raising his Pathan clan, and engaging, besides the Seetapore

Gwalior and Scindia.

The Nawab Raees of Farakhabad.

[1] *Sic.* The capital letters, of course, are numbers.—ED.

troops, deserters from the Nana and the Saugor Regiments. The latter, you know, passed up through the Cawnpore district. Our communications with Cawnpore by the Grand Trunk Road are again interrupted by the Nawab's troops. And our messengers are obliged to go *via* Etawah and Oreya. You will not fail to observe what Greathed says about the Cartooch being the invariably assigned origin of the rebel movements on all occasions of enquiry from deserters. His observations coincide, I think, with the opinion I strongly expressed in my last to you. I should like to hear your views on this point. A respectable native who was caught at Dehli by the outbreak, and was only able to get away lately, and had full and constant opportunity of conversing with the Sepoys on the subject, says "he could get no other assignable cause from them." He asserts that the Dehli people and Sepoys were not prepared for the inroad of our Mutineers from Meerut. But whatever may have been the views and machinations of some of the ringleaders, there can, I think, be little doubt that the fear of the cartridge, as the supposed [enemy of] (?) caste, was the motive that swayed the Hindoos. Mrs. Muir joins in kindest regards to Mrs. and Miss Tucker.—Yours affectionately,

Delhi had been unprepared for Mutiny.

W. MUIR.

DCXX.

W. MUIR, C.S., TO H. H. GREATHED, C.S., DEHLI.

AGRA, 14*th August* 1857.

MY DEAR GREATHED,—

. . . .

Α προγεκτ ις ον φοοτ φορ ραισινγ σομε οφ θε νιλδ villages *αγαινστ θε Ναιβ Σουβαχ ατ Αλυγυρχ. Γωβινδ Σινχ τακινγ θε λεαδ.*

W. MUIR.

Mr. Colvin's illness.

Mr. Colvin is not very well to-day, and I do not think you will have any letter from him.

DCXXII.

W. MUIR, C.S., TO GENL. HAVELOCK.

AGRA, 15*th August* 1857.

MY DEAR HAVELOCK,—Since yesterday we have had letters of the 9th and 10th from Dehli. The enemy appears to have become wearied of his self-destructive infantry attacks, and to have, for the time at least, abandoned them. On the 9th a battery of 8 or 10 guns was constructed by the rebels opposite our right, and caused us some annoyance. It is now their object to bring their artillery into play, and they have found a store of artillery belonging to our Dehli Magazine which they are using against us. But with all this "the enemy," Greathed writes on the 10th, "does not inflict material damage, *and they will be paid out when the time comes.*" Mark the allusion. **Attacks by Delhi Mutineers ineffective.**

The King, alarmed at the plunder of the Hakeem's house (I mentioned before that the Sepoys considered him implicated in the explosion of their powder manufactory, and attacked his house), has sent his family to the Kootub,—another significant circumstance. **King sends his family to the Kootub.**

Everything quiet towards the Punjaub. Richardes had collected at Paniput above 2½ lacs. Saharunpore quiet. Spankie managing well. 264 of the 1st Punjaub Cavalry under Captain Hughes had been sent to him. The postal communication with Meerut *via* Baghput had been interrupted. Cause not yet known. It was going round by Kurnaul. The infernal machines against the bridge of boats had been given up, Men on Mussucks had always been able to divert them before they had reached their destination. Health of the camp good. No news from Cawnpore later than the 5th. We are anxiously looking out for tidings of your movements at Lucknow.—Yours affectionately,

W. MUIR.

P.S.—I send this through Juswunt (?) Rao, a Tulookdar of Etawah. A messenger who took despatches from this on the 8th has returned, saying his despatch was plundered from him by the Rasdhan (?) Rajah. I have been of late writing you daily letters.

DCXXIII.

W. MUIR, C.S., TO J. W. SHERER, C.S., CAWNPORE.

AGRA, *16th August* 1857.

MY DEAR SHERER,—

You are to pay him [the messenger] our full reward of Rs.100. All well here. I opened and read your letter with Mr. and Mrs. H.[1] **Cossids' remuneration.**

. . . .

W. MUIR.

[1] Harington (?)

DCXXV.

W. MUIR, C.S., TO GENL. HAVELOCK.

AGRA, 17*th August* 1857.

MY DEAR HAVELOCK,—We have nothing to-day from Dehli. Our cossids must have been intercepted, as our last left Dehli on the 10th and reached this on the 13th. I have, however, just got a letter from Sir J. Lawrence, which contains his sentiments regarding Dehli, and your own movements in reference to it, and which you will be interested in having. He then asks after Lucknow, and his brother, of whose death he had not heard. (In another letter of the 6th, however, he speaks of his loss.) Sir John's views thus entirely agree with what has been urged from Agra. Probably his advice as to the occupation of a position in conjunction with the Meerut troops *οπποσιτε Δελι*, and threatening an attack in that direction, would do more than anything to paralyse the rebels. It would certainly cut them off from one half their present sources of supply, and would divert and distract their forces. You will have seen, however, that there is reason to hope for some early decisive measures against the City from the tenor of our last despatches. This week may possibly bring us some good tidings. If you were able to make an advance in the manner indicated by Sir J. L., any amount of heavy-size ordnance and ammunition could be sent over to you. By going up this Grand Trunk Road you would, by a better and more direct line, earlier reach the scene of operations.

Lord Lawrence's suggestion as to attacking Delhi.

Gwalior.

We have perhaps more than usually satisfactory accounts from Gwalior. A respectable person, employed there as Mohurrur in the Cotwalee, left the service in consequence of a great reduction of salaries by one half. He quitted Gwalior on the 13th. He states that the Indore troops are at Morar, but that both the Maharajah and the Contingent are displeased with them for the excesses they committed on their way up. The Maharajah also objects to accept their services, considering them rebels against Holkar. He has refused to furnish them with supplies. They have to buy their own. They are not allowed to pitch within the cantonment. Scindia has desired them to go away, promising them carriage but supplying none. They talk of going to Dehli direct *via* Dholepore. They consist of 12 regiments Infantry, 600 Cavalry, and several thousands of camp-followers, plunderers, Ghazis, etc. The Gwalior Contingent keeps to its cantonment and declares itself faithful to the Maharajah,

Indore troops.

Details of Indore troops.

Gwalior Contingent professedly faithful to the Maharajah.

ready to obey his commands and quite satisfied with the pay and largesses received.

The troops perform no regular exercises (?). But every night they post artillery round the cantonment for its protection. They have sold all their English artillery, accoutrements, etc., by auction.

Such is the present position of affairs. One cannot say how long it may last; but so long as it does it relieves us from additional anxiety.

I have an account of affairs at Dehli from the lips of a respectable Hindoo—former Vakeel of Jhujjer—and therefore acquainted with the state of things at Dehli, who was caught on a visit during the outbreak there, and left it only a short time ago. I am not sure whether the statement is worth sending you. I will see. It is remarkable as showing that he, having frequent means of communication with the Sepoys, could discover, in conversation with them at Dehli, no other cause of discontent than the Cartridge; nor could he trace any generally existing plot or conspiracy. He is also firm in believing that the King and Royal Family were taken by surprise at the incursion of the rebels, and that the King at first sincerely begged them to let him alone; though, he adds, it is not unlikely that the seductions of proffered power and wealth may have subsequently changed his feelings.

Cartridge the cause of discontent.

No plot traced.

King taken by surprise by rebels, and unwilling to join them.

A despatch from Dehli, dated the 12th, has just come in. News excellent. We charged the battery which I mentioned had been erected on our right, defeated the enemy, and took four of their guns with very little loss.

That was before our reinforcements arrived; so we shall see what they can do after the reinforcements come. Trusting that you will soon, by God's blessing, defeat the Nawab Raees and his allies.

Any news of little Mary and Bensley?

P.S.—By the way, my Dehli friend stated that, three or four days before the Bucr Eed, Bukht Khan, the rebel Commander-in-Chief, went to the King and told him that he must forbid the killing of cows at the Eed,—at the same time laying before His Majesty reasons in support of the lawfulness of such a course. The King consented; and that measure—coupled with the Army having been sent out on the Eed and for two days before—accounts for its passing off so quietly. This same point of killing cows has been a bone of contention between the Hindoos

Bukht Khan.

Killing of cows.

and Mahommedans of Dehli at the Eed from time immemorial. The fact shows the ascendency of "pandeeism." Mr. Wilson, Judge of Moradabad, in a letter just received from Meerut of the 11th, writes: "At Dehli the Hindoo Sepoys now have it all their own way. They threaten if their present attempts, viz. a battery at Kishengunge and a battery opposite the Metcalfe picket, fail, they will desert four regiments at a time, and spread all over the country. A small picket at Ghazeeuddeennugger sends out horsemen to kill our people at Moradnugger and Bolaina (?). The allowing the picket to remain unmolested is a disgrace to us, but we have no force with which to risk a general engagement within 8 miles of the Dehli Palace."

Power of the Sepoys at Delhi.

Annoyance from enemy's post at Ghazi-uddin-nugger.

This bears on the advisability of taking up the Shahdera position in force.

A requisition, Mr. Wilson adds, had come from Dehli to send over the Meerut riflemen there, but, he adds, there would be difficulty in the present state of the road *via* Kurnal in complying with the requisition.

W. M.

DCXXVI.

W. Muir, C.S., to C. Beadon, C.S., Foreign Secretary, Calcutta.

Agra, 19*th August* 1857.

My Dear Beadon,—It has been on my mind for some days to write to you with reference specially to a subject which appears to me of paramount importance, viz. our policy towards the subordinate States, in consequence of our altered military relations and the necessity for a far larger employment than we have ever before contemplated of European soldiery for the protection of India.

Future policy towards the subordinate States.

As the Supreme Power in India, encircling and shielding every State throughout the length and breadth of the land, the general responsibility for the peace of India has devolved upon us. It has been our task, and ours alone, to repel foreign invasion as well as to repress internal rapine and enforce international rights. In return for these services it has always been admitted that a reciprocal duty rests upon all the subordinate States. In acknowledgment of the security and peace they enjoy, allegiance is due to us, and it is equitable that tribute or contingent contribution, either in troops or money, should be rendered to us.

Where a money tribute is paid, we can of course employ it as we think best, either in the payment of European troops or otherwise.

Where the subsidy is in the shape of a regular contingent of native troops or the contribution, in seasons of necessity, of such troops, it seems to me that the time has come for revising the terms of our treaties.

Revision of treaties necessary.

In our present necessities, when our native army has melted like snow from our hands, reappearing as the sworn enemy of the paramount Power, and when good government has in consequence given place to anarchy and war throughout the North of Hindoostan, not one of the Native States on this side Jeend and Putiala has been able to render us the slightest effective aid. Wherever they have come out to our help, the cowardice or the treachery of their troops has left us worse off than if they had stayed at home. The clouds of Cavalry sent out by Bhurtpore, in conjunction with a force of all arms from Ulwar, with the view of guarding the Muthra Frontier and gradually advancing on Dehli, were paralysed by the appearance of the two paltry Companies of the 44th and 67th which had mutinied on the 29th of May at Muthra. They suffered the 150 Sepoys, unaccompanied either by guns or horse, to carry the Muthra treasure through their camp to Dehli, and the whole body of the allies became in consequence so mutinous that our officers were obliged to consult their safety in flight. A second Ulwar force, sent to atone for the misdeeds of the first, did us no better service. Its guns and, I believe, its horse went over to the Neemuch Mutineers. Similarly the Jeypoore troops, though probably more faithful, were unable to offer any material opposition to the Neemuch force; and, in respect to all the States of Central India, it is plain that they allowed first the Nusseerabad Mutineers and after them the Neemuch to cross the breadth of the land by two distinct routes without opposing to them the slightest serious obstruction. This was all that came of the stringent treaties binding them to come forward to aid us in our difficulties with their levies.

Native States west of Patiáli have given no aid.

Bhurtpore and Ulwar troops paralysed,

and mutinous.

Details of inefficiency of Native States, and inaction.

Our Contingents—the other form of assistance—have proved as treacherous and hostile as our own forces;—whether the Kotah or the Gwalior, they have all abandoned us.

Native States' Contingents treacherous and hostile.

It may readily be admitted the Native States are no more to be blamed for this than we ourselves are for the defection of our Army. It is their misfortune, not their fault. But not the less are they bound, when the deficiency has thus glaringly appeared, to remedy it, and to substitute a really effective contribution to the general internal defence of India.

We ourselves must retrace our steps. We can no longer rest our Empire almost exclusively on an Army composed of materials which, like our late Sepoy Regiments, crumble in a day. Whatever other changes are made, and whatever counterbalancing elements are introduced into the native Army, it would seem to be admitted on all hands that our reserve of European troops of every arm must be vastly multiplied. In the last resort it is only on them that we can trust. And European troops we must be prepared to maintain in effective force in India, even when our country is engaged in foreign wars and when we have been accustomed to drain India of them.

European troops must be multiplied.

Now, to meet the increased expense of so large an accession of British soldiery, it seems to me that all Native States are bound to assist who by the nature of their present engagements contribute any kind of aid. In cases where regular Contingents are already supported, it would be simple enough to substitute a fair amount of European troops as an equivalent for the Contingent; and where occasionally subsidies are provided, it would be reasonable to stipulate for a corresponding strength of Europeans to be regularly maintained.

We might perhaps go even beyond this, and in cases where no assistance is at present stipulated, or such assistance as is disproportionately small with reference to the Revenues of the State, insist upon the contribution of a fair amount, on the ground that protection by European troops is now shown to be indispensable. And refusal might be followed by the withdrawal of all guarantee of protection.

If moveable European columns with European Artillery were thus available at Gwalior, at Ajmere, and at one or two other points in Central India, the country would be secured from all reasonable apprehension of internal disturbance, while the general forces of the State would be valuably strengthened.

Native States must contribute to cost of defence by European troops.

On our part it would be no real hardship to any State, as the proportion of their own useless troops which the new arrangement would enable them to dispense with would far more than cover their contribution for our European Brigades.

I conclude that the points at which European troops will in future be massed will depend mainly on the lines of railway.

Agra as seat of N.W.P. Government.

The question has been mooted here whether Agra should continue to be the seat of Government in these Provinces. It no doubt stands in a very exposed position. Surrounded to the West and

South by foreign territory at short distances, it is liable in disturbed times to easy attack. Any point in the Doab would be more protected. Allygurh is Central, and has already the remains of a Fort constructed on modern principles of fortification. If it were contemplated at any future period to join Oudh to the North-West Provinces, then probably Furruckabad would be the most Central position; but it would need the erection of a fort, which is shown by the late proceedings to be an essential for every seat of Government. Furruckabad would otherwise be a good position if the railways from the East and South communicated directly with it. There is much, however, to be said for Agra. It has the prestige of name. And if the Jumna were bridged by solid masonry and Agra formed a point of junction on the main lines of the Eastern and Southern Railways, and if, as I conclude will be the case, large bodies of European troops of all arms are cantoned here, it may not be thought necessary to raise the question of a change of the seat of Government. Agra would then be perfectly safe and convenient in all respects.

Barracks for European troops.

What arrangements are contemplated for the cantoning of such immense additions to our European Army next hot weather? It will require time; and the locality and plans will need to be fixed as early as possible. The health of our British soldiery will be now a more essential point than ever. Is not the system of Barracks formed of separate houses for eight or ten persons the best plan? The shells of our new and old barracks are all standing here, and they can be roofed in rapidly.

Sir John Lawrence, in a letter to me of the 6th inst., says: "I think it would be well if intelligent military men were selected to raise levies," etc.

Difficulty in raising levies.

Want of funds.

Recruits in N.W.P. at present unreliable.

We have two difficulties in the way of raising such levies just now. First, funds;—we have just enough to go on with, and with the posts all closed find it difficult to borrow; while our collections are, and will continue till reinforcements come or Delhi falls, of little amount. Next, so long as the Military supremacy is not in our hands we are not sure of a single company recruited from these parts holding by us. If we arm them, they have a strong temptation to go off to Dehli, which is looked to as the centre of all that is attractive for the plunderer. A project is now under discussion for raising small levies through the Talookdars, for which levies the latter shall be responsible; but so long as our authority is confined within such very narrow limits and our enemies have the prestige of the Dehli palace and dynasty, not much could be done in this way. Even Teekwan Singh, for example, one of our best disposed Talookdars, when a "Naib Soobah" comes within five-and-twenty miles of him, begins to shake, to remember the ancient fidelity of his family to the house of Dehli, and to fear the wrath of the rebels if they should chance to gain even a temporary occupation of his estate. When Dehli falls this feeling will rapidly wear away, and we shall regain the moral ascendency required to ensure the faithful service of either police or military battalions. Meanwhile the protraction of the struggle is very trying to the loyalty of all parties.

Will you oblige me by taking an opportunity to mention to the Governor-General what I have said about the support of European troops in Native States, and any other points in this letter you may think deserving His Lordship's attention?

Natives of the Punjab should be enlisted for service in N.W.P.

You will, I think, be obliged to have a chief part of your force for the internal peace of districts composed of local Battalions, which will tend to break up the oneness and power of combination on the part of the national force. It might be a good plan if we could get down some of the Dogras or other Punjaub castes for such service.

A large proportion of low caste men should be enlisted.

In the Regular Army you will doubtless insist for the future on a large proportion of the lower castes being entertained.

Subscribing to missions by persons in power not offensive to the people.

What curious ideas have been started at home about the injurious effect of persons in power subscribing to Missionary Associations. So far as my observations go, Missionary efforts have, in these quarters at least, attracted no hostile feeling, nor would any amount of private support of Missionary Institutions be challenged as a grievance. It is too patent to the people that these institutions have no political and official standing to allow them to excite any jealousy. The wild and baseless rumour which stirred up the soldiery are utterly different in kind, and are connected not with Missionary operations, but (if arising at all out of any acts of ours) with the political effort avowed and pressed forward of late with redoubled energy for the civilisation and advancement of the nation. If Lord Ellenborough is prepared to leave India sunk in ignorance and barbarism, good and well; but if he demands, as all England has been demanding, that we shall use every effort for its social and political advancement, then he must be prepared for the recoil and indignation of the bigoted and interested classes;—classes interested in the continuance of things precisely as they are.

Cartridge rumour not connected with Missionary operations.

As regards the *immediate* cause of the outbreak, we can get no other clue by enquiries at Dehli and elsewhere *than the cartridge*. The fact is that the Sepoys had long been puffed up with the conceit that the Imperial fabric rested on their shoulders alone: they had constructed it; they maintained it. This filled them with an arrogant and independent feeling, which led to the constant feeling of grievance when they were not petted and humoured in everything. Here were the elements of disaffection and mutiny. The cartridge was used by the bad designing men of each regiment to inflame the otherwise contented soldiery, and when distrust was once infused our most solemn disavowals of interference with caste were disbelieved and met by the grossest fabrications and lies.

No other cause ascertainable than the cartridge.

Growing arrogance of the army.

I saw the arrogant spirit creeping through, though quite unintended, in a Sepoy of more than ordinarily quiet and respectful deportment, who was conversing with Mr. Colvin one day when he had assembled the Regiment privately to hear their grievances. The way in which he referred to the faithful Sepoys having conquered India from Ceylon to Peshawur *for us* showed the common trains of thought and conversation amongst the Sepoys.

As I said, we have perceived in these quarters no symptoms of any special ill-feeling against the Missionaries and their Institutions. They shared the same fate as others. Here there were perhaps fewer marks of antagonism against the Missionary than against other buildings. I saw some of the chapels in the bazaar with their doors and venetians uninjured. The crusade against Christians was a political one against the ruling castes. The real fear of the natives is against forcible conversion by political means to another caste; and they know from long experience that the Missionary efforts are entirely of another kind.

The Mutiny political, and attacked Christians as the ruling class.

Please God, when we have weathered the storm successfully the Government will be in a stronger position than ever to hold on its course of moral and political reform. Its religious policy should still be that of strict neutrality, but its officers should be left free to use their private influence as hitherto in the support of Christianity. It would be a grievous mistake to place any restrictions on the exercise of this influence. I believe it would injure and lower the character of our service.

Policy of neutrality, but private influence of officers not to be restricted.

I have been endeavouring, in private correspondence with Havelock, to keep him informed of all that goes on here. I enclose copies of some letters to him. Everything here hangs on the fate of Dehli. Whether an assault will be attempted, now that the reinforcements have arrived, seems doubtful. The tenor of

Everything at Agra hangs on the fate of Delhi.

the letters from the Cawnpore district seems to indicate that something of the kind is in contemplation.

Indore troops

At Gwalior things remain stationary. The Indore troops are not acknowledged by the Maharajah, and will probably leave as soon as they have a proper opportunity either for this, for Delhi, or for Cawnpore. Scindia prevents their departure for the present. The Contingent troops regard themselves as in the pay of Scindia, and are for the present under his control.

Gwalior Contingent.

The triumphant advent of Havelock restored the balance of opinion decisively in our favour in all these parts, and at Gwalior. But the failure of the expected reinforcements to arrive, and the check in the advance, have again caused doubt and apprehension. We earnestly trust that the reinforcements may not long be delayed.

Mr. Colvin's health broken down.

Mr. Colvin's health and spirits are greatly broken. I trust you may be enabled to facilitate his getting away for change. I had looked to his vigour and experience being of eminent service in the reintroduction of our rule, with such modification as altered circumstances may require. But I fear he must leave.

W. MUIR.

DCXXVII.

W. MUIR, C.S., to GENL. HAVELOCK.

AGRA, 18*th August* 1857.

MY DEAR HAVELOCK,—I enclose a letter received last night for you from Brigadier Wilson. The impression I gave in yesterday's letter of an attack by us on the enemy's battery on our right was erroneous. We always silence that battery, when it attempts to annoy us, by our superior fire; but we have not by the last account yet attacked it. I enclose the printed accounts taken from Greathed's letter. You will no doubt have particulars of the action from Brigadier Wilson. From a letter of Greathed's, dated the 13th, it appears that our loss on the occasion was greater than at first apprehended—19 killed and 90 wounded. I conclude that the cause of the first under-statement was that the greater part of the loss was in our native troops. In the same letter of the 13th Greathed writes: "We are all in high admiration of General Havelock's successes." He still alludes to the report as current of your having given up Lucknow to plunder. He states that "Rajah Goolab Singh is really dead; but that no apprehension is expressed of his death causing any complications. All tranquil in the Punjaub. The

Rajah Goolab Singh dead.

All tranquil in the Punjab.

disarmed regiments at Lahore are encamped; their lines have been demolished, and it is said that arms and ammunition were found concealed in them." He adds: "There were two attacks on the Metcalfe picket last night. The fusilade was sharp but ineffective, as the enemy kept at a respectful distance. You will find some particulars of the affair of the 12th, and the night attack, in a note from Anson which I enclose."

General Nicholson's Column. This morning we have a letter of the 14th. It reports that General Nicholson's Column marched in on the morning of the 14th in excellent order. It consists of the 52nd Light Cavalry —a wing of the 61st, and 2 Punjaub Infantry Regiments; a horse battery and 200 Cavalry;—a most important reinforcement.

Military position at Delhi. The enemy had been more quiet on the 13th. They must see that their new system of tactics makes no impression. The Teleewara Battery is not allowed to speak, being always shut up by our fire, and the skirmishing with light guns is of course ineffective against an entrenched position. Our pickets to the left, in advance of Metcalfe's house, were more attacked than formerly. They hold an impregnable position, and the fire of the enemy has ceased to command attention. **Nawab Raees applies to the King.** The Nawab Raees had sent a pressing application to the King for aid; but notwithstanding that it was accompanied by Nuzzers he got no reply. Greathed writes: "The idea here is that when the Pandies leave Dehli they will take the Gwalior road. I am opposed to the destruction of the Hindun bridge." The reason for the summons of the Rifles complained of in the extract I sent yesterday from a Meerut letter is explained. They are 200 strong, and are to be replaced by 700 Punjaub troops and a battery of 6 guns, which for their village excursions from Meerut ought to more almost than supply the loss. Of the Rifles at Dehli, CCL have been placed *hors de combat*, and they **Loss of the Rifles at Delhi.** number no more than 250, so that they can no longer take their position in the field as a Regiment. It was very necessary, therefore, to raise their numbers again. It is impossible, says Greathed, **Their excellent services.** "to overrate the excellent conduct of this Regiment. Nothing disturbs their discipline. **Revenue collections.** To the 10th nearly 3¼ laks of rupees had been collected in the Paniput district. They are well off for everything in camp, even music." All as usual here, excepting **Ghaus Mahomed.** that Ghous Mahommed at Allygurh has taken into his service 100 Sowars of the Saugor Regiments who were passing through Allygurh;—this has made the Zemindars I spoke of unwilling to attack him. An expedition with a part of our troops here is talked of in that direction.

Bombay news up to the 1st,—all well there. Five steamers had been sent to Suez to meet the reinforcements expected there. Nothing more from Neemuch. You will have heard that the wing of a Bareilly Brigade was disarmed there, but there is no reason yet to apprehend further disaffection.

Disarmament at Bareilly.

W. MUIR.

DCXXVIII.

W. MUIR, C.S., TO GENL. HAVELOCK.

AGRA, *20th August* 1857.

MY DEAR HAVELOCK,—I enclose a letter from Colonel Cotton for Gen. Neill. We have nothing more from Dehli,—the last was the 14th inst., of which I gave you an account in my letter of the 18th. I did not write to you yesterday.

A Meerut letter mentions that the guns we took on the 12th were two 9-pounders, one 6-pounder, and one 12-pounder Howitzer; we also spiked two others.

Disputes between Musulmans and Hindus. Bukht Khan.

Our accounts from Rohilkhund are that a serious split has occurred between the Mussulmans and Hindoos of Bareilly and Bijnore. Khan Bukht Khan has disappeared from Bareilly. And his army at Huldwanee which threatened Nainee Tal has dispersed. The Nawab of Rampoor goes on well with . . . The Nawab of Nujeebabad, who ruled Bijnore in the King's name, has been thrust out. A very small force would at this juncture have enabled our officers to return to their stations. The split will probably extend.

Expedition to Hatrass.

Our party for Hatrass moves out this afternoon. It consists of 150 European and some mounted Militia. We were glad to hear of your third victorious dash against the Lucknow Mutineers. We doubt not, now that the Dinapore people have been disposed of, that you will have speedy reinforcements to enable you to relieve Lucknow. God grant them strength to hold out.

DCXXIX.

W. MUIR, C.S., TO GENERAL HAVELOCK.

AGRA, *21st August* 1857.

MY DEAR HAVELOCK,—Our last from you is the 14th, written by Colonel Tytler. We are hoping that you have been able to do something with the parties North-west of you. We have tidings from Dehli up to 16th to-day. The enemy had

Operations at Delhi.

ceased firing round-shot at the stables in Metcalfe's grounds occupied by our picket. They had knocked down a corner of the building, but if they had succeeded in demolishing even the whole of the building it would not, Greathed says, "have been of any service to them, for they would still have had to face the breastwork—a sort of duty they do not relish. They have Mortars in Kishen Gunge.—Their Mortar is not so good as their Howitzer practice. The aim is true enough, but the shell do not burst." That is owing, I suppose, to the coarse and inferior nature of the powder which they manufacture.

Distribution of Delhi force made to secure Nicholson's services.

A new distribution had been made of the force. To Nicholson is assigned the command of a moveable column. The 1st Europeans with 1st and 2nd Punjanb corps. This arrangement made to secure his services (as he would otherwise have been superseded by his seniors) gives general satisfaction.

Captain Hodson. **Jhujjur.** **Patoudee.**

Capt. Hodson was out with his Cavalry watching the movements of the Party which had gone to Jujjur, and squeezed 1,60,000 Rupees from the Nawab. A troop of rebel Cavalry had gone to Patoudee, got some thousands of rupees from the Nawab, but they afterwards attempted to plunder the city and were set upon by the town people, who beat them off. The King disavowed their acts. It was intended by the Rebels to send those parties to raise the country on both sides of the river, but some one suggested that it was a device of the Hukeem to weaken the Garrison and betray the City.

Sikh Sepoys in Delhi.

The Rebels had formed all the Sikhs in the several Regiments into 2 Battalions. The real object of the movement is not yet known, but the Sikhs obtained it on a pledge to show the others the way to attack.

All quiet in Punjab. **Health of Cawnpore good.**

All quiet above. The disarmed Regiments at Lahore encamped opposite the 81st,—12 guns being on their camp. Health of Cawnpore good. Better than it ordinarily is at this season in quarters. Cholera disappeared. The last they had heard of you was up to the 1st inst., in letter from this.

Gwalior unquiet.

Things at Gwalior are unquiet. The Contingent wanted the Maharajah to pay the Indore troops as well as themselves. He refused. After some difficulties and threats on the part of the Maharajah, the Contingent took their pay, and so may be considered settled for another month. But the last letters, dated the 26th, indicated considerable *αυζιετι* & *αλαρμ* on the part of the *Δυρβαρ*, the cause not fully known yet. Meanwhile from Dholepore intimation has come in that the Indore Mutineers mean to march from Gwalior on the 19th, and reach Dholepore by the 23rd *ον θειρ ναι το θις ορ* to Dehli. The dates may be premature;

Aligarh powder manufacturers brought to Delhi.

but there seems little doubt that the Indore troops will soon leave Gwalior, and they may not improbably carry with them some of the Brigade and part of the Contingent also. I suppose they are afraid to go your way, as you have struck a salutary terror into the native mind. We shall probably have more accurate information soon. They must be hard-up for powder in Dehli, and for powder-makers. The Rebels sent down Sowars to Allygurh to bring up to Dehli the manufacturers who live there.

W. Muir.

Cossid seized

P.S.—I wrote to you yesterday, but not the day before. A Cossid with despatches from this dated the 11th was pulled up by the Futtehgurh people and his despatches seized.

DCXXX.

W. Muir, C.S., to H. H. Greathed, C.S.

Agra, 21*st August* 1857.

My Dear Greathed,—We have nothing later from Cawnpore than General Neill's of the 12th sent on to Brigadier Wilson, and Colonel Tytler's of the 14th. The intelligence of the latter was, I think, given in Mr. Colvin's of yesterday to you. But in case it may have missed, I add the following details. He said

General Havelock defeats rebels six times, and takes 66 guns.

that General Havelock had met and defeated the rebels 6 times, taking in all 66 guns. The last time was at [?] on the way to Lucknow, where they had entrenched themselves. We took 2 guns *ονλι, α φακτ* which *δελαιεδ ουρ αδυανς*, enabling *θεμ* to carry off the *ρεμαινδερ*. We *shouλδ σκαρσλι ἀνε συκξeeded* in *καπτυριvγ θεσε* II *ἀδ* it not been that as many of the Enemy's horses were killed they were disabled.

Havelock retires.

Circumstances have compelled the General to retire across the Ganges and [await reinforcements ?], but no check has been sustained by us. General Havelock found the enemy too strong for him to penetrate to Lucknow. Reinforcements are coming up the country, as the Mutineers from Dinapore have been destroyed or dispersed. Three Regiments will arrive by next month, and the remainder of the China Force will soon come in. General Grant, writing to him about the 13th July, said "that

Twenty-five thousand men promised from England.

within three months from that date 25,000 men would be landed in India, and if thought necessary more would follow. So much for Colonel Tytler's letter.

Things are unquiet at Gwalior. It would seem that the Indore Mutineers must soon be leaving it. The Maharajah refused to acknowledge or pay them. The Contingent demand to take in their own pay unless Scindia would also pay the Indore people;—this he refused to do. After considerable difficulty the Contingent took their pay. Gwalior unquiet.

As I write, a letter with capital news from Chester dated 15th. Lord Elgin has reached Calcutta with a large portion of the China Force (numbers not stated), *and the rest is daily expected.* "Shannon" and "Pearl" are named among the Steam Frigates arrived. Steam gunboat "Jumna" was at Benares yesterday; was to be at Allahabad on [?], and will probably come on to Agra. If no delay permitted, Lucknow, we pray, will yet be saved. Mr. J. P. Grant appointed Lt.-Gov. of the Central Provinces to Cawnpore, Benares, Allahabad, and Saugor Divisions. Lord Elgin reaches Calcutta with China Force. J. P. Grant, C.S., appointed Lieutenant-Governor of the Central Provinces.

The Calcutta dak arrives again with regularity. Havelock will no doubt immediately attack Bithoor. Jubbulpore, Saugor, Rewa, and Nagode all quiet. Behrampore (?) and Ghazeepore troops disarmed.

This all presumes (?) a speedy upward movement of English troops. They must be hard-up for powder at D., as they sent down urgently Sowars to Allygurh to seize and convey to D. the powder manufacturers there. Our expedition set out for Hatrass yesterday, and will reach it to-morrow morning.

. . . .

W. MUIR.

DCXXXI.

W. MUIR, C.S., TO SIR JOHN LAWRENCE, LT.-GOVERNOR, PUNJAUB.

AGRA, *22nd August.*

MY DEAR SIR JOHN,—Yours of the 5th regarding the movements of the reinforcements coming from the East towards Dehli arrived after your letter of the 6th on the subject of levies of native troops for service in the cold weather. Both were laid before Mr. Colvin, whose state of health is very uncertain,—one day fit for business, the next quite prostrate. He is much broken, and must seek restoration in change of country and entire cessation from the cares of State. He has already written to you on the subject of local levies, I believe, but he desired Reade, Thornhill, and myself to consider the subject further. I have not yet had Reade's views upon it. But there are two considerations which at present offer obstacles. Mr. Colvin ill.

Question of local levies.

First, we have little or no money for anything but ordinary expenses. The Agra Treasury is the only one saved from Meerut to Benares, and it has not much more than sufficient for 2 or 3 months' usual disbursements. When the daks are open again, and our power re-established, it will be easy enough to raise local loans and replenish the Treasury by granting bills of exchange. Our revenue collections, too, will soon regain their buoyancy, lightened of several heavy items under the heads of pensions. But just for the next month or two it would not be easy to devise the ways and means for the payment of extensive new levies. But even if we had the money our position is, to the outward eye of the multitudinous masses, so insecure just now that we have no hold upon our native levies so long as Dehli remains in the Rebels' hands, and we have occupancy of the country only by military posts, so far removed from each other as Meerut, Agra, and Cawnpore. The common people must regard ours as a doubtful if not a losing game, and self-interest, which looks forward, does not bind them to us. Until our military supremacy be in some measure vindicated, we cannot count upon the faithfulness of a single company of troops recruited in these parts. The likeliest plan is probably to raise some Hindoo troops through the most faithful of our Talookdars, they being responsible for them, and this will probably be tried on a small scale. But even our Talookdars, so long as they see us in this plight, are almost afraid to compromise themselves decidedly against the Hindoos of Dehli. The prestige of the Dynasty and ancient favours received from it begin to be remembered; not that they do not generally prefer, and long for, the re-establishment of our rule. But yet they feel an uncertainty as to who will win. For the levies themselves, the moment they receive arms in their hands they forthwith are exposed to the temptations of Dehli or any other centre of attraction for plunderers where high pay and other inducements are offered. We must therefore, I think, wait a little till our European troops have come up in this direction, and in some degree restore our shattered prestige before we can attempt local levies.

Want of money.

Recruits in N.W.P. not now reliable.

Talookdars even afraid to compromise themselves.

Sikh or Punjab levies suggested.

But could we not raise local levies of Sikh or Punjaub castes? I hear that amongst the hangers-on about the army at Dehli some troops have been organised there. If they had a hint that they would get service on coming here they might perhaps come in sufficient numbers for a small body of horse and foot. How far would the Dogras and other such Punjaub tribes relish service in local battalions in this part of the country? I conclude that we shall in future be dependent on local battalions chiefly for the work hitherto performed in the internal administration by the Sepoys. Our mainstay in the country must, of course, be European soldiers. I have sent a suggestion to Beadon that all our contingents and annual subsidies from Native States be connected with a fair equivalent of European troops to provide for two or more moveable columns of European troops being posted at different points in Central India.

Our mainstay in the country must be European soldiers.

Your other letter about the necessity of an early advance towards Shahdera I gave the substance of to Havelock, and it will no doubt assist him in forming his plans when the time comes. There are many advantages in the plan you mentioned, and we could send across any amount of large Artillery to join his force.

Lord Lawrence's proposal for early advance towards Delhi from down country.

Havelock's career of victories was checked—not by any want of fortune, for in eight engagements he had completely vanquished the enemy every time and taken 66 guns, but by the failure of the expected reinforcements to come up. They were detained by the three wretched Dinapore regiments, whom Lloyd neglected to disarm. And the enemy were in too great force between Lucknow and Cawnpore to allow of Havelock with only DCCCC Europeans penetrating to the former. This produced a feeling of much depression here, and the natives too don't understand the cause of the check in Havelock's advance. Our last, however, from Allahabad, dated 15th, is full of promise again. The Mutineer regiments have been greatly cut up, and the remainder have apparently taken the route through Rewa and Bundelkhund. The three European regiments detained by them have thus been set free, and if speedy movement be made upwards Havelock will be enabled to resume operations, and Lucknow will, we may trust, yet be safe.

Havelock's progress checked by non-arrival of reinforcements.

Meanwhile he will, we conclude, not be idle, as he has large bodies of the enemy about Bithoor and towards Futtehgurh to disperse. Sciudia has hitherto kept the Contingent quiet by payment of salary and largesses, and he expects to retain them so till the Dusserah.

Scindia keeps the Gwalior Contingent quiet.

The Indore troops, however, he refuses to pay and to recognise, and we are looking for them soon to leave Gwalior and do mischief somewhere. They are not, however, numerous; about 1100 foot and 400 horse with 7 light guns. The Malagurh Sooba has sent, as you will have heard, a Naib to Allygurh, who is canvassing for the Rebel cause and endeavouring

Strength of Indore troops. Malagarh Soobah sends a Naib to Aligarh.

Expedition from Agra.

to levy collections for Dehli. To counteract his efforts we have just sent an expedition of 150 Europeans and some Militia Horse. This will secure the immediate vicinity from attack, maintain the faithful Talookdars in their duty towards us, and bring in perhaps a couple of lacs of rupees, unless the [?] of the Indore Mutineers obliges us prematurely to withdraw. I have written at length, as you asked me occasionally to let you know what was going on. You will have heard that Mr. J. P. Grant was appointed Lt.-Govr. of the Central Provinces, Allahabad, Benares, and Saugor—Divisions which are at present cut off from Agra. A temporary measure, I presume.—Yours sincerely,

W. MUIR.

P.S.—News from Cawnpore up to the 17th just in. The effect of Havelock's advance on Lucknow was temporarily to relieve the City and enable the Government to throw in a month's provision. This is native report. No communication, General Neill says, has been received direct from the General since the 22nd of July. Havelock had attacked Bithoor and taken two guns, and was moving on to Sheorajpore. Reinforcements beginning to come in again at Allahabad.

W. M.

DCXXXII.

W. MUIR, C.S., TO GENERAL HAVELOCK.

AGRA, 22*nd August* 1857.

MY DEAR HAVELOCK,—

. . . .

I am delighted to hear that you are after the Bithoor people again, and that when the accounts left you were pursuing them and would probably go on to Sheorajpore.

. . . .

1st B.C. disarmed at Neemuch.

We hear that the first B.C. has been disarmed at Neemuch. I trust the Mutiny will not spread farther.—Yours,

W. MUIR.

DCXXXIII.

W. MUIR, C.S., TO GENL. HAVELOCK.

AGRA, 23*rd August* 1857.

MY DEAR HAVELOCK,—I enclose a letter from Anson, dated the 17th, which will give you the news. Also one sent by him from Mary, who, poor thing, is sadly distressed at the uncertainty and absence of information about dear Mary and Bensley. God grant them to hold out till you can relieve them. The siege train and ammunition from Ferozepore will be of essential service in the final stroke, which, when they know that you cannot come up soon, will probably not be delayed. A thousand waggons or carts are employed in bringing down the ammunition, etc.

. . . .

What has stayed the European (?) Regiments again at Benares ?—Yours affectionately,

W. MUIR.

DCXXXIV.

W. MUIR, C.S., TO GENL. HAVELOCK.

AGRA, *24th August* 1857.

MY DEAR HAVELOCK,—A letter from Becher up to the 20th to-day.

The following is our news of the 18th, and 20 letters. The arrival of the siege train is expected 25th. If by that time no expectation existed of your early advance, it was hoped that an advance upon the City might not long be deferred. Affairs at Delhi.

Train accompanied by a thousand waggons of ammunition. Eldest son of Golab Singh had succeeded without question,—friendly footing between him and Sir John Lawrence. He was following up his father's intention of sending four Regiments of Infantry and 6 light guns to our aid at Dehli. It is under R. Lawrence's command. He and the other officers accompanying will be able to see what stuff the troops are made of on the way. Sir John Lawrence is satisfied that they are good. Letters from Sealkote mention that camels had been sent to bring in the first instalment of the loan of 75 lacs promised by the new prince. Punjaub accounts continue most satisfactory. The King has conferred the Soobah of Rohilkhund on Bukht Khan, Commander of the Rohilkhund Brigade, and that of Goozerat (?) on Sirdhana Singh of the Neemuch Brigade! The Bareilly Brigade proposed to cross the bridge in order to recross and fall on our rear. But their object was suspected to be to return to Bareilly, and they were stopped. The bridge is sharply watched for deserters, but they leave by other roads. Succession of Rajah Goolah Singh's son in Kashmir. Kashmir Contingent under Major R. Lawrence. Loan of 75 lacs from Kashmir. King of Delhi appoints "Soobahs" of Rohilkhund and Gujerat.

The rebels still talk of sending a force *via* Allypore to our rear, but they have neither unity of counsel nor of action, and it is not anticipated that any such project will be carried out. Dissension is believed to be increasing. Rebels want unity.

The enemy have been quite quiet, Greathed writes, for the last few days. They have withdrawn their field guns from the front, and only fire occasionally from Kishengunge. Captain Hodson had been successful not only in destroying 23 out of 25 Sowars he came on in a village, but had a successful skirmish with a considerable body of the rebel detachment at Rohtuck. This party had, however, been withdrawn, as it was found difficult, in the present state of the country, to maintain connection with it, and it could not easily have been reinforced.

Captain Hodson's successful operations.

Mr. Greathed had a letter on the 17th from a Shahzadah, Mirza Ilahee Buksh, asking what he could do for us? Mr. Greathed would not, however, involve himself in any correspondence. Mohun Lal is at Meerut. He is believed to be friendly to us, but given to intrigue, and will be advised to go to Loodiana. The detachment that has gone out towards Hissar consists of 150 Hurianah Light Infantry, 900 horse, and 2 guns. They are inhabitants of Hissar, and are on their own hook. It was this force Capt. Hodson was watching.

Shahzada Mirza Ilahi Bakhsh offers his services.

Mohan Lal.

Rebel detachment proceeds towards Hissar.

The enemy have of late "hardly been firing at all." I fancy their stock of gunpowder is rather low. There are no spare Artillery in camp. To work the Siege Train now coming down, they have been obliged to withdraw Artillery men from Meerut where they are wanted. Indeed, Artillery men seem to be one of our greatest wants.

Great need of Artillerymen.

. . . .

In opposition to what Anson said in the letter I sent yesterday, he writes that sickness is not on the increase. Wounded doing well. Chumbul (Chamberlain?) "getting on famously" (?). Supplies as before [?].

Our expedition to Hatrass, finding Allygurh still occupied, has gone on, and is to-day expelling the Usurper, but we shall not have tidings of them till to-morrow.

. . . .

Major Williams, Commissioner of Meerut, writes: "Every native tells me that one Regiment marching up from the Eastward would bring the whole affair to a close." When are these reinforcements to come? What has stopped them at Benares?

P.S.—Major Macpherson's Dehli news-writer, who always colours in favour of the Rebels, reports advances of our troops against the Cashmere and Lahore Gates, which had caused great confusion and alarm in the city, and driven in the Rebels, and caused the gates to be shut;—he also reports daily desertion of small bodies of Sepoys. We shall see what facts these reports are founded upon when we get our regular despatches. Delhi rebels deserting.

DCXXXV.

W. Muir, C.S., to General Havelock.

Agra, 25*th August*.

My Dear Havelock,—General Neill's of the 19th has just told us of your success against the 42nd N.I., but he gives few particulars, and nothing of your further intended movements. General Havelock's success.

Our Party at Hattras, hearing that the rebels in Allygurh talked of an expedition to dislodge them, and had actually moved out of the city, advanced on Sunday night to meet them. They came up with the enemy about 3 miles on the side of Allygurh. They were about 3000 strong, chiefly composed of Ghazies, who came on wildly with their swords. But they got well beaten. Between 300 and 400 were left dead on the ground. We lost three killed, among whom were young Ensign Marsh and Mr. Tandy, indigo planter in the district; with 9 wounded—among the latter, Captain Longueville Clark. After the enemy had entirely disappeared our force retired to Hattras, ... Nothing fresh from Dehli, nor any news from Gwalior.—Yours affectionately, Affair at Aligarh. Ensign Marsh and Mr. Tandy killed. Captain Longueville Clark wounded.

W. M.

DCXXXVI.

W. Muir, C.S., to General Havelock.

Agra, 26*th August* 1857.

My Dear Havelock,—We have nothing more from Dehli; our cossids two or three days overdue. The Gwalior newsman professes to have accounts up to the 22nd, and represents the city to be more pressed than usual, and desertions more frequent—a body of 40 Cavalry going off in the night of the 21st. Much dependence, however, is not to be placed on this man, excepting that hitherto everything has been coloured in favour of the rebels. Rebels leaving Delhi in small parties.

Our Hattras expedition has produced good results. There are reports that the "Naib Sooba" has left Allygurh. At any rate, our authority is established for 40 miles in that direction. British authority re-established towards Aligarh.

. . . .

We ourselves would not attempt to hold any outpost in that direction if *α φορς οφ αυι* strength should threaten.

Troops at Gwalior.

It is time now to be looking seriously forward to the period when the Gwalior forces will be set free by the cessation of the rains and the occurrence of the Dusehrah.

Major Macpherson, the political agent, firmly believes that *Scindia will not be able to hold them back after that.* This gives just another month to prepare for them, viz. to about 26th September. There will be then some MMMMM men with a siege train within 80 miles of Agra—important fort & αρσεναλ. Should Dehli not have fallen by that time the position will be a very awkward one. It is a cogent reason if any men were yet wanting for pressing the march of troops υπυαρδς.

Lucknow will be of course your first consideration when reinforced, but what Sherer mentioned should also be borne in mind. The Indore troops may move before the Contingent does, as they are dissatisfied with Scindia's treatment of them; but should they not, which is quite possible, they will only tend eventually to swell the Contingent when it does move.

If Dehli should meanwhile fall, which God grant it may, the face of affairs would of course be instantly and entirely altered. —Yours affectionately,

W. M.

I wrote to you yesterday. Will you mention what I said about the Gwalior troops in your next communication with General Outram and with Calcutta? Lady Outram and son well here.

DCXXXVII.

W. Muir, C.S., to Genl. Havelock.

Agra, *27th August* 1857.

My Dear Havelock,—Last night I heard from Greathed, by letter dated the 21st. Cossids are still considerably overdue. The news continues satisfactory. The only untoward bit of intelligence is that a telegraphic message had been that morning received, intimating that the 10th L. C. had at last gone. They mutinied in a body at Ferozepore, and attempted to seize the guns. Failing to do this, they took the road to Dehli. It was understood that they had been dispersed and disarmed. The message is silent on this subject.

10th L.C. mutiny at Ferozepore.

Disorganisation in Delhi.

Greathed confirms the report that disorganisation increases in the city. "The authority of General Bukht Khan and Lall Khan is set at defiance, and the King is openly taunted in Durbar. A sense of common danger will probably keep them together, and no one wishes them to disperse." Altogether the feeling of confidence rises in our camp; while depression reigns in the city. There have been no attacks since the 12th, and not much distant firing. On the 20th we placed two light guns in the advanced Metcalfe entrenchment to dislodge a picket of the enemy, who in consequence opened their heavy guns at Selimgurh. But they did no damage, and our object was effected without loss. On the morning of the 21st (?) "they were trying to send rockets from across the river into the left of our camp, but it is out of range."

Greathed describes the party that has gone to Hansie as about 1000 strong—irregular horse, Hurianah Light Infantry, with two guns. They are believed to be residents of Hurianah, and their object to raise a local disturbance for their own interests. It is expected that Van Cortlandt, who is at Hansie, will be able to deal with them. Delhi rebels' expedition to Hansi. Van Cortlandt.

Of Hodson, Greathed writes that he had visited Rohtuck and defeated a band of insurgents of the city and neighbourhood. "He is generally well received by the people." Hodson.

The lady brought into camp was a Mrs. Leeson, not Tuson, a daughter of Mr. Collins, late Deputy Commissioner of Dehli. After being left for killed on the day of the massacre, "she was taken up after dark by a good Samaritan, one of the faithful, and was carefully tended by his family and conducted in disguise to our picket." Mrs. Leeson: her story.

Mozuffernugger is now in good order. Open outrage has ceased. "The roads are safe and the revenue is being collected." Seharumpore and Dera continue quiet. The entire revenue demand from Paneeput for the summer will soon be quite paid up. In the camp treasure chest there are 12 or 13 laks. Muzafarnagar in good order. Financial status in Delhi and neighbouring districts.

Mr. Greathed had received two or three messages from Shahzadas, "tendering their services, and vowing strong attachment. They meet with no response." Health of camp continues good. The reinforcements have lightened the duty in the camp. Shahzadas tender service.

Referring to the Sikhs in the city having at last had themselves formed into one corps, Greathed says, "This is an important incident;—as yet they have not evinced the line they intend to pursue. They were able to prevent the Sikh cossid who was arrested from being executed. He is now in camp." Sikhs in Delhi unite.

I will repeat here a portion of my letter of yesterday, in case it should miscarry, on a subject which is here felt to be one of daily increasing anxiety and urgency.

(All the part quieted about Gwalior.)

The contingency I have referred to will place Scindia himself in a most difficult position. No doubt when he promised to lead the Mutineers into action, after the Dussehra, he expected that we should be reinforced and out of danger by that time.

Military position at Agra. With 500 more Europeans we should be tolerably independent, and with a couple of troops of cavalry in addition quite so. But with our present small force the approach of any large body of the enemy, especially equipped with heavy artillery, would at once place us in a state of siege. We have letters and messengers from Gwalior up to the 23rd and 24th. All is quiet there at present. The Dehli Gwalior news-writer still speaks of numerous desertions. He mentions 50 Infantry having gone off on the night of the 24th to their homes "out of fear." This told to the King in Durbar. (Numerous desertions at Delhi.)

W. M.

DCXXXVIII.

W. Muir, C.S., to Genl. Havelock.

Agra, 27*th August* 1857.

My Dear Havelock,—This came after I had closed my letter. It would be useless, I fear, sending it on at once to Bensley and Mary Thornhill; but, please God, an opportunity may soon occur. I also enclose Anson's letter forwarding it. The accounts are up to the 22nd. There is no doubt the 10th Light Cavalry were formerly disarmed. One letter says that "some 100 of them have bolted towards Dehli on officers' and Artillery horses, which they seized." This is also supported by Greathed. The siege train seems not to be expected till about the 1st prox.; and "then," says the same writer, "let Dehli look out,—don't be uneasy about us. We are all very jolly here, and could, if necessary, stay on for the next 12 months, but I hope a week or two will see us inside the Imperial City." Anson's letter too breathes the same spirit. The writer from whom I have quoted, who is a very intelligent medical man, adds: "Our worst enemy by far is sickness, which increases by 150 cases a week. Nothing very serious, however,—chiefly fevers." He says they are very short of Doolies and bearers, and would be glad to have help in this respect from us. We could have assisted them if a detachment had been marching up, but as it is we are of course powerless. (Desertion of 10th Light Cavalry. The situation in Delhi camp. Sickness increasing in Delhi camp.)

Greathed, in a letter of the same date, says that dispositions have been made to intercept the men of the 10th Light Cavalry on their way to Dehli. The Punjaub continues perfectly quiet. The only element of anxiety are the disarmed Regiments, especially those at Lahore, which are in a sulky, restless state." They continue encamped in front of the European lines. (The Punjab quiet. Disarmed Regiments sulky.)

Rebels' operations at Delhi. **Disorganisation increasing.** **Jhansi Brigade leave Delhi for Malagarh.** **Zinat Mehal Begum offers her good offices.**

The Dehli rebels have erected a battery on the bank of the river opposite the Metcalfe picket. There was a rocket tube which became unserviceable on the 21st, and two 24-pounders which with a considerable elevation throw shots across the river. The attempt was not worthy of notice. They had thrown up breastworks at these batteries as if they apprehended that we might cross to attack them. There had been an intention on the part of the rebels to attack our camp on the morning of the 22nd, but it was not carried out. A large force was seen returning with their guns under cover of the Kishengunge battery. "Disorganisation," says Greathed, "is certainly on the increase." The Jhansie brigade had crossed to the Doab with the intention of going to Malagurh. As they have taken their women and wounded and their plunder along with them, it seems likely they will never return. They take their 3 guns with them, and consist of 5 companies of Infantry of the 14th Irregulars, and a band of Irregular Infantry. This party may possibly threaten Allygurh, as we hear the "Naib Sooba" has fled to Malagurh after our success of the 24th. If they move down to support him we must of course *ρετιρε*, as we cannot afford to *συππορτ* them from this. On the 21st a messenger came from Zeenut Mehal Begum, the chief Queen, offering her good offices. She was very properly told by Greathed: "We were highly anxious for her personal safety, and for that of all women and children, but that no communication could be received from inmates of the Palace."

Scindia and his Contingent.

Greathed concludes: "We are getting on well in camp, and I hope the news received from you to-day will determine the General to lose no time." He alludes, no doubt, to Mr. Colvin's intimation that no early *ρεινφορσμεντς* could be expected from you. If all goes well, the first week of next month should show some good work. Major Macpherson's news of this afternoon from Gwalior is again somewhat unsatisfactory. His correspondent tells him that Scindia is in trouble, and fears the Indore people will march after the Mohurrum, and that they will take the Contingent with them. We must wait quietly and see how matters turn.

W. M.

Macpherson seems to fear that the Maharajah has heard from Indore and Mhow that his motives in keeping the Mutineer Contingent are suspected, and that he is less forward in endeavouring to keep them back. I cannot pretend to enter into these inter-Political Agency matters.

DCXXXIX.

W. Muir to General Havelock.

Agra, 28*th August* 1857.

My Dear Havelock,—Nothing new from Dehli. I gave you all the news I could glean from various sources yesterday.

Dr. Mactier.

You may like to see the letter of Dr. Mactier's from which I quoted yesterday. Dr. Farquhar has allowed me to send it. I have hitherto taken it for granted that I have been doing right in keeping you constantly informed of all that is going on both in these parts and in Dehli. I do so as a private friend, though, of course, my letters can be made use of by you in any way you see fit. I shall be glad to know that they are of any service to you. We have a letter from Kurachee dated 13th August. It says that a P. & O. steamer with troops from the Cape was seen entering the Bombay harbour as the Kurachee steamer left. Colonel Stewart's column of 300 H.M. 86th had arrived at

All quiet at Indore. Five per cent. loan filling. Mutiny of the 27th at Kolapore.

Mhow on the 4th instant. All was quiet at Indore. The 5 % loan was filling at Bombay. At *Κολαπορε* the 27th *ἁδ* shown *συμπτομς* of *δισαφεκτιον*; *ον* the 2nd, CL of them had *πλυνδερεδ* the *τρεασυρε* and taken up a position in the town. They fled during the night, and 50 of them had been captured. Part of the 2nd Europeans were on their way there. Another portion of the same corps had landed at Goa *en route* to Belgaum, where

The Nizam giving help.

and at Dharnan all was quiet. The Nizam and his Minister helping us satisfactorily. All this, and probably later news, you may have had *via* Calcutta. Our little force has gone again to

Aligarh reoccupied. Major Greathed, R.E.

reoccupy Allygurh. A letter just in from Mr. Greathed's brother of the Engineers, who has been for some time past "Directing Engineer of the left attack." He writes in the highest spirits and in complete confidence of success,—so much so that he is glad of the disappointment as to the delay in your

His confidence of success at Delhi.

advance. The force now before Dehli he considers strong enough to beat any number of the enemy, while our artillery will entirely swamp anything they can bring against us. He says: "I look upon our success here as certain, and a speedy release of a large part of the force as assured." Though at one time harassed by the over duty of the camp, the troops are now in excellent spirits. Throughout the camp there is a feeling of

Confidence in Guides, Gurkhas, Coke's men, and Sikhs.

confidence in the Guides, Goorkhas, Coke's men, and Sikhs. "In proportion our enemy has lost in courage and vigour; his attacks for the last month have been made without any intention of winning." F. Williams, Commissioner of Dehli, says "the Mutineers are apparently going off in large bodies of 500 and 800, but generally without arms." This is all highly satisfactory. The heat is stated in another letter from camp to be extreme. Sickness is certainly to be dreaded, but we must hope that before the worst season comes on the matter will be over, and the main body moving elsewhere. News from Gwalior pretty much as before,—perhaps a little better to-day.

Mutineers deserting.

P.S.—Poor Lamb of the Artillery died 2 days ago. He had a grape wound in his thigh, and has been in a precarious state,—on the point of losing his leg ever since. He was a fine fellow, a brave officer, and excellent civil officer, and, I believe, a true Christian. D'Oyley and Lamb are two serious losses to the Artillery service.

D'Oyley and Lamb serious losses.

DCXL.

W. MUIR, C.S., TO F. WILLIAMS, C.S., COMMR. OF MEERUT DIVISION.

AGRA, 28*th August* 1857.

MY DEAR WILLIAMS,—As a cossid is starting for Meerut I send a line, and enclose one or two letters for (?)

The "Jumna" gunboat, at one time destined for Agra, has gone to Cawnpore from Allahabad. The "Megna" gunboat, expected at Allahabad shortly, will probably come up here. Mr. Colvin's health urgently requires a change. The ascending troops are all being detained at Benares,—we could not for some time understand why. It now appears probable that it is with the view of making a direct attack on Lucknow, from thence *via* Fyzabad. The Goruckpore Goorkhas from Nepaul might co-operate with effect in such a movement. From this cause reinforcements have ceased arriving at Allahabad, a party of the 70th Highlanders being the only troops they have lately received. But it does not matter; it will be all the same if we get them *via* Lucknow by and bye. No letters from Lucknow, but it is believed to be holding out well. The Natives report that they had laid in provisions there while the siege was temporarily raised by Havelock's movements. How will the deputation from Dehli of the Jhansi brigade to Malagurh affect your dealings with that place? Madras troops are marching up to Benares, and will be of great use there. The Nepaulese Goorkhas keep Goruckpore quiet. Mr. P. H. Grant, Lieutenant-Governor of the Central Provinces, was at Rungmahul on the 12th. Captain Peel's Naval Brigade of

Mr. Colvin's health.

Detention of European troops at Benares.

Madras troops.

Gurkhas keep Goruckpore quiet.

Captain Peel's Naval Brigade. Reinforcements expected.

600 Marines with 68-pounder Howitzers from the "Shannon" will be of wonderful service at Allahabad. The 90th will be up immediately. Three more China Regiments expected within the month. They were going to change their entrenched camp at Cawnpore, as it was within shell range of the opposite bank, and the enemy were creeping down there and could be seen bathing in the river. They wanted a quieter place for their hospital; the Garrison therefore for the present joins Havelock's camp, which is, I believe, on the Grand Parade. In his last rub with the 42nd and other Saugor and Fyzabad troops at Bithoor, Havelock had as usual a complete victory, capturing their only 2 guns, but he lost 6 killed and wounded. Altogether, he writes, 48 guns have been captured in the field by him; 20 seized at Bithoor, and upwards of 40 received in the Cawnpore Arsenal,—in all above 108! He is a noble fellow. Sir C. Campbell has remained in Calcutta. Sir Patrick Grant returns to Madras. . . . of the Bashi Bazooks has also arrived. The Nawab of Benda (?), who wants to collect an army, called on Narain Rao of Khirwee for a loan of five lacs. He of course refused. The Nawab said he would take it,—so both are (encamping?) their forces against each other, which is excellent for us. The electric telegraph is open again from Calcutta to Cawnpore—a great point! Let me have your views at length regarding the disarming question;—your letter, I told you, on the subject must have miscarried.—Yours affectionately,

Havelock defeats the 42nd.

108 guns secured. Sir Patrick Grant.

Narain Rao of Khirwan.

Telegraph open from Calcutta to Cawnpore.

W. M..

MAJOR G. W. WILLIAMS, Meerut.

DCXLI.

W. MUIR, C.S., TO SIR JOHN LAWRENCE, LIEUT.-GOVERNOR, PUNJAB.

29th August 1857.

MY DEAR SIR JOHN LAWRENCE,—An account of the Expedition to Allygurh, and of Cocks' triumphant entry there.

Raja of Mynpoory's excesses.
State of things at Gwalior.
Havelock's proceedings.
Cause of reinforcements being delayed.
Sir J. Outram's intended expedition *via* Fyzabad.
Reinforcements, etc., from Calcutta.
"Jumna" and "Megna" Gunboats.
Mr. Colvin might leave in the latter, but better, if possible, go to the Hills.

It has been suggested by several persons that when peace is restored there should be a general disarming. The best argument for it is the tranquillity pervading the Punjaub. But it could not be a partial measure. Whenever our villages are near to foreign States we should either have to allow them to retain their arms or require the foreign States to adopt the same course. How has this been arranged in the Punjaub? Is the measure imposed on the foreign and protected States?—and if not, how, for example, are the villagers of Thanesur expected to defend themselves against armed attacks? I should be much obliged by your favouring me with your sentiments on this point.—Yours very sincerely, W. M.

Proposal for general disarming.

P.S.—All India indebted for succour sent to Dehli, and admirable tranquillity of Punjaub nevertheless.

Acknowledges Sir J. Lawrence's aid.

DCXLII.

W. Muir, C.S., to Genl. Havelock.

Agra, *30th August* 1857.

My Dear Havelock,—Very cheering news has come in from Dehli, 26th. The Bareilly Brigade, followed by the N. Brigade, marched out of Dehli with the ostensible view of proceeding to Allygunge on the Paneeput road, and of attacking our rear (possibly with a view of engaging and renewing the temptation of civil discord [among] those troops during the Mohurrum, as you will remember they successfully did at Eed oo-Zoha).

Bareilly Brigade makes a sortie.

Intelligence of their movements reached our camp. Nicholson set out in the morning of the 25th at 4 a.m. with his Column with the view of intercepting them. He marched 18 miles over a cross-road much submerged, and came up with the enemy at 4 p.m. It was the Bareilly Brigade. It had crossed the Nujjuffgurh cut, and was encamped 2 miles north of the bridge. We attacked them at once, drove them off, and *captured 12 field-pieces.* Part of them rallied at a village on the way to the bridge, but they were driven out at the point of the bayonet, and fled in utter confusion across the escape. All their ammunition, camp equipage, and baggage were captured, and the day was concluded by the blowing up of the bridge. Lieutenant Lumsden of Coke's Regiment and Dr. Ireland[1] are killed, and young Low, who brings the intelligence, computes the other casualties at 40

Action of Najafgarh. The Bareilly Brigade defeated.

Lieutenant Lumsden killed.

Lieutenant (?) Low.

[1] Proved incorrect. Happily still alive. See p. 486, vol. i.—W. C.

or 50. The Column was expected back on the morning of the 27th. This is a very important victory. For the Bareilly Brigade, as immediately commanded by their Commander-in-Chief, is, I fancy, their crack corps. If anything had been wanting to decide our Chief there in making a final attack, this will surely do it. Greathed writes: "This signal success, and the intimation that General Havelock cannot be here for some time, will, I hope, determine the General in not delaying operations." This, as you will have noticed, is becoming the concurrent voice of the camp; and no doubt General Wilson only waits the arrival of the Ferozepore Siege Train before setting to work in earnest. The train was at Kurnaul on 26th, so that it ought to be at Dehli by the 1st. Greathed adds: "The Dehli Rebel detachment that went to Hissar has fared ill—it has been defeated on three occasions. Captain Hodson and his party of cavalry killed 88, chiefly irregular horsemen. This occurred at Rohtuk. He had killed 23 at Khurkhouda a few days before." We had this news before, but Greathed writes as if Hodson's party had not been withdrawn as Col. Becher said.

Bareilly Brigade the rebels' "crack corps."

Progress of siege train towards Delhi.

Captain Hodson's operations.

All was quiet in the Punjaub, a matter of great thankfulness. As regards the mutiny of the 10th Light Cavalry, it turns out that the guns were saved by the Invalids of the 61st. Their officer had heard a whisper of the intentions of the cavalry, and ordered his men to have their guns loaded. "The accession of these troopers to the rebel force," writes Greathed, "is of little present importance," but he expresses a just anxiety at "having so many unpardonable mounted rebels about the country when the neck of the rebellion here has been broken. They are chiefly from our N.W. stations, and many of them, chiefly in the Irregular Corps, belong to good families. But that is a future question, and sufficient for the day, etc." *General Lawrence* writes from Agra in much anxiety about Aboo, where his wife and son and daughters are. He had not heard from them since the 19th;—this letter is dated 27th. On the 26th Lawrence received a letter from Monck Mason at Joudpore, enclosing one from J. Conolly, Erinpoora, 22nd, calling for assistance, as he found the men of the Legion were about to mutiny. He said the Resaldar on command there [Anadia] had sent him an intercepted letter from the men of the Company lately sent on command, who writes: "We have fought the few Europeans and are securing ourselves,—join us quickly with the guns." There had been 100 men of Europeans at Aboo, but 50 had, against Lawrence's remonstrance, been withdrawn; and of

All quiet in the Punjab.

Invalids of the 61st save the guns at Ferozepore.

General Lawrence.

Monck Mason at Joudpore. J. Conolly, Erinpoora.

Aboo weak in force.

the remaining 50 many were sick, while there were 120 of the Legion and many bad characters in the bazaar. There were only 6 or 7 gentlemen there, and many ladies and children. But we must still hope for the best. Deesa is only 50 miles from Aboo, and assistance might reach from there. A squadron of the Lancers (?) was to march on the 28th for Erinpoora, but it would be, I fear, too late to be of any use.

Cocks, I mentioned, made a triumphant entry into Allygurh. The disaffected Mussulmans had all disappeared, and the remaining population were all delighted at the restoration of our authority. Muttra is held for us in peace and tranquillity by a Native Deputy Collector and Magistrate, a Mahommedan. So is the district of Etawah by loyal Talookdars, though, of course, in rather a loose fashion. What can prove more than these facts that the *country* is not against us, though no doubt many, thinking us down, endeavour to make the most of the movement; and the proclamation of a Mahommedan rule is a sore trial to all religious Mahommedans,—yet as a body the country is not against us, but, on the contrary, longing for the Mutineers' reign to cease.

Cocks triumphantly enters Aligarh.

A native officer holds Muttra in peace, and Etawah by loyal Talookdars.

Country is not against British rule.

Gwalior keeps as before. River still high. One of the Contingent Corps said to be ordered by Scindia into the interior, and to be about to go. Indore troops still restless; but if Dehli falls soon we shall, please God, be independent of them.

Scindia and his force.

DCXLIII.

W. Muir, C.S., to General Havelock.

Agra, 31*st August* 1857.

My Dear Havelock,—I enclose copies of my last three letters in case any has miscarried.

. . . .

Yesterday's news of Nicholson's victory over the Bareilly Brigade has put us all here in good heart. Even those who disapproved, and prophesied evil things, begin now to look for an easy and final success against the city.

Nicholson's success.

. . . .

That[1] is about the numbers of the enemy at Dehli which we had been estimating, and it is daily diminishing. Mr. Wilson, Judge of Moradabad, now at Meerut, gives a good instance of the manner in which Sepoys are dropping off. Between thirty and forty of them crossed at

Cracroft Wilson, C.S.

[1] The context does not give the figures. There is a hiatus.—W. C.

Mewattis plunder deserting Mutineers. Gurhmuktesur about ten days ago. The Mewattees set upon them by the way and plundered them of 1200 rupees. They complained to the Nazim of the Rampore Nawab, who reported the matter to Mr. Wilson; and the Mewattees also came to him, bringing 620 rupees of the plundered treasure. Mr. W. told them to keep the money and pursue the Sepoys; and he fully expected that they would either be killed or brought in alive.

Mr. Dunlop says he wrote a friendly letter to Bukht Khan (the Commander-in-Chief in Dehli), and that Mirza Mogul, the King's son, opened it. This occurred, he says, on the 22nd. I suppose it was intended to cast suspicion on Bukht Khan, and *may* be connected with his expedition to vindicate his character. **Revenue being paid.** Mr. Dunlop says his revenue is "being realised most satisfactorily," except in the pergunnahs within reach of the enemy's attacks. We have just got a letter from Capt. MacBean to Capt. Chalmers of the 24th, saying that Lucknow had been heard of on the 23rd. It is a great relief to us.

W. Muir.

DCXLIV.

W. Muir, C.S., to Genl. Havelock.

Agra, 1*st September* 1857.

My Dear Havelock,—One of the Cawnpore messengers reports that you are sick. I trust this may not be the case. There is nothing of fresh importance to-day, but I send a line as the enclosed letters are going at any rate. Major Macpherson's news from Gwalior is better to-day. Intelligence of our success at Nujjufghur over the Bareilly Brigade, and of the low state of **Gwalior and Maharajah Scindia.** the rebel cause at Dehli, had reached Gwalior, and apparently greatly strengthened Scindia's hands in holding the mutinous troops there in check. Macpherson has also tried to explain that the cause why no fresh advance is made by you is that an attack is probably being made from Benares on Oudh. Have you any fresh intelligence which you are at liberty to communicate to us on this subject? It is what not only puzzles and staggers the native mind, but depresses us all, not to hear what has become of all the reinforcements that have reached Bengal, and were expected to have been before this up the country. Do tell us all that you can on the subject. The Gwalior fellows are more likely to come here, according to their present talk, than go to Cawnpore. They have a salutary dread of Europeans.

Macpherson has got the Gwalior news-writer's report of Dehli up to Saturday the 29th. It is still filled with accounts of the defeat of the Bareilly and Neemuch Brigades (for the native account is that the Neemuch Brigade also was defeated), unless it be the statement of another later action, which is unlikely, of disorder in the City, of the departure of the Ghazees, and of the flight of troops to their homes. A hundred Cavalry and 200 Sepoys reported to have gone back that day. Our Europeans will stay on a few days longer at Allygurh. They are doing good service, and we are getting in some Revenue. Montgomery (Lahore), in a letter of the 18th inst., estimates that this week, including Goolab Singh's men (2500), there will be 15,000 men before Dehli by the middle of this month, even without further reinforcements from the east.

Disorder and desertions at Delhi.

Montgomery's estimate of force before Delhi.

He is raising Sikh horse and foot for use as Police in some of our Districts. He speaks of the tranquillity of the Punjaub as marvellous. The spirit of the people is excellent. They hate the Sepoys, and the moment a Regiment breaks up "the whole population is after them. The Sepoys are strangers in a strange land; they have no sympathy from the people, and are not protected or concealed." They are very summary and severe in their dealing. "Any one who talks treason is instantly hanged. We will not allow it to be breathed, and we have men mixed with the population to report it."

His account of the Punjab.

On your way up you will have to deal with the Rajah of Mynpoorie, who is endeavouring to enjoy a brief authority. He began by paying off some ancient scores against the Aheers of some villages faithful to us; and, finding himself joined by the Thakoor brethren, has been led on to assume an independent and probably hostile tone towards us. He is joined by many Rajahs or Talookdars. They had a great fight with the Aheers and beat them. He is reported now to have occupied Shekoabad. If he comes nearer he will probably burn his fingers, and I trust he will be well punished by yourself.

The Rajah of Mainpúri assumes authority.

Mary[1] writes in great dejection about Lucknow. God preserve the dear souls there.

W. M.

P.S.—With extra about Mutiny at Aboo of Joudpore Legion.

[1] Mrs. Charles Havelock, sister of Lady Muir and mother of Mrs. Bensley Thornhill. See note, p. 116, *ante*.—W. M.

DCXLV.

W. Muir, C.S., to Genl. Havelock.

Agra, *2nd September* 1857.

Havelock's retreat.

My Dear Havelock,—Yours of the 25th has just come in. We all here thoroughly appreciate the difficulties you had to contend against across the Ganges, and have full confidence that you acted rightly, however painful the step was in returning. A letter from Brigadier-General Neill of the 27th received yesterday announces the successful sally of the Lucknow garrison against the assaulting Ghazees and troops, and that they are well provisioned with corn. As they seem to have struck a terror into the besiegers, we may now look forward, I think, with confidence to their holding out till relieved.

Lucknow.

Nothing new from Dehli. I gave you yesterday the intelligence of a mutiny in the detachment of the Joudpore legion at Aboo. Nobody killed. Only young Lawrence (?) wounded slightly. All safe, with plenty of ammunition in the schoolhouse. Any tidings of Gubbins and Ommaney? We are very anxious to know. You would, of course, tell us if you heard anything of Bensley. What is the . . . who has set up in the Fort at Calpee? How does the Baonie Nawab behave? Sherer will perhaps answer these questions if you have not time. I have sent on yours of the 25th to Mary.

Mutiny of Jodhpore Legion at Aboo.

All quiet here. Allygurh expedition very successful. Things as before at Gwalior, but preparations for the Ram Leela are in progress. It looks as if there were a break in the rains.

Gwalior.

W. M.

DCXLVI.

W. Muir to General Havelock.

Agra, *3rd September* 1857.

My Dear Havelock,—I enclose a duplicate of Major Macpherson's message with Mr. Colvin's addendum for transmission to Calcutta, in case the original should not have reached.

Nothing new has come in direct from Dehli since Mr. Greathed's letter of the 26th, giving an account of Nicholson's victory over the Bareilly Brigade on the 25th. Our Cossids are now two or three days overdue.

But Mr. Colvin has had a letter from Mr. F. Williams at Meerut, the contents of which he has asked me to communicate.

Mr. Colvin himself is out of sorts to-day. He is not recovering his health as I should like to see. Williams writes as if both the Bareilly and Neemuch Brigades were attacked by Nicholson. His account tallies otherwise with that of Greathed; but, he says, we took all their guns, 13 in number, and "killed and wounded some 500 of them." He then goes on to say: "Fugitives who got to Dehli on the night (of the 25th) said our whole force must be out, and the 'Pahar,' that is, our camp on the heights, empty. About 10,000 men without guns turned out from the City in this hope and attacked our position briskly at first, but they were received so warmly the attack soon fainted away. They lost 700, about, then. It is calculated by some that in the two affairs the enemy must have lost about 1500 killed and wounded;—our loss was small, about 100 killed and wounded in both actions." I gather from this that the affair undertaken from the City, on the supposition that we had left our camp unprotected, took place on the day following that of the Nujjuffghur battle,—that is, on the 26th. It is curious that Greathed says nothing of it, [nor of?] any appearance of an attack from the City. The action must therefore have taken place in the afternoon, and Greathed probably despatched his letter in the forenoon. Williams adds: "The Jhansi Brigade, with its women, wounded, and plunder, is out on our side; but I am getting up a demonstration to send them flying from Malagurh, to which place it is said they are bent."

Mr. Colvin ill.

Najafgarh affair.

Attack on British position.

The Jhansi Brigade.

Our news from Allygurh continues good.

Heavy firing had been heard from Somna, a place about 16 miles north-west of Allygurh, on the 31st. This may possibly have been connected with Williams' demonstration. I gave you the last news from Gwalior yesterday. A summons from Dholepore had come for the Indore troops, but whether they will go there is another matter. Preparations for the Ram Leela going on. If you could make a demonstration our way, by moving a column out for any local object, and thus showing that there is the power of stretching your arm towards us, Macpherson thinks it would have the best possible moral effect in checking the Indore and Gwalior Mutineers. I can only mention this. You have, of course, many other considerations to weigh with you. But as reinforcements come up you might possibly, before you are in sufficient force to attempt Lucknow, be able to plan some sort of subsidiary expedition of this kind. It is astonishing what the effect of a small movement of this kind is. Our Allygurh detachment is magnified up country into a large army.

Indore troops summoned from Dholpore.

W. M.

Mutiny at Aboo.

Proceedings of Mutineers at Gwalior.

I enclose a little slip of a letter from Nusseerabad, dated the 29th August, which shows that the Mutineers at Aboo got the worst of it in their émeute, also a letter from Joudpore, dated the 25th August, about the Legion generally. Just as I was shutting this up I received the following from Macpherson:—"Yesterday morning the Indore Mutineers marched from Gwalior to the Residency. They had seized Havelock's dak from Agra, so he trusted no more to this one, but had written by Cossid. Of course we cannot tell, but the probability is they are all coming.

The Residency is the first march in this direction. They[1] may be bound either for Dehli or this. The Indore followers will probably halt at the Residency for a little, and endeavour to draw over the Contingent. Macpherson would like intelligence of this move to be telegraphed to Calcutta. The intelligence came after his packet was closed.

W. M.

DCCXLVII.

W. Muir, C.S., to Genl. Havelock.

Agra, *4th September* 1857.

Preparations at Delhi for assault.

General Wilson's determination.

My Dear Havelock,—Some important letters have come in from Dehli of the 28th and 30th ultimo. The whole tone of our communications from the camp is that of expectation of immediate offensive operations when the Siege Train arrives, and of being in possession of the City by the middle of the month. General Wilson himself, in reference to an application for help in the Doab, if no early assault were intended, has replied that he has no chance of immediate *ασσίσταυς* from the *Καυπωρ φορς*. He has determined, on the arrival of the Siege Train, to *βαττερ* and attempt an *ασσαυλτ* on the City; and, of course, every other consideration gives way to this. The arrival of the

Siege train delayed.

Good service rendered by Sikhs, Punjabis, and Gorkhas.

Siege Train had been delayed by rain at the Markhunda, but that difficulty had been got over, and it was expected at the latest from the 3rd to the 5th inst. "All are impatient," says Greathed, "for the day." "Volunteers have been called for from officers of Infantry and Cavalry to serve with Artillery in the trenches, and an important work has been commenced." He says that the Sikhs, Punjaubees, and Ghoorkas continue to do admirable service, and the best understanding exists between them and our men. The Insurgents on the left bank had sunk

[1] Neemuch men.—W. M.

our ferry-boat at Baghput. They are only 200 or 300, but now that we are looking at higher game they have it for the moment their own way. Greathed says: "The health of the force is still good, and I don't hear of any bad results from the exposure and privations to which the Column under Nicholson was exposed." On the other hand, Colonel Becher, in a letter of the 28th, says: "There is a good deal of sickness in camp, I am sorry to say, and it is on the increase, chiefly fever. Wounded all getting on very well." And Dr. Mackinnon speaks even more strongly in a letter of the 30th:—"The Siege Train will be here in 5 or 6 days, and I should suppose the trenches will be opened by the 10th at latest. We should be masters of Dehli by the middle of the month, unless we are disabled by sickness. At present nearly a φουρθ of our numbers are sick; but if they don't ινκρεασε we have force enough to take the place from the contemptible brutes who now hold it." Colonel Becher, in a letter of the 28th, gives additional information as to the affair of the 25th and 26th ultimo. Our troops, though fatigued by a long and harassing march, owing to the submerged state of the country, at once attacked the enemy and drove him from his position. They were apparently surprised, and could not take up quite the position they intended; their Artillery fire was rather heavy, but they could not stand the steady advance of our troops on the Serai, which was the centre of their position, and fled, leaving all their guns but two on the field. A very large quantity of ammunition was found and destroyed, and our native troops got plenty of plunder of every description. Our loss, about 20 killed and 40 or 50 wounded. The force consisted of—380 1st Fus., 420 H.M. 61st, 800 1st and 2nd Punjaub Infantry, three troops H.A., 100 Lancers, the Mooltanie Horse, and some of the Guides. "Lumsden killed. Lts. Gabbet and Elkington (61st) and Dr. Ireland dangerously wounded; the first since dead. All returned to Camp on the evening of the 26th."

Forecast as to fall of Delhi.
Sickness.

Affair at Najafgarh.

Lumsden killed; Lieutenant Gabbet dies of wounds; Elkington and Dr. Ireland dangerously wounded.

The attack from the City, as described by Williams in my letter of yesterday, is substantially correct. They thought that nearly our whole force had gone out with Nicholson, and trooped out, followed by women and the city rabble, to plunder and seize our camp. They were well thrashed, as usual; our loss small. It is reported that the Neemuch Brigade did not return to Dehli,—at least in an organised form. I fear the estimate formed by Williams of the enemy's loss was too great, at least as respects the Nujjufgurh fight. Colonel Becher says: "From all accounts the enemy's loss in Nicholson's fight was not very heavy,—a good

Attack from the City.

many were drowned in the swamp in trying to escape." Of Van Cortlandt's force at Hissar, he writes that "it drove back a body of the enemy who had been sent from Dehli to try and discover the family of some man attached to the King. They killed about 350 of them. Cortlandt is, I still believe, at Hansee, but we hear very little of him. Ricketts, at Loodianah, has caught and hanged some of the 10th Light Cavalry. The main body is not heard of." Macpherson has Dehli news, through the Gwalior news-writer, up to the 1st. The confusion in the City does not seem to decrease. The King had taken three lakhs from the bankers, and the troops were clamorous for pay. They threatened to attack the Fort. The King had forbidden the Tazeeahs to be taken out; which shows the ascendency of the Pandies! The Moslems' party must be disgusted. His accounts speak of the Neemuch force as still out 9 coss off, and as having erected entrenchments; our troops having erected counter batteries.

Van Cortlandt's operations at Hissar.

Ricketts hangs some of the 10th L.C.

Confusion in Delhi; King takes money from bankers.

King forbids Táziahs to be taken out.

Neemuch force.

Macpherson's Gwalior letters confirm yesterday's accounts as to the movements made by the Indore Brigade. He has a letter from the Durbar with message from Scindia, who had been reassured by his letters. It would seem by these accounts that a Shahzadah had come as from Dehli and been received by the mutinous troops with a royal salute. They wished Scindia to visit and acknowledge him. Scindia said that there had been so many "forged" Dehli Princes he could not acknowledge this one; that he heard the King and Royal Family were in a couple of months going to Mecca;—he would then pay his respects, nuzzerana, etc., to the King. The troops were displeased, and spoke of making the Shahzadah King of Gwalior, plundering the Lushkur, etc. After this, it would seem, they resolved to set off for Dehli. One of the Contingent Regiments (the 4th, I think) was inclined to fraternise with them. But another (the 5th, I think), along with the Artillery and the Cavalry of the Contingent, remained staunch to Scindia. If this be so, the move will be the best that could happen, for it will break up the Contingent. There was evidently a strong disposition to dissension in their camp. A day or two more will develop what is to be. Meanwhile the Indore troops without heavy Artillery cannot materially injure us, and they will, we may hope, be too late to be of any service to the Dehli Mutineers.

Shahzada from Delhi.

Dissension among the troops.

W. M.

Adding news of the émeute at Umballa by disarmed troops, etc., as in Greathed's letter of the 30th August.

DCXLVIII.

W. Muir, C.S., to Genl. Havelock.

Agra, *6th September* 1857.

My Dear Havelock,—I give you the intelligence of the *ινδορε* people as we have it to-day from various sources. Indore troops.
They marched from *μυραρ* on the 2nd inst. and halted at the *ρεσιδενσι*. It is said their object was to remain there a few days to tempt the *κοντινγεντ* to join them. On the forenoon of the 3rd a letter was received by them from *Δόλπορε*, saying that whoever came first, the British or the *Γυαλιορ* people, would get possession of the *φορτ* and *γάτ*, whereupon the Nawab[1] ordered off an advance body of 2 or 3 companies foot, 2 troops Cavalry, 2 guns, and some new levies, to proceed by forced marches and secure the Ghat. This they did, and crossed over on Friday afternoon. The main body moved on from *Γυαλιορ* on Friday morning, and halted half-way to the *χυμβυλ*, at which they probably are to-day. It may take them two or three days to cross. Their professed object is to proceed to *αγρα*, but, unless Coming to Agra.
they get the *κοντινγεντ* to follow them, one does not see what object they can have in knocking their heads against our fort. They might take up a *ποσιτιον νεαρ* to *υς*, and from thence attempt to *γαιν ουερ* the *κοντινγεντ*. Some say they will remain a few days at *Δόλπορε* in this hope. The force as it stands is a Details of Indore and Gwalior force.
small one. The 23rd from Mhow, say 800 men (some say that a number of these, say 100 or 150, lost their muskets on leaving Mhow); regular Cavalry, say 150 men; Holkar's ditto, 80 or 90 men; Holkar's foot, say 400, and his cavalry the same number; 1000 or so of Ghazees, etc., 7 guns, not of large calibre, and not largely supplied with ammunition or artillerymen. They talk of getting *ἑανι γυνς* from *Δόλπορε*, but there are not many to get there. They may pick up one or two heavy ones. No Regiment of the Contingent had up to Friday joined the force, but a few men from each Regiment—5, 10, 15—deserted their own corps and came on with them. It seems that the Scindia's hold upon the Contingent.
chief hold *Σινδια* has upon the *κοντινγεντ* is that about one-third of the men are residents in his territories; two-thirds are *Πωρβεας*, who are anxious to be off to *Δεχλι*. Moreover, some 9 of the chief *αρτιλλερι* officers are Jats of his territory, and entirely subject to him. The main *μαγαζινε* at *Γυαλιορ* has not Magazine at Gwalior.

[1] This is the Bhopal Nawab, whom they would seem to obey. They have also a "Shahzadah."

been touched or even opened. The *αρτιλλερι* refused the Indore men any part of it. The conclusion, then, which you might as well communicate to Calcutta, is that the *ινδορε* force will be *ουερ* the *χυμβυλ* by Wednesday, and will be probably marching *θις ναι* about that time, unless they remain at *Δόλπορε* to tempt the *κοντινγεντ ουερ* also. No fresh Dehli news in to-day.

At Delhi rebels driven within walls.

The Cossid who brought letters of the 31st says that we had pushed on our batteries to *τελεευαρα*, and all the rebels (at least on that side) were now driven within the walls. I have already told you of the great progress made on the night of the 29th in clearing a way on the right of our position. "A six-gun battery," Greathed writes on the 31st, "was at the same time constructed at the head of the trench 200 yards in advance of the advanced post." Everything was evidently getting into preparation for the arrival of the heavy train, when operations would be accelerated to the utmost. It is to be hoped that our Indore friends will find themselves checkmated from that quarter.

A Rampore Nawab, and Lucknow, send succour to the King.

I add the following additional particulars regarding succours brought to the *κινγ* from a *ραμπορε* Nawab and from *Λυκνου*.

Mr. Colvin seriously ill.

Mr. Colvin has desired me to ask that this information may be sent on to Lord Canning. Mr. Colvin himself is labouring under an attack of dysentery, and we are somewhat anxious about him. I do not think he will be writing direct to-day.

Nawab Kudratullah Beg.

"Nawab Coodrutoolla Beg," Greathed writes, "son of Nawab Mehndoo Khan of Lucknow, came into Dehli on the 29th with 1000 followers, and brought 1½ lakh of rupees.

Aga, son of Yacoob Ally.

On the same day *Aga*, the son of Yacoob Ally Khan, a relation of the Rampore Nawab, arrived with a band of men, and presented 10,000 rupees to the King. They have ill-chosen the time of their visit, for their own interests." From native sources it would appear that some of the Bithoor or Lucknow men beaten by you reached Dehli on the 29th, so Coodrutoolla's men may be made up of them. A Durbar report from Gwalior mentioned a deputation with a Nuzzur from Rohilkhund to explain the state of affairs there. It may probably have been from Bareilly or Rajpore calling for help against the Hindoos, who are getting the upper hand of the rebels in some parts. Greathed adds that one of his spies had been out at the bridge beyond Nujjufghur, and had returned on the evening of the 30th. Two rebel Regiments had been there. But hearing of the advance of our troops (a reconnoitring party on the 28th, under Hodson) they returned to Dehli. This spy intercepted 2 envelopes containing "roznamchas" or diaries from one Zabteh Khan Thannahdar of

Busunt Serai to the Dehli Foujdar. No other news of importance. Colonel Cotton will keep out the Hatrass detachment to the last safe moment, and we are taking every means to secure the earliest intelligence of the ινδορε movements. Colonel Cotton will not allow such a force to come within 5 miles of us without going out to fight them. Cotton is *well* chosen, and will, I am sure, prove equal to the emergency. Hatrass detachment.

W. M.

DCXLIX.

W. Muir, C.S., to Genl. Havelock.

Agra, *5th September* 1857.

My Dear Havelock,—Mr. Colvin has desired me to enclose copies of his despatch of yesterday. I add a note of additional Dehli news in a letter received this morning, dated the 31st. Regarding the operations alluded to in my letter of yesterday as undertaken on the night of the 29th, he writes that very considerable progress had been made in clearing to the right front, and the "covering (?) party drove the enemy out of their breastwork into Dehli, and the work proceeded without interruption. A six-gun battery was at the same time constructed at the head of the trench, 200 yards in advance of the advanced post." There are some other minor details which I can give you another day. Meanwhile we are all occupied with the movement upon Gwalior. News came in this morning that the advanced guard of the Indore troops had crossed the Chumbul with two guns; the whole Indore force marched on Wednesday to the Residency, opened the gates and began plundering the property. Scindia sent a body of his own troops to stop these proceedings—300 Infantry; and 300 marched on the 3rd, as a sort of advanced guard, half-way to Dholepore, and it is a detachment of them that yesterday crossed the Chumbul. It would seem probable that their object is to march and halt at Dholepore and tempt the Contingent to follow them. The 4th Regiment has sworn to stick by the Indore troops. They all declare that their object is Agra. Whether they can do us any real harm depends on whether they can tempt the Contingent to come with their . . . heavy guns. The 4th said that they would march with their guns, but that is only a light field battery. The Indore fellows have 7 guns, of which 4 are certainly light ones.

Progress of siege operations at Delhi.

Indore troops cross the Chambal.

Agra their objective.

W. M.

DCL.

W. Muir, C.S., to Genl. Havelock.

Agra, *7th September* 1857.

Advance of Indore force.

My Dear Havelock,—To-day's report as to the Indore force is little more than confirmatory of yesterday's. It is certain that an advanced guard of 2 or 3 companies, some Cavalry, 2 guns, crossed on Friday afternoon, taking possession of Kentra Ghat and the Dholepore fort. The main body marched from the Residency on Friday, and reached the opposite bank of the Chumbul yesterday. They are probably crossing to-day. Some say they are going to Dehli, others to Agra. They are likely to get some few heavy guns from the Dholepore Rana. Only a few volunteers or deserters from each of the Contingent Regiments have joined them. They will probably wait a day or two at Dholepore to see if any more will come. They got no part of the Gwalior Magazine.

[*So far also sent to Greathed at Dehli.*]

News from Dehli to the 3rd. Greathed says all are in great spirits in camp, and the best feeling prevails among the native troops. Fever patients come in and go out of hospital, but the sick-list is on the increase. He says he was on the top of Hindoo Rao's house one day when a body of Sepoys marched out on some duty; "their listless, slovenly way of moving was remarkable."

Mutineer Sepoys at Delhi.

The Sepoys clamour at Court for their pay, and there are violent altercations at Durbar about it. "The money received from Sowkars has been embezzled by the Shahzadas. They don't seem to have any idea of what is in store for them."

Shahzadas embezzle the money received from the bankers.

The siege train was at Raee on the 3rd, and was to be in on the 4th or 5th. With (it) are marching down 350 Europeans. Wild's Regiment of Punjaub Infantry is immediately in the rear, and the Cashmere Contingent of 4 Battalions and 6 guns and some Cavalry accompany, or follow, at a short distance. The latter, in charge of R. Lawrence, are under their own officers. "They are said to be serviceable soldiers," and all agree that they will be useful, when active operations begin, in occupying ground.

Siege train expected in on 4th or 5th.

Kashmir Contingent.

Major Richard Lawrence.

Lawrence requires 1 European Regiment to return to the Punjaub after fall of Dehli. Course to be taken by our troops after that.

Extract about Cortlandt at Hansee. 4 lacs in military chest. Jhansi Brigade at Boolundshuhur.

Extracts from Anson and Lt. Greathed's letters.

Now recaptured the three batteries.

I am concerned to say that Mr. Colvin's dysentery becomes more threatening. The medical men are very anxious about him, and I fear he is in serious danger.

Mr. Colvin dangerously ill.

DCLI.

W. Muir, C.S., to Genl. Havelock.

Agra, 8*th September* 1857, *morning*.

My Dear Havelock,—I write to say that Mr. Colvin has not improved during the night. . . . I much dread that our worst fears are about to be speedily realised, and that he is sinking under the continued attacks of the disease. The medical men do not conceal that they fear he is dying.

Mr. Colvin believed to be dying.

Mr. Thornhill will probably be sending a telegraphic message in the course of the day. Meanwhile, if this should reach first, you had better send on intimation to Mr. Grant to be forwarded to Calcutta.

Mr. Reade, as our Senior Civilian, takes charge of the administration, pending the Governor-General's orders. This is a necessity, and is also borne out by the precedent of Lord Dalhousie appointing Mr. Begbie (as Senior Civilian) to carry on the Government on Mr. Thomason's death.

Mr. Reade, Senior Civilian, takes charge.

Our last information from the Gwalior side is that the Chumbul rose so high that they were unable to cross, at least up to yesterday morning. No Contingent Regiment has joined them. The Indore men may possibly halt for a time at Dholepore.

W. Muir.

P.S.—Since writing you the above I regret to say that there are no symptoms of improvement. The disease continues, and as a necessary consequence Mr. Colvin's strength declines. The medical men appear to have almost no hope, and think he may not be able to live over the night. He is gradually sinking.

Mr. Colvin sinking.

With this I send one or two notes for Beadon, which please send on by post. Mr. . . .'s telegraphic Message I sent with the first copy of the foregoing letter. A duplicate has since gone, so I trust it will be sure to reach. Nothing new either from Dehli or Gwalior. All the Dehli news I gave you in yesterday's letter.

Sherer mentioned Sheo Pershad, Deputy Collector of Calpee,

Sheo Persbad. is under suspicion. So far as we know, his conduct was faithful, and he was told to proceed to Cawnpore and offer himself for Govt. service, either to the Military or Civil officer. His letters to us were free from suspicion; and Lt. Browne has a high opinion of his character and services. Of course we cannot say what he may subsequently have done, or by what means he may have rendered himself obnoxious to superiors. But there is one thing in his favour. His son was sent by him to the College here; and frequently comes to see Mr. Reade and myself. He has been to see us here since we have come into the Fort. I trust he may yet be found innocent and faithful.

Tantia. *P.S.*—Some of Browne's men say a dak plies from Bithoor to Jaloun, where the Goorserai Pundit, Tantia, lives, a relation of the Nana's. Suggests that Sherer might intercept it.

DCLII.

W. Muir to Genl. Havelock.

Agra, *9th September* 1857.

Announces Mr. Colvin's death. Indore force crosses the Chambal.

My Dear Havelock,—Announces Mr. Colvin's death at 4½ p.m. States that 4 Companies, 2 guns, etc., crossed at Dholepore on Monday, and all their force probably over by this time. Intentions not known. No Contingent Regiment joined them . . .

VOL. IX. OF INTELLIGENCE RECORDS.

TWELFTH SERIES.

MEMORANDA OF INTELLIGENCE

CIRCULATED FOR GENERAL INFORMATION AT AGRA.

September 1857 to January 7, 1858.

In making selections from these Memoranda for this Collection, matter elsewhere recorded in these volumes has been generally omitted.

A large number of them were originally circulated as "Extras" of the "Mofussilite" and "Dehli Gazette" newspapers.

W. COLDSTREAM.

MEMORANDA OF INTELLIGENCE

CIRCULATED FOR GENERAL INFORMATION AT AGRA.

DCLIII.

JUBBULPORE AND SAUGOR.—A letter from Major Erskine, dated the 25th August, gives an encouraging account of the state of things at Jubbulpore. For some time considerable apprehension prevailed there; but Major Erskine, by the judicious offer of double batta, prevailed on the 52nd, which was quartered there, and the 50th, which was at Nagode, "to remain quiet, and up to the present moment they have stood firm." Parties of the 50th and 52nd have been detached in the district, and "all have behaved well."

Major Erskine keeps peace at Jubbulpore and at Nagode.

"At one time the people commenced rising in Jubbulpore, so I ventured to send out detachments of the 52nd, and succeeded in completely restoring order, and there is now not a rebel in the Jubbulpore district.

The Bundelas rise.

"The Boondelas a few days ago invaded the Nursingpore pergunnah; the Nursingpore Thakoors drove them back. Jubbulpore, Mundlah, Seonee, Nursingpore, Nagode, Hoshungabad, and Baitool are now all quiet and well cultivated." The Rajas of Banpore and Shahgurh have incited the Boondela and Lodee Thakoors to rise, and caused the districts of Chundeyre, Saugor, and Dumoh to be in a disturbed state. The Lulutpore refugees are detained by the latter Raja.

Central Provinces quiet.

Rajahs of Banpore and Shahgarh.

"We still hold the towns of Saugor and Dumoh."

Brigadier Sage at Saugor.

At Saugor, "Brigadièr Sage and his Europeans are in the Fort. The greater part of the 31st, some 150 of the 42nd, and 150 of the 3rd Irregular Cavalry, have proved themselves staunch, and have not only fired on and driven away their rebel comrades, but five or six times fought well against the Boondelas."

Staunch Native Regiments.

Loyal troops at Dumoh. Captain Pinkney's successes.

After our officers left Dumoh the detachment there "held the Fort prisoners, town, station, and treasure." Captain Pinkney, on his way to Saugor, proceeded to Dumoh "with three companies of the 31st N.I. and recovered the station, etc., and found the treasure, Rs. 1,30,000, all right! He twice thrashed the rebels."

Dumoh was still held by Lieut. Nembhard with 5 Companies of the 31st and 42nd. But as the insurgents were in considerable force, Major Erskine had advanced to his aid with a column from Nagpore under command of Col. Millar, 33rd M.N.I. It consists of a European Company of Artillery with six guns; 100 of the 4th M.Lt. Cavry., 7 Companies of the 33rd M.N.I., and the Rifle Company of the 1st Nagpore Irregular Infantry; 2 Companies 28th M.N.I., and 2 Companies of the 52nd Bengal N.I. When he wrote Major Erskine was half-way to Dumoh. Major Erskine leads column to Dumoh.

W. MUIR.

. . . .

DCLIV.

THE FOLLOWING IS AN EXTRACT FROM A LETTER received from Meerut, dated the 1st September:—

"In my last I told you of the discomfiture of the Neemuch, Nusseerabad, and Bareilly Brigades, which went out on the 25th to go to the rear of the Dehli Camp, when the enemy lost all his guns (13) and a number of men, and how that in the hôpes we had sent out all our army to do this, and the camp was therefore empty, that was attacked next day (26th), when great loss was again inflicted upon the enemy; our loss in killed and wounded being altogether about 100 in both affairs, theirs estimated at 1500. The last news up to the 29th is that Bukht Khan, or Kum-bukht as we call him, who has been most wisely (?) suspected by the Mutineers of being as he is a traitor double-barrelled, was so taunted, displaced and spit upon, and threatened, for not fighting his best on that occasion, that at last he took his Brigade out again in the same direction with 8 more guns; and he is out now, well watched; and as Brigadier Wilson destroyed the bridge they used before, he (Kum-bukht) has to go 10 miles farther up to the escape, making a great arc and giving our moveable Column the choice of a short line to get at him. The Native report is that he has got into a swamp somewhere and stuck; and as there has been heavy rain to swamp him, and he wanted very little to damp his courage, this may be true. He has no chance of getting at the siege train, which, having been delayed, will be joined at Paneeput by 200 Rifles and 100 Artillery Recruits

Neemuch, Nusseerabad, and Bareilly Brigades defeated at Delhi.

Attack on camp at Delhi.

Bukht Khan.

Arrival at Delhi of siege train

and of Kashmir troops.

from here, and be in Camp on the 5th, about which time Golab Singh's men will be in too, and the last ball of the season ought to commence."

The Jhansi Brigade leaves Delhi.

The Jhansi Brigade, "with its women, wounded, and plunder, has left Dehli for good. It is said to be entrenching itself at Boolundshuhur. With the view of checking its movements a force has marched towards Hauper, and will no doubt give a good account of its movements. There is a little cholera about, in Meerut, but it is not spreading and is amenable to treatment; and the health of all here is generally good. All right above,

Unrest in Muzafarnagar.

but Moozuffernugger feeling a little the effects of disaffection below; crime appearing again, but Edwards has some more Goorkhas, and will have two Mountain Train guns, and will stop it. Referring to the Allygurh expedition, the writer says 'the fame of this exploit has done much good.'"

. . . .

DCLV.

. . . .

The mutiny of Jodhpore Legion at Erinpurah.

RAJPOOTANA.—A letter from Nusseerabad, dated the 4th instant, contains the following information regarding the mutiny of the Joudpore Legion at Erinpoorah:—

"Since my last, further particulars regarding the mutiny of

Mount Aboo.

the Joudpore Legion at Erinpoorah: no one was killed at Mount Aboo, and all the ladies and Europeans there are quite safe. After the Troops mutinied at Erinpoorah, they set fire to all the thatched buildings in the Cantonment, with the exception of Sergeant-Major Collins', who remained with the portion lately disarmed at Nusseerabad, under command of Captain Black. The Mutineers, after burning and plundering the Cantonment of Erinpoorah, moved on with a Camel Battery of 2 guns towards

Lieutenant Connolly and others taken prisoners.

Beawr and Nusseerabad, taking with them as prisoners, Lieutenant Connolly the Adjutant, Quartermaster-Sergeant Walters, his wife and three children, Sergeant Morton, his wife and two children; it is said the Infantry portion wished to murder the whole of the Europeans, but the mounted Sowars, of whom there are about 100, were opposed to taking their lives, and disputes arose, and even-

Europeans helped to escape.

tually the Europeans, through the instrumentality of the Sowars, made their escape from them, and have arrived, it is believed, at Aboo. The Erinpoorah Mutineers amount in all, Cavalry and Infantry, to about 700 men, and they were a day or two ago within about 17 miles of Beawr, encamped somewhere near the entrance to that Pass which lies between the range of hills running between Burr and Beawr, and Brigadier-General Geo. Lawrence was waiting to intercept them with a portion of H.M. 83rd Regiment, Horse Artillery, and 1st Lancers; and, as I understand arrangements have been made for hemming them in on all sides, I think it is very unlikely that many of them will escape, and the Camel Battery will be almost useless to them on account of the almost constant heavy rain we have had lately, which has put the roads into such a state that camels are next to useless as draught animals."

General George Lawrence.

"All appears to be quite quiet now at Neemuch. Colonel Jackson of the 2nd Cavalry is now in command of the Station, which was kept in a state of excitement a short time ago by a wandering faqueer hoisting a green flag at Mundasoor and announcing himself as the son of the King of Dehli—whose raj he proclaimed, getting as many rabble and budmashes, of whom there is now no scarcity in all parts of the country, to join; but I believe it is not likely to come to anything serious. All is quiet at Ajmere."

Colonel Jackson at Neemuch.

"Nusseerabad is very quiet now." The Subadar and Jemadar of the 12th N.I. had been sentenced to imprisonment. A party of officers had started for Agra on the 24th, but been recalled on account of the scarcity of carriage. It was thought they would leave again on the 8th.

Nusseerabad quiet.

"The dak continues between this and Bombay to be very irregular, and sometimes a letter occupies 20 days in transit."

Postal communication with Bombay difficult.

DCLVI.

Cawnpore.—In a letter of the 5th instant it is said that the reinforcements for Lucknow were expected on the 10th instant.

. . . .

The son of the Goorserai Chief, Tantia, who holds the Fort of Calpee, had sent in Messrs. Griffith and Passana. Extracts of a letter from the latter are given below. Notwithstanding this service, the Mahratta chief is hostile to our Government.

Tantia sends in Griffith and Passana.

. . . .

Extracts from Mr. Passana's Letter, dated Cawnpore, 16th September:—

"On the approach of the Jhansie Mutineers I left Oorai with my family and Griffith's on the evening of the 14th of June.

Fate of Passana, Griffith, Heming, Double.

My poor mother, who I thought would be safe in disguise, was pointed out by some of our Burkundazes and cruelly murdered. Heming, who had been wandering about in a state of distraction, was found near the camp of the Mutineers and murdered. Mr. Double and his family were brought over from a village where they had taken refuge; the Mutineers took them on to Chowk, near Calpee, and are said to have released them, but they died from heat and fatigue. Mr. D.'s son alone was found alive. The Goorserai Rao has assumed possession of the district, appointed his own officers, and is levying forced loans from all the Mahajuns and men of substance; his eldest son, who has taken Calpee and other pergunnahs as his share, is said to have realised upwards of 30,000 Rs. from the town of Calpee alone."

Goorserai Rao assumes rule of Orai.

Calpee plundered by Tantia.

"We unfortunately fell into the hands of the Company which had escorted treasure to Gwalior. We had put up at Koodaree; they encamped at Baugra, and, hearing of us, made a 'dour,' plundered all our property, and made us prisoners for six days; as soon as we got out of their hands we were detained by the Rao's people at Oorai, and made over to the Mutineers from Lulutpoor. By the mercy of God our lives were spared. The Rao's son, Tantia, at Calpee, then seized us and was sending us to the Nanah at Cawnpore, but the defeat of the Nanah prevented him; since then we were treated with civility and taken care of as prisoners. I managed to communicate with General Neill at Cawnpore, who wrote several letters to the Rao to send us over to Cawnpore. After a deal of hesitation and delay he did so at last, and we arrived here on the 4th instant."

Tantia sends in refugees.

"We lost everything that we possessed, our houses being plundered and burnt; we are in great want."

. . . .

Insurrection at Mandesaur.

JEYPORE, *September 8th.*—"The postal communication *via* Indore has been closed since the 23rd ultimo, owing to the insurrection at Mundusore. The Mahometans threw off their allegiance to Scindia and set up a government of their own. But from Mr. Rose's account they seem not to have any decided plans. They have, however, systematically set to work to cut off our dak communication. This is from Mr. Rose, who adds, "Bazaar rumour has it that 50 Dragoons with 3 guns have left Mhow for this place (Neemuch) some days ago! He says it is quite possible, as Durand had been applied to for reinforcements some weeks ago."

Captain Denny and his party had left that morning for

Ajmere. It was expected that the Nusseerabad party of officers would not at present travel this way. Captain Denny's party.

"It would not surprise me if the Jodhpore Mutineers formed a kind of nucleus for the disaffected in Rajpootana,—and even for Goozeerat."

MHOW, *August 10th.*—The 14th Dragoons arrived here with other Bombay troops about a week ago. I don't think any forward movement, at least with Artillery, can be expected until after the rains from this quarter. We have here now two European batteries, a wing of 14th Dragoons, and 250 H.M. 86th Foot, besides 25th Bombay N.I., and some Nizam's Cavalry, the latter splendidly mounted. British force at Mhow.

DCLVII.

GARRISON ORDERS.

BY LIEUTENANT-COLONEL COTTON, COMMANDING.

FORT AGRA, *September* 12, 1857.

FIELD OFFICER OF THE DAY (TO-MORROW).—Col. Ramsay.
NEXT FOR DUTY.—Col. Glasfurd.
SUBALTERN OFFICER OF THE DAY (TO-MORROW).—Lieut. Hailes.
NEXT FOR DUTY.—Lieut. Henderson.
COUNTERSIGN.—"Etawah."

1. Lieut.-Col. Cotton, Commanding at Agra, has much pleasure in publishing to the garrison the following extracts of a despatch from Major Montgomery, commanding a detachment at Hatrass. Major Montgomery, in command of a party consisting of three guns and 61 Artillerymen, 154 of the 3rd European Regiment, of all ranks, and 22 Militia Cavalry, with a party of Jat Horse, on the 24th ultimo attacked and totally routed, near Allygurh a force of the insurgents numbering between 5000 to 6000 men under Ghose Mahommed Khan, Naib Soubah of the King of Dehli. The defeat was most signal, and Lieut.-Col. Commanding offers his congratulations to Major Montgomery on his able conduct in the field; he assures the troops of his high appreciation of the gallantry of all, and he will have great satisfaction in forwarding Major Montgomery's report for the information of the Commander-in-Chief. The following is a list of the killed and wounded:— Major Montgomery routs Ghaus Mahomed Khan.

KILLED.

J. O'B. Tandy, Esquire, Indigo Planter.
Ensign Marsh, late 16th Grenadiers.
Lance-Corporal William Armstrong, 3rd Compy., 3rd Eur. Regiment.
Private Nicholas Fitzgerald, ditto. ditto.
Private Patrick Laving, 8th „ „

WOUNDED.

Lieut. Clarke, late Gwalior Contingent, severely (three sword-cuts).
Artillery.—Sadler-Sergt. Robert McGill, severely (gun-shot).
Gunner Robert Lockhart, mortally, since dead (ditto).
3rd Eur. Regt.—

Private James Fitzgerald,	No. 2	Compy.,	very slightly	(gun-shot).
Colr.-Sergt. John Ryan,	„ 3	„	severely	(ditto).
„ „ Patrick M'Carthy,	„ 3	„	ditto	(ditto).
„ „ Nicholas Hand,	„ 3	„	very slightly	(sword-cut).
Private James Leahey,	„ 3	„	dangerously	(gun-shot).
„ Alexander Nixon,	„ 3	„	very slightly	(sword-cut).
„ Isaac Mulrooney,	„ 3	„	ditto	(ditto).
„ Robert Adair,	„ 8	„	severely	(ditto).
„ John Brown,	„ 8	„	slightly	(ditto).
„ James Cochrane,	„ 8	„	severely	(ditto).
„ John FitzSimmons,	„ 8	„	ditto	(ditto).
„ Francis MacDonnell,	„ 8	„	ditto	(ditto).
„ John Nesbitt,	„ 8	„	slightly	(ditto).
„ Patrick Quinn,	„ 8	„	very ditto	(ditto).
„ Charles Parker,	„ 8	„	ditto	(ditto).

Militia Cavalry.—Mr. Byrne, wounded accidentally (gun-shot).

CONTUSED.

Captain Murray, late Gwalior Contingent, received severe contusion, from sword-cut.

Mr. Volunteer Hennessey also received contusion, from sword-cut.

Jat Horse under Captain Murray.

The Jat Horse under command of Captain Murray had Kurruck Sing, nephew of Thakoor Gobind Singh, very severely wounded, and three Sowars wounded.

Total:—killed, 5; wounded, 23; contused, 2.
Grand total . . . . . 30.

EXTRACTS.

Major Montgomery's action near Aligarh.

Lieutenant De Kantzow.

"Having secured the baggage, etc., my greatest care and anxiety, I commenced the action by attacking, with the Militia Cavalry under Lieut. De Kantzow and the Jat Horse, a large body of Cavalry, chiefly Irregulars, who threatened our left and rear. This duty was most gallantly and promptly performed, and our left and rear having thus been cleared from the enemy's Cavalry, who were driven back to the rear of their main body, I brought the guns into position under cover of skirmishers and opened fire, which was sharply replied to by the enemy from behind the garden walls, against which I found Artillery of little avail. Information was now brought to me by Mr. P. Saunders, who considerately and kindly placed his services at my disposal, that the enemy were in great force on the right of the garden. I immediately directed Captain Murray to move round to the right with the Jat Horse and cut off the enemy on the general assault, and carrying their position with the Infantry, at the same time ordering Lieut. Griffin to move up two of his guns in the same direction. This movement took some little time, evidently occupying the attention of the enemy and enabling me to make arrangements for the assault. Leaving a sufficient number of men under Captain Strover to protect the gun on the left, and all being ready, I gave the word 'Forward,' and went to the front accompanied by Lieut. Clarke, and followed by No. 8 Company of the 3rd European Regiment under Lieut. Blake. On reaching the garden wall, a large party of fanatical Mussulmans, headed by Moulvees, rushed forward, sword in hand, from the right corner, and there ensued a most desperate hand-to-hand encounter, which terminated in their total destruction, and where we met with our chief loss. Lieut. Griffin moved up his two guns, and getting well to the right opened fire with terrible effect on their reserve, killing great numbers and completely dispersing the remainder. Captain Murray, at the same time taking advantage of an opening in the wall, dashed forward with part of the Jat Horse, entered the garden and cut up the Ghazees who remained in it; among whom was the chief Moulvee Abdoolzaleel, who was cut down in a hand-to-hand encounter with that officer. The field was now our own, after two hours' fighting, the enemy having been completely routed and dispersed in all directions, leaving at least 300 dead, thus terminating a decided victory against great odds and with comparatively small loss on our side; considering the strength of their positions and the number of Ghazees, who fought with the utmost desperation and contempt of life. My best thanks are due to the Civil Authorities, and to all the Officers and men under my command. To Captain Strover, second in command, who in quarters and in the field has rendered me every assistance, and to the Officers, non-Commissioned Officers, and soldiers of the 3rd European Regiment, who behaved with the valour of British soldiers. To Lieut. Griffin, non-Commissioned Officers, and men of the Artillery, for the promptitude with

Mr. P. Saunders.

Captain Murray kills Moulvee Abdoolzaleel in single combat.

Ghazis' desperate valour.

Lieutenant Griffin, R.A.

which my orders were carried out, and to whose energetic exertions I attribute in a great measure the success of the day. To Lieut. De Kantzow and the Militia Cavalry, who, with the Jat Horse under Captain Murray, rendered important service by successfully attacking and dispersing a large body of Irregular Cavalry at the commencement of the action. Of the conduct of the Militia Cavalry, both in the field and in quarters, I cannot speak too highly. To Assistant-Surgeon McKellar for his judicious medical arrangements, and his assiduous and humane attention to the wounded. To Lieut. Blake, 3rd European Regiment, and Lieutenant Clarke of the late Gwalior Contingent, who behaved with conspicuous gallantry, the latter being severely wounded. Ensign O'Donnell, 67th Native Infantry, who, during the march and in the field, assisted me very greatly. Mr. Volunteer Hennessey, who greatly distinguished himself, shooting five men; and as he was also present in the action of 5th July, and is the son of an old and deserving officer, I respectfully solicit that the services of the youth may be specially brought to the notice of Government, with a view to his obtaining Military employment.

Lieutenants Blake and Clarke, Ensign O'Donnell, Hennessey.

Praiseworthy conduct of the Rev. Mr. Kellner.

I beg to bring prominently forward the praiseworthy conduct of the Rev. Mr. Kellner, who gratuitously accompanied the Detachments, and for whose humane and unremitting attention to the wounded during the action and under fire too much praise cannot possibly be bestowed. I am also greatly indebted to Mr. Cocks for his cordial co-operation and assistance on all occasions, particularly on the day of the action, and for the very accurate information he obtained when the most conflicting and contradictory accounts were spread abroad, evidently with the view of discouraging and throwing difficulties in the way of an advance; also to Mr. Paterson Saunders and Messrs. Lane and Colvin, of the Civil Service, whose services I cannot speak too highly of in carrying orders throughout the heat of the action. To Captain Fanshawe, in charge of the carriage, etc., for his admirable management in providing ample carriage for the detachment and energetic exertions in the Postal Department, as also for the very accurate information he has at all times procured. To Mr. Daniell, C.S., to whom was assigned the responsible duty of protecting the baggage with the Jat matchlockmen.

Mr. Cocks.

Mr. Paterson Saunders. Messrs. Lane, Colvin, and Daniell, C.S. Captain Fanshawe.

Mr. Tandy and Ensign Marsh killed.

"I deeply lament the loss of J. O'B. Tandy, Esq., and Ensign Marsh, 16th Grenadiers, both of whom were Volunteers,—the former fell whilst attempting, quite alone, to enter the walled enclosure."

. . . .

3. The Officer Commanding the Militia is directed to place the services of Mr. J. E. Elis, No. 1 Company, and Mr. J. Smith, No. 3 Company, Agra Militia, at the disposal of Mr. Coulston, until further orders.

4. Divine Service will be performed for the Troops in Garrison to-morrow morning, agreeably to previous orders.

5. The Financial Commissioner is authorised to advance the sum of Co.'s (3000) three thousand to the Garrison Engineer, for the purposes of his Department.

DCLIX.

MEMO. FORT AGRA, 7 *a.m.*, *Sept.* 14*th.*

. . . .

PUNJAB.—All was tranquil in the Punjab.

There had been a petty local disturbance at Murree, when the neighbouring villagers attacked the station, but did no harm besides plundering two houses. Several of them were killed. Troops had gone up from Rawul Pindee, and all was quiet again. **Disturbance at Murree.**

. . . .

W. MUIR.

DCLX.

MEMO. FORT AGRA, 2 *p.m.*, 15*th Sept.*

DEHLI.—10*th Sept.*—Col. Greathed's Despatch.

. . . .

[*The most of this despatch is printed in No. LII., p.* 88, *vol. i.*]

Their mortar on the other side the Jumna has been moved opposite Koodsia Bagh, and throws a shell in occasionally. **Operations at Delhi.**

"To-day Eaton (Rifles), Randall (Coke's), Murray (Engineers) have been wounded.

"I don't see any indication of a flight. There is at present some bewilderment at the nature of our attack, but the full effect has not been developed.

"All is quiet on this side (the Jumna) to Kurnal and upwards."

. . . .

W. MUIR.

DCLXI.

MEMO. FORT AGRA, 8 *a.m.*, *Sept.* 16.

. . . .

Operations at Delhi.

On the 10th instant another correspondent writes: "Our fire is kept up at present chiefly on the Moree and Shah Bastions, which have been a good deal knocked about. There has been sharp musketry firing in the direction of the Cashmere Gate, where we have parties under grape from the Gate bastion; but our casualties since yesterday morning (9th) have not exceeded 50. Two officers wounded: Lieut. Murray, Engineers, lost left arm; and Eaton, 60th Rifles, slightly. Troops in excellent spirits, and working admirably."

Murray and Eaton wounded.

On the 11th he adds: "Our large mortar battery in Metcalfe's Garden opened this morning, and is throwing shell into the enclosure of, and behind, the Cashmere Gate.

"All our batteries have not yet opened. Casualties last night rather heavy; returns not yet in. Lieut. Gillespie, Artillery, wounded.

"All well in the Punjab, and above this. Telegraph line nearly completed into camp."

ALLAHABAD.—Latest letters, *September 7th.*

Advance on Lucknow.

A letter from General Outram, dated the 5th instant, intimates that half the troops for the advance had marched the previous night, and he was himself to follow with the remainder that evening. They hoped to be assembled at Cawnpore by the 11th, and would lose no time in pushing on to Lucknow. He also mentions that they expect further reinforcements at Cawnpore by the end of the month, and arranged to send on a considerable force here.

. . . .

CAWNPORE . . . .—"On the whole, matters are looking much brighter every day. Our entrenchment here has been much strengthened. It is a little open to shells on the river side; but where are the shells to come from when Havelock crosses the river?

Death of Captain Sheehy.

"Cholera has almost disappeared. The last case was Captain Sheehy, 81st Queen's, on duty with the Volunteer Cavalry."

. . . .

NAINEE TAL.—*September 6th.*

All well there.

"The last account from Bijnore makes one believe that the Hindoos have suffered in a late engagement. I am inclined to attribute their defeat to their having been attacked in detail. After their first victory at Nugeena they must have separated, instead of keeping in one body. **Bijnore.**

"It is to this failure to combine, and to keep united after a first combination, that I also attribute the want of success of certain Hindoos in Bareilly, who commenced acting offensively, but who, after a first victory at Fureedpore, had to retreat into Shahjehanpore. These men had counted on the combined attack by Thakoors on the Rampore side of Bareilly, and by others on the Budaon side; but both those last parties hung back when the time came. I have only learnt this to-day by the mouth of some men who have brought up 2000 Rs. and 100 Goldmohurs from Bareilly." **Hindus at Bareilly attack rebels.**

There was no apprehension as to money and supplies at Nainee Tal. The Nawab of Rampore continues friendly. **Nawab of Rampore friendly.**

Letters from Mahomedans were beginning to come in. "So the lesson at Cawnpore has taken effect. **Mahommedans submitting.**

"I hear of 150 of the Irregulars from Saugor having arrived at Bareilly, but undecided yet as to taking service with Khan Bahadur Khan.

"The Hindoos within Bareilly have suffered much in pocket and caste-insult. I learn that a large number of the population have left the town; and now desertion of their house is followed by attachment, and sometimes by its destruction." These facts should open the eyes of the Hindoos to the real object of the rebellion, and show them what they have to expect from their Mahomedan fellow-countrymen. **Hindus at Bareilly oppressed by Mahommedan rebels.**

HATTRASS.—15*th Sept.*—All well.

"Three Sowars, formerly chuprassies of Government, were executed, as it was proved that they had taken part with Ghous Mahommed in the battle against us. **Ghaus Mahomed.**

"Mr. Daniell had visited Allygurh, and found everything in excellent order. A box has been seized belonging to Ghous Mahommed, containing important documents, which may throw light on the mutiny and rebellion."

W. MUIR.

DCLXII.

FORT AGRA, 4 *p.m.*, 17*th Sept.* 1857.

DEHLI.—A letter, dated the 12th, has just been received. It states that "our firing was going on pretty steadily, though even then all the batteries had not opened."

It was expected that the next day all would "be well *en train*, and then for the grand smash, which will soon take place."

"All well in camp. Sickness less to-day."

FORT AGRA, 7 *a.m.*, 18*th September.*

Details of bombardment.

DEHLI.—12*th September.*—The following additional particulars of the proceedings of the 12th are from Mr. Greathed's letter of that date.

It was before reported that the 18-gun battery, No. II., in front of Ludlow Castle, had, with the aid of the heavy mortars, quickly silenced the Cashmere Bastion.

"That bastion has not since replied, and heavy salvos are continually directed against it. No. I. battery continues to fire into the Moree; it is a heap of ruins, but the gunners manage to fire light guns from different parts.

"No. II., at the Custom House, has not yet opened. Some alterations had to be made in it. It is expected it will be ready this evening.

"The enemy have not made any more sorties, but they keep up a brisk fire of musketry in front of the bastions from rifle pits and among the jungle, and they have a flanking fire from field-pieces on the right, and from a heavy gun and mortar on the other side the river. Suleymgurh and the Water Bastion also fire on the left and centre batteries. Rockets are occasionally fired from a Martello Tower in front, and there are single light guns on two others.

"All this does not retard the progress of the siege, or lead to any interruption of fire. And, though the delay about No. III. is certainly a disappointment, there is still every reason for congratulation. A position has been seized and maintained for breaching purposes, which, if worked up to according to rule, would not have been ours for some time, and our fire is very destructive.

"A party of the enemy's Cavalry, two hundred in number, got across the cut of the Canal yesterday to cut off our camels. They retired on seeing a force coming against them, and might have got off, but they were met by 80 of the Guide Cavalry under Capt. Sandford, and two Ressaldars and 25 Sowars were killed on the field. The rest got off to Dehli. Loss of the Mutineers.

"The sense of impending danger has roused the energies of the Pandies, and they talk of nothing but defence, and are making Dumdumahs near the Magazine, and between the Cashmere and Cabulee Gates. But experience has hitherto shown that these energies fail when the moment of action arrives; and I think it is generally a source of congratulation that the rebels are not availing themselves of the many avenues of escape. The population appears quiescent. Their preparations to withstand assault.

"Major Campbell of the Artillery was wounded by a grape shot in the leg in battery, and Lieut. Lockhart is also wounded. The enemy was quieter last night, and the casualty return for the last 24 hours is, I hope, moderate. The erection of No. III. costs a good many men.

"All quiet above."

FORT AGRA, 8 *a.m.*, 18*th September*.

A letter from Mr. Cocks, dated Hatrass, September 17th, afternoon, gives the following particulars regarding the fugitive regiments at Khoorja, and the rumoured fall of Dehli on the 14th. Dependence cannot, of course, be placed on the rumour until confirmed by our own letters. First news of fall of Delhi.

"A man I sent to Khoorja for news has just returned, and says that two and a half regiments have reached Khoorja, being fugitives from Dehli, and swearing they are off to Lucknow, where is their home, and where they will die. The Sepoys are very badly off for arms, and even for 'lotas,' although they have money.

"The city was, it is said, stormed on Monday, and the entrance made, and the streets knee-deep in blood. This has been corroborated by Muhajans' letters; and I fancy there can be no mistake that the city is ours, if not the Palace."

W. MUIR.

DCLXIII.

FORT AGRA, 6 *p.m.*, 18*th Sept.* 1857.

DEHLI.—*September* 14.—Mr. Greathed writes:—

"Dehli was stormed this morning, and the British Forces are in possession of the line of defences from the Water Bastion to the Cabul Gate, including the Cashmere Gate and Bastion, and News of fall of Delhi reaches Agra.

the Moree Gate and Bastion, the English Church, Skinner's House, the College, and the ground about. Preparations are being made to turn the guns from the captured bastions on the city, and to bring up other guns and mortars to commanding points.

"The enemy for the present retain the Lahore and other Bastions, the Palace, Suleymgurh, and the chief part of the city; but our hold of the position that has been secured appears firm, and the fall of the remainder is to be expected.

Nicholson, Campbell, and Reid wounded. "General Nicholson, Colonel Campbell, 52nd, Major Reid, Sirmoor Battalion, are among the wounded officers, who are numerous. Lieut. Bradshaw, 52nd, and Fitzgerald, 75th, were killed. Bradshaw and Fitzgerald killed.

"A body of troops was observed to march off by the bridge, but pursuit is impracticable until Suleymgurh and the river front have been occupied.

"The chief losses were experienced in attempting to reach the Juma Musjid and to penetrate beyond the Cabul Gate."

. . . .

DEHLI.—*Sept.* 13.—Mr. Greathed's report of the 13th instant has just been received.

"After I wrote yesterday, the left batteries opened against the Water Bastion and Curtain, with one gun bearing on the causeway leading to the bridge, and have continued in full play. They have to endure a warm musketry fire from the walls, and shot and shell from Suleymgurh, and from across the river.

Captain Fagan, R.A. "The army has suffered a severe loss in the death of Captain Fagan of the Artillery. He was an admirable officer, and has been the life of the Camp. His daring was unbounded, and he could not be restrained from exposing himself over the breastwork to observe the line of fire from the new battery, and was shot through the head.

Earle and Chancellor wounded. "The other casualties are Lieut. Earle, Artillery, and Chancellor, 75th, wounded. The loss among the men is held to be moderate.

"The centre batteries have continued an increasing fire against the Cashmere Bastion and Curtain, and the Mortars keep up a searching fire on its neighbourhood. No. I. still grinds away at the Moree.

"The enemy have mounted a heavy gun in two places on half-moons in the wall, and are persevering in their enfilade from the right, and are doing their best to defend the place.

"The Officers never leave the batteries, which are open to

the sky. But the only men who are dispirited are those whom sickness or wounds keep in Camp.

"It is very arduous work; there is only a partial relief for the Artillery men.

"*On donnera l'assaut demain, ou apres demain, ou plus tard.*

"I have had no intelligence from the town since the evening of the 11th.

"General Nicholson will command the moveable column to be sent from this.

"I shall consequently remain here with General Wilson. I should wish, as I have before said, to be allowed to return to Meerut. Saunders is on the spot, if Williams is not to come here, and he has excellent qualifications.

"The latest from you is of the 7th, 4 p.m. The Expense Magazine in the Water Bastion has blown up, and an ammunition waggon of the enemy's on the right flank has also been destroyed. The battery has been very steady all day."

We may expect to hear of the assault in a day or two.

. . . .

CALCUTTA.—A letter has been received *via* Cawnpore, dated the 4th instant, of which the following is an extract:—

"Peel's Battery will be at Allahabad in 10 days, and will set free all the Military force now kept there for the defence of the place; 500 men of the 90th and 5th are on their way up the Grand Trunk Road, and will be at Allahabad by the 17th. The other China Regiments are hourly expected." **Peel's Battery advances from Calcutta.**

ALLAHABAD.—*September 9th.*

"Yesterday a troop of Irregular Cavalry, the 'débris' of the 12th 'Holmes' Regiment, passed through *en route* to Cawnpore. **Troops coming up country.**

"They are chiefly Afghans, and it was expected it would be of essential service to General Havelock.

"Companies of H.M. 53rd should be arriving here after the 12th instant,—one Company each day until the whole wing has arrived. Captain Peel's Naval Brigade ought to arrive by the 20th instant at latest. The Madras Regiments coming up will be placed under Mr. Grant's orders, and employed in regaining our lost districts: first, the Transgangetic Pergunnahs of Allahabad, then Goruckpore.

"The Dinapore Mutineers are at Banda, coquetting with the Nawab. Koour Singh is near Drummond Gunge in this district, with the Ramgurh Battalion. Osborne is watching him." **Kunwar Singh.**

. . . .

W. MUIR.

DCLXIV.

FORT AGRA, *midday*, 21*st Sept.* 1857.

DEHLI.—*Sept.* 15*th.*—The Cossid who left Dehli on thé 15th arrived only to-day (21st), in consequence of the infested state of the roads. Mr. Greathed, writing on that date, says:—

"No serious attempt has been made by the enemy to recover the valuable line of defences they lost yesterday. On our part, measures have been adopted to consolidate the conquest, and to add to it. The Magazine is the first point. Batteries have been turned against it, and 10 heavy mortars are playing on the city. The Camp, which remains on the old ground, has not been molested. The enemy's retention of the suburb of Teleewara prevents it being advanced under the walls of the city. Our Flag floats over the CASHMERE-GATE, and Head Quarters are established in Col. Skinner's house. Suleymgurh still continues to send an occasional discharge of shrapnel or grape into the Church square, and there is a desultory fire of musketry from tops of houses in the distance.

Progress in occupation of the city.

"Two Regiments are reported to have left the city last night by the Rewaree Road. An organised body of troops was seen marching off yesterday morning over the bridge soon after the attack.

Strength of assaulting column.

Casualties.

"The column that entered the city yesterday consisted of 2000 Europeans and 2000 Native soldiers. The casualties amount to nearly 650. The loss among the Officers has been very heavy:—Nine Officers of Engineers, eight of H.M.'s 8th, nine of the 1st Fusiliers. The heaviest misfortune is the wounding of General Nicholson. He may perhaps survive, but is in great danger.

Nicholson.

"The killed and mortally wounded among the Officers are:—

"Fitzgerald, 75th; Bradshaw, 52nd; Murray, Guides; Rosser, Carabineers; Tandy, Engineers; Jacob, 1st Fusiliers; McBarnett, 55th N.I.; Davidson, 26th N.I.

"This is the correct list. Thirty-nine were wounded."

News up to the 15th has also reached us through Jeypore. The following are extracts from a letter dated from "*Head Quarters, Skinner's House*":—

"You will be delighted to hear that we are at last within the walls of Dehli. The assault took place yesterday morning soon after daybreak, and the storming was entirely successful, and we were soon in possession of all this end of the Fort, with the Cashmere, Cabul, and Moree Gates, which we now hold with the Church, College, and other large buildings near this one, in which Head Quarters are.

"The part of the city we now hold is very compact, and preparations are being made for heavy batteries to knock the Mutineers out of those parts of the city in which they now are. This we hope to be able to do, with very little loss of life to ourselves, in three or four days.

"Many of the city people have come in to ask for quarter, which has been given them; but Sepoys who wanted to come in have not been permitted.

"A great many of the Mutineers, particularly Cavalry, left last night in the direction, it is said, of Rewaree. **Mutineers leave Delhi.**

"All our news from the Punjab and the rear generally, and Meerut, etc., satisfactory.

"Among the wounded Officers, besides the names already given, are mentioned General Nicholson's brother, 31st N.I.; Greville, 1st Fusiliers, severely; Major Baynes."

Another letter of the same date states that "we are in possession of the Cashmere, Moree, Cabul, and Lahore Gates; adding that we were going to shell the Palace and Suleymgurh that day."

P.S.—Since the above was sent to press, a despatch of the 16th has been received from Dehli. It is highly satisfactory, and shows continued steady progress. Details will be given shortly.

DCLXVI.

FORT AGRA, *September 24th*, 9 *a.m.*

DEHLI.—*September* 18*th and* 19*th.*—We have just received despatches from Mr. Greathed of the 18th, and from Col. Becher of the 19th. On the latter date Mr. Greathed was dangerously ill of cholera; so, for the present, we shall be deprived of his valuable bulletins.

. . . .

Writing on the 19th inst., Col. Becher says:—"To-day we have taken possession of all they left towards the Palace, of the block of buildings which extend to the Chandnee Chouk. To the right again we have pushed forward, and now hold (8 p.m.) the *Burn* Bastion, which gives us as good as the command of the

Progress in occupation of Dehli.

Lahore Gate. Our line therefore extends clearly to the Chouk, and our position is strong and as good as it could possibly be. Please God, I shall ere long have to tell you of a complete and signal success. This must be the speedy end of what now is done.

"We have steadily shelled the Palace all to-day, and all the city in the vicinity of the Juma Musjid.

"Our Cavalry made a reconnaissance round the city to-day, and say that a large camp is standing near the Dehli Gate" (*i.e.* the Gate near the extreme south-east corner of the city).

General Nicholson is reported to be in a very precarious state.

RETURN OF ORDNANCE CAPTURED IN DEHLI.

Abstract.[1]

	PIECES.
Magazine	161 (159 ?)
Cashmere Bastion	13
Water ditto	9
Moree ditto	9
Round Tower	1
Gateways	2
3-Gun Battery	3
Kishengunge	5
	203 (201 ?)

W. MUIR.

DCLXVII.

AGRA FORT, 2 *p.m.*, 27*th September*.

Capture of Dehli complete.

On the 21st instant the Palace of the Kings of Dehli was occupied by the British troops, and the capture of the city was complete.

GOD SAVE THE QUEEN.

A Royal Salute is about to be fired from the ramparts of the Fort.

[1] Details of weight of each piece of ordnance given in original, but here omitted.—W. C.

MONDAY MORNING, *28th Sept.*—Our Despatches from Dehli of the 20th and 21st have not yet come to hand. But since yesterday's Memorandum was issued, further accounts have come in which show that the Palace and city were occupied as early as the 20th instant.

Writing from Umballa on the 20th, Mr. G. C. Barnes (who is in telegraph communication with our camp at Dehli) says that we had then still possession only of the Northern half of the city, including the Chouk. But the Mutineers were fast evacuating Dehli. The stand they yet made was to cover the retreat of their baggage and plunder, which they expected to overtake. The King was believed to have fled from the Palace.

On the same day, the 20th, but probably at a later hour, Mr. Saunders (who in consequence of the lamented decease of Mr. Greathed, on the night of the 19th, had taken charge of the office of Agent to the Lieut.-Governor) writes "that the Mutineers have evacuated the place; that we have taken possession of the Palace, after blowing in the gate; and that we occupy the Juma Musjid, the Lahore Gate, and the Ajmere Bastion." **Death of H. H. Greathed, C.S.**

The enemy's camp, he adds, was still standing outside the Dehli Gate; but it was empty, and we had sent to take possession of it. The King was then said to be at Humaioon's Tomb, and there was every expectation of his either giving himself up or being apprehended.

A force was about to be sent to the Hindun, and a party was to meet it from Meerut in order to clear the communication with that place. "Having got possession of the Palace, the bridge of boats is, of course, under our control."

. . . .

The district of Moozuffernugger is in a disturbed state, owing to the outrages of a large body of rebels. The fall of Dehli will already have set at liberty troops for the suppression of these disturbances. **Muzafarnagar District disturbed.**

. . . .

On the 19th instant Captain Showers, with a small party of H.M. 83rd and some Bombay troops, attacked Neembhera, an outlying possession of Tonk. They could not enter, as the gate which they endeavoured to force was afterwards discovered to have been bricked up. "Night stopped our operations." **Captain Showers attacks Nimbhera.**

[*The rest of the account is contained in No. LXXIX., pp.* 116, 117, *vol. i.*]

Fugitive Mutineers reach Muttra.

MUTTRA.—Several thousands of the fugitives from Dehli, with a good many light guns and some baggage, reached Muttra on the 24th, 25th, and 26th instant. They are said to have about 2000 sick and wounded with them; many are ill off for arms and accoutrements, and the whole bear in their faces the marks of a dispirited and broken force. They are preparing a bridge to cross the Jumna, and speak of Oudh as their destination. It is to be hoped that the pursuing column will reach Muttra before they can effect a passage. The Hattrass Detachment has fallen back on Khundowlee, but only to make a still more outward movement after being reinforced.

The Indore troops are still at Dholepore. They are said to be contemplating a junction with the Mutineers at Muttra.

Scindia controls Contingent.

The Contingent, by the latest accounts, continued at Morar obedient to Scindia. The Maharaja has removed all the boats on the Chumbul from the Ghats on the Agra Road.

W. MUIR.

DCLXVIII.

FORT AGRA, *28th September* 1857.

DEHLI.—Our regular despatches for the 20th instant have just come in.

Mr. Saunders' report of occupation of Delhi.

Mr. C. B. Saunders writes:—"I am glad to be able to report that our troops have this day taken possession of the Palace and fort of Selimgurh, and of the Juma Musjid, of the Lahore Gate, and of the Ajmere Bastion." Although we have not yet received news of the actual occupation of the Dehli Gate by our troops, there is no doubt that the whole of the City has been evacuated by the Mutineers, and that we have got complete and undisturbed possession of the City and its defences.

Dispersion of rebels.

"The Mutineers have gone off in different directions, but the main body, after blowing up their surplus ammunition, marched, it is said, with light guns in the direction of Muttra and Agra. The general belief is that they will ere long scatter and disperse to their homes, being perfectly disorganised and dispirited. The King and his family are said to be either at Humaioon's or Nizam Ood Deen's Tomb, and there is every prospect of his giving himself up or of his being captured."

Another letter states that in the final operations there was "little or no loss" incurred by our troops.

MEERUT.—On the 22nd instant a force of Sikhs, Rifles, and Carabineers, with four guns and mortars, started early in the morning for Mozuffernugger. They will no doubt inflict exemplary punishment on the insurgents of Thanahbhowun in that district who have committed so many outrages. Expedition against Muzafarnagar.

W. MUIR.

DCLXX.

September 29th, 1857.

. . . .

CAWNPORE.—*22nd and 23rd September.*—Mr. Sherer, in a letter of the 22nd instant, writes:—"The crossing was effected in first-rate style on Saturday and Sunday:—the troops the first day, and the Commissariat the next. The enemy brought down a gun and opened fire, but Olpherts waited upon them with one or two of his field-pieces, which have been newly horsed, and they withdrew the gun to Mungulwara. The force marched on this latter place yesterday at daybreak, and about 7 o'clock we heard a heavy cannonade, which lasted about an hour. They went right on, and, not meeting with much opposition at Onao, as we suppose, pushed for Buseergunge, where it is thought they encamped last night. Advance on Lucknow.

"Futtehpore is reoccupied by 200 Europeans—to be increased to 500 directly. Fattehpur reoccupied.

"Dinapore troops still at Banda."

On the 23rd Mr. Sherer says:—"We have had a letter from the Lucknow Force, dated Monday evening (21st). They took seven guns at Mungulwara on Monday morning, *and only lost one man.* They went straight on, and had seen nothing more of the enemy up to Buseergunge." He adds that news had been received of the safety of some families near Lucknow for whom fears had before been entertained. Affair at Mangalwara.

Another letter of the 23rd gives the following extract of a communication from the Camp, dated the 21st:—

"The enemy were prepared to oppose us at Mungulwara with seven or eight guns planted at the villages on each side of the road, and a 'Moorcha' on the road itself, but were driven off after exchanging a few shots, leaving four of their guns. They were followed up for several miles, and two more guns were taken. They were slaughtered like sheep. I have only heard of two killed, and six or eight wounded:—no Officers. We have moved on to Busarut Gunge, 16 miles from the river."

Lucknow garrison.

The Cawnpore letter adds:—"The force was all in high spirits at Bunni-bridge yesterday (22nd), and the Lucknow garrison was all safe and sound on the 21st, and able to hold out a fortnight or more."

W. Muir.

DCLXXI

Fort Agra, 30*th September* 1857.

. . . .

Advance on Lucknow.

Cawnpore.—*September* 24*th*.—Letters have been received at Cawnpore from the force proceeded to Lucknow, dated the evening of the 22nd instant. It was then encamped at Begum Gunge, fourteen miles from Lucknow. On the 21st we halted twenty miles from Cawnpore, and on the 22nd marched fourteen miles.

The enemy were flying before us.

"Their retreat was too precipitate to allow them to destroy Bunnee Bridge; only four more guns taken (total *ten*), but many are said to have been thrown into wells, as only four passed over the bridge.

Relief force approaches Lucknow.

"Firing at Lucknow distinctly heard; a Royal Salute by our 24-pounders, to announce our approach to the Garrison there.

"Our army will have arrived at Lucknow either last night or this morning."

Another letter says:—"After Mungulwara, a very feeble resistance, instantly overcome, at Oonao, was all that our force had heard of the enemy. The flight was so hasty that they had no time to destroy the bridge over the Sye at Bannee, and only four guns were carried by the enemy over the Nuddee. Of the remainder, four came into our hands (I suppose they were left on the road), and the rest were thrown down wells previous to our advance. Tremendous rain had been encountered, but our troops were marching capitally, and all were in high spirits. The General fired a Royal Salute of 24-pounders at Begum Gunge, to let our friends in the Garrison know the army was close at hand.

Fattehpur reoccupied.

"Futtehpore is quite reoccupied. Mr. Probyn is going as Collector, Mr. Edwards as Judge, and Mr. Macnaghten, Assistant

Deputy Magistrate; also Mr. William Glyn. 300 Europeans in the shell of Mr. Edmonstone's house."

A telegraph message from BENARES states that "parts of the 23rd, 82nd, and 93rd Regiments with 300 Artillery had arrived in Calcutta within the last few days,—in all 2000 men; and the remainder of these Regiments is daily looked for. Some of the 89th had arrived at Bombay; and the rest, with the 95th Regiment, daily expected from the Cape." Reinforcements arrive from England.

W. MUIR.

DCLXXII.

FORT AGRA, *2nd October* 1857.

THE account given yesterday on native authority of a signal victory gained by Col. Greathed's column at Boolundshuhur on the 28th ultimo is substantially corroborated by a despatch received from Mr. Sapte, the Collector and Magistrate of that district, dated the 29th idem. He states that the force is composed of the following regiments:—8th and 75th H.M.; two Punjab Infantry and three Punjab Cavalry regiments; 9th Lancers; 18 guns and two mortars. Colonel Greathed's column.

"We arrived at daybreak," says Mr. Sapte, "and found the rebels, consisting of the Jhansi Brigade, and Wallidad of Malaghur's levies, entrenched on the road in the station close by my compound. They fired as we advanced, and, after two hours' pounding or more, we drove them from their position, *killing* some 150 of them, and losing ourselves some 50 killed and wounded—among the latter, six officers. Action at Bulandshahr.

"We took one 9-pounder gun and one 3-pounder; two 9-pounder ammunition waggons, a quantity of small-arm ammunition, and 25 barrels of gunpowder.

"I am sorry to say, during the action Wallidad escaped from his fort and has gone to Rohilkhund. The Nana Sahib" (it is concluded that the Nana's *brother* is meant, who lately arrived at Malagurh wounded) "was said to be with him. We took possession of Malagurh this morning, and it is now being mined preparatory to being blown up." Wali Dad escapes. Malagarh occupied.

The Jhansi Brigade was believed to have still three guns with it, but little ammunition. The discomfited Mutineers were flying towards Rohilkhund. Our column was to follow them up to Anoopshuhur, and then march *via* Debhaee to Allygurh. Fugitive Mutineers.

Mr. Sapte states that another column "was out on the other side under Capt. Showers."

Bulandshahr quieting down

Regarding his own district, he writes:—"I am establishing the Police, and hope the mail-cart will be running in a very short time. The road between this and Meerut will be quite safe in a few days."

. . . .

W. MUIR.

DCLXXIII.

FORT AGRA, 3rd *October* 1857.

Colonel Burn appointed Military Governor of Delhi.

DEHLI.—A letter has been received from Dehli, dated the 28th ultimo. Colonel Burn, 1st N.I., is appointed Military Governor of the City; and Col. Jones, 60th Rifles, Commandant of the Palace.

A small force under Brigadier Showers had proceeded towards Humaioon's Tomb and the Kootub, the bad characters from Dehli having congregated at both places. Brigadier Showers had apprehended and sent in two of the King's sons, Mirza Mendoo and Mirza Bukhtawar Shah, who were to be tried by a Military Commission. The King and Zeenut Muhul are prisoners in the Palace.

The King prisoner.

"General Penny writes from Meerut, that the fall of Dehli has had a marked effect in the Meerut district:—Revenue being brought in rapidly.

"Two hundred of the Beloch Battalion and some Cavalry left Meerut yesterday (27th) for Gurhmuktesur, where they expect to meet the Nana."

DCLXXIV.

FORT AGRA, 3rd *Oct.* 1857, *evening.*

LETTERS have been received from Cawnpore up to the 27th. The letters from Lucknow had been intercepted by a few Sowars on the road at Nawabgunge. Immediate news expected.

Mutiny at Nagode.

The 50th mutinied at Nagode and burnt the station; but all our Officers escaped. The ladies arrived safely at Mirzapore.

Cawnpore quite quiet. Telegraph and dak regularly open again with Calcutta. There had been some, apparently casual, interruption for a few days.

Mutineers at Muttra.

Information has been received this evening that the Nusseerabad Brigade has followed the Bareilly troops across the river;

leaving the Neemuch force alone, or about ¼ of the entire fugitive troops at Muttra.

The Neemuch Brigade had sent on its advanced guard to Furrah, which the main body would reach during the night, thus entirely evacuating Muttra. The Neemuch Brigade, it is supposed, will march *via* Futtehpoor Sicri to join the Dholepoor Mutineers.

DCLXXV.

FORT AGRA, *Oct. 4th*, 1857.

LUCKNOW HAS BEEN RELIEVED AND THE GARRISON RESCUED.

The following is an extract from Mr. Sherer's letter, dated Cawnpore, 1st of Oct., 10 p.m.:—

"Letters just in from Lucknow. Bellee Guard relieved on the 25th, and garrison rescued apparently by an advance made on the left of the Goomtee. Lucknow Garrison rescued.

"Progress being already made towards the possession of the whole city.

"On the 29th the right quarter occupied, and 7 guns taken.

"Man Singh, contrary to expectation, has taken an active part against us, and has been wounded in two places." Man Singh.

Our despatches, dated 27th ult., announcing the complete fall of Dehli, had been received at Cawnpore.

W. MUIR.

DCLXXVI.

FORT AGRA, *Oct. 5th.*

DEHLI.—28*th Sept.*—Brigadier Showers' Column was to proceed from Humaioon's Tomb and the Kootub towards Rohtuck or Goorgaon, to restore confidence and enable us to reorganise our Police and Revenue establishments in those districts. A letter had been received from Mr. Ford announcing that he had arrived at Rohtuck with a portion of Van Cortlandt's force, and had re-established our authority in that district. Arrangements are also in progress for the reoccupation of Goorgaon, where Mr. Ford will probably return. Mr. Guthrie is likely to go to Hissar. Sir T. Metcalfe will take charge for the present of the Dehli district. Everything is quiet about Dehli, and the division is settling into order Brigadier Showers' Column. W. Ford, C.S. Van Cortlandt's force. Delhi Division settling down.

Besides Mirzas Bukhtawur Shah and Mehndoo, Mirza

Trial of King's sons. Jewun Bukht had been apprehended, and was to be tried along with them.

MEERUT.—The troops deputed to Mozuffernugur found that the insurgents had evacuated Thanah Bhowun. They were said to have gone towards Shamla and Baroti. Our force is in pursuit of them, and arrangements are also being made in the Meerut district for their interception. It is feared that they will disperse and elude apprehension.

Meerut loyalty. At Meerut, Mr. Williams writes on the 25th:—"All well here, and loyalty the order of the day. The City to be illuminated to-night."

Mr. Assistant Donald. Sirsa quiet. SIRSA.—A letter from Mr. Assistant Donald gives an encouraging account of the recovered condition of the district. Crime was rare, deserted villages being reoccupied, and the country fairly under cultivation.

. . . .

W. MUIR.

DCLXXVII.

FORT AGRA, *October 6th*, 1857.

Advance of Colonel Greathed's Column. COLONEL GREATHED'S Column reached Allygurh yesterday morning. He was opposed by the Mussulman fanatics and rabble, who, it will be remembered, a short time ago expelled It occupies Aligarh. our adherent Gobind Sing and his followers from Allygurh. The town was cleared of them all. "Two 5-pounder guns fell into our hands. The Cavalry did most excellent service, and cut up fully 400 men with arms in their hands." The Column was to march next day to Akrabad, a stronghold of fanaticism and revolt, which deserves a signal chastisement.

Lieutenant Holm, Engineers, killed at Malagarh. In the operations for blowing up Malagurh, Lieut. Holm, Engineers, lost his life by the explosion of a mine which was fired too soon.

. . . .

Entrenchments at Cawnpore CAWNPORE.—*September* 30*th*.—"Our little fort is nearly finished. We could man eight guns; and position is very strong.

and Fatehgarh. "They are making an entrenchment also at Futtehpore, and 300 Europeans are located there."

MIRZAPORE.—From this station there is news up to the 28th ultimo. Captain Osborne, the political agent at Rewa, had re-Nagode. occupied Nagode with a body of the Rajah's troops. The rebels had fled at the false alarm of the approach of a European force.

"A body of Madras troops of the Kamptee Column has had an engagement with the Mutineers of the 52nd N.I. at Jubbulpore. The Madrassees defeated the latter, killing upwards of 200 of them. The Mutineers have fled to Myhere. Engagement at Jabbalpur.

"The remnant of the 50th N.I. from Nagode came into Mirzapore this morning under Major Hampden. They are located in the Rajah's House and grounds on the opposite side of the river. Their number is about 220. They are considered very staunch men.

"The 5th Irregulars and others were by the Soane two or three days ago. They are coming, it is supposed, by Bijegurh, and so on to Ghorawul. They have with them a lac of rupees and jewellery plundered from the temple and pandoos of Deegah. This ought to make the Hindoos very enraged at them. They will be hemmed in now very likely, and will be obliged to come near Mirzapore."

Major Ellis is at Pannah. The Rewa, Pannah, and Chrakara Rajahs continue well affected. Rewa, Pannah, and Chrakara Rajahs, well affected.

The wing of a Madras Regiment is at Mirzapore.

The Naval Brigade had been detained for some days, but was expected at Benares.

Benares.—A letter from Benares, dated the 27th ultimo, states that "we have just heard of the landing of 2000 men in four days at Calcutta, and another 1000 are long overdue by sailing ships." Troops arrive at Calcutta.

. . . .

W. Muir.

DCLXXVIII.

Fort Agra, *Oct. 7th*, 1857.

Cawnpore.—A letter from Mr. Sherer, dated the 2nd instant, gives the following additional particulars regarding the relief of Lucknow:—

"The great fight was clearly on the 25th, when the sick and wounded were left at Alum Bagh, and the main body marched on the town, keeping to the right as much as they could, but not crossing the Goomtee as I erroneously supposed. The officers killed are detailed as follows:—General Neill, Major Cooper, Artillery; Packenham, 84th; Bateman, 64th; Wild, 40th Relief operations at Lucknow. Officers killed.

N.I.; Warren, 12th Irregular Cavalry. The following are *incidentally* mentioned as all right in the Baillie Guard:—J. Anderson, the Taylors, Coupers, Gubbins, Mrs. Ommaney and family, Mrs. Fletcher Hayes."

Saved in the Baillie Guard.

It is believed that the Nana was present. All quiet about Cawnpore.

BOOLUNDSHUHUR. — *4th October.* — Mr. B. Sapte left Col. Greathed's force at Koorjah, and returned to Boolundshuhur on the 4th. He is supported by 220 Beloch troops, 200 Pathan Horse, and two Horse Artillery guns. At Boolundshuhur a greater amount of ammunition was captured than at first reported. Mail-carts are running in both directions from that station. The line to Dehli is open. Wulleedad escaped to Bareilly. Many of his followers have been caught. His Tehseeldar was to be hung on the 5th.

Jang Bahadur sends two Goorkha Regiments.

NYNEE TAL.—A letter has been received, dated the 22nd ult., stating that Jungbahadoor was sending two Goorkha regiments and 15 recruits to Almora. Major Ramsay thus reinforced would probably commence offensive operations on Rohilkhund.

W. MUIR.

DCLXXIX.

FORT AGRA, *8th October.*

Account of relief of Lucknow.

THE following additional particulars regarding the relief of Lucknow have been received in a letter from Lucknow, dated the 26th instant:—

On the 25th General Havelock's force, having left the sick and wounded with a Detachment at the Alum Bagh, forced their way into the City under serious opposition.

After crossing the Charbagh Bridge the troops skirted the City, to avoid the enemy's defensive works prepared through the entire length of the main street leading directly to the Residency. Still, much opposition had to be encountered, till we reached the Residency in the evening. Our loss was severe, estimated at from 400 to 500 killed and wounded.

On the 26th the troops were occupied in taking the batteries bearing on the Garrison, which were held till assaulted, and continued till then to fire on the Residency, after our troops had relieved the Garrison the night before. Many thousands of the enemy had deserted the City. The late King's sons had fled to Fyzabad.

The list of Officers killed, as before given, is correct. The following is a more accurate list of the persons and families incidentally mentioned as being safe with the Garrison:—"J. Anderson, the Fayrers, Ogilvies, Gubbinses, Coupers, widows and families of Major Banks and Mr. Ommaney, Mrs. Hayes." Safe with the Garrison.

. . . .

W. MUIR.

DCLXXX.

FORT AGRA, *9th October* 1857.

DEHLI.—Letters received up to 5th instant. General Wilson left the day before for Meerut and Mussoorie, on medical certificate. General Penny arrived on the 5th to take the command. Colonel Becher had left several days before for Simla. General Penny succeeds General Wilson in command at Delhi.

Brigadier Showers' Column was supposed to be at Goorgaon on the 5th.

The reinforcements for Colonel Greathed's Column were to march on the 6th.

All being quiet at Dehli, H.M.'s 52nd marched towards the Punjab. Three European Regiments, the 60th, 61st, 1st Europeans, remain at Delhi with the 4th Sikhs, Guide Infantry, and Sirmoor Battalion, and two troops of Horse Artillery. Troops at Delhi.

CAWNPORE.—*3rd October.*—Stores under a convoy of 300 men were being despatched to Lucknow. Cawnpore would be reinforced from Futtehpore; and that again from Allahabad, where the Naval Brigade was expected next day. The road between Lucknow and Cawnpore was still infested by plunderers, who interrupted our communications.

Major Ellis was safe at Punna; and Mr. Coles, the Superintendent, had returned to Nagode.

DCLXXXI.

FORT AGRA, *Oct. 12th*, 1857.

LOCAL INTELLIGENCE.—The Indore Mutineers left Dholepore on the 6th instant, having procured some heavy guns there in addition to the seven field-pieces which they brought with them. Indore Mutineers advance on Agra. Information having been received of their advance in the direction of Agra, Col. Greathed's Column was directed to hurry on from Akrabad by forced marches. The whole Column arrived in Agra on the morning of the 10th instant. Colonel Greathed's Column arrives.

The Mutineers, apparently in ignorance of this rapid movement, marched upon Agra on the same morning, and reached the Cantonment about 10.30 a.m. They opened a heavy fire upon our Camp, which was soon returned by our two troops of Horse Artillery and our two field Batteries. Their Horse, which at the first alarm had penetrated into our Camp, were repulsed with great loss to them, and trifling loss to ourselves. Their attack was soon turned into a complete rout, our guns following them up steadily, and the Cavalry cutting up all within their reach on both sides of the road. The pursuit was continued all day up to the banks of the Kharee, the whole of their guns, thirteen in number, being captured, including a prodigious brass piece of 18-pound calibre. Their camp, their baggage, and plunder, all fell into our hands. The guns are now in the Fort.

Mutineers attack camp at Agra; are routed.

Casualties. French. Jones.

The casualties on our side, in the accomplishment of this brilliant success, were comparatively few,—though they include the lamented death of Captain French, and the severe wounding of Lieutenant Jones of the Lancers.

Wali Dad.

ROHILKHUND.—Waleedad, with the remains of his Malagurh force and of the Jhansi Brigade, is said to have fled to Bareilly, which he reached on the 5th instant.

W. MUIR.

DCLXXXII.

FORT AGRA, *Oct. 13th*, 1857.

Dispersion of rebel force.

THE rebel force which was discomfited on the 10th appears to have broken up, and not to have re-formed in strength in any quarter. Some of the fugitives sought refuge at Bhurtpore, but were seized by order of the Durbar, and an attempt made to disarm them. They resisted, and are said to have been attacked, some of them killed, and the rest dispersed.

. . . .

Troops come up country.

BENARES.—*4th October.*—"The head of the Column of troops is just going to begin to show itself in earnest. Regiments have already begun to arrive from the Cape, and the regular supply from England will be in Calcutta by the time these are drained off. It has been settled that the great bulk of men is to come up the Trunk Road to Allahabad by bullock train: 150 a day, and 50 a day by horse carriage dak—6000 a month. Anything over and above that is found to be in the way at Calcutta will be sent up, marching along the Trunk Road. The steamers are supposed to carry up the baggage."

Towards Bengal, the Brigade which left Alleegunj to march up the Grand Trunk Road, viz. a wing of H.M. 53rd Foot and 27th M.N.I., has beaten the Ramgurh Mutineers near Hazareebagh. Affair near Hazaribagh.

W. MUIR.

DCLXXXIII.

FORT AGRA, 14*th October* 1857.

CAWNPORE.—8*th October.*—Mr. Sherer mentions the receipt of letters from Lucknow, dated 6th instant. General Outram now holds important positions in the city itself. The strong post at Alum Bagh has been victualled and reinforced from Cawnpore. No lists of the garrison have yet been received, but the tenor of the statements would lead to the confident belief that casualties have not been numerous during the period of their siege. Outram's position in Lucknow.

BENARES.—The following notices are from Mr. Henry C. Tucker's Memorandum of Intelligence, dated the 2nd Oct.:—

JOUNPORE.—"The party of Goorkhas with Mr. Lind have taken Moobarukpoor and its Rajah Iradut Jihan, who has since been hanged." Rajah Iradat Jehan hanged.

AZIMGURH.—"The Goorkhas have been similarly successful against the fort of Atrowlya, but Rajah Benee Madho and Madho Purshad escaped during the night. The Goorkhas pursued, but only succeeded in capturing one wall piece. Moozuffur Jihan has fled from Mahol." Fort Atraulia taken.

"BENARES is quite quiet. Extensive preparations are being made for the troops expected from England—3000 new carts are to be constructed by the end of November, with 4000 sets of bedding; and large supplies of grain are being laid in."

W. MUIR.

DCLXXXIV.

FORT AGRA, *Oct.* 16*th*, 1857.

DEHLI.—12*th October.*—Mirza Bukhtawur Shah, Mirza Mehndo, sons of the King, were condemned by the Military Court, and sentenced to be shot. The execution was to take place on the morning of the 13th. King's sons condemned.

The King will be arraigned before a Military Commission next week. The prosecution will be conducted by Major King's trial.

Harriott, Deputy Judge Advocate-General. His life was guaranteed to him at the time of apprehension.

. . . .

MOZUFFERNUGGER.—*October* 11*th.*—All was again quiet in this district. The rebels appear entirely to have dispersed. Mr. Edwards was still at Thanah Bhowun with the district force, and the land revenue was coming in rapidly.

GWALIOR.—The Contingent, it is reported on good authority, has moved from Gwalior, and taken an eastward course. It started on the 14th or 15th.

News of the victory of the 10th had reached Gwalior, and created a great sensation there.

The Maharaja, now relieved of his difficulties, will publicly reopen political communications with the Governor-General's Agent.

Indore Army disperses.

LOCAL.—The Indore army has been totally dispersed; they have broken up in parties of from 100 to 500 in all directions. The feeling of the country is now openly hostile to the fugitives. Supplies are withheld from them, and in several quarters they have been actively attacked.

Composition of force which attacked Agra, 10th October.

From a quantity of baggage and camp equipage which has been seized and sent in from Shumsabad, in this district, it appears that with the Indore force there were men of the 4th Contingent Infantry, of the 1st Laswara Cavalry, and Scindia's 2nd Cavalry, present on the 10th. Among the plunder obtained in the field was a splendid necklace valued at from 20,000 to 40,000 rupees.

W. MUIR.

DCLXXXV.

FORT AGRA, *Oct.* 18*th*, 1857.

CAWNPORE.—*October* 10*th.*—All is quiet about this station; though communication with Lucknow is still interrupted by the enemy's horse on the road.

Reinforcements are now beginning rapidly to arrive. Mr. Sherer mentions that two or three bodies of our men are between Allahabad and Cawnpore on their way up.

. . . .

Hope Grant takes command of the moveable column.

AGRA.—Brigadier H. Grant, C.B., has arrived at Agra, and proceeds this day to take command of the Moveable Column, which is now more than half-way to Mynpoory.

Fifteen fugitives from the Indore force were apprehended by

the Bhurtpore authorities, and reached Agra this morning under an escort of Bhurtpore Cavalry. **Bhurtpore seizes Mutineers.**

Captain Nixon returns this evening with the same escort to Bhurtpore as Political Agent.

The following messages were published in the Calcutta papers by the Government:—

"*From Benares, Friday, 2nd October, 10 p.m.*
From the LIEUTENANT-GOVERNOR,
To Calcutta,
To the GOVERNOR-GENERAL.

"LETTERS from Captain Osborne of the 1st tell how the 52nd N.I. posted themselves at Kalinger (Kuttinghee?) to oppose the march of the Kamptee Column from Dumoh to Jubbulpore. The Mutineers were met marching up the road in column of sections. Our guns opened upon them and swept through them, putting them into utter confusion. They were followed up for five miles. The guns, after stopping to unlimber, fired a few rounds of grape. The Cavalry, Rifles, and Infantry all combined in cutting them up. Some were made prisoners and executed. They are said to have lost 125 men. Lieutenant MacGregor has been murdered by them; his body was found near Kalinger. On our side, Lieutenant Watson, one trumpeter, and two or three camp-followers were wounded; the Officer slightly. Captain Osborne's position at Rewah seems to improve. Reports from Mirzapore lead to the belief that Kooer Singh with the bulk of the 5th N.I. is at Banda." **Action at Kalinjar.** **Lieutenant MacGregor murdered.**

"*From Shergotty, Saturday, 3rd October, 9.23 p.m.*
From LIEUTENANT STAUNTON.

FOLLOWING message received from Major English at Chuttra:—"I had a severe engagement yesterday with the Ramgurh battalion; defeated them, taking four guns complete and 45 cart-loads of ammunition. I have had 45 men killed and wounded."

W. MUIR.

DCLXXXVI.

FORT AGRA, 19*th October* 1857.

. . . .

A LETTER from Lahore, dated the 10th instant, states that all was well throughout the Punjab.

An official Memorandum from Lahore of the same date gives the following information:—"The arrest by Mr. C. Richards, at a village on the Jumna, about 20 miles from Kurnal, of the notorious Ahmud Ali Khan, with 28 of his people and some papers, is also reported."

Arrest of Ahmad Ali Khan.

. . . .

AGRA.—A letter from Brigadier Grant's Column, dated Shekoabad, the 17th instant, says that "The crops are splendid; and, except for burnt bungalows, one would not know that anything extraordinary had occurred."

Position at Alam Bagh.

CAWNPORE.—*October* 12*th.*— . . . The detachment at Alum Bagh is described as well off in all respects; they had returned to Cawnpore 150 elephants, for which they had not sufficient fodder, under a guard of about 100 men, so that the obstructions in the road cannot be of any strength.

W. MUIR.

DCLXXXVII.

FORT AGRA, *Tuesday, October 20th,* 1857.

Position at Lucknow.

CAWNPORE.—13*th October.*—A letter from Cawnpore of that date mentions that "the ladies are all well at Lucknow. We are in possession of ¾ of the city." The rebels shelter themselves in the buildings of the remaining quarter, and will not meet us in the open country.

Further reinforcements will soon be sent from Cawnpore, as troops are now arriving rapidly there.

No list of the Garrison of Lucknow has yet been received at Cawnpore.

Troops are conveyed from Allahabad by the Railway so far as it goes, and onwards by Bullock Train waggons. There are 60 pairs of bullocks posted at each stage for the purpose.

. . . .

W. MUIR.

DCLXXXVIII.

FORT AGRA, 21*st October.*

LUCKNOW.—The following list of persons present in the Baillie Guard when relieved on the 25th September was received last night in a letter from Mr. Sherer, dated Cawnpore, October

16th. It is the copy of a list attested by Mr. Couper, the Chief Commissioner's secretary. Names of persons relieved in Lucknow Residency.

"*List of the surviving Officers, Ladies, and Children of the Lucknow Garrison.*

"GENERAL STAFF.—Brigadier Inglis, Captain Edgell, Captain Wilson, Lieut. Hardinge, Lieut. James, Major Marriott, Paymaster; Lieut. Birch, Lieut. Barwell, and Mr. Couper, C.S.; Capt. Carnegie, Provost Marshal.

ARTILLERY.—Lieuts. Thomas, Bonham, J. Alexander, and MacFarlan.

ENGINEERS.—Lieuts. Hutchinson, Anderson, and Innes.

7TH LIGHT CAVALRY.—Col. Master, Capt. Boileau, Lieuts. Warner, Farquhar, and Dr. Campbell.

32ND FOOT.—Captains Lowe, Bassano; Lieuts. Lawrence, Edmonstone, Foster, Harmer, Cooke, Clery, Browne, Charlton, Payell; Paymaster Giddings; H. M. (Qr.-Mr.?) Stribling; Doctors Scott and Boyd.

84TH FOOT.—Lieutenant O'Brien; M'Grath.

13TH NATIVE INFANTRY.—Captains Waterman, German; Lieuts. Aitken, Chambers, Cubett, Thain, Loughnan, and Dr. Pitt.

41ST NATIVE INFANTRY.—Major Apthorp, Captains Kemble, Sanders; Lieuts. Ruggles, Darrah, Inglis, Keir, Hewitt.

48TH N.I.—Col. Palmer, Major Bird, Captain Green; Lieutenants Huxham, Smith, Ouseley, Fletcher, Hay, O'Dowda, Ward, and Dr. Wells.

71ST NATIVE INFANTRY.—Captains Strangways, Dinning; Lieuts. Langmore, Sewell, Worseley, two Campbells, and Doctor Brydon.

Capt. Stewart, 3rd N.I.; Lieut. Tulloch, 58th; Ens. Inglis, 63rd; Capt. Weston, 65th; Ens. Dashwood, 18th.

OUDE IRREGULAR FORCE.—Brigadier Gray, Capt. Forbes, Dr. Greenhow, Dr. Partridge, Lieut. Graham (Cavalry), Lieut. Clarke (1st Oudh), Lieut. Soppitt, Dr. Harlan, Captain Hawes, Apothecary Thompson, Lieuts. Graydon, Watson, Mecham, and Vanrenen; Dr. Darby; Captains Hearsey, Orr, and Messrs. Birch and Harris; Drs. Ogilvie and Fayrer.

CIVIL SERVICE.—Messrs. Gubbins, Martin, Benson, Capper, Lawrence, Thornhill, Boulderson.

LADIES AND CHILDREN.—Mrs. Hayes and one, Edgell and two, Marriott, Inglis and three, Barwell, and one child of Lieut. Thomas (Mrs. Thomas dead), Lewin and one, Radcliff and two, Boileau (7th Cavalry) and three, Case and Miss Dickson, Mrs. Stevens, Giddings, Bruere and four, Germon, Aitkin, Pitt and one,

Apthorp, Darrah, Bird, Huxham, Ouseley and three, Dashwood and two, Wells and one, Mrs. and Miss Holford, Strangways and three, Brydon and two, Banks and one, Stewart, Fullerton, Mrs. and Miss Birch, Barlow, Forbes and one, Graham, Gale, Barbor, Clarke, Soppitt, Orr and one, Harris, Polehampton, Ogilvie, Fayrer, Gubbins, Ommanney, two Misses Ommanney, Couper and two, Martin, Benson, Thornhill, Boileau and three, Eldridge, Staples, Miss Schilling, Mrs. Anderson, Kendell, Burtram and one.

Clerks.

UNCOVENANTED SERVICE, ETC.—Cameron, merchant; Mr. Hill, ditto; Mr. Parry, Dehli Bank. Extra Assists.—Williams, Garland, Collins. Clerks.—Messrs. Cavanagh, Wittenbaker, Lincoln, Phillips, French, Anthony, M'Grenan; Apothecary Higgins.

CIVIL ENGINEERS.—Marshall, J. May, and very many more—in fact, very few have been killed; names will be communicated hereafter."

In a previous letter Major Burrell and Lieut. Preston, of H.M.'s 90th, were mentioned as killed in the attack on the city.

News of the victory gained here on the 10th had reached Cawnpore on the 15th, and been telegraphed the same night to Calcutta.

Rebel fugitives.

The main body of the Dehli fugitives have turned off, it is believed, from the Trunk Road, about Kanouge, and crossed over into Oudh. A portion had previously gone off towards Bareilly, and another portion joined the Raees at Furruckabad.

Position at Lucknow.

Besides the list, no fresh news has been received from Lucknow; "they hold strong positions in the city, and do not mention that they are hard-up for supplies."

The Alum Bagh detachment, as before stated, is well off in every respect.

The Nana, it was believed, had not yet ventured across the Ganges into the Doab.

NYNEE TAL.—A Mussoorie letter of the 16th mentions that the Bareilly army which had invaded Huldwanee and menaced Nynee Tal had again retreated.

W. MUIR.

DCLXXXIX.

FORT AGRA, 22*nd October* 1857.

. . . .

Maharajah of Jyepore.

THE Maharaja of Jyepore has just sent through the political agent, Captain Eden, the sum of Rs. 250, which he requests may be received as a donation towards the Widow and Orphan Fund at Agra. This a gratifying mark of the Maharaja's good feeling towards us.

BOOLUNDSHUHUR.—*October* 20*th.*—47 guns have been collected in this district by the Magistrate, some of very large calibre. Several of the Mutineers of the 23rd N.I., 14th Irregular Cavalry, and other Regiments, have also been captured. The district is quiet, and the Revenue being fast collected. **Guns collected.** **District quiet.**

All to the north-west is quiet.

BEWAR.—21*st October.*—The Column reached Bewar on that day without opposition. The troops of the Raees had fled two days before.

"We are received here," writes Mr. George Campbell, "in a very friendly way, and all the people are ploughing their fields at the roadside in perfect confidence." **Feeling of the people.**

W. MUIR.

DCXC.

FORT AGRA, 24*th October* 1857.

. . . .

NYNEE TAL.—14*th October.*—Letters of that date report all to be well. Major Ramsay had gone down with a small force a few days previously, and had decoyed the enemy's Cavalry across the Gola Canal. He nearly succeeded in cutting them off; but when they saw the trap they galloped back, and fled across the bridge before he had time to occupy it, and so got away without much loss. In the night-time the whole force moved off. **Major Ramsay attacks rebel cavalry.**

. . . .

BRIGADIER GRANT'S COLUMN.—This force by a long march of 29 miles reached Goorsahaigunge on the 22nd instant. The rebels at Furruckabad appeared to have expected an attack on that city, and were making preparations for a retreat into Rohilkhund. Some of the troops were also surprised at Goorsahaigunge on their flight down the Trunk Road, and a few of them cut up. **Rebels at Farakhabad.**

The Column will reach Cawnpore on Tuesday the 27th.

Brigadier Grant mentions that "at Mynpoory a number of mail letter-bags were discovered in the Fort, apparently unopened; they have been given to the Post Master for distribution."

W. MUIR.

DCXCI.

FORT AGRA, *24th October* 1857.

. . . .

Hope Grant's success at Kanauj.

BRIGADIER GRANT'S COLUMN.—This force has achieved another brilliant success, though upon a smaller scale, at Kanouge, on the 23rd instant.

A portion of the forces discomfited (see this morning's Memorandum) by the Cawnpore troops, composed apparently, in part at least, of the Dehli fugitives, were making for Futtehgurh as our Column was advancing from Goorsahaigunge. Some of their guns were left, in the hurry of their flight, with the Nawab's Tehseeldar at Kanouge, and these we took possession of.

On learning the approach of our Column, a body of about 300 of the enemy, with five guns, endeavoured to effect an escape towards Oudh. 200 of the Lancers and Native Cavalry were sent in pursuit, and, a smart firing being immediately heard, Brigadier Grant followed with a second squadron of the Lancers and two guns of Bouchier's Battery. The enemy attempted to form on crossing the Kalee Nuddee, and fired on our Cavalry. They soon gave way before the guns, when our Cavalry at once crossed and followed them up. The fugitives were now hemmed in between the Kalee Nuddee and the Ganges, and but few of them escaped. Some, both Cavalry and Sepoys, were drowned in attempting to swim across the Ganges. Nearly 200 were cut up, the remainder taking refuge in the fields.

We captured their five guns, of which two (a 24-pounder Howitzer and a 6-pounder gun) turned out to be our own.

The Cavalry were the 15th Irregulars.

On our side, Lieutenant Watson received a slight injury in the hand, and two Sowars were wounded.

The rapidity and the completeness of this affair will produce the best results on both banks of the Ganges.

W. MUIR.

DCXCII.

FORT AGRA, *26th October* 1857.

CAWNPORE.—Letters of the 18th and 20th instant have been received, and contain the following account of the affair which was noticed, on the authority of native reports, in the

Memorandum of the 24th:—A portion of the Dehli fugitives having moved down the Trunk Road to within twenty miles of Cawnpore, and it being apprehended that the Nana would cross over and put himself at their head, an expedition was arranged to start on elephants from Cawnpore on the night of the 17th. It consisted of two battalions of 325 Europeans each, and six guns with Royal Artillerymen, about 60 Sowars, and 100 of Captain Bruce's newly levied musket-men. Delhi fugitives approach Cawnpore.

This force reached Sheorajpore on the 18th, at about 3 p.m. "The enemy," writes Mr. Sherer, "opened fire on them from a 12-pounder and a mortar placed on the road outside the village, but as soon as our Artillery (under Capt. Moir) came to the front and opened in return a fire, which is described as being beautifully precise, the enemy *en masse* took to flight, and our forces advanced without further opposition on to the village, and pursued a couple of miles beyond it; Capt. Bruce carrying on with Sowars for perhaps a mile and a half further. But it was found quite impossible to come up with them." Affair of Sheorajpore.

We occupied Sheorajpore that night. Next morning (19th) the troops started for a Ghat four miles distant, where it was reported that the enemy were attempting to cross. The road was found to be very heavy, and the bullocks, "not being regular gun bullocks, were done up." The force accordingly "returned through Bithoor, having burned down a Sepoy village, and arrived safely" at Cawnpore on the morning of the 20th.

The flight of the enemy up the Trunk Road was so hasty that they left a gun at Bithoor, which has no doubt been picked up by Brigadier Grant's Column. It was a portion of the same fugitives who were so thoroughly beaten by the Column, and their guns captured, at Kanouge on the 23rd.

The Nana is still at Futtehpore Chowrassee. It seems he was too afraid to cross the Ganges. The Nana.

A letter of the 17th speaks of a part of the 93rd and wing of the 53rd being then between Cawnpore and Allahabad.

The same letter adds:—"Our troops at Lucknow hold the Baillie Guard, Motee-Muhal, and other surrounding and intermediate buildings; and we have a strong party this side the city three miles in Alum Bagh. The strength of the enemy is near the Kaiser Bagh." Position at Lucknow.

A private letter from Cawnpore, of the same date, says, "All goes on well at Lucknow, and Man Singh is trying to negotiate. A letter came from him this morning—a sure sign he is done up." Man Singh.

Mr. Sherer states that the "Golden Fleece" has reached Calcutta with 900 troops on board. He says that the appearance of the 500 sailors (styled "Jehazies") and 500 of the 93rd in kilts is "acting very strongly on the public imagination at Allahabad. A coachman of the Mail Cart Department told me that the 'Jehazies' were four feet high and four broad, and that they carried 9-pounders and 12-pounders in their arms, as a coolie would a bundle. The men in 'jangiyas' also (as they call the kilt) are described as being very red and hairy, and terrible people." Such reports, no doubt, will rapidly spread, and strike a salutary dread into our enemies.

Bluejackets and Highlanders at Allahabad.

MIRZAPORE.—17*th Oct.*—A letter of that date contains the following passage:—"A detachment of M.N.I., and two guns Madras Artillery, manned by Europeans, have left lately this place for the Kuttra Pass, which I believe they now hold. A regiment M.N.I., 6 guns, manned by Europeans, and 150 of the Ramgurh Cavalry, are here to-day *en route* for the Kuttra Pass also. The force is being assembled to overawe the Jageerdars of Rewah, who have risen against the Rajah, who has gone to his Fort at Gobindgurh, and also to overawe the Rajahs to the south-east of Rewah."

Jagirdars of Rewah rise.

. . . .

SAUGOR.—*September* 21.—The Banpore Rajah having advanced with some 2000 men to within 10 or 11 miles of Saugor, our little force of 500 men and officers, with 3 guns, went out to dislodge them. The enemy was, however, too strongly entrenched, our ammunition fell short, and the troops retired on Saugor. Col. Dalyell of the 42d was killed, and Lieut. Campbell of the 31st; and Lieut. Prior of the 33rd M.N.I. badly wounded. "Several Sepoys were killed and about 40 wounded." "We are waiting," the writer says, "for the arrival of the Madras Column to attack the Rajah again."

Banpore Rajah.

Colonel Dalyell killed. Lieutenant Campbell killed.

The garrison seems to be secure in the Magazine, which is strongly defended with guns, and the town well affected; in proof of which it may be mentioned that 150 boys were still attending the Government school under Mr. Wiggins.

Government School open.

The following extract of a letter from Bombay may be of interest at the present juncture:—"When the whole of the troops now under despatch reach India there will be eleven Regiments of Dragoons and fifty-seven Regiments of Infantry of the Queen's Service, besides 4500 of the Royal Artillery and four Companies of Engineers. This force, together with the Company's European Infantry and Artillery, makes a total

Strength of European force in India.

European strength of about 85,000 men. This is exclusive of Officers, and of additional European Artillery for the Company's service, which is not yet raised,—but it supposes all the Queen's Regiments to be of their full complement of men, whereas I suppose that the Regiments may be set down on an average of 200 men short of it. This would reduce the total number by about 12,000; but, after making every deduction, there will still be about 70,000 European troops in India.

W. MUIR.

DCXCIII.

FORT AGRA, 27*th October* 1857.

CAWNPORE.—*October* 22*nd*.—Letters had been received from Lucknow under date the 18th instant. Matters remained pretty much in the same position as before, but Grant's Column must now be on its advance from Cawnpore to Lucknow. It was to have reached Cawnpore on the 26th.

"A portion of H.M.'s 53rd and 93rd," writes Capt. Bruce, "are now *en route* from Allahabad. The stream of troops had commenced to arrive there; and, with bullock train, dak carriage, and occasional steamers, it was expected that 700 a week would be the average. The 'Golden Fleece,' 'Thebes,' and 'Queen of the South,' all powerful screws, had reached Calcutta with about 1600 men; and as these vessels left England in the midst of a fleet of 15 or 18 similar ships, exclusive of the sailing clippers, I imagine many others must be close at hand." Troops streaming up from Calcutta.

W. MUIR.

DCXCV.

. . . .

FORT AGRA, 29*th October* 1857.

LOCAL.—A force was despatched on the 27th instant, under command of Colonel Cotton, to dislodge from Futtehpore Sicree a body of Indore fugitives, who had for some days taken refuge there. Our troops reached Futtehpore Sicree at 7 yesterday morning.

The great body of the Rebels had fled during the night or early in the morning. But a few desperate men still held a very strong position in the Tehseeldaree and other buildings on the Affair at Fattehpur Sikri.

high ground. We began by shelling the Tehseeldaree, after which the place was stormed. The advance was made through the Eastern Gate of the Durgah, on which a 9-pounder was brought to bear. The large gate of the Tehseelee, from the loopholes around which the rebels kept up a sharp musketry fire, was soon burst open. The men inside fought desperately, but were speedily overpowered. Twelve of them were killed, and five were cut up by the Cavalry outside the town. Seven or eight on our side were wounded, "most of them slightly"; among these is Lieut. Glubb, who was shot through both legs. There was little opposition in the town itself.

W. MUIR.

DCXCVI.

FORT AGRA, *30th October* 1857.

Mandesaur insurgents at Jiran.

NEEMUCH.—*25th October.*—On the 22nd October, intelligence having been received that the village of Jeerun, 10 miles from Neemuch, had been occupied by a portion of the Mundessore insurgents, a reconnaissance was ordered under Capt. Tucker, 2nd Bombay Cavalry; and on the following day a small force, consisting of 50 H.M.'s 83rd, 100 Bombay 12th N.I., and 200 Bombay 2nd Cavalry, with 2 guns and a mortar, proceeded in the same direction.

Affair at Jiran. Captain Tucker killed.

The reconnoitring party encountered the enemy close to Jeerun, where Capt. Tucker was killed. It retired upon our advancing troops. When the detachment reached Jeerun it found the enemy drawn up in force, with 6 or 7 standards, outside the town. They are now known to have comprised all the really fighting troops possessed by the rebels of Mundessore. Our guns and mortar were brought into play, and the Infantry attacked the town. They were, however, obliged to fall back by the overpowering numbers of the enemy, and the mortar was for a short time in their hands. The Cavalry soon returned to the attack, and the Infantry followed, retaking the mortar. The enemy were driven into the Fort, and their fire entirely silenced. We remained in possession of the heights close to the town; but our Artillery not being strong enough for the capture of the Fort, the detachment returned in the evening to Neemuch. The effect of this attack was most favourable; for the enemy the following day evacuated the place, which is now held by us.

In these operations we lost, besides Capt. Tucker (whose body was recovered), Capt. Read, H.M.'s 83rd, killed. Five Officers: Capt. Simpson, 2nd Bombay Cavalry; Capt. Laurie, 21st N.I.; Capt. Soppit, 12th N.I.; and Lieuts. Blair and Le Geyt, 2nd Bombay Cavalry, were wounded. Ten men were wounded. The loss on the part of the enemy must have been considerable. Captain Read killed. Other casualties.

LOCAL.—Col. Cotton's detachment is now at Achneyra on its way to Furrah. The loss to the enemy at Futtehpore Sicree was larger than at first reported. Forty persons, chiefly Ghazies with two Sepoys, were killed. Colonel Cotton's detachment.

CAWNPORE.—25*th October.*—Brigadier Grant's Column arrived at Chowbeepore, a short march from Cawnpore, on that morning.

Letters had been received from Lucknow up to the 21st There had apparently been no more serious fighting since the 27th. But on that and the two preceding days the losses were very heavy. The following additional names are given of the killed:— Fighting at relief of Lucknow.

Colonel Bazeley, Artillery.
Lieutenant Crump, Madras Artillery.
Surgeon Bartman.
Major Simmons, 5th Fusiliers.
Lieut. Haig, 5th Fusiliers.
Lieut. Poole, H.M.'s 84th.
Lieut. Webster, H.M.'s 78th.
Lieut. Joly, H.M.'s 32nd.
Lieut. Moultrie, H.M.'s 90th.
Major Halliburton, H.M.'s 78th.
Lieut. Gibant, H.M.'s 84th.
Lieut. Gumme, Madras Fusiliers.

Among the wounded are—

Colonel Campbell, 90th Foot.
Major Stephenson, Madras Fusiliers.
Major Perrin, H.M.'s 90th.
Col. Tytler, Quarter-Master General.
Capt. Havelock, Adjutant General.

CALCUTTA.—A letter from an official source, dated the 19th October, states that "The troops from England are now arriving daily. One hundred men a day go up by the bullock train; and from the 1st of November the daily despatch will be two hundred. So that by Christmas we shall certainly have, at and above Benares, 8000 more Europeans than we now have; and with such a force success is everywhere certain." Arrival of English troops.

W. MUIR.

DCXCVII.

FORT AGRA, *2nd November* 1857.

Hope Grant's Column reaches Cawnpore.

CAWNPORE.—Letters have been received up to the 28th ultimo; Brigadier Grant's Column marched into Cawnpore on the morning of the 26th.

93rd Highlanders reach Cawnpore.

Four hundred of the 93rd Highlanders reached on the 27th: "splendid fellows," writes Mr. Sherer, "and in excellent heart and health, longing for an early opportunity of distinguishing themselves." Besides, "200 of the Naval Brigade and a lot of Artillery" were expected immediately.

Koer Sing.

Koer Sing, with "a wretched undisciplined rabble," had reached Calpee with the view of crossing over to Oudh. The

Gwalior Contingent.

Gwalior Contingent is moving heavily and slowly towards Calpee. It is said to intend to deposit its magazine in the Jaloun or Calpee Fort.

The Commander-in-Chief left Calcutta on the 27th ultimo, and was expected at Cawnpore on the 1st.

Order has again been restored in the Rewa country.

Flight of Bareilly force.

NAINEE TAL.—A letter from Major Ramsay, dated the 20th ultimo, states that three Companies had been sent down towards Huldwanee, on which the entire Bareilly force, said to number some 5000 men, again ran away.

Colonel Cotton's Column.

LOCAL.—Colonel Cotton's Column is now at Muttra, having inflicted merited punishment on Beyree and some other refractory villages near their route. At Beyree about 150 armed men were cut up; and a considerable number of matchlocks with ammunition, swords, etc., and a small brass cannon, were taken.

Loyalty at Muttra.

The party was received with every demonstration of pleasure at Muttra, and a general illumination of the city followed.

Attack on Adhaura.

ALLYGURH.—On the 31st ultimo a party of Europeans and Sikh Infantry and Jat Horse set out very early in the morning for Adhoura, a village about 9 miles from Allygurh notorious for harbouring some of the most hostile of the Mahometan faction. They reached this village at daybreak; and, by pushing on the Jat Cavalry, took it so entirely by surprise that very few shots were fired. The greater part of the disaffected inhabitants were either captured or killed. Three of the chief rebels were amongst the killed, and three amongst the wounded. About 50 altogether were killed, and the same number taken captive. Five hundred head of cattle were also captured. The effect of this necessary severity will be excellent throughout the district.

LAHORE.—29*th October.*—All quiet in that direction.

. . . .

W. MUIR.

DCXCVIII.

FORT AGRA, 3*rd Novr.* 1857.

LAHORE.—31*st October.*—A telegraphic message mentions that all is quiet in the Punjab.

DEHLI.—31*st October.*—"The Furrookhnugger Nawab has been arrested, and sent in a prisoner to Dehli to take his trial." Furrukhnagar Nawab arrested.

CAWNPORE.—Letters from Grant's Column speak of the crops all along the road from this to Cawnpore as excellent—both the Khureef and Rubbee. "The ruins of the Police Station-houses and of the Sarais at the halting-places, and the absence of the telegraphic wire, were almost the only things on the line of march indicative of the storm that has lately passed over the country." Crops excellent.

. . . .

W. MUIR.

DCXCIX.

FORT AGRA, 4*th November* 1857.

. . . .

CALCUTTA.—A letter of the 23rd ulto. states that "Troops are beginning to arrive daily now. About 5000 men are already come by screw round the Cape within the last few days, and are being pushed up as fast as possible." Arrival of troops from England.

Postscript, midday.—Cossid has just arrived with a despatch from Mr. Sherer, dated Cawnpore, 31st October.

"Brigadier Grant's Column," he writes, "crossed the river yesterday, and encamped about a mile up the bank. They left for Lucknow at 2 a.m. this morning, reinforced by 400 Highlanders—first-rate men. The 75th went on, notwithstanding fatigue, etc. Mr. John Power accompanies as Civil Officer." Hope Grant's Column advances towards Lucknow. John Power, C.S.

A thousand men are on the road between Allahabad and Cawnpore.

"Col. Berkeley's Column has reached Allahabad, and Brigadier Carthew, with a Kamptee Column, has been ordered to march direct on Cawnpore, which he will do, I presume, by way of Kalinjer."

W. MUIR.

DCCI.

FORT AGRA, *6th November*.

. . . .

Fort of Dhar.

CENTRAL INDIA.—It is reported through Gwalior that the Fort of Dhar, in which the insurgents had taken refuge, was, after being shelled by our troops, evacuated during the night. In the affair reported in the last Memorandum we are said to have taken three guns.

GWALIOR.—The 5th Regiment has followed the rest of the Contingent to Jaloun.

W. MUIR.

DCCII.

FORT AGRA, *9th November* 1857.

CAWNPORE.—Letters have been received up to the 4th instant.

Banda rebels.

The Banda rebels, who have been ravaging the Futtehpore district, were attacked on the 2nd instant by a detachment consisting of the Head Quarters H.M.'s 53rd, 200 of Peel's Naval Brigade, one Company of the 93rd Highlanders, and 100 Sappers and Miners. Our troops came up with the enemy at Kujwa, 20 miles to the N.W. of Futtehpore. The insurgents, who were in great force, numbering, it is said, 3000 with 3 guns, were entirely routed. Two of their guns were taken on the field; and they fled in such confusion that they abandoned the third.

Affair at Kujwa.

On the 3rd instant the fugitive rebels were flying through Ghatumpore towards Calpee. Many were attacked and plundered of their spoil by the villagers. Col. Powell of the 53rd was killed in this affair.

Colonel Powell killed.

Sir Colin Campbell reached Cawnpore on the 3rd instant. He was to hold a levee on the 4th.

Sir Colin Campbell reaches Cawnpore.

Brigadier Grant's Column reached Nawabgunge on the road to Lucknow, without opposition, on the 1st instant. The Column is waiting there, it is believed, for the Commander-in-Chief, for whom an escort of Cavalry and Horse Artillery had been left behind at Cawnpore.

. . . .

W. MUIR.

DCCIII.

FORT AGRA, *11th November* 1857.

CAWNPORE. — *9th November.*—"We expect," Mr. J. Power writes, "Captain Peel and the remainder of his Brigade in to-morrow morning. The first portion came in two days since, dragging their 24-pounders as if they were nothing. The 93rd, 53rd, 84th, 5th, and portions of several other regiments are here now, or rather, made one march towards Lucknow this morning." The only difficulty now in the daily arrival of troops at Cawnpore is carriage. **Naval Brigade.** **Advance of troops on Lucknow.**

The Gwalior and other insurgents in Bundelkhund are said to be in so great a state of alarm at the reported approach of our Column that they have broken the Bridge at Calpee.

W. MUIR.

DCCIV.

FORT AGRA, *November* 16, 1857.

CAWNPORE.—*11th November.*—"We still pour on towards Lucknow all troops that arrive here. Yesterday the Head Quarters of the 23rd arrived, and were pushed on this morning. To-day some of the 82nd arrived, and move on to-morrow. The whole of the 82nd is between here and Allahabad. To-morrow Brigadier Carthew with his Madrassies and six guns. He comes, I think, from Mirzapore, where he has been holding the Kutra Pass." **Troops pouring through Cawnpore to Lucknow.**

BRIGADIER GRANT'S COLUMN.—*November 6th.*—"Yesterday the greater part of the force escorted the convoy we brought with us to Alum Bagh, and returned. **Hope Grant approaches Lucknow.**

"The sick and those wounded before General Havelock's force reached Lucknow were brought back by our force, and have been sent with an escort to Cawnpore."

November 9th.—Five miles from Alum Bagh.—"To-day we have shifted our camp one mile nearer Lucknow, and our main picket must be within three miles of Alum Bagh, into which our large convoy was safely escorted two or three days ago. Part of the Naval Brigade with four 24-pounders arrived yesterday. The sight of the *tars* was most refreshing and encouraging." **Arrival of Naval Brigade.**

"NANGUNGE.—*10th November.*—We are still near Bunnee Bridge, but the Commander-in-Chief has arrived, and we move on Thursday, the day after to-morrow." **Arrival of Commander-in-Chief.**

Strength of Sir Colin's force.

With the troops at Alum Bagh, and excluding the 2000 men in Lucknow, the Column would be above 6000 strong, besides Artillery. They have eleven heavy guns, two 8-inch mortars, two 18-pounders, and eighteen field guns. The force, too, was being daily strengthened by reinforcements from Cawnpore both in Infantry and Artillery.

The disturbance in Googaira.

LAHORE.—11*th November.*—The Chief Commissioner states that "the disturbance in Googaira is coming to an end."

Arrival of troops at Bombay.

BOMBAY.—4*th November.*—"The remaining portion of H.M. 95th arrived on the 31st October. The whole Regiment now forms part of the Garrison of Bombay." The 3rd Dragoon Guards and the 72nd Regiment Foot are expected shortly. Three Regiments of Infantry and detachments, two of Cavalry, and a troop of Horse Artillery, will follow.

"The Mhow Field Force will be reinforced by the Head Quarters of the 14th Dragoons, a Native Infantry Regiment, and 250 of the 3rd Europeans. This reinforcement may be expected to reach Mhow in eight or ten days."

W. MUIR.

DCCV.

FORT AGRA, *November* 19, 1857.

Colonel Gerrard's Column.

DEHLI.—*November* 18*th.*—After the return of Showers' Brigade to Dehli a new Column was formed for service under Col. Gerrard.

This force left Dehli on the 9th instant, and marched, *via* Goorgaon, towards Rewaree, with the view of intercepting the Joudhpore Legion, which, joined by the Jhujjur, Ranghur, and other Cavalry, had appeared in Sheekhawattee, and was supposed to be making for the Mewattee tract in Goorgaon.

On the 13th the Column, then at Rewaree, received intelligence that the enemy was still at Narnoul.

From Rewaree our troops marched towards Kunoud, and the enemy would appear simultaneously to have marched in the same direction.

Affair near Kunaud.

On Sunday the 15th (the letters seem erroneously to make it the 16th) our Column no sooner reached its encamping ground near Kunoud,[1] about 11 a.m., than the rebel force moved up to the attack. They were 5000 strong, with 5 or 6 guns. Our Column (composed of 1st Bengal Fusiliers, the Crimean Squadron of Carabineers, the Guides Cavalry, 400 Mooltan Horse, 200

[1] Really near Narnoul. See DCCVI., *post.*

Pathan Horse, one troop H.A., and two 18-pounders) numbered about 1500.

The action began about midday. The cannonade on both sides was heavy. The enemy was strongly entrenched in a serai, and his Cavalry fought obstinately. The Carabineers and Guides Horse made a splendid charge, and the conduct of all our troops is praised in high terms.

The Rebels were, after several hours' hard fighting, dislodged from their position, and all their guns taken. By sunset they were in full flight. Our loss is stated at 70 killed and wounded. Colonel Gerrard was mortally wounded, and soon after died. Wounded: Lieut. Craigie, Guides, badly; Lieut. Kennedy, ditto, slightly; Captain Pearse; Lieut. Humphrey, Sappers; both the latter doing well.

Colonel Gerrard killed.

. . . .

LOCAL.—Colonel Riddell's Column was yesterday at Secundra Rao, on the Grand Trunk Road. The Allygurh force was at Kasgunge, and after taking a circuit by the Kutchla Ghat on the Ganges would return to Allygurh.

Colonel Riddell's Column.

The Rao Bhowany Singh, who was left by us in charge of Mynpoory, has been obliged to leave his post in consequence of the return of Rajah Tej Singh.

Rao Bhowani Singh.

Rajah Tej Singh.

From Secundra Rao, Colonel Riddell writes:—

"The country is looking well, and is to all appearance as highly cultivated as before the outbreak. The want of traffic on the Trunk Road, however, is very apparent."

W. MUIR.

DCCVI.

FORT AGRA, *November 20th*, 1857.

DEHLI.—18*th November*.—Demi-official despatches regarding the defeat of the Joudpore Legion have now been received.

The engagement took place, not at Kunoud, but near Narnoul, where the enemy had been for some time encamped.

The only additional name given among the wounded is Wallace.

The date is still mentioned as the 16th, which, if correct, would make the action to have occurred on Monday, not (as stated in the private correspondence from which yesterday's Memorandum was taken) on Sunday.

. . . .

CAWNPORE.—Our Cossids, bearing despatches of the 14th from Cawnpore, are believed to have been arrested by the rebels about half-way. From the statement of two who escaped, it will appear that no intelligence of any action at Lucknow had been received up to the 14th.

LOCAL.—All was well yesterday with our two Columns in the Allygurh district. Their appearance has had the effect of making the enemy evacuate Puttialee.

W. MUIR.

. . . .

DCCVIII.

AGRA, *November 23rd*, 1857.

CAWNPORE.—*November* 18*th*.—From despatches just received by Cossid of that date it would seem that some of Mr. Sherer's letters must have miscarried.

Sir Colin Campbell occupies environs of Lucknow.

Mr. J. Power writes, on the supposition that we had already heard "of Sir Colin Campbell's force having taken the Fort of Jellahabad, the Martinière, and the park of Dil Khoosha." In the former affair the enemy deserted and left the Fort and 4 guns to us an easy prey. The Fort was destroyed, and the guns carried off to camp. In the taking of the Dil Khoosha we have not heard what our entire loss has been. Lieutenant Manye[1] of the Horse Artillery, and Lieutenant Wheatcroft of the Carabineers, doing duty with the 9th Lancers, were the only casualties amongst our Officers.

Lieutenants Manye and Wheatcroft killed.

The telegraph had been established between Cawnpore and Alum Bagh on the 17th; but a few hours afterwards met with an accident.

Strong position at Cawnpore.

The Gwalior Contingent had apparently not yet summoned courage to cross the Jumna. Our position at Cawnpore, both as regards the fortifications and number of troops, is rapidly increasing in strength. "We have," says Mr. Power, "3 miles out of this, at the junction of the Calpee and Cawnpore Road, 800 Madras troops, 600 Europeans, and a European troop of Madras Horse Artillery; and by the end of the week we shall have 1500 more Europeans in."

W. MUIR.

[1] Mayne (?).

DCCIX.

AGRA, *November 23rd.*

NEEMUCH.—Through Jyepore it is reported that Neemuch was safe up to the 13th instant.

JYEPORE.—*November 19th.*—The party of Officers from Nusseerabad arrived there on the 18th, and were to leave for Agra on the 21st. **Officers from Nusseerabad.**

ALLYGURH.—On the 19th of November, the Allygurh Column, under command of Major Eld, moved up to the Kutcha Ghat, and, finding a body of the Rohilkhund insurgents occupying the opposite bank, opened fire upon them. Our practice was excellent, and the shells soon forced the rebels to fly in great confusion. They had 28 killed (including 3 Sepoys) and about 30 wounded; some horses were killed, and an elephant knocked down. Though the enemy had 3 or 4 guns (including a 12-pounder, which is believed to have burst), no one was touched on our side. **Major Eld's action at Kutcha Ghat.**

On the following day, under the protection of a 9-pounder, our people brought over all the boats from the other bank. "It was gratifying in the extreme," Major Eld writes, "to witness the cordiality and heartiness of our reception by the Hindoos of every class. Sorun is a very large and populous town, and hundreds upon hundreds crowded round us, every one with a kind word, hailing us as deliverers, and praying that we might conquer and free them from the state of anarchy and confusion from which the whole country had for months been suffering." **Attitude of Hindus at Sorun.**

CAWNPORE.—The following items are gleaned from a "Memorandum of News" by Mr. Thornton, "published under authority of Captain H. Bruce, Superintendent of Police," Cawnpore, November 12th.

LUCKNOW.—The Commander-in-Chief with the European troops arrived this morning (the 12th) at Lucknow. **Commander-in-Chief arrives at Lucknow.**

LOCAL.—To-day eight horsed field guns Royal Artillery, and a Regiment of Cavalry (Military Train), arrived here. The 23rd Fusiliers will be here in the course of to-day and to-morrow; and the Madras Brigade under Brigadier Carthew are expected on the 14th instant. There are also one horse field battery Royal Artillery, and the 13th Light Infantry on the road between this and Allahabad. **Troops pouring into Cawnpore.**

Since the Commander-in-Chief left Cawnpore, 15 guns and upwards of 1500 men have passed towards Lucknow.

The fugitives of the Dinapore Mutineers were seen proceed- **Dinapore fugitives.**

ing towards Nanamhoro Ghat. One hundred and fifty of their wounded men joined the 1st Division of the Gwalior troops, which had arrived at Calpee with a few light guns.

Thirty-six vessels arrive at Sandheads with troops.

" CALCUTTA.—Thirty-six vessels, with about 12,000 European troops, have arrived at the Sandheads, near Calcutta, and more are expected daily."

The above came by the regular dak of the 15th. I have had no Cossid despatched from Cawnpore of later date than the 11th instant.

W. MUIR.

DCCX.

AGRA, *November 24th.*

DEHLI.—*Nov.* 23.—The Moveable Column remains for the present in the vicinity of Rewaree. The defeated rebels have fled eastwards in two bodies, the Cavalry *via* Tapookra, the Infantry by way of Toojara.

Intelligence by electric telegraph has just been received to the effect that two bodies, supposed to be the same as those alluded to, are crossing the Dooab, one above and the other below Allygurh.

Captain Drummond proceeds to relieve Hutteen with Coke's Corps, Kumaonis, Tawana and Hodson's Horse. Affair at Roopraka.

A small detachment of two Companies of Coke's Corps and Kumaonies, with about 100 of the Towana and Hodson's Horse, under command of Captain Drummond, proceeded on the 19th from Sonah in the Goorgaon district to relieve Hutteen, which had been attacked by the Mewatties. At Roopraka, 3500 of these insurgents received the detachment with a sharp discharge of matchlocks. Our troops reserved their fire till within a hundred yards, then poured into them a destructive volley, and charged with the bayonet. Fifty were killed in the village, and some four hundred by the Cavalry outside.

Colonel Seaton appointed to command.

Colonel Seaton has proceeded to Rewaree to assume command, *vice* Colonel Gerrard killed in action.

The Ulwur troops are reported to have had a brush with the Joudpore fugitives.

NEEMUCH.—Captain MacDonald, writing from Deolee, says: —" Intelligence has been received from Neemuch down to the 16th. All well; the enemy has hardly fired a shot for two days."

BOMBAY.—*Nov.* 11*th.*—" The 'Genghis Khan,' which left England on the 11th August, arrived this morning at Bombay with 289 men of the 3rd Dragoon Guards, and 98 of the 86th Regiment and 16 Officers. The remainder of the 3rd Dragoon

Guards and 200 Artillery may be daily expected, as they left England a week previous to the departure of the 'Genghis Khan.'"

SAUGUR.—*Oct.* 27*th.*—"We are quite safe here, and I feel confident we shall never see a shot fired."

CAWNPORE.—*Nov.* 16*th.*—"Sir Colin Campbell's Army has been in communication with Sir James Outram for some days by means of a semaphore, which works well upon both sides. On the 14th we occupied the Dil Khoosha Park and House, together with the Martinière, pushing a picket across the Canal." **Advance on Lucknow.**

LOCAL.—Colonel Riddell's force is to-day at Sasnee, in a good position, it is hoped, to cut off the Joudhpore fugitives. **Colonel Riddell's force.**

4 p.m., LUCKNOW.—A Cossid with despatches from Cawnpore to the 10th instant brings the following Intelligence:—

"On the 16th the Commander-in-Chief's Army advanced across the Canal and carried the Secundra Bagh, the enemy suffering enormously; 1500 dead Sepoys were counted in one place alone. The Military Barracks were also seized. On the 17th, Shah Mujjill[1] and Mess House, both very strong positions, were carried by assault, and the Motee Mahal seized.

"Sir James Outram and Sir H. Havelock then came out and met His Excellency the Commander-in-Chief, and a junction was formed. **Sir Colin Campbell relieves Lucknow.**

"The Kaisur Bagh (King's Palace) was being commanded, and was most probably taken on the 18th.

"We have 5 Officers killed and 30 wounded.

"Sir Colin Campbell is so slightly wounded that it does not interfere with his duties.

"*List of Officers killed and wounded on the* 16*th and* 17*th November* 1857, *in the relief of the British Garrison at Lucknow*:—

"KILLED.

"Midshipman M. A. Daniell, Naval Brigade.
Captain Harley, Royal Artillery.
Captain Dalzell, 93rd Highlanders.
Captain Lumsdan, 30th N.I., attached to 93rd Highlanders.
Lieutenant Frankland, 2nd Punjab Infantry.

"WOUNDED.

"General Sir C. Campbell, G.C.B., Commander-in-Chief, slightly.
Major Alison, Military Secretary to the Commander-in-Chief, severely.
Captain Alison, Aide-de-Camp to the Commander-in-Chief, slightly.
Captain A. N. Anson, Aide-de-Camp to Brigadier-General Grant, severely.
Lieutenant Salmond, Naval Brigade, severely.
Midshipman Lord Clinton, Naval Brigade, slightly.

[1] Probably "Shah Najaf."

Captain Travers, Royal Artillery, slightly.
Brevet-Major Pennycuick, ditto, ditto.
Lieutenant Ford, ditto, ditto.
Lieutenant Milman, ditto, ditto.
Assistant-Surgeon Veale, ditto, severely.
Captain Hammond, Bengal Artillery, severely.
Captain Walton, H.M.'s 53rd Regiment, severely.
Lieutenant Munro, ditto, dangerously.
Major Barnston, H.M.'s 90th ditto, severely.
Lieutenant-Colonel Ewart, H.M.'s 93rd ditto, slightly.
Captain Borroughs, ditto.
Lieutenant Cooper, ditto, severely.
Lieutenant Walsh, ditto.
Lieutenant Goldsmith, ditto.
Lieutenant Wood, ditto.
Ensign Macnamara, ditto.
Lieutenant Dobbs, Madras Fusiliers, slightly.
Lieutenant Watson, 2nd Punjab Infantry, dangerously.
Lieutenant Paul, 4th ditto, severely.
Lieutenant M'Queen, ditto, ditto.
Lieutenant Oldfield, ditto, severely.
Lieutenant Halkett, Hodson's Horse, ditto.
Lieutenant Wynn, H.M.'s 90th Regiment, slightly.
Lieutenant Powell, ditto, ditto."

The Contingent was said to have intended to cross at Calpee on the 19th, but it was thought unlikely that they would move over unless the Nana joined them.

W. Muir.

DCCXI.

Agra, *November 26th*, 1857.

Central India.—The Mhow Column is said, by intelligence received through Gwalior, to have been at Kuchroud on the 18th inst., on its way to Mundessore. Its advance had been delayed by the mutiny of the remaining portion of the Mehidpore or "United Malwa Contingent."

Subscription for relief.

Jyepore.—A sum of about 2000 rupees has been remitted by Captain Eden, being the amount of subscription from Jyepore for the relief of the sufferers from the Mutiny. Of this, Rs. 1000 are contributed by the Maharaja Sowai Ram Singh Buhadur; and the remainder by persons attached to the Court and City.

Flight of Jodhpore Legion.

Local.—The Joudhpore Legion have fled so rapidly that they have hitherto eluded pursuit. Another body of these fugitives is reported to be following in the same direction.

W. Muir.

DCCXII.

AGRA, *27th November* 1857.

NEEMUCH. — *22nd November.* — The enemy on that date retired from Neemuch. Enemy retire from Neemuch.

On the morning of the 21st the rebels attempted an escalade, but were repulsed by the brave garrison with great loss to the enemy. They abandoned their scaling ladders and a green crusading flag, which were brought into our fortifications. The insurgents suffered much from our musketry, shell, and grape. Upwards of 200 were killed.

Although the enemy had, it is stated, 5000 foot, 1000 cavalry, and three guns, they attempted nothing further, and evacuated the station on the morning of the 22nd. It is probable that their retreat is connected with the advance of the Mhow Column on Mundesore on the 21st instant.

No one on our side was killed throughout the siege. Two officers, Barnes and Williams, were wounded, both slightly; and about six men of the 12th Regiment, but only one severely.

The conduct of all our troops is greatly applauded as "cool, steady, and collected as could be desired." The 12th Bombay N.I. "behaved splendidly," and some of their men had been promoted for their gallantry.

AJMERE.—*23rd November.*—"All well in this quarter."

LUCKNOW.—*19th November.*—By letters received at Cawnpore from Lucknow of that date the operations of the 18th would seem to have gone on successfully, though no details have yet been communicated. On that day they were busy removing the women, the wounded, and the treasure from the Residency. The insurgents appeared to be flying, as firing in the city had almost entirely ceased. The telegraph was open to Alum Bagh from Cawnpore. Mr. De Vere was killed on the road, while attempting to travel along the line towards Cawnpore without an escort. Mr. De Vere killed.

CAWNPORE.—*21st November.*—Troops now arrive regularly from below. The 82nd and 34th Regiments were about to arrive. They all, as they come in, join the Camp at the head of the Calpee Road. The Gwalior Contingent appeared to be delaying their movements until we shall be fully prepared for them at Cawnpore. Troops arrive at Cawnpore.

"Whilst I am writing," says Mr. Sherer, "General Depuis has ridden in with a troop of Gentlemen gunners."

The following is taken from Mr. Thornton's "Memo. of News," dated Cawnpore, 20th November 1857:—

Nana is at Fattehpur.

"The Nana is still at Futtehpore (Oudh); he has never crossed into this district since he was driven out of it by Sir H. Havelock, nor indeed has he left Futtehpore Chowrassie at all, except on one occasion to visit Lucknow, where he was not well received. Many of his followers and several of his relatives have passed towards Calpee, whither he may doubtless attempt to fly as soon as Oudh becomes too hot for him."

Colonel Wroughton defeats the Oude rebels.

JAUNPORE.—Colonel Wroughton, with the Goorkha troops, defeated again, on the 29th ultimo, the Oudh rebels near Jaunpore; the enemy were 5000 strong and had 7 guns, while the force under Colonel Wroughton only numbered 1200 men and had 2 guns. Five hundred of the enemy were killed, and 4 guns, with their camp stores, were captured by the Goorkhas.

Arrival of Troops in Calcutta since the 14th instant:—

Per "Alnwick Castle" . . .	402 men 19th Regiment.
" "Octavia"	231 Recruits.
" "Adventure"	334 2nd Batt. Rifle Brigade.
" "	76 42nd Regiment.
" "	76 37th Regiment.
" "	265 19th Regiment.

It was expected that a brigade would shortly be organised at Cawnpore to proceed towards Mynpoory and Furruckabad.

W. MUIR.

DCCXIII.

AGRA, *November 28th.*

Jodhpore Legion.

THE fugitives of the Joudpore Legion have entirely disappeared from this part of the country. None seem to have ventured nearer than 25 or 30 miles from Agra. A large body of them was met at Etawah, on their way probably to join the Nana's forces.

AGRA FORT.—*November 28th, 4 p.m.*—Since the above was printed, a report has been received of a further body of rebels being at Nohjheel, on the left bank of the Jumna, in the Muttra district. Colonel Riddell's Column remains at Saidabad for a day or two, with the hope of catching them.

Colonel Riddell's Column.

W. MUIR.

DCCXIV.

AGRA, *December* 1.

CAWNPORE.—*November* 25.—"The Contingent have shaken off their vacillations, and are steadily advancing. They have got over their heavy guns, after all; but they came last of everything across the bridge. Gwalior Contingent advances on Cawnpore.

"The first Division, with Koer Singh's men and six guns, arrived this morning at Sucheindee, which is only twelve miles off, and six from our camp; but this must be a blind to cover the advance of the two Divisions towards the Ganges or Bithoor. We have two thousand Europeans with Enfields watching for the first Division at the canal bridge, six miles from here; and if the infatuated fools advance another step they advance to certain destruction."

On the 26th, I learn from the statements of the Cossids who brought the above despatch, there was an engagement between our troops and the advanced Division of the rebel Army. The action was fought near the Pandoo Nuddee, in advance of our Camp; two out of four guns which the enemy had in the field were taken, and he was driven back some way from Sucheindee. As our messengers state that they were eye-witnesses of this action, their report may be accepted, without reliance on its details, as founded on fact, pending the receipt of further despatches. Action near Pandoo Nuddee.

The Commander-in-Chief would seem to have been still at Lucknow, arranging probably for the carriage of the sick and the women and children to Cawnpore.

W. MUIR.

DCCXV.

AGRA, *3rd December* 1857.

MUNDESSORE.—28*th Nov.*—A despatch has been received of that date from the Mhow Column encamped at Mundessore. The proceedings there have been attended with complete success.

The Army of the Shahzada having attacked Mehidpore on the 8th ultimo, and having been joined by the Mutineers of the Malwa Contingent, was proceeding with the Mehidpore Artillery to Mundessore, when on the way they were attacked by our Hyderabad Contingent Horse. "Our Cavalry dashed at them at once," etc.[1] Action (at Ravul) near Mandesaur.

. . . .

[1] The action is fully described in No. CCXXV., p. 293, vol. i.

NUSSEERABAD.—28*th Nov.*—The Head Quarters H.M.'s 83rd with guns, etc., from Deesa, marched in on that date.

DCCXVI.

AGRA, *December 7th*, 1857.

Troops expected at Karachi.

LAHORE. — *Nov.* 30*th.* — "Three Regiments of European Infantry, one of Dragoons, and a lot of Artillery are every day expected at Kurrachee, and will be sent up to Lahore as quickly as possible."

Road to Cawnpore from Agra disturbed.

The road to Cawnpore is so beset by plundering parties that our Cossids have not been able of late to get through with any letter.

DCCXVII.

AGRA, 12*th Dec.* 1857.

CAWNPORE.—A despatch has been received, dated the 3rd instant, but without any mention of our engagements with the Gwalior Contingents. The letters on that subject have evidently miscarried.

Lucknow families sent down country.

The Commander-in-Chief appears to have reached Cawnpore from Lucknow on the 30th ultimo, with the families, sick, etc., for whose immediate passage to Allahabad arrangements were speedily made. So soon as they were well in the rear on their journey down the country, operations were to commence for the attack and dispersion of the rebels who occupied the environs of Cawnpore and a portion of the town itself.

Gwalior Contingent defeated at Mogul Serai. Balla Sahib wounded.

Intelligence has been received, through the Gwalior news-writer at Calpee, that a most decisive action took place on the 6th or 7th instant, which ended in the entire discomfiture of the Contingent and other insurgents, in the capture of all their Artillery, baggage, and in driving them back towards Calpee, in the fort of which place the Balla Sahib (brother of the Nana), who was himself wounded, has taken refuge. The villagers are said to have refused shelter to any of the fugitives.

In the absence of our own despatches, this grateful intelligence may be received as authentic; for the Gwalior news has always been, in the main, trustworthy.

AJMERE.—6*th December.*—"We hope to have a good force up here soon. A European Dragoon Regiment, a complete one of Infantry, a troop of Horse Artillery and natives, with some European Sappers and Miners, are our expected reinforcements."

W. MUIR.

We have been favoured with the following translation of the statement of the Gwalior news-writer, referred to in the above Official Memorandum :—

Letter from Maharajah Scindia's News-writer at Calpee, to an Officer of the Maharajah, dated Tuesday the 8th Dec. :—

Native description of fight near Mogul Serai.

"Three Hurkarus came straight from Cawnpore to-day, and reported that the Gwalior Contingent rebels having collected all their force and stores at Bhoti, advanced thence to a place two coss nearer to Cawnpore, and left there, with 50 or 60 men, their camp and bazaar. The whole force, including sepoys and chiefs with their followers of all sorts, amounted to 15,000 men. Their plan was to fight with their guns up to 12 p.m., and then to assault and carry the entrenchments. At Mogul Serai, near Cawnpore, the English had a battery, and there the fight began. The rebels fought very bravely up to 12 p.m., when the English began to retire, and the rebels followed them until they were two coss from the rebel camp. Then 500 English with two guns advancing on the Allahabad Road attacked the rebel camp and captured it, with all that was in it. Leaving a guard there, they then attacked the rear of the rebels, when the retiring English turned and attacked them in front. The rebels could not endure this double attack, and fled; and the English chased them to Sucheindee, and took on the road their guns, baggage, magazine—everything. Meanwhile, the two great guns which the rebels had sent for with ammunition from Calpee having reached Renniah, the English marched thither also and captured them. The three Hurkarus who report this were in the action, and with great difficulty saved their lives, but none of their property. And of the flying sepoys, no village would admit a man within its walls—not even if it were his own home. The Hurkarus put up in the village of Muttabelpore, and there, at twelve o'clock at night, came Koor Dowlut Sing, but the people would not let him halt there. I cannot tell how many were slain, but shall hear to-morrow. The English fought in this battle as Roostum and Isfendiar alone fought before. The Sahibs dismounted amid the fire of the guns and slew the gunners with their swords, and, rushing upon the gunners, stopped them as they applied the match. While the English so worked their guns that winking is a slow operation compared to the rapidity of their fire, they fired after the fugitives as their noise directed, and if they but saw a head that head was crushed. The blood of the dead and wounded flowed in streams.

Kunwar Daulat Sing.

"Whoever shall hear this news will rejoice; for these men, who injured and trampled on high and low, have received punishment from God proportioned to their cruelty. And great as was their bravery, as signal have been their flight and destruction. The dead are doomed to *dozukh.*"[1]

DCCXVIII.

AGRA, *Dec.* 15*th*, 1857.

Colonel Seaton's Column's success at Gangeri.

ALLYGURH.—The Column from Dehli, under Col. Seaton, after halting on Saturday the 13th at Allygurh, made a double march on Sunday, and yesterday proceeded to Gungeree, a town about 30 miles east of Allygurh, and 12 miles west of Kassgunge, at which latter place Wuleedad, with a force from Furruckabad, had for some time been posted.

Wali Dad.

The insurgents, apparently in ignorance of Col. Seaton's movement, and expecting to find at Gungeree only Colonel Farquhar's small force from Boolundshuhur, had also advanced from Kassgunge to a plain on the banks of the Neem Nuddee (an affluent of the Kalee Nuddee), which runs close to Gungeree on the east.

Col. Seaton, finding them posted there in great force, lost no time in organising an attack. He led the way with the Cavalry and the guns, Major Eld following with the Infantry. After a short conflict the rebels fled, but not before we had three Carabineer Officers killed and one wounded. The enemy lost 150 killed, and we captured three of his field-pieces—one 9-pounder, the others 6-pounders.

Major Eld.

The above is founded on a telegraphic message received from Major Eld.

W. MUIR.

DCCXIX.

AGRA, *Dec.* 17*th*, 8 *a.m.*

CAWNPORE.—*December* 10.—Our regular despatches are still wanting; but a demi-official letter, under date the 10th instant, received from the Commissariat Department at Cawnpore, contains incidentally the following important information:—

The women and children from Lucknow leave Cawnpore.

The women and children from Lucknow, with the sick and wounded, left Cawnpore (as we have been informed by a brief Memorandum from Mr. Sherer dated the 4th instant) on the night of Thursday, the 3rd. The present letter states:—

"Thank God, they are, I trust, in safety by this, and on their way to Calcutta."

[1] Bottomless pit.

The references to our military operations entirely confirm all that has been before published. The discomfiture of the Contingent and other rebel bodies before Cawnpore was most complete. "They have lost everything,—magazine, guns, camp, supplies; and their force scattered. Such a blow they have never received, and will not get over." Discomfiture of the Contingent.

In driving the insurgents out of Cawnpore we took 17 guns. We then pursued them to Bithoor, and dislodged them from thence, capturing 17 more guns, "which, with those taken by Genl. Wyndham, gives us a total of 38." Rebels driven out of Cawnpore and Bithoor.

In these operations our loss has been small: "About 20 killed and wounded in both attacks, here and at Bithoor."

Mr. Sherer's note of the 4th says that "Sir James Outram is at Alum Bagh, with 3000 men." The present letter adds that the troops there are doing well, and that the insurgents have not had the courage to venture on an attack in the fields. Sir James Outram at Alam Bagh.

The magnitude of the force available for service at Cawnpore may be judged of by the Commissariat preparations ordered for its support from here. We have to get in readiness supplies for 10,500 men, of whom 8500 are Europeans.

W. Muir.

DCCXX.

Fort Agra, 18*th Dec.* 1857.

Cawnpore.—Regular despatches have now been received up to the 10th instant. On that date, after an intermission of 16 days, letters from Agra had again begun to reach Cawnpore.

Mr. Sherer writes:—"Yesterday, the 9th, Brigadier Hope (Grant?) had a great success at the Ghat near Sheorajpoor. He captured 15 of the enemy's guns, and great stores of ammunition. I have not been able to pick up details yet, but am told we did not lose a man." Hope Grant's success at Sheorajpore Ghat.

"Brigadier Inglis commands our fort, and General Wyndham goes up country, towards his own division, Sirhind."

The town has suffered very little, considering what it has undergone.

"The ladies and children of Lucknow have, thank God, arrived in perfect safety at Allahabad. All the civilians have accompanied them."

All well at Alumbagh. Outram has not been attacked since Sir Colin left.

A letter of the 7th instant gives the following particulars regarding the previous engagements

In the first action, of the 26th ult., we captured two 8-inch Howitzers and a 9-pounder. The success in this engagement, admirably conducted by General Wyndham, was not exaggerated in the Cossid's report given in the Memo. of the 1st of December.[1] On the 27th and 28th there was fighting again, and, although our small force retired into its entrenchments, on the latter day we took two 18-pounders and a 9-pounder, besides spiking 5 guns.

On Sunday the 29th the Commander-in-Chief arrived from Lucknow, and offensive operations were stayed until the families and the sick were well out of the reach of the insurgents.

Dispersion of the rebel forces.

On the 6th the Commander-in-Chief attacked the enemy. They have all dispersed—a great number, I think, gone towards Bithoor, some towards Calpee, some across the Ganges into Oudh. Their force is very large—the whole Gwalior force and Cavalry; Neemuch Brigade, Dinapore Mutineers, most of those we fought under Greathed at Agra; and about 4000 men with guns, who came from Oudh, and some men under the celebrated Nana.

The Nana.

On that day we took 5 mortars, two 8-inch Howitzers, three 18-pounders, and 6 smaller guns.

ALLYGURH.—The Column marched on the 15th to Kassgunge, which was found to have been evacuated by the enemy. Some 60 or 70 Sepoys and Jehadies were, however, cut up in the vicinity by Hodson's Horse.

On the 17th the force was to march to Puttialee, where the rebels were said again to have assembled.

Death of Lieutenant Vyse.

Of the two Officers mentioned as wounded in the Memo. of the 15th, Lieutenant Vyse died, and Lieut. Head is doing well.

The loss on the enemy's side at Gungeeree is now represented at 400 or 500 killed.

W. MUIR.

DCCXXI.

AGRA, *19th Dec.* 1857.

Defeat of the Farakhabad rebels at Patiáli.

ALLYGURH.—On the morning of the 17th the Column marched against Puttiallee, as stated in yesterday's Memo. The following telegraphic message, sent by Col. Seaton on the afternoon of the 17th, contains the gratifying intelligence of the entire defeat of the Furruckabad rebels, who had entrenched themselves at Puttiallee.

[1] See p. 225, No. DCCXIV., *ante*.

"Found the enemy strongly posted, facing the west, with the town in rear. They opened on our videttes from two guns, but as the Column approached, unmasked several others.

"I advanced Horse Artillery flanked by Cavalry, Infantry bringing up the rear. Charged and took all their guns,—eleven, camp, and park. Pursued them for seven miles. Enemy lost not less than six hundred, among whom are many Chiefs.

"Our loss very trifling. None yet reported as killed."

W. MUIR.

DCCXXII.

FORT AGRA, *21st Dec.* 1857.

CAWNPORE.—All was well at Cawnpore, by despatches dated up to the 14th instant. The Commander-in-Chief was still there.

Sir Henry Havelock died from an attack of dysentery, and was buried at Alumbagh. **Death of Sir Henry Havelock.**

Mr. J. B. Thornhill, of the Civil Service, died at Lucknow of wounds.[1] . . . Lieut. Dashwood also died during the siege. Among the killed in the late engagement before Lucknow, Mr. Benson, C.S., and Ensigns F. F. Oldfield and Dashwood, are mentioned. **Death of J. B. Thornhill, C.S. Death of Lieutenant Dashwood. Mr. Benson, C.S., Ensigns F. F. Oldfield and Dashwood, killed.**

W. MUIR.

We have just received authentic intelligence of the mutiny of the troops at both Dacca and Chittagong. A detail of Native Foot Artillery and two Companies of the 73rd N.I. were stationed at the former place, and three companies of the 34th N.I. at the latter. **Mutiny at Dacca and Chittagong.**

We are not in possession of any particulars, our letters having miscarried, but, as the troops were but few in number, we trust their mutiny has not been attended with the usual atrocities.

DCCXXIII.

AGRA, *Dec. 25th*, 1857.

ALLYGURH.—*Dec. 25th.*—Mr. Wilson writes:—"The Hardy family, seven in number, and thirteen other Christian refugees, safe in my camp." **The Hardy family and other Christians saved at Aligarh.**

The guns captured by Col. Seaton's Column, 17 in number,

[1] He was wounded when he had gone out to meet Havelock's Column. See No. DCCXXIII., *post*.—W. C.

were brought into Allygurh by Major Eld, who had returned with his detachment.

Effects of victory at Patiáli.

The effects of Colonel Seaton's victory at Puttiallee have been most complete and decisive. The insurgents are believed to have rested nowhere till they reached Furruckabad. The number killed, as stated in the telegraphic message, is, by later accounts, considerably below the reality.

CAWNPORE.—*Dec.* 19*th.*—Letters have been received up to that date, but without any fresh particulars of public interest. A westward movement, however, was expected at an early date.

General Outram continued to hold Alum Bagh with 4500 men.

Mr. J. B. Thornhill received the wound of which he died, after the junction with Sir Henry Havelock.

DCCXXIV.

AGRA, 28*th Dec.* 1857.

Walpole's Column,

CAWNPORE.—A strong Column under Brigadier Walpole left Cawnpore on the 18th instant, and reached Akberpore, half-way to Calpee, on the 19th. It remained there for two or three days, engaged in settling the surrounding country, which has been so long disorganised by the insurgent troops.

Composition of.

With this Column are the Rifle Brigade, 2 Battalions; 38th Foot; Bouchier's Battery, and Blunt's Troop Horse Artillery; 1st Punjab Cavalry; and 3 Squadrons of the 9th Lancers. It will proceed towards Etawah.

Sir Colin Campbell's Column.

With the Commander-in-Chief, when His Excellency moves westward, will be the following Regiments:—Remington's Troop Horse Artillery; Smith's Battery Royal Artillery; the Naval Brigade, with six 24-pounders, two 8-inch Howitzers, and eight mortars; two Companies Sappers and Miners; Bengal ditto; and two Companies Punjab ditto, the Cavalry which went down with Grant's Column; the 8th Foot, 23rd Fusiliers, 42nd Highlanders, 53rd, 64th, 82nd Foot, 93rd Highlanders, with a Regiment of Punjab Infantry.

The 32nd, 34th, and 88th Foot remain at Cawnpore, with

Loyalty of the Lucknow Native Corps.

"the faithful remnants of the Lucknow Native Corps, who behaved with great gallantry and fidelity."

Sir J. Outram's force at Alam Bagh.

With Sir J. Outram at Alum Bagh are one Royal Battery; two Bengal Field Batteries; a heavy Bengal Battery; a Company of Madras Sappers; the Military Train (2 Squadrons) as Dragoons; some Irregular Cavalry; Her Majesty's 5th Fusiliers, 78th Highlanders, 84th Foot, 90th Light Infantry; Madras

Fusiliers, and Ferozepore Regiment. There is a detachment of Horse Artillery and troops at a station midway between Cawnpore and Lucknow.

The 7th Hussars are about to be formed at Allahabad, where horses are being collected for them.

A strong Brigade under Col. Franks has been organised at Benares for service in the Eastern Frontier of Oudh. The 20th and 97th Foot, with wing of the 10th and a Royal Troop and Battery, will form part of this Force, with Madras Troops and Goorkhas. **Brigade under Colonel Franks.**

MYNPOORIE.—The following message, announcing the re-occupation of Mynpoorie yesterday, has just been received by telegraph *via* Allygurh :—

MYNPOORIE.—27*th Dec.*, 3 p.m.—"Found the enemy, this morning, posted behind some high trees a mile west of the city. He opened with four guns as I advanced. **Affair at Mainpúri.**

"I sent the Horse Artillery guns a détour to the right, supported by the Cavalry; the heavy guns and Infantry following. The enemy, finding his retreat to the city cut off, soon began to retreat.

"Took all his guns, six; and cut up 250. As yet none reported killed on our side."

W. MUIR.

DCCXXV.

AGRA, *Dec.* 30*th*, 1857.

. . . .

MEERUT.—*Dec.* 28*th*.—Mr. Wilson writes "that Mr. Samuel Edward Erith, Head Writer, Budaon Collector's Office, has been rescued, and that he is safe in his camp." **S. E. Erith rescued.**

W. MUIR.

DCCXXVI.

AGRA, *Jan.* 1*st*, 1858.

ETAWAH was occupied by Brigadier Walpole's force on the 29th ult. The insurgents fled to Furruckabad. **Walpole's Brigade occupies Etawah.**

The Commander-in-Chief was at Meerunkee Serai on the 30th ult. The rebels are believed to have broken the bridge over the Kalee Nuddee at Khoda Gunge. Captain Hodson with 100 Horse had opened a communication with the Head Quarters Camp, and returned on the 30th. **Captain Hodson.**

W. MUIR.

DCCXXVII.

AGRA, *Jan.* 5, 1858.

HEAD QUARTERS CAMP.—A communication dated the 3rd instant states that on the previous day His Excellency the Commander-in-Chief had an engagement with the rebels, and took seven guns. The force, which on the 3rd was encamped at Karoulee, two or three miles on the Furruckabad side of the Khodagunj Bridge, was to march immediately on Futtehgurh.

Commander-in-Chief engages the rebels.

Walpole's Column.

ETAWAH. — *Dec.* 31, 1857. — Brigadier Walpole's Column "reached Etawah on the 29th instant. The rebel force, consisting of seven guns, 1500 matchlockmen, and 350 horse, some of whom were Mutineers, hastily abandoned Etawah under their leaders, Aladad Khan, Mewatee, and Gunga Sing Bhudoseea. But some of them, with Taj Khan, Mewatee, a subordinate leader, were surrounded by Kaour Zor Sing's people in the Tehseel, where they were killed by a part of the Column on the morning of the 29th. They had two telegraph guns, and resisted to the last. Three riflemen were wounded on the attack, one badly."

MYNPOORIE.—H.M. 28th Regiment with guns and 200 of Wale's Horse remain for the present at Mynpoorie.

BOMBAY.—*Dec.* 28*th.*—"The Head Quarters and 350 men and 24 Officers of the 56th Regiment arrived yesterday. They will go down to Belgaum to relieve the Head Quarters of the 86th, which will join the wing of that corps now at Indore."

INDORE.—Sir Robert Hamilton, writing on the 23rd ultimo, says:—"Holkar blew away a leader on the 20th.

Amjhera Rajah sentenced to death.

"The Amjhera Rajah, his kamdar, and three officials were tried before me and a Court of eight vakeels on the 21st, found guilty, and sentenced to death. The execution of the Rajah is suspended; the kamdar and two officials were hung on the 21st; one sentence commuted to transportation for life.

"Two other men were tried, found guilty, and executed.

"Eight Mutineers arrested were tried, and blown from guns. To-day three Mutineers have been found guilty and executed.

Sir Hugh Rose assumes command in Central India.

"Sir Hugh Rose has assumed command of the Field Force in Central India. We shall move on Saugor as soon as equipped.

"All quiet at Mundessore. Baba Apta hung four of the officials who had gone over to the rebels.

"I am opening the postal line and telegraph with Gwalior; open with Bombay and Surat."

CAWNPORE.—*Dec.* 29*th.*—The telegraph has been completed along the Grand Trunk Road to the boundary of the Furruckabad district. The present supply of wire will, however, hardly suffice to stretch it to Mynpoorie.

The district of Cawnpore is becoming more settled; and, after a long intermission, the revenue begins to come in. Cawnpore District settling down.

A Moveable Column, of all arms and of considerable strength, is being organised for service wherever required in the vicinity of Cawnpore. The Magistrate and Collector will probably make a circuit of the district in company with this force. Cawnpore Moveable Column.

BENGAL.—The Sylhet Light Infantry Battalion met the Chittagong Mutineers on the 20th ultimo, and "drove them back into the Tipperah jungles with considerable loss. Unfortunately, Byng, the Commandant, was killed by one of the first shots; but the Battalion behaved admirably. The Mutineers are now so hemmed in that it is next to impossible they should escape." Chittagong Mutineers. Byng, Commandant, killed.

DCCXXVIII.

AGRA, *Jan. 7th*, 1858.

HEAD QUARTERS.—The action of the 2nd instant was more important in its results than at first anticipated.

The enemy appear to have moved out in strength from Futtehgurh. About 9 in the morning they opened a cannonade on Hope's Brigade at the Khodagunge Bridge. Reinforcements were immediately pushed on from the camp at Goorsahaigunge, 4 or 5 miles distant from the Bridge. The engagement continued till nearly 3 in the afternoon, when the insurgents, having been dislodged, commenced a rapid flight towards Futtehgurh. They were pursued by the Cavalry, who cut up some 300, and captured 7 guns. Affair at Fatehgarh.

That night the Nawab Raees and most of the troops are said to have evacuated the town and escaped across the Ganges. On the following day, the 3rd, our troops advanced, and are believed to have occupied the city without any opposition. No details have been received; but it is understood that we were in quiet possession of the place on the 4th.

W. MUIR.

We have ourselves received two letters from Futtehgurh of the 4th and 5th instant, and from these extract the following intelligence:—

"Our Division (Wyndham's) left Head Quarters on the 28th to take a small Fort, which we did without opposition, the enemy having bolted ere we came up.

"We remained there two days blowing it up.

Rani of Tiroora.

"After this we paid a visit of congratulation to the Ranee of Tiroora, who has held out for Government all along. We rejoined Head Quarters on the 1st at Goorsahaigunge. A Brigade was sent six miles on to repair the suspension bridge, 14 miles from this place: they commenced work on the 1st, and by morning of the 2nd had finished it, all but one or two planks, which they were laying down; when the Chief saw the villagers come out of the village opposite he desired some one to go and tell them not to be afraid as they would not be hurt, when all of a sudden bang came a round shot from amongst them, which killed four men of the 53rd. The enemy were then discovered to be in force; the Naval Brigade soon opened upon them, pitching into the village for about two hours; they returning it with an 18-pounder and 9-pounder.

Action near Fatehgarh.

"When the firing commenced we were all sent for, the bridge was soon finished, and then the Chief with his force crossed, turned them out of the village, and pursued them with Cavalry and Artillery for about 8 miles. The Naval rockets blew up a magazine of theirs very prettily, and knocked over a 9-pounder; this and another gun they left in the village. The Cavalry captured 4 more, one an 18-pounder, and plenty of ammunition; in all, 6 guns that day. Our loss was Younghusband of the Seikhs, shot through the lungs, and Maxwell of the Artillery, shot through the thigh. General Grant was slightly touched, and a spent ball hit the old Chief on the stomach, but did not injure him; 4 men of the 53rd were killed, and 6 or 7 of the 8th were also knocked over by a shell; no others wounded. We encamped at the 12th milestone from here, and started again yesterday at 11 a.m. The Cavalry the night before came upon a body of the rebels in the open, and cut them up . . .; we counted 50 bodies in a few fields, all Sepoys. We came near Futtehgurh about 3 p.m., and to our disgust found the enemy had decamped during the night! They had an 18- and 24-pounder ready loaded, and were entrenched on the Grand Parade; also an entrenched camp (our Brigade is in it now) outside the Fort. They left all their guns but 2, ammunition, etc., and merely made off with all the treasure and two guns to protect it. All the rest we have got. Two we found here, 5 in the Fort, and 3 or 5 others on the road. Those in the Fort are two 24-pounders, two 18-pounders, and one 9-pounder.

Younghusband and Maxwell killed.

"The Nawab burnt his own house, set fire to the Camp, and looted Furruckabad before leaving. In the entrenched

Camp we found most of the furniture, buggies, etc., belonging, we suppose, to the Officers who were here when the Mutiny broke out.

"We are all encamped in a circle on the Grand Parade. I fancy a large force will be left here, whilst we, I believe, go on to Bareilly; when, I don't know. We never know 5 minutes before we start where we are going to. The Chief is as close as wax. The country everywhere is under cultivation, just as if nothing had happened, and splendid crops they are. The country appears to have perfectly settled down between this and Calcutta. Coming up, we used to go out shooting 6 and 7 miles from Camp, but never met with any adventure. Cawnpore is a fearful sight, smashed to pieces by ours and the enemy's shot and shell. The "slaughter house" was blown up before we left. The Highlanders and Sailors look so jolly. The 93rd and 42nd both wear bonnets, kilts, hose and gaiters, exactly the same as at home."

. .

DCCXXX.

AGRA, *11th Jan.* 1858.

ALLAHABAD.—"A strong party marched out from the Fort on the 4th, I think, and beat back the Nazim, who had ventured too near the bank, killing some 250 and losing only one man, but having 17 horses disabled.

"It was the intention of the Nazim to creep down to the river and attack the steamer with the ladies on board; but his plan was frustrated, and the ladies have received permission to go down by bullock train."

CAWNPORE.—*8th Jan.*—"All well at Alumbagh. They remain unmolested. The road is a little stormy between here and there in places; but parties of 4 and 6 Military Train come over on messages without danger."

Extract from "Cawnpore News Letter," dated 2nd January 1858.

GORUCKPORE.—"Jung Buhadoor, the Nepaul Commander-in-Chief, with his army of 10,000 Goorkhas, composed of 14 Regiments of Infantry and 4 Batteries of Artillery of 6 guns each, arrived at Segowlee, on the 21st ultimo, to co-operate with the British Troops against the rebels.

Jang Bahadur brings a Nepal force to co-operate against the rebels.

"On the 26th ultimo Col. Rowcroft attacked the rebels at Sobunpoor, in the Goruckpore District, and totally routed them,

Colonel Rowcroft attacks the rebels at Sobunpoor.

taking 3 guns and the whole of their tents, baggage, and ammunition. The enemy numbered about 5000 men, while the force under Col. Rowcroft, with the Naval Brigade under Captain Sotheby, and two Goorkha Regiments, amounted to about 1000 men. On our side only one camp-follower was killed, and a Goorkha Soobadar wounded. The enemy left about 40 killed on the field, besides a large number of wounded."

DCCXXXI.

AGRA, *14th Jan.* 1858.

Bijnor insurgents checked at Moyapur by Captain Boisragon.

MEERUT.—12*th Jan.*—The Bijnore Insurgents, who have been attempting incursions into the Seharunpore and Mozuffernugger districts, three days ago received a decisive check at Moyapore, near the head of the Ganges Canal in Seharunpore.

Captain Boisragon, with only 70 Seikhs and Goorkhas, 10 Europeans, and 2 guns, fell in with a thousand of the rebels at that place, and completely discomfited them. A hundred were killed, and the Moyapore Dam having been opened to cut off escape, many more were drowned.

A man of rank, supposed to be Nawab Ahmedoolla, was wounded. His nephew was killed by Captain Boisragon himself.

. . . .

W. MUIR.

DCCXXXII.

AGRA, *Friday, Jan.* 15*th*, 1858.

FROM the Commander-in-Chief's Camp, Futtehgurh, 13th January, we have received the following :—

"Walpole's, the Rifle Brigade, have gone to the Ramgunga to repair a Bridge. The 64th marched this morning for Allygurh, where they are to remain for the present. The Chief had a review of the Cavalry on the opposite side of the river this morning.

"We have reports, which are very generally credited, that Lucknow is taken by Outram, and that Maun Singh is now anxious to come to terms. The Nana Sahib is not far off, trying to make a bolt of it, with about 600 men. He will be hanging in our Camp before many days are over, if he does not look out very sharp. The Convoy came in this morning from Bawur. I hear that the ladies and several Officers leave for Cawnpore to-morrow. The Chief moves ground to-morrow, but only goes a short distance."

INTELLIGENCE DEPARTMENT, AGRA.

THIRTEENTH SERIES.

LETTERS WRITTEN DURING THE MUTINY, PRINCIPALLY TO AND FROM AGRA.

THE twelve preceding series of letters and documents compose the Intelligence Records as contained in nine volumes in official or demi-official form; eight volumes are in manuscript: the Twelfth Series consists of a collection of printed bulletins circulated in Fort Agra (Vol. IX.).

This (Thirteenth) Series comprises letters written mostly by officials (a majority being addressed to Mr. (now Sir William) Muir), giving accounts of the condition of the country, of the progress of the Mutineers, of the military operations for relief, and the restoration of order. Parts of some of these letters, having been copied at the time in the Manuscript Intelligence Volumes, appear in one or other of the foregoing series.

Some 46 letters of this (Thirteenth) Series were originally grouped as Vols. X. and XI. (see p. 24, *ante*). After this grouping had been made, a large number of letters which had been lent to Sir John Kaye and Col. Malleson, for use in the preparation of their classical histories, came into Sir William Muir's hands on the death of Col. Malleson. Many of these belonged to the same series of correspondence as the letters in (so-called) Vols. X. and XI., and have now been included in one series with the latter.

This Thirteenth Series is in fact composed of (1) the letters grouped originally as Vols. X. and XI.; and (2) the Kaye-Malleson letters just mentioned.

As in the case of the last series, matter elsewhere recorded in these volumes has been generally omitted.

W. COLDSTREAM.

ABSTRACT OF LETTERS IN SERIES XIII.

1. From Agra, by W. Muir, C.S.
2. From Sir John Lawrence, Chief Commissioner, Punjab.
3. From Amballa.
4. „ Rohtak.
5. „ Hissar.
6. „ Dehli.
7. „ Meerut.
8. „ Bulandshahr.
9. From Naini Tal.
10. „ Etawah.
11. „ Cawnpore.
12. „ Allahabad.
13. „ Moveable Column.
14. „ Mirzapore.
15. „ Captain Gowan (in hiding).
16. „ Calcutta.

1. LETTERS FROM AGRA, BY W. MUIR, C.S.

[*These Letters have a special importance,—some as giving a detailed account by a writer on the spot, of the outbreak of the Mutiny as experienced at Agra, and others as giving views on important points of policy.*]

DCCXXXIII.

To the Editor, "Bombay Times."[1]

AGRA, 13*th June* 1857.

MY DEAR SIR,—I propose to give you some account of our proceedings here at the present crisis, and to continue it from time to time as circumstances may permit.

It will only be necessary for me very briefly to recount the earlier events,—and that chiefly with reference to their bearing on Agra, which is naturally the centre of my intelligence and views.

On Sunday night, the 10th of May, telegraphic information reached us of the tragic scene that was being enacted at Meerut. But the serious sequel of this tragedy in reference to Dehli was not made known to us by any direct communication. The news therefore did not at first excite that deep concern which a full appreciation of the extent of the calamity would have caused. Many, indeed, did not know that anything unusual had occurred till Tuesday. **First news from Meerut.**

Meanwhile the telegraph was stopped with Meerut, and of necessity with Dehli also (for the wire to Dehli passes through Meerut). The daks of Sunday came in as usual on Monday, both from Meerut and from Dehli,—but after that the dak ceased. **Post and telegraph stop.**

Rumours of the fearful truth—exaggerated as regards Meerut,

[1] This letter did not reach its destination. See Editor's Note in *Bombay Times* of 3rd July prefixed to letter next following, which was printed in that issue.—W. C.

VOL. II.—16

in regard to Dehli they could hardly be exaggerated—began to come in on Tuesday. Continued silence, the fear of the unknown, caused apprehension to grow hour by hour. It was a period of intense anxiety and alarm till Thursday, when news from Meerut let us know that at any rate the European troops there were safe.

Meanwhile the Government shared in the general apprehension of danger. A railway official fled from his post at Palwul, across the Jumna to Allygurh, with tidings that the Mutineers were marching in force on Agra. It afterwards appeared that these were mere flying parties of marauders. The Government apprehended that the conspirators, having struck a blow at Dehli by the murder of the British, were probably about to try the same game by a dash at Agra. The danger was at one time (though on insufficient grounds) deemed so imminent that the families of civil officers were ordered into the Fort.

Families of Civil officers ordered into Fort.

Holding these views as to the probable approach of a force down the right bank of the Jumna, the bearing of the Lieutenant-Governor was manly and determined. It was resolved to go out and meet the enemy, and a spot was actually selected beyond Secundra, 5 or 6 miles on the Muthra road. Our real difficulty was then felt, though not yet known in its full extent. It was doubtful whether our two Native Regiments were well affected. In this extremity the Lieutenant-Governor ordered a parade, and addressed each of the Regiments. He promised the native troops that the obnoxious cartridges should not be served to them, and asked them whether they were satisfied and would fight with us; if not, they might go to their homes. An occasional assent was given, and as the Lieutenant-Governor left they all joined (at a suggestion given to that effect) in loud and reiterated cheers.

Bearing of Lieutenant-Governor.

Doubts as to loyalty of Native Regiments.

Troops paraded.

Things began now apparently to mend a little. Communications were received both by dak and telegraph with Meerut. A body of some 1500 Bhurtpore Horse was engaged to protect Muthra. A force from Ulwur subsequently joined it, and advanced some 30 or 40 miles towards Dehli, thus partially restoring order on the right bank of the Jumna.

Advance of Bhurtpore and Ulwur troops towards Delhi.

A couple of hundred horse and six guns of the Gwalior Contingent joined us here. The horse were mostly detached to strengthen the position at Allygurh. Scindia, in a very friendly manner, sent over his bodyguard—a small force of all arms—for Mr. Colvin's special protection.

Scindia's loyalty.

One or two proclamations were issued by the Government to

Proclamations issued by Government.

reassure the people and to encourage the Sepoys to lay down their arms and retire peaceably to their homes.

It became evident that the Mutineers had no present intention of leaving Dehli, excepting the few who were skulking homewards. All eyes turned towards the army that was to advance on Dehli. People expected that it might be there a fortnight after the occupation of the City by the Mutineers. It was a time of expectation. The effect of delay was dreaded on the country at large, and on the other Sepoys especially.

As regards the country generally, though the shock was great it soon appeared that nothing was to be feared from it alone. There was not the semblance of a rising anywhere. The question was one simply between the Government and its native soldiery.

The rising was only of the native soldiery.

Suddenly the 9th Native Infantry gave way. Its headquarters were at Allygurh, within 80 miles of Meerut and fifty of Agra. A detachment was at Mynpoory, 70 miles from Agra on the road to Cawnpore; the remainder at Etawah, 60 or 70 miles down the Jumna. Allygurh and Mynpoory are most important points, being the stations at which the line strikes off to Agra from the Central Trunk Road from Dehli and Cawnpore respectively. Anything going wrong there breaks up communications west and east.

9th Native Infantry gives way.

The solicitations from Dehli, and the temptation of joining the rebels rioting in their success there, proved too much for the fidelity of the Allygurh Regiment.

A spy was brought up by the Sepoys themselves, and was hung by a Court-Martial assembled by order of Government. He was a high Brahmin. The fact was made the most of by the disaffected. Excitement arose, and the men who had stood out for ten days mutinied. It was late in the evening. The officers hesitated too long to bring upon the Mutineers the Gwalior Horse, and it is doubtful whether they would have attacked them. It was resolved to retire on Hatrass, 20 miles on this side Allygurh. No lives were taken by the Sepoys.

Aligarh troops mutiny.

It is now admitted that they ought not to have retired so far. For the Sepoys, having plundered the Treasury, set off without delay for Dehli, and our officers and horse might at once have reoccupied Allygurh. We were now again cut off from Meerut by dak; and the telegraphic wire was irretrievably mangled.

Emissaries from Allygurh soon reached Mynpoory; and in a couple of days the same scene was enacted there, with this

Also those at Mainpúri.

Captain De Kantzow. Mr. Power, C.S. Rajah Bhewani Singh.

difference, that, mainly through the exertions of a young German officer, De Kantzow, a few Sepoys remained staunch, and the gallant Magistrate, Mr. Power, whose prowess cannot be too greatly applauded, continued firm at his post. He was aided by Bhewani Singh, a neighbouring Rajah, into whose fort they at first retired. They saved thc Treasure and the Jail. They long held their position, a mere handful of officers and men; they have since been recruited by Gwalior Horse. They have shown many feats of bravery, and repeatedly repulsed bodies of Mutineers.

Mutiny at Etawah. Mr. A. D. Hume, Magistrate.

The tidings of these events shortly reached Etawah. The Magistrate, Mr. Hume, strove to stay the mutiny by taking the men across the river, but was only partially successful. The residents were safe there; but the Sepoys rose, and committed the ordinary enormities in the station, and went off, excepting a very few. The Grenadier Regiment of the Gwalior Contingent arrived a day or two after these events, and has since remained there, so that security is restored.

Lieutenant Greathed leads the Aligarh column.

Another 8 or 10 days passed in expectation. The larger half of the Gwalior Horse at Hatrass, on the plea of not being supported, as promised, by artillery from Agra, mutinied and went off to Dehli. But a considerable party of Volunteers, officers and clerks—headed by Lieutenant Greathed of the Engineers—set out from this for Allygurh. Their primary object was to liberate an indigo planter near that place; but they have remained ever since in the vicinity, sometimes obliged to leave Allygurh by the stray bands of Mutineer Horse and Foot passing through to Dehli,—and have proved of the most essential service in keeping open the postal communications.

This letter brings us nearly down to the end of the month. In my next I hope to resume the thread of the narrative there.

DCCXXXIV.

To the Editor of the "Bombay Times."[1]

AGRA, *16th June.*

DEAR SIR,—I resume the statement of affairs at Agra commenced in my previous letter.

Mutinies throughout the country.

The few last days of May are crowded by important movements throughout the country. Mutinies occurred almost

[1] This letter appeared (under date of "Agra, 18th June") in *Bombay Times* of 3rd July 1857.—W. C.

simultaneously at distant quarters. In some places, as at Nusseerabad, Neemuch, Lucknow, and Rohilkhund, they were evidently the result of the successful example held out to them at Dehli, and of letters and emissaries from thence.

At Agra the crisis was brought on by another cause. A detachment from one of our Native Corps here guarded the Treasury at Muthra. A company of the 67th Native Infantry had been for some time performing this duty, and anxiety was felt in consequence of the temptation of six or seven lacs of rupees thus placed in their power. It was resolved, when the guard was next changed, to bring over to Agra a portion of the treasure under escort of the returning Company.

On Saturday the 30th of May the relieving Company of the 44th reached Muthra, and in the afternoon the treasure was ready to be brought back to Agra by the Sepoys of the 67th. Unexpectedly the two Companies combined and attacked their officers;—killing one (Lt. Burlton) and shooting at the others and at the Civilians who were present. The latter escaped to the camp of the Bhurtpore force, about 40 or 50 miles on the road to Dehli.

Native soldiery rise at Muttra.

Civilians escape to Bhurtpore.

The Sepoys with the treasure tumbrils took the same road.

Tidings of this mutiny reached Agra before midnight. It was soon determined that no confidence was to be reposed in those Regiments of which Companies had behaved in so treacherous and traitorous a manner. A parade was directed early next morning, Sunday the 31st, and it was resolved to disarm both the Native Corps.

We were fortunate in having the means for carrying this resolution into effect. In other stations without European troops the authorities are helpless and have been forced to maintain a show of reliance on the native soldiery even after doubts had grown into actual mistrust. But with our 3rd Europeans and our European Artillery the Native Corps dared not offer any resistance. The disarming was performed promptly and without resistance. But it was a season of anxiety, and all the European inhabitants were during that morning assembled at their various rendezvous. The native troops were double the number of the Europeans; and they must still be overawed in their lines.

Native troops disarmed at Agra.

Our large fort had been partly secured already by throwing into it, at an early stage of this eventful period, a Company of Europeans. Still, the Sepoy guard might have offered resistance.

Fort garrisoned by Europeans.

Another element of great apprehension was in our Central

Danger feared from Central Jail. Jail with its nearly 4000 prisoners. Much excitement prevailed amongst them, and it was suspected that efforts had been made to tamper with the strong guard of some 300 men which protects the prison. Any mishap here might have placed the whole station at the mercy of this vast concourse of the most daring and abandoned characters in the country.

A couple of guns and a small detachment of Europeans had been before stationed on a neighbouring eminence commanding the Jail. And all was thus kept quiet.

Dr. Walker's vigilance. Special credit is due to the Superintendent, Dr. Walker, for the incessant vigilance with which he has watched over his anxious charge.

City of Agra loyal. The City with its population of above 125,000 persons, though of course excited and apprehensive, remained perfectly tranquil and loyal throughout these events. Indeed, the alarm of the inhabitants was at what the Sepoys might do, and at the anarchy which would ensue if they should rise. A feeling of satisfaction and security pervaded the City immediately they were disarmed. The same feeling was strongly expressed by the Gwalior Durbar. (Good effects of the disarming.)

A few days after, as the plots of the Sepoy Regiments were seen to thicken, it was deemed prudent to desire all the men of the 44th and 67th to proceed to their homes. This they did without demur. And not a Sepoy now remained in or near Agra. (44th and 67th N.I. dismissed to their homes.)

In carrying out all arrangements relating to the city and district of Agra, the Honble. R. Drummond, our Magistrate and Collector, displayed an admirable combination of courage and judgment. In repressing by his front of confidence and authority the first risings of panic, in the unceasing vigilance with which he has provided for the watch and ward of the city, and for the ascertainment and for the checking of any spirit of disaffection, in the prompt raising of a police battalion, and in the putting down of all attempts at plunder and riot through the district, his efforts have been conspicuously successful, and entitle him to the thanks of the whole community. It is not too much to say that but for these efforts, wisely supported by the Lieutenant-Governor, consternation on the part of the European and Anglo-Indian community might have spread amongst the native population, and been productive of the worst results at times when our position was really critical. (Great services of Hon. R. Drummond.)

The mutiny of the two Companies at Muthra, by giving us a fair and sufficient occasion to disarm our Sepoys, may have been of real and essential service. It enabled us to anticipate evils which came suddenly and unpreparedly on other stations.

There was a report that on that very day they intended to rise on us while at church. It is remarkable that it was the same Sunday of the rising at Lucknow and Shahjehanpore.

Rumour of intended rising at Agra.

Our joy at the repeated and decisive success gained by the small Meerut force (which had moved out to Ghazeeooddeennugger, 10 miles on the Allygurh road from Dehli) on the 30th and 31st of May, over the Mutineers from Dehli, who attacked their position, was damped by the daily news of disaffection and mutiny on all sides.

On the same Sunday morning (the 31st) on which we disarmed our Sepoys the native troops rose at Lucknow, and a large portion of them, cavalry and infantry, was expelled from thence. They struck across the country towards Dehli, passed the Ganges, and joined the Grand Trunk Road near Canouj. They marched up that road line, threatening Mynpoory and Allygurh. They destroyed all our postal arrangements, and also the electric wire, and thus about the beginning of June completely cut off our communications with Cawnpore and Calcutta.

Native troops rise at Lucknow.

March of the Lucknow rebels.

Agra cut off from Cawnpore and Calcutta.

Shortly after, one of the corps of Oudh Irregular Cavalry, which had volunteered for duty against the Mutineers, and had been deputed to the Trunk Road between Cawnpore and Allygurh, itself mutinied and killed all its officers, including Captain Fletcher Hayes, Military Secretary to the Chief Commr. This produced a severe shock in Mynpoory and Furruckabad, and added to the bands of lawless soldiery now laying waste the Dooab. The district of Etah lying between Mynpoory and Allygurh was in consequence abandoned.

Captain Fletcher Hayes murdered.

Etah abandoned.

It is remarkable, notwithstanding, that the 10th Native Infantry at Furruckabad have stood loyal up to the present moment. Surrounded on all sides by disaffection and riot, they still guard the treasure and enforce order in the station of Furruckabad. It was at one time deserted by its civil and some of its military officers, who fled in a panic at an anticipated attack. Yet, contrary to all expectation, the 10th holds on.

Conspicuous loyalty of the 10th N.I. at Farakhabad.

During the first week of June rumours of the loss of Shahjehanpore came in, and they were soon confirmed by news of the arrival at Meerut of the civil officers from Moradabad. So far as can be gathered from native report (regarding Shahjehanpore and Bareilly, we have nothing else to go upon), the facts are these.

Shahjehanpore lost.

All the troops in Rohilkhund, consisting of Native Infantry, Artillery, and Irregular Cavalry, had, since the catastrophe at Meerut and Dehli, been in an excited state; but this had calmed down, and it was believed by the officers that they would continue quiet unless any party of Mutineers came upon them from without. Indeed, the 29th Native Infantry at Moradabad had shown some direct and active signs of loyalty in putting down revolt in some part of the district, pursuing a body of the Sappers and Miners who had escaped from Roorkee, and actually forcing them on pain of being fired on to surrender their arms.

29th Native Infantry.

Mutiny of 28th Native Infantry at Shahjehanpore.

At Shahjehanpore the 28th Native Infantry, without exhibiting any such loyalty, had so well concealed their murderous designs that their officers had confidence in them to the end. It was the morning of Sunday the 31st (the day of the disarming here), while some of the officers were at church, that the Regiment rose. An attack was made, and one officer at least shot in the church. Mr. Ricketts, the Magistrate and Collector, was assassinated either there or in his own house. Five officers are said to have been murdered. One escaped wounded, and with him another unhurt. Another account states that a party both of ladies and gentlemen escaped to Mohumdee, an adjacent station in Oudh, but were attacked there also.

Mr. Ricketts, C.S., murdered, and other officers.

The Treasury was plundered and the Jail broken. The Government Dispensary and public offices were burned. The insurgents made off for Bareilly.

Rising at Bareilly.

Of the rising at Bareilly we have but meagre information. The ladies had previously proceeded to Naini Tal. It is probable that, if not already concerted with the Shahjehanpore troops, the revolt did not take place until their arrival at Bareilly. It is said that the officers were conducted in safety by the troops to a distance from the station; that the Magistrate and Collector escaped, and that the Commissioner was wounded. But the names of several of the civil officers are given as murdered.

Mutiny of 29th N.I.

In consequence of these events, and of emissaries from the Mutineer regiments, the 29th followed their example. Having before sworn to defend their officers, they conducted them safely to Naini Tal. The civil officers got off to Meerut (after a narrow escape from the wrath of the Sepoys, who found less treasure than they expected), and gave us intelligence of these proceedings.

The Civil officers of Bareilly escape to Meerut.

The Mutineer troops concentrated at Bareilly are said to have set up a sort of Government there, headed by an old Sudder Ameen, chief of the Hafiz Rehmut family. They sent a detachment to Budaon, which pillaged the Treasury and forced the

Magistrate and Collector to take refuge on this side the Ganges. It is not known whether they have attacked Bijnore. That the rebel troops have stayed in Rohilkhund is a fortunate circumstance. They will find plenty of employment in the local dissensions of the province until, please God, we are at leisure to call them to account for their treacherous and bloody deeds.

No out-station in these parts (excepting Furruckabad) has now escaped. **Mutiny general in N.W.P.**

We became at this time entirely exposed towards Dehli on the right bank of the Jumna, as we had been on the left until the Meerut troops marched out to the Hindun. For our famous Bhurtpore Horse, with the troops of the Ulwur Durbar, proved **Alwar.** unequal to oppose the two Companies of Mutineers from Muthra on their way to Dehli! They either actually sided with them, or showed in so significant a manner their unwillingness to fight for us, that our officers, Civil and Military, about 30 in number, quitted the camp and took refuge with a neighbouring well-affected Ressaldar. The force broke up and returned to Bhurtpore and Ulwur, leaving all anarchy again in the districts of Muthra and Goorgaon. **Anarchy in Muttra and Gurgaon.**

The Treasury and buildings, public and private, at Boolundshuhur were plundered, and the booty carried off to Dehli. **Bulandshahr plundered.** Rohtuck was also plundered by a detachment sent by the Mutineers **Also Rohtak.** from Dehli. About the beginning of the month emissaries were sent to Hissar (between Dehli and Sirsa), who raised the troops **Outbreak at Hissar,** there, murdered (it is said) every European, and carried off the treasure to Dehli. These exploits, however dastardly and inhuman, are reported to have raised the spirits of the Mutineers within Dehli after their discomfiture at Ghazeeooddeennugger.

The Bengal Infantry and Artillery, which had mutinied at Nusseerabad, took the road to Jeypore. **at Nusseerabad,** It was for some time doubtful whether Agra or Dehli was their object. At last they diverged to Dehli.

We were not surprised at Neemuch going, as the 72nd left **Neemuch,** this station a few months ago in a very disaffected state. But in its mutiny the troops of the Gwalior Contingent went also,—an **of the Gwalior Contingent.** unfortunate precedent!

To encourage us amongst these daily reports of revolt and disaffection, despatches came to us from the Headquarters of the Army, giving us most satisfactory accounts as to the Dehli force, which, though painfully late, was now positively advancing in a high state of efficiency, and promised to be before Dehli by the end of the first week of June. It was also becoming evident

Object of the Mutineers only Delhi and plunder.

Revolted regiments becoming demoralised.

that the mutinous Sepoys had as yet no common object but Dehli and plunder. The exception at Bareilly of a local government was encouraging rather than otherwise. Besides, deprived of their officers, the revolted regiments were everywhere becoming demoralised, and wherever met in action had proved unequal to any steady attack, if not positively weak and cowardly. We began to see, or to think that we saw, the elements of our strength, under God's good providence, in their scattered condition, and the objectless character of their movements.

The serious mutinies to the eastward I reserve for my next letter.

DCCXXXV.

Letter from W. Muir, C.S., to the Editor, "Bombay Times."

(*Draft Letter.*)

Fort Agra, *7th July* 1857.

Dear Sir,—I recommence my task of communicating the state of affairs at Agra, which I brought down, I think, to the mutiny at Gwalior.

The whole Gwalior Contingent, after some delay (which it is difficult to account for and was of great benefit to us), followed the example of the Regiments at Nusseerabad.

Nusseerabad troops join the rebels at Delhi.

The Nusseerabad Corps marched with its artillery right across Rajpootana and joined the rebels about the middle of June. They were engaged in the great fight before the walls on 23rd, and one of their regiments is said to have been almost entirely cut up on that occasion.

Neemuch troops march on Agra,

The Neemuch troops, namely, the 72nd N.I. Indore, a Gwalior Contingent Regiment, and troop of 6 guns, left their Cantonment with the expressed determination of proceeding to Agra. This resolution they continued to give out by the way, as we know by various official reports forwarded to us. The 72nd, who had only a few weeks before reached Neemuch from Agra, vaunted much that they knew the Fort, and could take it in a few hours.

via Tank and Deoli.

They came by Tonk and tried, but not successfully, to pick up some of the Forces of that petty State; then they reached Deolee, the Cantonment of the Kotah Contingent, where they got two guns of the Contingent and some of the troops. They came

Halt at Biana.

on by Hindun and halted at Biana 2 or 3 days. Some Subadar of note died there, and they performed the funeral obsequies with great state. Up to this time it continued uncertain what route they would take. They had communications with Bhurtpore, but seem to have been discountenanced in that quarter.[1]

. . . .

DCCXXXVI.

From W. Muir, C.S., to Sir Henry Lawrence, Chief Commissioner of Oudh, Lucknow.

(*Draft Letter.*)

Fort Agra, *Monday, 6th July* 1857.

My Dear Sir Henry,[2]—The Neemuch Mutineers have at last come upon Agra, and forced us to take refuge in the Fort. They halted for a few days at Biana, and it was for some time uncertain whether they were not going to Dehli. On, however, they came, and by the 1st inst. were at Futtehpore Sicri. We had, besides our Europeans (650) and Artillery, 200 or 300 Volunteers, foot and horse, the Kotah Contingent troops from Ulwur, and a party of Kerowlee Horse and Foot levied by Sayfoolla Khan. On Saturday (the 4th), the Mutineers being reported half-way from Futtehpore Sicri, an advance was ordered in the early part of the night. The Kotah Contingent marched out of the Station in accordance with these arrangements in the afternoon, and at its first halt mutinied, firing at its officers and killing a sergeant. Our Volunteers, who were picketed near, seized and brought back their guns and ammunition, and pursued the Corps, cutting up a few.

Neemuch Mutineers come to Fattehpur Sikri, and advance towards Agra.

Kotah Contingent mutinies.

In the morning our Kerowlee Horse left (but by permission, and after having performed much good service in the district), and we heard nothing more of the Ulwur Contingent. So we had nothing but our European Foot and Artillery and the Volunteers to fall back upon.

Kerauli Horse leaves.

On Sunday forenoon our pickets came in saying the enemy had come within three miles of the Station. About midday we advanced: the action began between 2 and 3, and lasted above two hours. The Mutineers had taken up a strong position at the village of Putroulie.

We were driving them before us when our ammunition

Action at Agra.

[1] The rest of this letter is quoted at page 7 *et seq.* of vol. i.

[2] Sir Henry had died at Lucknow on 4th July, four days before this letter was written, of a wound received on 2nd. See No. IX., p. 67, vol. i.—W. C.

failed, and a slow retreat was ordered. The retrograde movement was executed with all the coolness and steadiness of a parade, and the troops reached the Fort in the most excellent order. One, if not two tumbrils were exploded by the enemy's shot, and we were obliged to abandon one of our guns, the carriage of which was blown up by the accident. The Mutineer Artillery was excellently served. Poor D'Oyley is badly wounded by a grape shot through the bowels,—I fear fatally. Lamb of the Artillery also badly wounded, and will lose his leg. Young Oldfield, the Assistant Secretary, was dangerously wounded in the chest while making a gallant cavalry charge with the Volunteers. Williams of the 72nd also lost his leg. The night passed off quietly.

Troops retire on Fort.

D'Oyley, Lamb, R.A., Oldfield, C.S., Williams, 72nd, wounded.

To-day it is given out that an attack is contemplated on the Fort, but we are all ready for them. As far as we know, they have little more than 6-pounders. The weight of the two guns they got at Deolie we do not know. Some think they had 9-pounders in the battle, but report says their ammunition is done. They could get more from Bhurtpore without much delay.

We are greatly crippled by having no regular Cavalry.

The Militia did well, but they are raw and few. 200 or 300 Carabineers would probably have changed the face of yesterday's action. Even now they would make us tolerably independent.

As it is, we are virtually in a state of siege, and must, I fear, remain so till aid reaches us.

Agra besieged.

Press forward the advance from Cawnpore. The prestige of the Empire is sadly affected by the seat of Government being reduced to these straits.

Buildings in flames.

We have *no* footing out of the Fort at present. Bungalows and public buildings are in flames all around. They began with H. S. Reid's Normal School! We could see the savage Sowars cantering round the flaming building.

Bodies of Mutineers in the districts round.

We broke the Pontoon bridge on Sunday morning on the opposite side. There are bodies of Mutineers, Horse and Foot Artillery, in the Allygurh, Mynpory, and Etawah districts. Pearson's battery of 9-pounders is either hovering about in the Allygurh road or gone to Dehli. Raikes' and Alexander's mutinous troops of Gwalior Horse are also over the river. The regiments at Gwalior are said to be, by the last intelligence, a little way out of Gwalior on the Agra road. The Chumbul, however, has risen, and there would be difficulty in crossing heavy artillery even if Scindia wished. There was a native report that a regiment of Sepoys is marching up the right bank of the Jumna, but it wants corroboration.

But we must expect, after our retreat into the Fort, to be the object of concentrated attack, and it is the more necessary that we should have the earliest possible relief.

Mr. Colvin has, I regret to say, been for the last two days totally unfitted for any public business by an attack of his head. He is better, but still forbidden to attend to any State matters whatever. The loss, however, is felt the less just at present, as our councils must for a time be almost purely military. I trust that the arrival of reinforcements has entirely relieved your own apprehensions for Lucknow as well as Cawnpore; but we have no particulars yet, except that European Foot and Artillery were at Allahabad some time ago. **Mr. Colvin indisposed.**

Monday evening, 6th July.—No attack to-day. Report says that the enemy, having had a notion given them of our Europeans' fighting, have gone off to Furrah and Dehli, not relishing an attack under our Fort guns. I should have thought they would have hung about, a nucleus of disaffection; but if they have gone, so much the better.

Tuesday morning, 7th July.—Another quiet night. No signs of the enemy about.

From later information it would seem that the enemy is beyond Pithoulee, and intend staying there. This sounds likely; and they will form a nucleus for Gwalior and other Mutineer troops. It is therefore of essential importance that we should have early relief.[1] **Enemy at Pithauli.**

DCCXXXVII.

From W. Muir, Esq., to H. H. Greathed, C.S., Dehli.

Agra, *6th September* 1857.

Mr. Colvin is suffering, I am sorry to say, from an attack of dysentery, and I doubt whether he will be writing to-day. I therefore send a few lines regarding the movements of our Indore friends. Our information from various sources is that no Contingent Regt. has joined them. They consist of the 23rd, say 800 strong; some 150 reg. Cavry.; quatre cents Holkar's Infy.; and quatre cents of his Cavry.; a thousand Ghazees *et id genus*; seven guns, but artillerymen superior in numbers and discipline, **Indore Mutineers. Details of Mutineers.**

[1] This is a draft letter, partly in Mrs. (Lady) Muir's handwriting and partly in Mr. (Sir William) Muir's. It is unsigned in the draft.—W. C.

and small store of ammunition. Some 5 or 10 men from each of the Contingent Regiments had deserted to join this expedition. They halted on the 2nd at the Residency, and appear to have intended to halt there 2 or 3 days with the view of seducing the Contingent. But on the 3rd they got a letter from Dholepore saying that whoever came first, the British or they, would secure this Ghat and the Fort. The Nawab (from Bhopal) immediately ordered off three or four companies, two troops, and two guns, which proceeded accordingly, and crossed over on the evening of the 4th. The main body marched on the 3rd halfway to the Chumbul, and are probably crossing now. They will not be able to get all over till the 8th, and on the 8th or 9th talk of marching this way. They talk of getting heavy guns at Dholepore. They may pick up a few. They say their object is Agra, but unless they get some heavy artillery they cannot do us any sensible harm, though they will unsettle the District and alarm the City. We trust operations will be so accelerated at Dehli that they will find themselves checkmated by Genl. Wilson's force. Colonel Cotton will not suffer them to come near Agra without attacking them. The detachment at Hattrass will not be withdrawn till the last safe moment.

(Signed) W. Muir, Secy. to Govt., N.W.P.

They have also a Shahzada. They suspect his genuineness.

DCCXXXVIII.

W. Muir to H. H. Greathed.

Agra, *7th September* 1857.

Movements of Indore rebels.

To-day's report as to the Indore is little more than confirmatory of yesterday's. It is certain that an advanced guard of 2 or 3 Companies, some Cavalry, and two guns crossed on Friday afternoon, taking possession of the Kentree Ghat and the Dholepore Fort. The main body marched from the Residency on Friday and reached the opposite bank of the Chumbul yesterday. They are probably crossing to-day. Some say they are going to Dehli, others to Agra. Only a few volunteers or deserters from each of the Contingent Regiments have joined them. They will probably wait a day or two at Dholepore to see if any more will come. . . . .

I have a letter from Tucker of the 26th from Benares;
Outram and Mr. Grant expected there the next day. Outram's **General Outram.**
idea of a direct advance on Lucknow through Jaunpore had been **J. P. Grant,**
abandoned, and all available troops were now being pressed **C.S.**
upwards with the greatest despatch. The 5th and 90th were
being moved upwards. Havelock was again beginning to receive
reinforcements. 200 Highlanders were to reach Cawnpore,
Sherer writes on the 1st. The Nana had come back from Luck- **The Nana.**
now dispirited. They would have nothing to say to him. He
went to Jursa Singh's fort at Futtehpore Chowrassee, but Jursa **Jarsa Singh.**
Singh is dead, and his sons are said to be cool towards their
guest, and to wish themselves well rid of him. Nasir Ali is all
right. Ghazeepore, Tucker says, is going on beautifully, revenue **Ghazipur.**
all collected, and the district rather better than usual. Benares **Benares.**
quiet. A very strong fort has been built, armed, and partially
provisioned at Rajghat. Most of the ladies had left, but Tucker's
wife and daughter were still with him. Mirzapore going on **Mirzápur.**
beautifully under St. George Tucker, who has great credit for the **St. George Tucker.**
brave manner in which he has acted all through. He tried to
intercept the Dinapore Mutineers 20 miles from Mirzapore, but **Dinapur Mutineers.**
he only killed 4,—they ran off so fast towards Khyroghur, where
they were stopped by the Tonse. They have, however, crossed
that river. Chunar has been strengthened and fully provisioned. **Chunar.**
Jaunpore totally disorganised by bands from Oudh too strong for **Jaunpore.**
our people. After the Goorkhas left Goruckpore the station was **Gorakhpore.**
held for a while by young Bird, but "finally abandoned."
Azimghur is now kept quiet by the Goorkhas, and our officers **Azimgarh.**
are resuming their duties there. Our Hattrass party all right,
but we shall probably be obliged to recall it, as we must go out
and fight those Indore fellows if they come anywhere near. The
sooner your grand finale comes off, you see, the better for
numberless most weighty interests. I am sorry to say Mr.
Colvin's dysentery continues and is assuming a more threatening **Mr. Colvin.**
aspect. We begin to get very anxious about him. Anson's of the
2nd with yours of 3rd received,—thanks for both. Your brother's
to Mr. Colvin also came to hand. I will see about his writer.
We are very anxious about Lucknow. God grant reinforcements **Lucknow.**
may now arrive in time, and that Havelock may have a speedy
advance. It is a thousand pities the troops were ever diverted
from the direct course.

W. M.

DCCXXXIX.

FROM W. MUIR, ESQ., TO H. H. GREATHED, ESQ.

AGRA, 9*th September*.

Mr. Colvin's death.

MY previous letter will have prepared you for the intelligence of Mr. Colvin's death. He sank gradually, and expired quite peacefully at 4½ this afternoon.

E. A. Reade, C.S.

Reade is conducting the administration, as Senior Civilian, pending the Governor-General's orders. I am sure that this great loss will be deeply felt by you, both in your public and private capacity. I can bring myself to add little more in this letter.

Indore troops.

The Indore troops crossed over quatre Companies and deux guns more on Monday. They are probably all on this side the Chumbul by this time. We are not yet fully certain of their intentions. They may either come this way, march yours, or stay for a time at Dholepore. Letter from Cawnpore up to the 4th. Outram to march that day or next from Allahabad with above 1300 troops, so that an advance will now be made speedily on Lucknow. The garrison was holding on bravely, acting, indeed, on the offensive. It had sprung a mine against the enemy, made a sally, spiked a gun, and killed many of them,—so that we may hope for news now of its relief, say within the next fortnight.

Lucknow.

(Signed) W. MUIR, Secy. to Govt., N.W.P.

DCCXLI.

FROM W. MUIR, C.S., TO CECIL BEADON, C.S., CALCUTTA.

AGRA, 17*th Sept*. 1857.

MY DEAR BEADON,—

. . . .

Death of Mr. Colvin.

The death of Mr. Colvin has made a sad change in our state here. We had looked to his comprehensive and vigorous mind and large administrative faculties to guide us successfully through the multitude of difficult questions that will attend the reintroduction of our rule into these provinces. But this may not be.

Things are going on steadily under Mr. Reade's judicious

management. The truth, however, is that just at present there is little for the Civil power at Agra to do. The fall of Dehli, tidings of which may now be daily looked for, will rapidly open the country, and set at liberty the troops necessary for the restoration of order and Civil Government throughout the Doab. The Dehli, Meerut, and Agra Divisions will first fall into order. Rohilkhund must follow the chances of the military proceedings, which may be complicated by the movements from Gwalior. If the rebels from Dehli retire in force on Rohilkhund, the operations there may be prolonged. The rebels there may possibly make a stand, in co-operation with those in the jungles of Oudh. Otherwise, the moment a small column is at liberty to go in that direction, our authority could be at once re-established throughout the Division.

Prospects for the re-establishment of Civil power.

It is not, however, of much use yet speculating on operations that will mainly depend on the course the fugitives may take from Dehli. In Bundelkhund there will, I fear, under any circumstances, be a protracted campaign; so many forts and strongholds abound there, and chieftains with wild marauding clans about them. Has the question been entertained at all of a general disarming of our population on the restoration of order? It has many advocates here; and the success of the system in the Punjab is a strong argument in its favour. Such a measure will prove the more useful now, because, for a time at least, the troops for securing internal tranquillity and suppressing affrays, petty disturbances, etc., will be scarce. Europeans can hardly be afforded for such work; and it will take some time to supply the vacuum caused by the collapse of the Sepoy army. The system of disarming would, no doubt, greatly aid the police, and lend to the restoration of peace and quiet. In all future internal political movements it would also give the military arm a more complete hold of the country. On the other hand, it would render the people, where well affected, less able to resist the aggression of Usurpers or Invaders. But this, even under the present system, they have seldom had the mind or ability to do.

Bundelkhund.

Disarming the people.

The main difficulty in enforcing the plan would be found in the districts on the right bank of the Jumna. In the Doab and North of the Ganges the whole territory is ours. But south of the Jumna we have a foreign frontier, and our villages are intermixed with those of other States. The idea could not be entertained of rendering these villages liable to attacks from their armed neighbours, which they, having been disarmed, would

Difficulty in disarming south of the Jumna.

be unable to repel. If we, for example, disarm the villagers of Muthra and Agra, those on the frontier of Bhurtpore, Dholepore, and Gwalior must equally be disarmed. Should we be justified in insisting that the villagers in those Native States, say within a distance of 5 miles from our frontier, should be disarmed? We could certainly, I think, not ask more than something of that kind. It would be too great an interference with the internal administration of the States to proceed further; and, what is of even greater moment, it would deprive the subjects of such States of the check which they now have against misrule, and of their chief means of resisting oppression and exaction. Even limited to the tracts north of the Jumna, the disarming would be productive of an immensely sedative and quieting effect. Is there any likelihood of its being attempted?

Prospects for Civil administration.

Has anything been said or settled about the future machinery of Administration in these provinces? The effect of Mr. Colvin's illness was to make him take a desponding view, both of our present position and of our future prospects. He could not see how the Government was to be carried on against so many and various adverse interests. I never would admit his premises. The rebellion has originated in a military discontent, not in the least in any popular discontent. That the anarchy, consequent on so widespread a mutiny, should have dragged into the whirlpool all the restless spirits of the land—all who had hopes of making anything of the opportunity—was a natural and necessary result. That the proclamation of the King of Dehli's reign should unsettle the allegiance of the Moslems was to be expected from the singularly close combination of the political and religious elements in the system of Islam. But the mutiny once crushed, and the crown of Dehli dashed to the ground, both causes of opposition will cease. It may take some little time for the waves of rebellion that now run so high completely to subside; but I do not see reason for doubting that, almost immediately our military supremacy is restored, a calm will ensue; things will speedily return into their old established channels, and the administration be as easily conducted as before. We shall find no lack of natives of both persuasions, for offices of trust, who will be perfectly faithful to us.

The rebellion military, and not a rebellion of the people.

Difficulties ahead; unsettled state of property; destruction of records.

But there will be at first some serious difficulties, mainly from the violent and unlawful unsettlement of things and transfer of property during these disturbances, and also from the general destruction of the Record of Rights, etc., from which the previously existing status of property could have been otherwise discovered. The extent to which the violent usurpation of property of all kinds has taken place will, I fear, be found in all quarters of these Provinces prodigiously great. During the absence of Government each man helped himself according to his own strength and the weakness of his neighbour. People sought to enforce old claims, to revive ancient feuds, and to re-enter on properties from which they had been legally dispossessed. The seller has ousted the man who fairly purchased his lands, the mortgager his mortgagee, the old proprietor the auction purchasers of their estate; and, even where there existed no claim or quarrel whatever, the times afforded great temptation to the powerful to seize on the rights of the helpless. To restore things to the status of May or June last, or of a period anterior to the outbreak, in any district of disturbances (except where such status has been altered by natural succession, or by voluntary and lawful act of the proprietors), will, I presume, be the principle on which all such cases will be adjusted. But this will take immense time and labour to carry out, and will probably require the undivided energies of a single officer within a moderate tract for some period.

As illustrative of the amount of work these proceedings will involve, I subjoin the extract of a letter from Cocks, now at Hatrass, regarding the state of things in Allygurh. "The great bulk of cases which we shall eventually have to try and dispose of are of dispossession by former zemindars of present holders of estates. I have petitions from auction purchasers, and such like, by hundreds, even in the well-disposed Pergunnahs of Hatrass and Sassnee: what will be the number elsewhere? We shall in many instances have to resort to harsh measures to give back possession. It will be a labour of years." Allygurh was less likely to suffer in this way than other districts. We managed long to maintain a half-hold of the District; and in Hatrass and some other adjoining parts our Tehseel and Thannah offices have *uninterruptedly* held office and to some extent enforced their authority. In other districts in which the rebellion has raged unchecked for many months, the revulsion and unsettlement must have been much greater. I take it for granted that the Government will hold itself bound to restore to possession all who have been wrongly and violently ousted. For example, the Government has given a good title to an auction purchaser, and the old proprietor turns him out. The purchaser should be able on summary complaint to obtain a summary order

Civil authority in Aligarh during rebellion.

for reinstatement. And the same summary remedy should be afforded to all who have suffered violent ejectment. Will it be not advisable to have a separate Commission for this work? as well as for the reconstruction of the Record of Rights? or Settlement Papers showing the status of proprietary and cultivating occupancy with its incidents, where that has been destroyed?

Proposed Commission.

Punjab system proposed.

And until, at any rate, some degree of system has been reintroduced, would it not be advisable to have these Provinces under the Punjab plan of Government—every branch of the Administration being superintended by the one controlling head of the district? This would greatly strengthen his hands. A separate machinery for the disposal of Civil causes can hereafter be reintroduced (only it should be more simple, rapid, and inexpensive than the old). But, for a couple of years at least, it does seem very advisable to unite the whole authority in the hands of the Magistrate and Collector.

Local Battalions.

Has any proposal been yet entertained for the organisation of local Battalions? How would it do to have a corps of from 300 to 500 Nujeebs and 50 to 100 horse in each district—the Headquarters, with a reserve, being at the Commissioner's station—the men being periodically shifted? Small detachments would probably be required at the most troublesome Tehseelies, for a time at least. The European Officers on district command might be required to fit themselves for usefully assisting the Magistrate and Collector in the Civil Administration.

Detective Police.

The detective police should be distinct from the Battalion. It was a mistake in Lord Ellenborough's system, making the Tomandars, Havildars, etc., also Police Officers, in suppression of the ordinary police. Their training and qualifications did not in the least suit them for the duty. The system failed eminently in Bundelkhund. The Thannahdars, etc., with a small police and detective establishment will still be required.

There would be European Artillery needed to a small extent at the Headquarters; for I conclude that arms will henceforth be exclusively European. A force of this kind would amply supply all the ordinary wants of the country—suppression of outrage, carriage of treasure, and enforcement of order.

Treasure will, I suppose, never be allowed to accumulate in large quantities in the out-stations, but be constantly remitted from thence to the Central Treasuries, which should always be under European Guard, and be available at convenient points over the country.

Reade has asked me to take exclusive charge of the Intelligence Department, and it occupies nearly all my time. (I have not much to do, as you may imagine, in my capacity of Member of the Sudder Board.) The hearing the statements of messengers and informers from various quarters, maintaining correspondence daily with Dehli and Cawnpore, and keeping up the record of intelligence so obtained (which I undertook to do at Mr. Colvin's request soon after we came into the Fort), employs almost my whole day.

Intelligence Department.

Then one conducts business in the Fort under considerable difficulty. A single room was assigned to us (with our 5 children and proportionate complement of Dyes and Ayahs), as bedroom, dining-room, drawing-room, and nursery. The Cudbert Thornhills have a still smaller adjoining room; so we curtained off a portion of ours as a mess-room for us all. When there is anything to be done in writing or business and our room is occupied for one of its various purposes, one is obliged to migrate from room to room seeking an empty corner in a friend's. We have *no* office rooms of any kind.

How business was carried on in the Fort.

I trust Lord Canning will not disapprove the manner in which intelligence is now made known. It had long been felt that the partial and scanty communication of news made the public anxious and suspicious; and the vacuum was filled up by all sorts of unfounded and alarming rumours. Everything of importance affecting our position is now published (and, as far as possible, in the words in which received), if there be no military or private reason for holding it back, or if it is not likely to create unnecessary or injurious panic. The effect is also good on the native mind. Many of course do not believe our news, but many do. It supports our well-wishers, and the leaven spreads through society.

Publication of intelligence.

I fear Lord Canning must have felt harassed by the frequency and urgency of the solicitations we used to make for the more prompt advance of troops in this direction. The position of affairs below was not at the time fully appreciated. It is now quite understood that every nerve was strained by the Governor-General, and everything done that could have been done to push on men.

Calls from Agra for aid.

. . . .

Has the point ever been mooted whether the damage done *by the people* in the late outrages could with justice and propriety be recovered from the offending district, pergunnah, or town? It is reported here that, when the Loodiana Mission was plundered, Lawrence assessed the damage done upon the inhabitants. Where the evils have been committed, not by Mutineer or other troops, but by the people themselves, the punishment would appear to be a fitting one, and would certainly go some way to vindicate the prestige which has been sadly hurt by the scene, long before the eyes of the people, of scattered doors, lintels and furniture, books, boxes, papers, and even Government records (the débris of which latter are still strewed about the roads near our offices). The difficulty would be to make the burden fall upon the proper shoulders. Here, for example, there is no doubt that the burning and plundering was the work of a portion of the community. A few Sowars of the Neemuch force rode about inciting them and leading the way by setting fire to some of the houses. But, excepting this commencement, the excesses were exclusively committed by the restless, low, and fanatic part of the inhabitants. To punish these to any extent would be a right thing to do. But the measure I speak of could not discriminate the guilty; it must include the whole population within specified limits—like a fine on a county or borough for losses occasioned by a riot. A property tax would assess the most respectable most severely, and those who had least hand in the business, though they may not have used as they ought their influence and restraining power.

Assessment of loss caused by Mutineers. *Destruction of property.* *Burning and plundering at Agra.*

A poll or house tax might answer, but would be a very insignificant penalty for the really guilty. The Mewatties, butchers, and [*paper torn*] were the main offenders; but you cannot introduce a *class* punishment. Altogether I like the principle, though I do not see clearly the way of carrying it into effect.

Losses heavy.

The most grievous sufferers have been widows and other helpless persons, whose only capital consisted of one or more houses. Poor people, their sole source of income has suddenly stopped. Of the larger holders, Reade, Raikes, and myself are the chief sufferers. My house alone was worth above 20,000 Rs. I bought it from Sir H. Elliot. But our losses don't so much signify

Fall of Delhi anticipated.

The mind of the public here is on the extremest stretch, waiting for news of the fall of Dehli. You will, please God, hear of it before this reaches you, by electric telegraph. How nobly our brave soldiers and officers have behaved! The result proves the wisdom of those who held back till the proper moment. The very instant Wilson had a sufficient force and sufficient artillery he set to work.

. . . .

Cocks is getting on famously at Allygurh and Hatrass with a [mere handful ?] of men, proving that the *country*, rural as well as urban, is *not* against us. **A. Cocks, C.S.** **Country not against us.**

Kindly lay any points of interest I have mentioned before Lord Canning at any fitting time.

I began this on the 17th, but from other occupation and interruptions only finish it to-day, the 22nd.

W. MUIR.

DCCXLII.

FROM W. MUIR, C.S., TO H. HARINGTON, C.S., CALCUTTA.

AGRA, *30th November* 1857.

MY DEAR HARINGTON,—

. . . .

I am glad to say that Colonel Fraser, at Reade's suggestion, has invested Williams with the authority to investigate the conduct of all our police, revenue, and other functionaries and establishments. He is, as you know, eminently fitted for ferreting out the actual circumstances of the second week of July, and he has the advantage of coming amongst us without the strong bias which almost every one has acquired one way or the other. **Major Williams to investigate conduct of officials.**

. . . .

Fraser has also, I think, judiciously issued, or is going to issue, an order, fixing for all who have absented themselves a period of 40 days within which to come in, on pain of immediate dismissal from their posts. I am afraid, however, that the cause of the alarm was, with some at least of the officials, the course pursued in certain cases.[1] The execution of Ameer Khan, which I before alluded to, will, whether it was a right or wrong act, have this unfortunate tendency. **Officials summoned to their posts.**

. . . .

It is notorious that the present troubles have broken up families into the most opposite lines of conduct. Wilson and Williams both can testify that they have worked with confidence

[1] The wording of the MSS. copy is here defective ; the words given here probably convey the sense intended.—W. C.

with men on our side whose nearest relatives have been with the enemy. It is not so much for Mohbeen's own sake I regret his being placed in confinement; Fraser will, I feel confident, take care that no harm comes to him without just cause. It is the effect on those without. It will, I much fear, unduly alarm men, such as the Principal Sudder Ameen and others who have expressed their desire to come in, and whose presence, besides other reasons, is exceedingly desirable for the full and complete investigation Major Williams has in hand; Major Williams feels this much himself. His proceedings are otherwise all *ex parte*. I greatly regret, for the interests of calm justice (which, besides being right, is evidently the most expedient course for the future success of the administration), that you are not here.

. . . .

H. Cocks, C.S., at Aligarh.

The principles on which Cocks is proceeding at Allygurh are the true ones for the just and successful administration of the country at this juncture. His object is to show the people "that we can distinguish between the good and the bad; and that, although we do not fear to seize and punish any one, we are still open to reason and consider each man's circumstances, whether he could or could not help himself." I wish we had fifty Cockses. It is so rare to find men combining, as he does, justice, moderation, and energy.

. . . .

Friend of India.

The *Friend of India* has impugned the proceedings at Dehli, and seems to think that this Government is responsible. It would be well that it should be known that ever since Mr. Colvin's death the administration of the Dehli Division has been conducted exclusively under the orders of Sir John Lawrence.

Sir John Lawrence's orders for trial of King of Delhi.

Yesterday Saunders sent a copy of the orders, under Sir John Lawrence's instructions, for bringing the King of Dehli to trial, that course "having been considered desirable, as well for the satisfaction of Government as for that of the public." The Court is not to pass any decision if it finds the King guilty, as his life is guaranteed. The Court is to consist of "a Military Commission." I regret much that the mixed Commission, originally nominated by the Supreme Government, was not reverted to. Unless the Military Commission is carefully selected, there is great hazard of its being composed of men unused to sift and weigh evidence. The same Commission is to try the Nawabs of Jhujjur, Dadree, and Furrookhnugger, and the Rajah of Bullubgurh, on the charge of "complicity in the late

Nawabs of Jhujjur, Dadree, and Furrookhnugger, Rajah of Balabgarh.

rebellion," with authority, in their case, to pass sentence on conviction. Colonel Harriott, Deputy Judge Advocate-General, is to conduct the prosecution.

. . . .

The stories regarding the manner of the King's confinement are, I understand, quite unfounded. Indeed, from H. S. Reid's accounts, I should rather think that the wretched old man was sometimes the object of decided disrespect from the visitors. **Manner of the King's confinement.**

Dr. Farquhar and Lowe have just gone to Dehli to see for themselves the state of things there. Farquhar, as you know, is a genuine philanthropist, though he has no sympathy for mutineers and traitors. The object of this visit is simply to see whether the reports of the misery of the unsuspected portion of the population, who are said to be in extreme distress, many of them without shelter, persons brought up in comfort and seclusion dying of exposure and cold, etc., are exaggerated or not. **Dr. Farquhar and W. Lowe, C.S., go to Delhi.** Dr. Anderson, the Professor of Moral Philosophy, spent some days in Dehli, and saw a great deal of the better affected classes amongst the Hindoo Students, whom he was before acquainted with while lecturing at Dehli a few months before the outbreak. The impression his statements give, confirms the hardships of our well-wishers. I will let you know the result of Farquhar's observations. **Dr. Anderson.**

. . . .

We are anxious for news of the successful evacuation of Lucknow. Our last from Cawnpore is of the 24th, they had not had a line from Lucknow later than the 19th, and apparently were not aware of the resolution to withdraw. I conclude that the silence was intended to keep them in the dark, as the enemy would no doubt have availed himself of the chance of annoying us if the secret got abroad. We only knew of it by a letter from Sir J. Outram to Lady Outram. The retirement will be a difficult operation, and the effect upon the country of the Lucknow movement will be *serious* if a *prompt advance* be not made upwards. The first measure will, of course, be to crush the Contingent. The next, I trust, to attack the rebels at Furruckabad, and to occupy that post and Mynpoorie. That will re-establish our name; but, if it be not speedily done, the withdrawal from Lucknow, misrepresented by our ill-wishers into a reverse and expulsion, will dangerously unsettle us again to the North-West. I trust, however, that the Commander-in-Chief will display such activity, the moment he has returned to Cawnpore, as to neutralise the ill effects of the movement.

Oude abandoned will have one advantage—of drawing off the rebels and disaffected from all quarters, and giving them a place to stay in quietly for a time till we have leisure to attack them.

. . . .

W. MUIR.

DCCXLIII.

AGRA, 16*th Dec.* 1857.

MY DEAR HARINGTON,—

. . . .

I hope my letter, with draft of a bill for restoration of possession to the status existing prior to the rebellion, reached you; Fraser directed that it should be sent to the Supreme Government with his concurrence.

. . . .

General disarming recommended.

I trust the Government of India will direct a general disarming of the population throughout these provinces. Such a favourable opportunity, with a reason which the people will themselves appreciate or understand, will not occur again. The present disarming Act seems intended for limited tracts and to be temporary. Provisions of more universal applicability and more stringent penalties are needed.

Whole country to north-west quiet.

It is wonderful how quiet the whole country has become to the North-West, with the handful of troops here and there, and the opposite bank of the Ganges bristling with insurgents—daks as regular as before the outbreak—revenue in general punctually realised. Allygurh has been a little unsettled, but far less than we expected, by the advance of the Furruckabad rebels within 35 or 40 miles. It is one of the many providences which we have had to mark with gratitude that Colonel Seaton's force was able to advance on Gangeree at the very time that the enemy, apparently in ignorance of its presence, was moving on Colonel Farquhar's little band of 500 or 600 men and two guns. Wullee Dad was with or near the force, and any further inaction on our part would no doubt have made him move onwards to his old haunts in Boolundshuhur and again thrown us into confusion.

Revenue realised.

Farakhabad rebels.

Colonel Seaton.

Wali Dad.

For above a fortnight we had no news from Cawnpore, and became very anxious. Up to this moment we have nothing later from Sherer than his letters of the 25th ultimo and the 4th inst.; but a private letter has confirmed the news which I had already ventured upon native report to publish of the discomfiture of the Contingent on the 7th inst. What the Commander-in-Chief is now doing, or what he proposes to do, we cannot learn; and this prevents our co-operating, which we might otherwise be doing with Seaton's Column and our own troops, which could be escorting the carriage and supplies which have so long been waiting here.

The Raikeses left yesterday to go by the Punjaub. The Unwins who had been going the same way have been detained.

. . . .

Williams has been getting on well with his investigations; many of his results are satisfactory. There seems no evidence, but the reverse, of any invitation on the part of our officials to the Neemuch army, though when they drew close to Agra, a day or two before the fight, there is reason to suspect two or three of the Police Officers entering into communication with their emissaries. The enquiries have hitherto tended to clear —— and ——. —— and others are, however, gravely implicated. **Major Williams.** **Conduct of officials.**

. . . .

It will be an enormous work replacing our last record. The great loss is of the village plans. We must set the Putwarrees hard at work again. **Loss of records.**

Farquhar and Lowe spent a week at Dehli. They found a mass of misery and disease in the multitudes who have taken up their temporary residence in such places as the Kootub, Nizamooddeen's Tomb, etc. The practical results I have communicated privately to Sir John Lawrence. Farquhar strongly urges that the artificers of the Hindoo classes should be readmitted into the city at once. It is the poorer classes who are suffering the most intensely. The richer can procure comfort of some sort, but those of a lower grade are destitute of shelter, clothes, and often of food. The Prize Agency still goes on ransacking the houses for plunder. Officers take "tickets" for so many days' hunting, and all quarters are exposed which have not been ransacked. The principle has been laid down that the jurisdiction of the Agency does not extend to real property, but a ransom is required to secure the houses from further search. They have, however, been so thoroughly ransacked that the people are now not disposed to pay much for the ransom. And it would be well if the Agency proceedings in this respect were stopped, for, apart from their effect on the people, they are, Farquhar is convinced from what he saw, very disorganising to the morale of the officers,—and that will **Dr. Farquhar's report at Delhi.** **Treasure hunting at Delhi.** **Search of houses.**

extend, only in a stronger form, to the soldiery. But I must stop. I have written all this to Sir J. Lawrence. Mrs. Harington, as you will have learned, left this on Saturday last for the Punjaub on to Calcutta. I wish she had waited till the direct road was open. We are looking anxiously for tidings from you.—Yours affectionately,

W. Muir.

---

2. LETTERS FROM SIR JOHN LAWRENCE, CHIEF COMMISSIONER OF THE PUNJAB.

DCCXLIV.

Lahore, *5th August* 1857.

Sir John deprecates retreat from Delhi, and promises support.

My Dear Sir,—I saw a note from Mr. Colvin deprecating the retreat of the Army from Dehli, and asking what reinforcements I was sending. I quite concur in Mr. Colvin's views—I consider that defeat and ruin would follow a retreat. I have sent, and shall send, every soldier we can spare. But, though the country is friendly, we have a long border to guard, and, above all, upwards of 20,000 Hindostani Soldiers to guard. The majority of these men are desperate. We have lately sent off large reinforcements. Between the date of Mr. Colvin's letter and the 15th of August I trust that full 3000 troops will reach Dehli, probably 1200 more shortly after. I am not sure, however, that these will suffice to enable an army to storm. It is possible that we shall have to wait until Havelock arrives. I am not sure that this officer will be able to get up to Dehli soon. It is possible that he may be detained by the state of Lucknow; or not have the force necessary for such an advance.

Native army in Punjab.

Unless it be necessary to go round by Agra and Muttra in consequence of the bridges over the Hindun being broken, or for any other good reason, I should say that Havelock would do well to march straight up the Doab, and take up a position at Shahderah, opposite to the Palace, so as to make the attack from that side. His advance up the Doab would do much good.

We are very quiet in the Punjaub, and have got the Poorbiah and Hindostani troops well under our control. We have destroyed 4 Regiments of N.I. and dismissed the greater part of the rest. But none of them are to be trusted. If you can

Four regiments destroyed.

hear any authentic news from Lucknow, kindly send me word. Send my brother also a copy of this letter.[1]

I am raising Cavalry for service down below. Good horsemen, however, are not to be made in a day.—Yours sincerely,

JOHN LAWRENCE.

W. MUIR, ESQ., Agra.

DCCXLV.

LAHORE, *6th August* 1857.

MY DEAR SIR,—I heard last night of the death of my poor brother Henry. It will be a grievous blow to his family, and all of us, and a real calamity to Government. I do not know a man in India who, at this juncture, might not have been better spared. But the ways of the Almighty are inscrutable. **Death of Sir Henry Lawrence.**

I hope General Havelock will be able to remain in Oude and reduce it to order, especially if Sir Patrick Grant is coming up.

I think it would be well if intelligent military men were selected to raise levies of horse and foot in the North-West. I write to you on this subject, because I hear Mr. Colvin is ill. During the next two months a body of Mawatees, Bundeelas, Rajpoots, and Juts might be raised, who would prove very useful, and afford great aid during the ensuing cold weather to our European soldiers. These might gradually be increased as reinforcements arrive from England. Cavalry in particular will be greatly required. I have already raised 10 new Regiments of Punjaub Infantry, and am still going on. I send all my old Regiments down to Dehli, so far as I can spare them, and hold the country with the new ones. We have raised a large body of horse, but these are not of much value except in their own locality—I am now beginning to raise better horsemen, and as I succeed shall pay up and discharge a good many of the Levies. By retaining them in our pay, we keep the country quiet, and they serve to overawe the disarmed Poorbeeah Regiments. If Mr. Colvin is equal to any business, kindly show him this note. I hope to send a large Contingent of Maharaja Goolab Sing's down in a few days to Dehli.—Yours, etc. **Suggestions for raising levies in North-West.** **Sir John raises 10 regiments of infantry.** **Sends all his old regiments down to Delhi.** **Raising cavalry.**

(Signed) J. LAWRENCE.

To W. MUIR, ESQ., Agra.

[1] Sir Henry Lawrence had died in the besieged Residency at Lucknow on the 4th July, or about a month before this letter was written. See next letter.—W. C.

My Dear Sir,[1]—This is copy of a letter I sent you yesterday, *via* Meerut. We are all well here.—Yours sincerely,

John Lawrence.

W. Muir, Esq., Agra.

DCCXLVI.

From Sir J. Lawrence, Chief Commissioner, Punjab, to H. H. Greathed, C.S. Commr., Dehli.

Lahore, *7th September* 1857.

You quite take me aback when you ask me for a Police Battalion and 500 Police Horse. If you give me three months, I have little doubt but that I shall be able to supply them, but at once I could not do so. These Levies would be of little use. The Corps of Infantry must be well selected, and well put together, or they will disgrace me and do you no good. We have a great many mounted Levies; the majority, however, are the followers of border Chiefs, without discipline, order, or habits of obedience. Such men would give more trouble than they are worth.

Sir John's proposals as to furnishing levies.

I wish you had told me, six weeks ago, what you required. I could pick up a couple of hundred old Sikhs, dismounted horsemen, if you could manage to mount them. This is the way I have supplied Williams. The Dehli Territory used formerly to have plenty of horses and mares; I should hardly think you would fail to get animals,—while you were doing this, I could collect more. I would also call for Volunteers from the flower of the Mounted Levies whom I considered fit for the work; could in this way supply 300 horsemen,—even this would, however, take time.

When Dehli falls, I would suggest that you call on the heads of all the respectable villages to furnish men for policemen. The Jat, Aheer, and other Hindoo villages could supply plenty of men, for which each village should be responsible. The men would be a little awkward at first, but this would soon wear off. I think in this way you would be able to manage.

I will set to work at once and call for Volunteers from among the Mounted Levies, and in the meantime do you let me know if you can mount any number of Sowars I may send you.

[1] Appended in Lord Lawrence's writing to the foregoing letter, which is a copy. The despatch of a copy was for safety's sake in those troublous times.—W. C.

I think, on reflection, that Nicholson would be a better man for the pursuit than for Dehli. If Government want to follow and cut up the insurgents, he has not his equal in the force. Unless the pursuit be conducted with vigour and promptitude, the insurgents will get breathing time, rally, and collect again.—Yours sincerely,

Nicholson recommended for command of pursuing column.

(Signed) J. LAWRENCE.

DCCXLVII.

COPY OF TELEGRAPHIC MESSAGE FROM SIR JOHN LAWRENCE TO C. B. SAUNDERS, ESQRE., AND GENERAL WILSON. DATED LAHORE, *20th Septr.*

I AM sorry to hear of Mr. Greathed's death. I think it is an excellent arrangement that Mr. Saunders should officiate as Commissioner. If General Wilson considers that I can be of use in the present emergency, I am willing to carry on the administration of the Dehli territory through you as Commissioner, subject to the wishes of Mr. Reade and the orders of the Supreme Govt. My sole object in this proposal is to facilitate the public service. I shall be happy at any moment to resign the duty.

Sir John offers to administer Delhi.

DCCXLVIII.

LAHORE, *4th Oct.* 1857.

MY DEAR MR. MUIR,—I forgot to ask you about a matter of some importance. You know how well the Maharajah of Putialah and Rajah of Jhind have obeyed.

Loyalty of Patiáli and Jhind.

. . . .

The Maharajah of Putialah wants to send down 500 men or so, to help to put Dholpore in order. I told the vakil that I would write and ascertain the state of affairs at Dholpore, and enquire whether Colonel Fraser was agreeable to this measure before I could say anything. Perhaps you will kindly let me have the necessary information.—Yours sincerely,

JOHN LAWRENCE.

W. MUIR, ESQ.

DCCXLIX.

LAHORE, 10*th October* 1857.

Sir John assumes charge of the Delhi Division.

MY DEAR FRASER,—At General Wilson's request, I had taken on myself to look after the Dehli Division. We had previously to the fall of the city reconquered Hissar, Hansi, and Sirsah, and occupied Rohtuck just afterwards. I will do whatever you like, viz., go on managing it, pending the orders of Government for which I applied at the time, or make it all over to you. We have an Irregular Force of about 2500 under General Van Cortlandt in Rohtuck and Hissar. I can look after the Division without much difficulty, having served some thirteen years in it, but I have no wish to interfere unless you desire it.

We are all well in the Punjaub, thank God; but Dehli did not fall a day too soon.—Yours sincerely,

JOHN LAWRENCE.

COLONEL FRASER, C.B.,
Chief Commissioner, Agra.

P.S.—Please send your answer through Mr. Saunders, and let him know your wishes. J. L.

DCCL.

CAMP, GUJERANWALLAH (40 miles from LAHORE).

11*th November* 1857.

Rajah of Mundee.

MY DEAR MR. MUIR,—The little Rajah of Mundee is alive and well. If he died, no one could be placed in his position, without our officers knowing. I have told the Maharajah of Putialah that he can send troops to Dholpore.

Police.

I quite agree with you, that a Superintendent of Cantonment Police cannot effectively look after the work between Dinapoor and Peshawar. What I intended to explain was merely that I did not find that an Inspector of Police Battalions answered.

Cantonment Police.

As regards Cantonments, I think that Government should take the opportunity of the present vacancy, and the late revolution, to place the police in our Cantonment on a totally different footing. We should have a very strict police system introduced, which should be carefully and judiciously enforced by a Superintendent of considerable ability and administrative talent. Our Cantonments have too often been very "Alsatias," the refuge of criminals. The Cantonment Magistrates were not under proper control. They had little or no training, and did pretty much as they liked. Between the Brigadier and Commissioner they were virtually independent. . . . was in many respects a good man, and did something to improve the system. But he had not the knowledge, nor the ability, and indeed not the power, to place matters on a proper footing. I would allow no native to live in Cantonments who had no employment or was not a good character, and would enforce a strict system of surveillance. Look at the Sudder Bazaars of Meerut and Cawnpore; they were sinks of iniquity, and most of the atrocities perpetrated during the late convulsion were committed by their inhabitants.

Sir John's opinion as to Cantonment administration.

Sudder Bazaars.

We are all feeling anxious for news from Lucknow. Our disturbance in Gogaira is coming to an end.

Gogaira.

What is the force which the Insurgents have at Futtehgurh? Could not Meerut and Agra combine their available means for an onslaught on these wretches?—Yours very sincerely,

JOHN LAWRENCE.

WM. MUIR, ESQ.

DCCLI.

LAHORE, 30*th Nov.* 1857.

MY DEAR MR. MUIR,—I was taken quite by surprise at your news that we are to give up Oude for the present. It seems to me doubtful policy. We shall certainly lose prestige by the move, but we may gain in power. And, if this be the case, it would probably be judicious; on the other hand, it will delay for a long period the punishment of all these rascally Mutineers. On the whole, if after a careful consideration it is admitted that we have the means of holding on at Lucknow, I should be for doing so, even if we only held that place and the surrounding country.

Sir John's views on vacating Oude.

If we have not the means of subduing our own Mufsids and reoccupying the country in strength, it will be best to leave Lucknow for another year.

I enclose a note for my nephew G. L.; will you kindly send it to some civilian at Cawnpore to forward on? We have never had a line from him since the beginning of the outbreak.

I wrote off some notes on M. for Williams' police paper, which I gave to Arnold[1] to put together. This he did, but is now making a few additions at my suggestion. I hope to despatch it two days hence. My idea is that the military organised police should be left quite separate from the detective force, and be no larger than is absolutely necessary. The one should be under military men, few in number but carefully selected; the other, entirely under the Magistrates.—Yours sincerely,

Sir John advocates separation of detective and military police.

(Signed) JOHN LAWRENCE.

WM. MUIR, ESQ.

DCCLII.

LAHORE, 15*th Dec.* 1857.

MY DEAR MR. MUIR,—By all means, open any letters which come for me from the Commander-in-Chief or any other person, when you want information.

. . . .

I have addressed the Supreme Government officially, and the Governor-General individually, several times about the prize agents and their doings, but I can get no response. I have written also several times to General Penny, but he will not interfere authoritatively. I wrote to him also, both officially and privately, in Ramchunder's case. The fact is, that when a man has power he is attended to, and even when on the spot he may influence people; but, when neither possessed of power nor present, he can do little. I quite believe all that Farquhar says, for I know him to be a trustworthy fellow.

Prize agents.

Ramchunder.

Dr. T. Farquhar.

I marched this morning for Multan, where I hope to be early next month to see my wife off. I shall then return to Lahore.—Yours sincerely,

JOHN LAWRENCE.

WM. MUIR, ESQ.

[1] W. Arnold, son of Dr. Arnold of Rugby, the first Director of Public Instruction, Punjab.—W. C.

3. FROM UMBALLA.

DCCLIII.

FROM G. BARNES, C.S. COMMISSIONER, UMBALLA,
TO C. THORNHILL, C.S., AGRA.

UMBALLA, 26*th* (*May* or *June*).

MY DEAR THORNHILL,—Will you please tell Mr. Colvin that we are unable to send any Puteealah Horse to Meerut. But I have sent the Raja of Jheend and an Asst.-Comr., Capt. M'Andrew, to Paneeput with orders to feel his way down as close to Dehli as he safely can. The Comdr.-in-Chief will not move onwards without his siege train, which I am getting up from Philour with police and political escorts.

I have sent some Hindostanee troops to Spankie's aid at Saharanpore. He is a gallant and active Magte

. . . .

I suggested to Le Bas to send an Asst. to Mozuffernugger, and the C.-in-Chief gave me a body of 85 Hansee Horse to accompany him. Mr. Richards has been sent, as the district is utterly disorganised. The 5th L.I. here has behaved very badly, and through weakness has not been punished. All is quiet here and in the Punjab. Our Cis-Sutlej Chiefs behave with great spirit and loyalty.

G. Campbell is at Kussowlee. Have you any message for him?

---

4. FROM ROHTUK.

DCCLV.

FROM W. FORD, C.S.

CAMP ROHTUCK, 30*th Sept.* 1857.

General Van Cortlandt. Biwanee illuminated.

MY DEAR SIR,[1]—General Van Cortlandt and his force arrived here on the 26th after having visited Biwanee, which was illuminated on the occasion. Since my arrival here I have

[1] This letter is quoted in a fragmentary way in No. CXLIII., p. 183, vol. i., but, as giving an account of a Civil officer's efforts to re-establish order in a District soon after the fall of Dehli, it is given here in full.—W. C.

Re-establishment of Civil government. re-established the Tehseels and Thanahs, and laid the dak to Dehli. I have also hung thirteen highway robbers who were taken with arms in their (hands) and attempted to escape, firing on our Sowars. The large villages have tendered their sub- Revenue collections. mission, and my collections are going on very well indeed. The roads are now opening for travellers. In addition to this I have assumed the office of Offg. Customs Commissioner, and am Customs line. laying down the line, which will soon be completed to Rohtuck. Several of the officers have joined. I had intended to have proceeded from this to Dehli to assume charge of the Goorgaon District, but Sir John has ordered me back to Hansie, to again Mr. Ricketts. take charge of that District until relieved by Mr. Ricketts, whose Colonel Clarke. place will be supplied by Col. Clarke, who is now on his way from Kurrachee. This will retard my arrival in the Goorgaon District, of which Mr. Clifford, my Assistant, could assume charge Rao Toolaram in arms. after Rao Toolaram, who is in arms against our Govt., has been put down. It would also be necessary for any one taking charge of the District to be supported by a Military Force, since the Meos are troublesome. Meos of the District are likely to give a good deal of trouble. It is very important that the high road through Pulwul and Hodul should be kept open. This part of the country is now pretty quiet, but it will require a Military Force for some time Disloyalty of Mahommedan population. to keep the people down, the Mahommedan population having been particularly opposed to us. Trusting that matters are prospering at Agra.

---

5. FROM HISSAR.

[*This series of three letters, descriptive of the unsettled condition of the District a fortnight after the outbreak at Meerut, and the surprise of the residents at Hissar, has a special and melancholy interest. The writer, his wife, and other residents were killed shortly after the date of these letters. A monument to their memory stands at Hissar.*]

DCCLVI.

FROM JOHN WEDDERBURN, B.C.S., OFFG. MAGTE., HISSAR,
TO THE SECY. TO GOVT., N.W.P., AGRA.

HISSAR, *Friday*, 22nd *May*.

SIR,—I continue my journal, tho' from what Bindrabun the Inspector of Post Offices reports from Bhewani, there seems little probability of its due receipt at Agra. He says that the zemindars of the Coy.'s Territory thro' which the dak was laid are so hostile that he was forced to change the line from Rewari in Goorgaon, and send the dak round by Seekur and Jyepoor. I hope this route may continue open. I have received nothing in reply up to this date, so all is uncertainty. My dak of camels will run a poor chance; as yet I have received nothing from the Lahore side to forward. I have got in safely all the money at the Tehseels, about which the Tehseeldars were in great alarm. I believe the Police and Tehseel Establishments are great alarmists, and that at the bottom the popular feeling is not very unfriendly. No doubt, if these Establishments have been oppressive, they are now in just fear of being paid off. Mr. Hallet of the Customs, who went to Hansi last night and returned this morning, reports that the zemindars on this road were civil enough, having heard of the report of the recapture of Dehli. Disturbed state of Hissar District.

Owing to reports that the Hansi and Kurnal and the Hansi and Bhewani dak was threatened and obstructed by the zemindars, I have sent a few of my slender force of Sowars to keep the line open. I hear that the communication down country from Umballah is open and that all is quiet, but this bears date some days back. Up to this time, 2 p.m. of the 22nd, we have no authentic confirmation of the recapture of Dehli, tho' it is generally believed. It strikes me that at this time a suspension of the regulations and plenary powers conferred on Magistrates would have a good effect. Captn. Robertson tells me he is raising 500 or 600 Matchlockmen to keep his District quiet.

4½ P.M.—No further news yet from the side of Dehli. I fear the report of its recapture was premature. There is a general feeling that the roads are unsafe and that robberies are going on, tho' only a few trifling cases have been reported. Possibly the sufferers, not expecting redress at this time, do not complain; but we shall hear them loud enough when peace shall be restored. Some zemindars of the frontier towns towards Bikaneer say that they hear that the Minas, Sheikhawaties, Salchelies, and other predatory tribes are preparing for incursions into this territory, which is very likely. I expect to hear of them every day. Hansi, Hissar, and Futtehabad are secured, I hope, but many places must be open to their attacks. I have been grossly misled about the facility of raising a body of Cavalry; we have not got 40 yet. The dak (police) from Rulten (?) is still interrupted; the Sowars sent to enquire have not returned.

DCCLVII.

FROM SAME TO SAME.

HISSAR, *Saturday, 23rd May.*

Alarm at Hansi.

SIR,—This morning I hear from Hansi that they are in great alarm there, owing to the report of the Mutineers of the 45th N.I. from Ferozepore being somewhere about the country. The Thanadar seems to have acted like an idiot, and quite contrary to his instructions in the way of communicating with the people. The intelligence was directed to be quietly communicated to the villagers, but that Dogberry seems to have beat a tom-tom in the town, and frightened the Bunyahs out of their wits: such is the inconvenience of the Sudder Station being at the smaller of these two large towns, and the Cantonment at the other; this has been a source of the greatest embarrassment from the beginning, and I hope the arrangement may be amended when matters are straight again. I have written to the Tehseeldar, and am sending over the Dy. Collr. to restore confidence.

9 A.M.—Just received despatches from Sirsah containing a Circular of the Judl. Comr. of the Punjab announcing all quiet there throughout the country, but very anxious for news from Agra, and asking if the double dak is ready. I shall send a pilot letter to-day or to-morrow to see if the camels are at their posts, but I much fear that, owing to the rumoured disorganisation of the Goorgaon District, the camels will not be left at peace in Riwaree and Nageena any more than the dak runners; meanwhile I shall forward any Punjab despatches by Bindrabun's dak *via* Seeker and Jyepore.

They say the communication by dak and telegraph is open down country from Umballah and Meerut even to Calcutta, but are without news from Agra. Further, that the Mutineers, after plundering Dehli, have moved off towards Muttra; we have not heard this direct from the Dehli side yet. Mr. Loch of Rohtuk holds no communication with us, tho' he might forward valuable intelligence. I have written twice to him, but got no reply yet. I don't know what he is doing, but he has stuck to his post like a man.

Reports of security in the Punjab.

Lieut. Elphinstone, Dy. Commr. of Gogaira, writes that the Govt. is well centralised in the Punjab; daily district reports are sent direct to the Judl. Comr., and daily circulars are compiled in his office of the general state of the country and distributed to the Districts; the disarming at Meean Meer has had the best effect, and the villagers are aiding in the arrest of deserters. Disarming at Meean Meer, salutary effects of.

HISSAR, *23rd May.*

P.S.—The roads are unsafe now for small parties of one or two, and the Bunyahs are all in panic; at Futtehabad a Pensioner Nawab did good service in securing the town. No news from Dehli, but the native reports continue to say it is in possession of the English.

DCCLVIII.

FROM SAME TO SAME.

HISSAR, *Tuesday, 26th May.*

SIR,—The police reports are now full of cases of petty plundering on the roads, and even on a larger scale, one village driving off a number of cattle belonging to another village, and so on. In some of these the robbers have been seized, and the police hold their own pretty well, but in others they are obliged to content themselves with recording, and taking proofs of the cases for future consideration. No confirmation of the state of things in Rohtuk yet, but the dak is stopped; we are consulting about a reconnaissance in force with our horsemen in that direction. Post towards Rohtak stopped. I am advancing money for the use of the new levies under Mr. Barwell. Nothing has reached me from Agra yet; there is a capital dak from Lahore *via* Gogaira, Fazilka, Sirsa to this, and I have to-day laid eight camels on the road to Kurnal,—thus we Post open to Lahore. shall have a double line there, and the Bhewani-Seekur one besides; it is to be hoped all will not fail; letters for the Lieut.-Govr., Agra, and Mr. Secy. Edmonstone, Calcutta, were forwarded from the Punjab by to-day's dak *via* Kurnal; a second heavy despatch went by Rhewary. The C.-in-C. has ordered the 57th N.I. and remnant of the 45th to be turned out of Ferozepore without a fraction of pay; they will increase the plunderers in our rear, even if they don't come down in a body.

It is now a fortnight since we heard of the outbreak, and a dreadful one of suspense it has been; we look for brighter tidings soon. There certainly has been something wrong at Rohtuk, tho' by whom or to what extent still uncertain.

6. FROM DEHLI.

DCCLIX.

FROM H. H. GREATHED, C.S., AGENT TO LT.-GOVERNOR, WITH DEHLI FIELD FORCE, TO W. MUIR, C.S.

CAMP BEFORE DEHLI, 13*th July* 1857.

Neemuch Mutineers had applied to the King for siege guns.

MY DEAR MUIR,—Your letter of the 7th brought me the intelligence of the ravages committed at Agra by the Neemuch Mutineers. I had hoped this disaster would be averted, for I knew that the Mutineers had applied to the King for siege guns and Sappers and Miners, and that they had been refused, but the treachery of the Kotah Contingent must have decided them to attack. I lament the loss of such an excellent officer as D'Oyly, and few are more warmly regretted; and the loss of property is very much to be deplored; but these misfortunes will not affect the issue of the contest. Our honour has not been compromised, and the Fort and Magazine are safe.

Loss of D'Oyly, R.A.

Neemuch Mutineers at Muttra.

The messengers who brought your letter inform us that they saw the Mutineers at Muttra, so that there can be no doubt that we shall make their acquaintance before long. We hear that the 17th is fixed for their next attack, and suppose that it is arranged the Neemuch Mutineers shall take the lead in it. The last was on the 9th, and the Pandies were severely punished. Our defences have since been much improved, and I trust that greater loss will be inflicted, with fewer casualties on our side.

The Honble. J. R. Colvin.

Mr. Colvin's illness is a source of much anxiety to all who know him. At present the services of Civilians are of small account in their ordinary capacities, but the time for reorganisation is not very far off, and we should look to Mr. Colvin then.

Assault must be deferred.

I believe the time for the surprise and assault of Dehli with our present Force is gone by; at least the Pandies must break their heads and spirit against our position and weaken their strength before the project will be renewed. A chance was lost on the 12th June, which it has seemed impossible to recover. The troops have been engaged in a most arduous contest, and have carried it on with an admirable spirit. The Goorkhas, Guides, and Seikh Regts. fight nobly. These regiments have been purged of their Poorbeeas, and Renny's Troop of H.A. were relieved of their guns yesterday. The men will be employed in the Batteries with Europeans. The Hindoostanee Irrgr. Cavalry are nearly all out of Camp. Brig.-General Chamberlain will

Hindustani Sepoys.

reply to the application for reinforcements; as the work of mischief has been accomplished, and the Fort is beyond the means of any force, it may be anticipated you will be left alone. The movement of the Gwalior Contingent is still a subject of anxiety on your account as well as our own. We shall have large numbers opposed to us; it seems possible their supply of caps may fall short. The appointment of Williams to the Meerut Commrshp. is still a mystery to me. I am not certain whether he will insist on assuming my functions. It will quite alter my position.

F. Williams, C.S.

DCCLX.

From Same to Same.

Camp before Dehli, *16th July* 1857.

My Dear Muir,—

. . . .

Gwalior Force.

The attitude of the Gwalior Force leaves us in anxiety about Agra; we know the Neemuch and Kotah men were seen at Muttra, and suppose they are coming here, but they have not yet arrived; but once within the vortex of Dehli they are not likely to retrace their steps. It is useless for me to say anything about reinforcements, profitless to revert to what might have been done in the first days of our occupation of the Ridge; I gave my deliberate opinion that the assault should be made, and I believe Genl. Barnard determined in favour of the project solely on political grounds. I can only say now that we are not in the same relative position we were then, and that the question has to be viewed in a different light. The Mutineers are now nearly in the full pride of their strength; they have for upwards of five weeks been vainly endeavouring to drive us from our position; their aim and object is to do this. They know as well as we do that strong reinforcements are on their way up country, and that, if they cannot destroy this force within a certain time, their cause is up. They have missed their aim in regard to the arsenals, and their only chance is to destroy the force in the field. As long as we hold our own until the Calcutta troops arrive, our game is sure; consequently an attack on Dehli or the reduction of our means of defence would be to incur a risk which the situation of affairs does not justify. It is needless to say how gratifying it would be on every ground to contribute to the safety of the Fort of Agra and its inmates; the question is whether the risk to which you are exposed from

Question of early assault of Delhi.

Mutineers in full pride of strength.

Attack on Delhi not then justifiable.

Question of relief of Agra.

the Gwalior Force justifies the risk of the existence of this Force which is keeping at bay all the other Mutineers in the country. The Jhansee men have reached Dehli; they came by Allyguhr. The 46th N.I. and 9th Cavalry mutinied at Sealkote a short time ago; 300 of the former have been destroyed by the moveable column, and as all the boats in the Punjab rivers are now at our own posts, it is unlikely any will reach this. The 50th have been disarmed, the 14th nearly all destroyed, the 33rd, 35th, and 59th and 10th Cavalry have been also disarmed. At present there are only 3 Pandy Regts. in the Punjab. "Pandy" is no slang term; it has become the generic name of the Bengal Sepoy; and Pandyism expresses in one word the indescribable spirit that actuates them. There was an attack in full force on our right on the 14th. They passed the whole day in fruitless efforts to penetrate our lines, and were beginning to retire in disgust, having caused but few casualtics, when at 4 p.m. a column under direction of Brig.-Genl. Chamberlain advanced to their attack. They fled in confusion to the City, pursued by our people; but too far, for they came under grape from the City walls. Chamberlain had his arm broken, et a peu pres deux cent furent blessés. Monsr. le Genl. Read a la fievre. Nous manquons de Generaux, mais les troupes se comporterent toujours bien, et il ny'a pas de crainte.

Jhansee men reach Delhi. Mutiny at Sealkote. Disarming only three Hindustani regiments in the Punjab. Pandy and Pandyism. An attack on camp. Chamberlain's arm broken.

. . . .

Sir John Lawrence is exerting himself to supply the army with funds, and has sent a lac to Mussoorie. Intelligence of Sir Hugh Wheeler's movements is the all-important object. Our loss in killed on the 14th was fifteen; the minor casualties were from spent grape, but the loss is large. General Read leaves to-morrow. Brig. Wilson will be placed in command. The arrangement inspires confidence.

Sir John Lawrence. Anxiety about Cawnpore. Brigadier Wilson takes command.

[*Most of this is in "Agra Bulletin" of* 21/9/57, *p.* 13, *vol. ix., Series Twelfth.*]

DCCLXIV.

From Same to Same.

Dehli, 15*th Sept.* 1857.

My Dear Muir,—My letter yesterday announcing the triumphant entry of our troops into Dehli was addressed to poor Mr. Colvin. Shortly after sending off my despatch I had yours of the 8th, and your letter of the 9th has confirmed all the fears it excited. I think with deep regret of the ruin that has overtaken our Civil administration, and now of the loss of the Ruler who had done so much to invigorate it. It is impossible to recall one unkindly thought towards Mr. Colvin. Pray offer my condolements to his son Elliott. **Colvin's death.**

. . . .

The column that entered the city yesterday consisted of 2000 European and 2000 Native soldiers; the casualties amount to a peu pres six cent cinquante. Les pertes parmi les Officiers sont tres graves. Neuf Officiers du Genie, huit du huitieme Regt., neuf du premier Fusiliers. On compte quarante Officiers morts ou blessés. Des telles pertes decouragent les soldats. Le plus grand malheur est la blessure du Genl. Nicholson. Il echappera peut être a la mort, mais il y'a grand danger. **Composition of assault column.** **Casualties.**

My brother Welby is doing well; the radius of the right forearm is broken, and the same bullet cut him across the chest. This occurred as he was advancing to the breach. **Welby Greathed wounded.**

The killed or mortally wounded among the Officers are—

Fitzgerald	75th.	Tandy	Engineers.
Bradshaw	52nd.	Jacob	1st Fusiliers.
Murray	Guides.	M'Barnett	55th N.I.
Rosser	Carabineers.	Davidson	26th N.I.

This is the correct list. Trente-neuf furent blessés.

DCCLXV.

List of Officers Wounded on the 14th Septr. 1857 at Dehli.

Staff	Brig. Nicholson; Capt. Anson, A.D.C.
Engineers	Lts. Greathed, Salkeld, Maunsell, Home, Pemberton, Medley.
Artillery	Lts. Lindsay, Elliott.
Cavry.	Lt. Cuppage.
8th Foot	Major Brooke, Major Baines; Lts. Pogson, Stebbings.
52nd Foot	Col. Campbell, Capt. Bailey, Capt. Atkinson.
60th Foot	Lts. Curtis and Waters.
61st Foot	Col. Deacon.
75th Foot	Col. Herbert (slightly); Lt. Armstrong.
1st Fusiliers	Capt. Greville; Lts. Wemyss, Owen, Lambert, Speke, Caulfield (3rd N.I.), Graydon (last 3 doing duty).
2nd Fusiliers	Captain Hay (60th N.I.), doing duty; Lt. Elderton.
Sirmore Batt.	Major Reid; Capt. Boisragon.
1st Punjab Infantry	Lts. Nicholson, Gambier (38th N.I.), Gustavinski.

Kishengunj has been evacuated. The enemy left 4 heavy guns and mortars, which are being brought into Camp

DCCLXVI.

Return of Ordnance Captured in Dehli.

Magazine.

5 32-Pr. Guns.
4 24- „
25 18- „
1 12- „
5 4- „
11 3- „
3 10-Inch Howitzers.
5 8- „ „
1 10- „ Mortar.
2 8- „ „
—
64

8 68-Pr. Carronades.
38 24- „ „
40 18- „ „
5 9- „ Brass Guns.
—
91

Unserviceable.

3 24-Prs.
2 18- „
1 10-Inch Howrs.
—
6

Cashmere Bastion.

1 24-Pr.
2 18- „
1 12- „
1 6- „
2 10-Inch Howrs.
2 10- „ Mortars.
4 8- „ „
—
13

Water Bastion.

2 24-Prs.
2 18- „
2 8-Inch Mortars.
1 5½- „ „
1 6-Pr. Brass Gun.
1 3- „ „
—
9

Moree Bastion.

2 24-Prs.
2 18- „
1 12- „
1 10-Inch Howr.
1 10- „ Mortar.
1 8- „ „
1 6-Pr. Brass Gun.
—
9

Round Tower.

1 12-Pr.

Gateway between Moree and Cabul B(astion).

1 12-Pr.

3-Gun Battery.

1 18-Pr.
1 12- „
1 24- „ Howr.
—
3

Cabul Gate.

1 12-Pr. Gun.

Kissengunj.

4 18-Prs.
1 10-Inch Mortar.
—
5

Total.

Magazine . . .	161
Cashmere Bastion . .	13
Water Bastion . .	9
Moree Bastion . .	9
Round Tower . .	1
Gateways . . .	2
3-Gun Battery . .	3
Kissengunj . . .	5
Total . .	203

DCCLXX.

FROM LT.-COL. KEITH YOUNG[1] TO CAPTAIN EDEN, JYEPORE.

DEHLI HD. QRS., SKINNER'S HOUSE,
15th Sept. 1857.

MY DEAR CAPT. EDEN,—You will be delighted to hear that we are at last within the walls of Dehli. The assault took place yesterday morning soon after daybreak, and the storming was entirely successful, and we were soon in possession of all this end of the fort, with the Cashmere, Cabul, and Moree Gates, which we now hold; with the Church, College, and other large buildings near this one in which Headqrs. are. The attack yesterday was in three columns, with a reserve column, and another strong column under Reid of the Goorkhas was to have cleared out the suburbs of Kishengunge and march into the City by the Lahore Gate; but this movement was unfortunately an entire failure. . . . .
Had it not been for this contretemps we should in all probability have been in entire possession of the city, as the enemy were all ready for a bolt; but their success outside gave them heart to hold on at the Lahore Gate, and Reid being unable to advance as was intended, our other columns were unable to push on so far as was intended; and it was perhaps just as well that it was so, as the part of the city we now hold is very compact, and preparations for heavy batteries to knock the Mutineers out of those parts of the city in which they now are; this we hope to be able to do, with very little loss of life to ourselves, in 3 or 4 days.

There has been no message from the King as yet that I am aware of, but many of the city people have come in to ask for quarter, which has been given them; but Sepoys who wanted to come in have not been permitted. Our casualties yesterday, I am sorry to say, were very heavy—not less, I fear, than 600 kd. and wdd.: amongst the former I have heard the names of 5 officers—Tandy, Engrs.; (no Artillery Offr. kd. or wdd.[2]); Murray, 42nd N.I., with Guides; Bradshaw, H.M. 52nd; Fitzgerald, H.M. 75th; M'Burnett, 55th N.I., with 1st Fusrs. Of officers wounded, I have heard the names of Greathed, Engrs., severely; Brig. Nicholson, very severely, and his brother, 31st N.I.; Reid, Sirmore Batt., severely; Jacob and Greville, 1st

[1] The well-known Judge-Advocate General of the Army.—W. C.

[2] A mistake; see p. 283, *ante*.—W. C.

Fusrs., severely; Major Baynes (?) and Lt. Pogson,[1] very severely; Rosser, H.M. Carabin., dangerously. I trust you will, in the course of two or three days, receive accounts *via* Agra of the whole place being in our hands. A great many of the Mutineers, particularly Cavalry, left last night in the direction, it is said, of Rewaree. All our news from the Punjab, and the rear generally and Meerut, v. satisfactory.—(sd.) K. Young. Stewart writes me (15th) that we are in possession of Cashmere, Moree, Cabul, and Lahore Gates; he says, "As our men from working and fighting incessantly so many days are regularly knocked up, we are going to shell the Palace and Selimghur to-day; our loss heavy; I fancy there must be 50 Officers kd. and wdd."

DCCLXXII.

From Chas. B. Saunders, Offg. Agent to the Lt.-Governor N.W.P. at Dehli, to W. Muir, Esq., Member of the Bd. of Rev.

Dehli, *20th September* 1857.

My Dear Sir,[2]—It is with feelings of the most sincere regret that I have to report, for the information of His Honour the Offg. Lieut.-Govr. of the North-West Provinces, that Mr. H. Greathed, his Agent with the Army before Dehli, was attacked with cholera yesterday morning, and expired at about midnight last night. He rose in good health, but at about 9 a.m. the disease attacked him, and he never rallied, but gradually sank until death closed his sufferings.

. . . .

Three Regts. on the 14th, when we first made good our entrance into the City, crossed the bridge of boats, and marched down the Doab towards Allighur, but with the avowed intention of crossing the Ganges at the Anoopshuher Ghat with a view to join the insurgents in Oude. I will write again to-morrow more fully, but must now ask you to excuse more at present, as I have had a great many letters to write, and am of course anxious to attend Mr. Greathed's remains to the grave this afternoon. It will be as well to look out at Agra to prevent any of the defeated army cut(ting) off in detail any of the European inhabitants who

[1] Major Baynes lost his leg; Lt. Pogson was killed,—both of H.M. 8th Foot.—W. C.

[2] Parts of this letter have been given in No. LXXXIV., p. 121, vol. i.; and in *Bulletin* of 28th Sept., Twelfth Series, *ante*.—W. C.

may not reside in the Fort, in the event of their taking the direction of Agra on their way to effect a junction with the Gwalior and Indore troops.

The King and his family are said to be at either Hamayoon's or Nizam's Tomb, and there is every prospect of his giving himself up or of his being captured.

DCCLXXIII.

FROM C. B. SAUNDERS, C.S., DEHLI, TO W. MUIR, C.S., AGRA.

22nd Sept. 1857.

. . . .

I have replied by telegraph to Sir John Lawrence's telegram, to say that, in the event of Sir John Lawrence assuming charge of the Dehli Territory administration, I begged, with the concurrence of the General Commanding, to place myself under his orders, and was prepared to act in the position pointed out, subject to the approval of Mr. Reade and of the Govt.[1]

. . . .

DCCLXXV.

FROM CHARLES B. SAUNDERS, C.S. (TO W. MUIR, C.S. ?)

DEHLI, *28th September*, 1857.

MY DEAR SIR,[2]—The Moveable Column which, according to the General's original intention, was to have gone down towards Agra on the side of the Jumna, is now at Boolundshuhur or in its immediate neighbourhood. There was some little delay in organising and despatching the Moveable Column so as to (ensure ?) their intercepting and cutting off the fugitive Sepoys who evacuated Dehli on the 20th. **Moveable Column.**

. . . .

Few of the European Regiments, after the severe losses entailed by the siege, by the assault, and by sickness, which has laid many low, could muster more than from 250 to 300 men. **Weakness of European regiments.**

[1] See p. 124, vol. i.

[2] Parts of this letter contained in No. CXXXVI., pp. 171, 172, vol. i.—W. C.

Retreat of rebel army.

The intentions of the retreating Army as disclosed to us by every one who came in, were evidently directed to Lucknow, and although it appeared doubtful at first whether they would not have gone down towards Gwalior to effect a junction with the troops of that State, and also with the Indore force.

. . . .

Cossids who have come in from Agra state that they have crossed chiefly at the Jewur Tuppul Ghat and are making for Anoopshuhur. The Moveable Column are now at Malagurh, where Wulleedad Khan is still said to be; and I understand from parties who have come over from Meerut to-day that firing was heard early this morning from that direction. Everything is quite quiet here. The King and some of his family, including Mirzas Bukhtawur Shah, Mehndoo, and Jumma Bukht, are in confinement, and the latter will stand their trial before a Military Commission. Mirzas Moghul Beg, Khizr Sooltan, and Aboo Bukkur were caught at Humayoon's Tomb and shot on the spot, as their complicity in the rebellion was beyond all doubt, from the prominent part which they were known to have taken in it.

Affairs at Delhi.

. . . .

Sir John Lawrence telegraphs that he is anxious to make as few changes as possible, until he knows the wishes of the Government of the North-West Provinces with reference to his assuming the administration of the Dehli Territory as a temporary arrangement.

DCCLXXVI.

From Charles B. Saunders, C.S., to W. Muir, C.S.

Dehli Palace, *4th October* 1857.

. . . .

Persian and Arabic books.

I am afraid a great number of valuable Persian and Arabic books have been most wantonly destroyed by our soldiery, who for the first 10 days after entering the City were almost beyond all control, and entirely without discipline; but the Prize Agents have recovered a few valuable books, and I have no doubt that there are others which may even yet be secured. I read to Ram Chunder the portion of your letter which referred to him, and he was much gratified at your recollection of him. I will employ him in making a Catalogue of some of the best works in the possession of the Prize Agents, and will set him to work to

Ramchunder.

try and recover the copy of the "Seerut Hishamee" to which you allude. "Seerut Hishamee."

The burial-ground near the Cashmere Gate had been but very little injured; some of the tombstones had been broken and defaced, but not to any great extent. One of our breaching batteries was erected at the rear of this burial-ground, and some of the tombs were, I doubt not, injured by our shot and shell as well as by the brutality of our enemy. Until we obtained possession of the City none of our dead could of course be interred in this ground, as it was completely under fire from the City Walls. After taking possession of the place, poor Greathed was the first to be interred there, General Nicholson the second—two men of mark and deservedly first-rate reputations. Burial-ground near the Kashmir Gate.

DCCLXXVII.

From C. B. Saunders, C.S., to W. Muir, C.S.

Dehli Palace, *5th October* 1857.

My Dear Sir,—I am afraid that you have not received such regular accounts from this place since it fell into our hands as before, but the fact is, that the work of the Civil Officer did not in reality commence until Dehli was taken. My time has been, as you may suppose, occupied from morning to night without cessation, and I am afraid that I have not sent off as many Cossids with accounts of what has been done and is being done as I might have done had my time been but at my disposal. Position of Commissioner of Delhi.

The telegraph having been at my disposal from the day of the final assault and capture of the Palace on the 20th, and the communication being direct and uninterrupted with Lahore, I have obtained almost immediate instructions from the Chief Comr. on all matters of importance, and I have consequently been in more close communication with Sir John Lawrence on all official matters than with Agra. I have now got a personal assistant in Lt. Waterfield of the 23rd N.I., who will assist me with mere routine work, and I hope to be able to send you more constant accounts of what is going on. General Wilson left this yesterday morning, being greatly knocked up with the constant work and responsibility which have fallen to his lot for the last 3 or 4 months. General Penny arrived from Meerut to-day to supply his place; and will make this the Headquarters of the Meerut Division for the present. The Moveable Column under Col. Greathed was expected, from infor- Sir John Lawrence. General Archdale Wilson relieved by General Penny.

mation received, to have arrived at Allygurh to-day, and will be in a good position, I presume, to intercept the Mutineers' force on its way across the Doab from Muttra.

Sir John Lawrence ordered Mr. J. S. Campbell (who volunteered for service) to Rohtuk, and that officer has undertaken the charge of that District subject to confirmation at Agra. He has a considerable force at his disposal, consisting of Patiala and Cashmere troops, 300 Mooltani Horse, and a portion of Van Cortlandt's force. A Moveable Column under Brigr. Showers is to-day at Goorgaon, and is on its way to Rewaree to coerce Rao Toolaram and to disperse a small force of Rangur Irregr. Cavry. and others whom he had collected in that neighbourhood Sir Theophilus Metcalfe has gone out, in the absence of Mr. Ford at Hansi, with the Column. On Genl. Van Cortlandt's return to Hansi and Hissar, Mr. Ford will return to Goorgaon, his old District. Mr. Guthrie, who was ordered to join Mr. Greathed by instructions from the late Lt.-Govr., is on his way down from the Hills and will go to Hissar. I have obtained the orders of the Chief Comr. with reference to the above dispositions of Officers. I am anxious to know whether the employment of Military Officers as Assistants to the Officers in charge of Districts will meet with the concurrence of the Chief Comr. of the North-West Provinces, as under present circumstances it appears almost impossible to obtain the services of young civilians until the communications with Agra and Calcutta are again opened out.

Force at Rohtak under J. S. Campbell, C.S.

Showers' Column.
Rao Toolaram.

DCCLXXVIII.

From C. B. Saunders, C.S., to W. Muir, C.S.

Dehli, *6th October* 1857.

My Dear Sir,—I have just received your letter of the 3rd by Cossid. We were in hopes that authentic news of the Relief of Lucknow might have reached you in time to have been communicated in your present letter. Everything remains quiet at this place, and our arrangements are being carried out for the reorganisation of our police and revenue establishments. The Moveable Column under Brigr. Showers encamped to-day at Patoudi *en route* to Rewaree. Their object is to disperse any force which Rao Toolaram may have still around him, and to destroy any bodies of Rangur Irregular Cavalry which they may come across. The Nawab of Bahadurgurh has written

Showers' Column.

Nawab of Bahadurgurh.

to-day to me to inform me of there being in his Dadree Pergunnah a force of about a thousand Irregr. Cavalry men, who are plundering travellers and creating disturbances in that neighbourhood. Genl. Van Cortlandt has marched back at Sir John Lawrence's desire to Hansi, to take up temporarily the Civil charge of that District in addition to his military duties, with a view to relieve Mr. Ford and enable him to return to Goorgaon. The City of Dehli is placed entirely under Military Government. Col. Burn of the 1st N.I. is Military Governor. In connection with the above, it is a curious incident, that when Lord Lake first occupied Dehli, we entrusted the Govt. of the City to a Col. Burn, some distant relative, I believe, of the present occupant of the post.[1] General Van Cortlandt. Delhi under military government. Colonel Burn, military governor.

. . . .

Mirza Bakhtawur Shah and Mendhoo, two of the King's sons, have been tried by a Military Commission, which has this afternoon completed its session and reported its decision; the latter, however, will not be made known until confirmed by General Penny, but, from the amount of documentary evidence which I furnished against them, I fancy there can be but little doubt of the result. King's sons tried by Military Commission.

DCCLXXIX.

FROM C. B. SAUNDERS, C.S. [TO W. MUIR, C.S., AGRA ?].

DEHLI, *8th October* 1857.

MY DEAR SIR,—I have just received your intelligence by Cossid of the Relief of the Garrison of Lucknow by General Havelock's force. The news has of course given very great satisfaction, and some of the heavy guns on our City Bastions, lately in the hands of our enemies, will in a very short time thunder forth a salute to intimate the glad tidings to the surrounding country. We hope to receive further details shortly of the state of the Garrison, and, if possible, the names of the survivors. News of relief of Lucknow.

General Wilson having 2 or 3 days since been relieved of his duties by General Penny to enable him to take leave to the Hills for change of air, I opened Col. Fraser's letter and showed it to the General now Commanding, before forwarding it on to Genl. Wilson at Mussoorie.

The General has begged me to state with reference to the request made by the Chief Comr. for the Column under Brigadier

[1] Other parts of this letter in No. CXLIX., p. 190, vol. i.—W. C.

Showers' Column cannot be spared.

Showers, now out in the Goorgaon District, to be sent on down the right bank of the Jumna to Agra with a view to render that place secure, that he regrets much that he cannot accede to the proposal. The Column is only about 12 or 1300 strong, and is urgently required to restore peace and tranquillity in the neighbourhood of Dehli, and to prevent the possibility of the Mutineers' Irregular Cavalry and the numerous defeated but not yet entirely disbanded adherents of the King once more gaining head in this part of the world. It is believed that the presence of the Moveable Column in the Goorgaon District will have a most salutary effect in restoring tranquillity for a long distance to the South of Dehli. The force is at the present moment beyond Rewaree, where Rao Toolaram is still at the head of nearly 4 or 5000 Aheers and Rangur Cavalry, and the General does not consider it advisable that they should proceed further in the direction of Agra, but, as soon as they have completed the work on which they are at present engaged, considers that they should return to this neighbourhood, when they will again be employed, according to the advice of Sir John Lawrence, in a combined movement against the Rebels in Jhujjer and Dadree. The Column consisting of 1200 being reinforced by the Jummoo troops (such as they are), and by a force detached from Genl. Van Cortlandt's Brigade at Hansi, will be sufficiently strong to clear the territories of the Jhujjer and Dadree States of the rebels who have left our territories to seek protection under foreign rule, and who are now subsisting to a great extent on plunder.

Rao Toolaram.

Numbers of troops at Delhi overestimated.

Our numbers at Dehli are greatly exaggerated elsewhere, and it is, I believe, generally believed that we were in a position, after taking the place, to move off strong Columns in every direction, and to clear the whole of the Doab as well as the Districts towards Agra of the enemy, and to send them flying before our victorious troops.

Condition of troops after assault.

Those only on the spot know the difficulties with which our Commanders had to deal. The whole Army was utterly and completely disorganised, and within 3 or 4 hours of the assault discipline was almost at an end. For several days a great majority of our European troops might almost be said to be suffering from delirium tremens. The Native troops were almost if not equally demoralised from similar causes, and from the plunder which fell into their hands.

General Wilson expressed his inability to despatch two Columns, and it was with considerable difficulty that one was organised and got ready to march under Col. Greathed. I advocated, in the first instance, strongly that the Columns should be sent down the right bank to follow up and destroy the enemies flying or rather fugitive Columns before they could cross the Jumna. When, however, I found day after day pass and no Column was prepared to pursue them with vigour, I changed my opinion and considered, with by far the great majority of the Military Officers, that the proper direction for the Column to take was the Grand Trunk Road down the Doab, with a view to intercept the Mutineers on their way to Oudh, for all the accounts we received pointed out Lucknow and not Agra as the point to which their steps were directed. I am still of opinion that the General was right in adopting the course which he did, on finding that he was unable to organise a Column to pursue the Mutineers immediately on their evacuating the City, and think that Col. Greathed's Column ought to be able, if properly handled, to intercept and cut off, or at any rate to harass and fall upon the rear of, the fugitive troops before they cross the Ganges. The Palace and Magazine are held as Military positions, and the Gates and Bastions of the City are held by our troops. Without unnecessarily disclosing the poverty of the land, I may mention that the Cavalry force at the disposal of the General since the departure of the Column under Brigdr. Showers amounts to a number very considerably under one ὑνδρεδ, and the Infantry, though more numerous, are somewhat in proportion after you have deducted the forces of our native Allies. It will therefore be apparent to the Chief Comr. that our authorities would not be justified, after all the troops have gone through for the capture of this place.[1]

Question of the route for Greathed's column.

Weakness of force at Delhi.

. . . .

DCCLXXXII.

FROM C. B. SAUNDERS, C.S., TO W. MUIR, C.S.

DEHLI PALACE, 12*th October* 1857.

MY DEAR MR. MUIR,—

. . . .

I have not failed to lay your letters before Genl. Penny, but he begs me to assure you that with every wish to relieve your

[1] Sentence left unfinished in original. The rest of this letter in No. CXLIX., p. 190, vol. i.—W. C.

position at Agra from the difficulties with which you appear to be surrounded, it is, for the reasons which I have before detailed to you, a matter of impossibility to detach from the force another Column to march down the right bank of the Jumna.[1]

Impossible to detach another column.

. . . .

DCCLXXXIII.

From C. B. Saunders, C.S., to W. Muir, C.S., Agra.

Dehli, 13*th October* 1857.

My Dear Mr. Muir,[2]—

. . . .

P.S.—The two Princes were shot this morning by the banks of the Jumna.

DCCLXXXV.

From C. B. Saunders, C.S., to W. Muir, C.S., Agra.

Dehli, 15*th October* 1857.

My Dear Sir,—I have just received your letter of the 11th, again calling urgently for reinforcements with a view to render your position at Agra more secure, and enable you to dispense with the presence of Col. Greathed's Column. I have duly brought the contents of your letter, as of all previous ones, to the notice of the General, and am again under the painful necessity of informing you that he regrets his inability, as far as Brigr. Showers' Column is concerned, to comply with your requisition. He was in hopes that the signal victory gained over the Indore troops, the capture of all their guns and ordnance stores, and the utter dispersion of the force, would have rendered your position completely secure, and have enabled you to send on Col. Greathed's Column to Cawnpore, its original destination.[3]

Showers' Column cannot be sent to Agra.

. . . .

When Showers' Column has effected the objects for which it has been detached from this force and returned to Dehli, the General will, I doubt not, take into consideration the require-

[1] The rest is mostly contained in No. CLV., p. 199, vol. i.—W. C.

[2] Part of this letter is given in No. CLX., p. 204, vol. i.—W. C.

[3] Part of this letter in No. CLXII., p. 207, vol. i.

ments of Agra with a view to send you down further reinforcements. He has, however, determined at once to send you a detachment of 500 Seikh Muzbee Sappers and Miners, who are well armed and equipped and have done excellent service during the late Siege. Capt. Taylor of the Engineers, who was second in that branch of the Service during the Siege, being Col. Baird Smith's chief adviser, will leave this to-morrow morning *en route* to Agra in command of the above party, which will, I trust, prove a seasonable reinforcement. Capt. Taylor is without doubt one of the ablest and most valuable officers with the force, and his services will be much missed. He deserves a very considerable share of the praise which must be conferred upon the Engineering branch of the Service present at Dehli for the admirable manner in which the latter operations of the Siege were conducted by them.

Sikh Muzbee Sappers ordered to Delhi.

Captain Alec Taylor, R.E.

. . . .

DCCLXXXVI.

FROM C. B. SAUNDERS, C.S., TO W. MUIR, C.S., AGRA.

18th October 1857.

MY DEAR MUIR,—The Column under Col. Gerrard has routed the Joudhpore Legion at Narwal, but not without severe loss.

Jodhpore Legion routed.

. . . .

I am sorry to say that poor Col. Gerrard was killed, and our losses in Officers appear to have been considerable.

Colonel Gerrard killed.

DCCLXXXVIII.

FROM CHARLES SAUNDERS, C.S., TO W. MUIR, C.S., AGRA.

DEHLI, *21st October*.

MY DEAR MUIR,[1]—

. . . .

There are a great number of Mehwaties collected at Sonah and in the neighbourhood. The natives declare that they number 20,000, but that is an exaggeration. Our troops will have to be employed in dispersing them.

Mewattis collected.

[1] Most of this letter is contained in No. CLXVIII., p. 218, vol. i.

DCCLXXXIX.

CORRESPONDENCE ON PRIZE PROPERTY.

FROM C. B. SAUNDERS, ESQ., OFFG. COMMISSIONER AND AGENT TO LIEUT.-GOVR., TO MAJOR-GENERAL N. PENNY, C.S., COMMANDING AT DEHLI. DATED, PALACE, DEHLI, 27*th October* 1857.

SIR,—I have the honour to forward for your information a copy of a letter to my address from the Offg. Secty. to the Chief Commissioner enclosing an extract from his letter, No. 72, dated
Prize Property. 20th instant, to the Supreme Govt. on the subject of Prize Property.

If you coincide with me in considering that it is desirable that the views of the Chief Commissioner, as to what description of property should or should not be considered as Prize Property, should be made public, I shall feel obliged by your forwarding copies of the enclosed documents to the Prize Agents and to the Military Governor of Dehli for their information and guidance, together with such instructions on the subject as you may consider it advisable to issue, with a view to prevent property which does not appear to be legitimately claimable as Prize by the Army being brought to the hammer.

(*Enclosure* (1).)

FROM LIEUT. E. H. PASKE, OFFG. SECRETARY TO THE CHIEF COMMISSIONER, PUNJAB, TO C. B. SAUNDERS, ESQ., OFFG. COMMISSIONER OF DEHLI. LAHORE, 23*rd October* 1857.

SIR,—I am directed to annex extract of my letter, No. 72, d/ 20th inst., to the Supreme Government, conveying the Chief Commissioner's views as to what description of property should or should not be considered as Prize Property, and to request that, pending the orders of Government in any doubtful cases, the property be placed under sequestration, but be not sold.

(*Enclosure* (2).)

LAHORE, 23*rd October* 1857.

Extract Paras.: 6 and 7 of letter No. 72, dated 20th October 1857, from the Offg. Secretary to the Chief Commissioner, Punjab, to the address of the Secretary to the Government of India, in the Foreign Department:—

Political Secret.

6. It would appear from the Papers in the Appendix that some definite rule as to what shall be considered Prize Property at Dehli is necessary. The Prize Agents claim the jewels of the ex-King, as well as all horses and arms which may have been subsequently collected in the country. The Chief Commissioner has suggested that, pending the orders of the Govt., all such property be either kept in deposit, or sold to the best advantage, and an account rendered to the Agents. It would also, the Chief Commissioner considers, be expedient if Government declared to what extent the property in the City of Delhi is to be considered the right of the captors. It would appear to him that it ought not to extend to any real property, whether inside or outside the city; nor to any personal property not actually captured by the Army. As the ex-King and his jewels were actually seized by Lieut. Hodson, the latter would probably come within the category of Prize Property.

Prize Property. **Claims of the Prize Agents.** **Sir John Lawrence's views.** **King's jewels.**

7. The booty acquired in war is the property of Government and not of the Army, and, though it is usual to make such booty over to the captors, Government can clearly place a limitation on its extent. All moveable property which belonged to the Mutineers, or to citizens of the town who joined in the insurrection, may fairly be declared Prize Property. But it seems very questionable if this claim should extend to the goods and chattels of peaceable citizens, of men who, it must be notorious, were in no way implicated, but on the contrary suffered severely in consequence of the outbreak. The Chief Commissioner considers that the property of Merchants, Traders, and Saukars, Artisans and the like, unless they joined in the war, should not be considered as booty. Unless this be done, the whole of the inhabitants of Dehli, whether guilty or innocent, will be reduced to pauperism, and the trade of the country paralysed. In the

Goods of peaceable citizens.

analogous case of Mooltan private property was not, it is believed, so considered; nor in that of Bhurtpore.

True Extract.

(Signed) E. H. PASKE,
Offg. Secretary.

True Copies.
(Signed) CHAS. B. SAUNDERS,
Offg. Commr.

DCCXCI.

FROM C. B. SAUNDERS, C.S., TO W. MUIR, C.S.

DEHLI, *16th November* 1857.

MY DEAR MUIR,—Your letter of the 20th of October relative to the views of the Military Authorities upon Prize Property, together with your letters of the 21st, 22nd, and 23rd of October, did not come to hand until the 3rd of November: I ought to have replied to it at that time, but the subject having become somewhat out of date, and having but very little leisure, I did reply to it as quickly as I ought to have done (*sic*).

Sir John Lawrence. Prize Agents. I have from time to time submitted to Sir John Lawrence, for the expression of his opinion, several points with reference to the views and proceedings of the Prize Agents, and have communicated the replies I received to the General Commanding for communication to the Prize Agents.

You are quite correct in supposing that the chief ground for preventing the reoccupation of the City at an earlier date without much danger (*sic*), but this view of things was not Commissioner's difficulty in preserving property from plunder. shared by the Military Authorities, and it has been with great difficulty that I have succeeded to any extent in preserving the property of staunch adherents to the British Govt. from plunder.

Secondly, with regard to the difficulty of distinguishing the evil from the well-affected citizens, I confess that the difficulty has been a great one, and no very great trouble has been taken to discriminate between the two . . . . General Wilson ordered that no Protection tickets should be held to be valid unless countersigned by him, and the consequence was that but few obtained anything like protection for their property—no guards could be furnished, and before 2 or 3 days had elapsed there was not a house which had not been ransacked and plundered of its contents, friends and foes of the Govt. suffering to an equal extent. The chief wealth of the citizens, however, had been carefully buried or secreted in closets which had been ingeniously bricked up and plastered over. The Seikhs and others with the force very soon learnt the artifice, and a very considerable amount of plunder has been carried off, which will not enrich the Prize Fund. The Prize Agents have since been busily engaged in ransacking the houses of the rebels and others who have enjoyed a reputation for wealth or disloyalty to our Govt. It has been considered by the Prize Agents that with regard to loyalty the *onus probandi* was with the parties whose property is subjected to search, and that all must be considered to be enemies who cannot satisfactorily prove that they have done anything to show that they are our friends. **Plundering general.** **Disloyalty presumed.**

Thirdly, the Prize Agents and the Army generally were rather anxious to lay it down as a rule that the whole city had become the property of the Army, having been taken by assault, and were anxious to dispose of real as well as personal or moveable property. This was a view of the question which could not be supported. I protested against the doctrine, and Sir John Lawrence has given his opinion very strongly against it. I do not think that the Prize Agents have any idea now of trying to enforce their doctrine further, and it appears to be generally conceded that their claims can only extend to moveable property. They do not therefore attempt to ransom household property as such, but they have, on the payment down of a certain sum by the inhabitants of a street, ransomed its wealth, or rather guaranteed it from search and plunder; and they were anxious to carry out the plan further, but numerous difficulties have arisen to prevent its general adoption. The Neel ka Kuttra, the richest quarter in the town, was thus ransomed and guards placed to protect its inhabitants from further molestation. The consequence has been that all the wealth of the City which has escaped the clutches of independent plunderers has been transferred by its owners at night-time to this quarter, and the guarantee has been abused. The city has now been so thoroughly ransacked and plundered that parties are not willing to pay much for their effects still remaining untouched, and the sooner the operations of the Prize Agents can be brought to a close the better it will be, I think, for all parties. **Real property.** **Views of Sir John Lawrence.** **Ransom by streets.** **Nil ka Kuttra.** **City thoroughly plundered.**

I hope I have answered your questions as fully as you

require. I shall be happy to give any further information you may be in want of on the subject, but I must inform you that the authorities here have not gone upon any very fixed principles, but on the contrary the whole question has been (as all similar misappropriations of property always must be) marked rather by a want of principle than anything else. I enclose you copies of letters on the subject of Prize Property, which show what Sir John Lawrence's views on the question were.

Want of principle in disposing of property.

P.S.—I communicated the contents of your letter to Genl. Penny.

DCCXCII.

From Offg. Commr. Dehli, Wednesday, 18*th November* 1857, to Chief Commr. Lahore; Commrs. Jullunder and Umballa; and C. Lebas, C.S., Kurnaul.

It is 6 a.m., Novr. 18th.

Letters from Ford at Narnoul and from Capt. Dwyer at Kanound of the 16th have just been received by express forwarded from Jhujjer by Capt. Lawrence. They report the defeat of the Joudhpore Legion on that date at Narnoul after a severe fight, with the capture of all their guns, 6 in number. Our troops arrived on their ground about a koss from Narnoul at about 11 a.m., and the fight continued until sunset. The enemy came out to meet our force in advance of Narnoul, and the Carabineers and Guides made a splendid charge against the rebel guns and cavalry; the latter fought well. We took the Seraie occupied by the enemy towards sunset, and now occupy it. The enemy had about 5000 men in the field. All our men did well. The 1st Fusiliers, as usual, splendidly. Ford writes that we have lost, he fancies, about 70 killed and wounded, but Capt. Dwyer states our loss in officers alone at 24, which I trust is a mistake. I regret to say that poor Col. Gerrard was mortally wounded, and has since died. Among the wounded officers, the only names mentioned are Pearse (doing well), Humphreys of the Sappers (doing well), Craigie of the Guides (severely), Kennedy in the hand, and Wallace. Ford adds that there may be other officers wounded about whom he had not yet heard. Col. Gerrard is the only one yet mentioned as killed. Money had a horse killed under him. Ford adds that if the rebel force had not been

Defeat of Jodhpore Legion at Narnaul.

Colonel Gerrard killed.

Pearse, Humphreys, Craigie, Kennedy, Wallace, wounded.

defeated, it would have raised the whole country. They fought with great pluck. The amount of the enemy's loss not yet ascertained. We occupy the Seraie where they had entrenched their guns. Capt. Dwyer writes that the enemy, after having been driven back, had, as far as he could ascertain, bolted southwards. Further particulars when received will be communicated.

DCCXCIV.

FROM C. B. SAUNDERS, C.S., TO W. MUIR, C.S., AGRA.

23rd November 1857.

MY DEAR MUIR,—

. . . .

I think you asked me some time ago whether Ramchunder was being employed to advantage here, and if not, recommended that he should be sent down to Agra to officiate as Mathematical Master in the Agra College. Ramchunder has for some time past been employed in collecting and arranging the books which were found in the city, and endeavouring to secure for Govt. any books of the Library of the Dehli College which are forthcoming. His services have been very useful here, as he has also assisted in translating State Papers for the different trials which are taking place or are about to come off before a Military Commission. If, however, you consider that his services are more required at Agra, I will send him off without delay. He is a very intelligent good man.

Ramchunder employed in collecting and arranging books, etc.

7. FROM MEERUT.

DCCXCV.

FROM J. CRACROFT WILSON, ESQ., C.S.,
TO C. THORNHILL, C.S., AGRA.

MEERUT, 11*th August* 1857.

MY DEAR THORNHILL,—

. . . .

Naini Tal. Major Ramsay. Khan Buhadur Khan has sent a force to attack Nainee Tal. Ramsay has sent away all the ladies and children to Almorah, and is prepared to receive the villains. He has, I believe, 700 Goorkhas and 100 Officers. Ramsay will serve out the brave army well. Nawab of Rampore behaving well. Yoosuf Alee Khan, the Nawab of Rampore, is behaving well, but he has no control over his Pathan soldiers. On the 27th ulto., one Abdoollah, a Moradabad Sayud, mildly expostulated with one of the Pathans doing duty at Moradabad, begging him not to oppress a gardener who was selling vegetables in the Bazar. In return for this expostulation the Pathan wounded the Sayud in two places. The Sayud then took refuge in the house of a respectable Mohamedan. The Pathans followed, and demanded that the wounded man should be delivered over to them. The Mohamedan refused. By this time the Cotwal came up, and he was taking the wounded man off in a doolie to the Dispensary when the Pathans set upon him and finished him. The Sayud's relatives exposed his corpse to the public gaze. The people of Moradabad, Hindoos, and Moosulmans united. It is said there were 15,000 of them came armed to the Nawab's uncle, who is in personal charge of Moradabad. He did not dare give them redress, so the Moradabad men killed 36 Pathans upon the spot, and took possession of the boats on the Ramgunga to prevent reinforcements arriving from Rampore. The next day the Nawab's uncle called the principal inhabitants of the town, and at their suggestion the peace of the town has been entrusted to a fine fellow, a Rajpoot, who lives in the Kutgurh Mohullah. Dhonkul Sing. One, Dhonkul Sing, a Kutgurh, headed this movement against the Pathans. I had received, days before, accounts of the oppressive conduct of the Nawab's Pathans, and I anticipated a row. In truth, if the Nawab's life is not taken by his own rascals, I think we shall be very fortunate. Yoosuf Alee's death, unless we at once arrived with a strong European force (I have the battle at Futehgunj, where the Rampore men almost annihilated a European Regiment in 1794, vividly before my eyes), would be a great calamity. And now for . . . . . .

. . . . He has been playing us false throughout. He, as you know, will not answer our letters, and, while sitting in Bijnore himself, sent his soraral nephew to Sheerkot and demanded one lakh of Rupees. The demand was refused, and then the nephew with the aid of 2000 men surrounded the town. He contrived by different means to induce the Choudhrees to point out where their wealth was hid, and in this way he secured some 50,000 Rs. By this time three days had elapsed, and all the other Hindoo talooqhdars united and drove the nephew back to Nujeebabad, where they have surrounded him. I feel certain that the Hindoos will oust ——— from the govt. of this district. Oh that a force was at my disposal, and authority from Govt. that I might go over and put a stop to all the horrors now going on. Shakespear has just written to me to say that, in the paper which he gave to ———, he never authorised his demanding Revenue. So that plea even is not available for his conduct. ——— had no ungovernable mutinous army. The men he is now drilling and converting into soldiers have all been entertained since Shakespear quitted the district, and there is not a shadow of any excuse for his conduct. Shakespear will quit Munsoorie the moment he hears of the fall of Dehlee, and take up his quarters at Meeruth, ready to accompany the Brigade, which may be ordered into Rohilkhund. I think now I have told you of all that is going on across the Ganges. Stay, I forgot to say that a Rajpoot zummeendar has opposed the Moosulman interest in the Budaon District, and he has set himself up as king of the country. As to money, the Meeruth Tehseeldar has just reported to me that he has only 37,000 Rs. now due. I know too that there are more than two lakhs in the Meeruth treasury. I propose going out shortly to the Northern portion of the district and collecting Revenue in connection with Palmer in Mozuffernugger. The Revenue of the Mowana tehseeldaree is also coming in very fairly. In both these pergunnahs I have been at work.

Budaon District.

Revenue being collected in Meerut.

. . . .

At Dehlee the Hindoo Sepahees now have it all their own way. They threaten, if their present attempts, namely a battery at Kishengunj and a battery opposite the Metcalfe picket, fail,

At Delhi.

they will desert, four Regiments at a time, and spread all over the country. A small picket at Ghazeeoodeennuggur sends out horsemen to bully our people at Moradnuggur and Bolainee. The allowing the picket to remain unmolested is a disgrace to us, but we have no force with which to risk a general engagement within 8 miles of the Dehlee Palace. Do you know what has become of a very fine chestnut Arab horse sent up to the Govt. Stud by Colonel Scobie, the Remount Agent at Bombay, and which was at Agra before the Neemuch Mutineers arrived? If the horse was stolen by the Mutineers I will look out for him at Dehlee. He is the horse to carry me after the Goojurs.

DCCXCVI.

FROM F. WILLIAMS, C.S., MEERUT, TO C. THORNHILL, C.S., SECY. TO GOVT., AGRA.

(*In F. Williams' handwriting.*)

MEERUT, *Septr. 22nd*, 1857.

Delhi.

MY DEAR CUD.,—I send you a copy of a letter just received from Saunders at Dehli. *Dehli is ours entirely.* The Rebels have *all* left it, mostly down the right bank of the Jumna. The King, it is said, is at Humayoon's Tomb. There is no news of any Moveable Column having started after them, and General Wilson writes to the General here that he can send no Column to this side. This is not in consequence of any loss in the final capture of the city, for the Mutineers and Rebels evacuated the place, and General Wilson wrote on the 20th. By this time a Column may be after them. You will see by Saunders' letter that Greathed died of cholera at midnight of the day the City became ours—this has almost damped the joy here that would otherwise have been felt. I would not interfere with Saunders. Both Greathed himself, before he died, and General Wilson, wished Saunders should take charge there.

Death of H. Greathed, C.S.

C. B. Saunders C.S.

(*Rest of letter wanting.*)

DCCXCVII.

FROM FLEETWOOD WILLIAMS, C.S. COMMR., MEERUT,
TO C. THORNHILL, C.S., AGRA.

MEERUT, *23rd or 24th Septr.* 1857.

MY DEAR CUD.,—This[1] came in after I wrote to you this morning. I am afraid Walee Dad will not be hung on his own bastion, after all. His ladies and traps are over the Ganges, and he will follow them directly he hears of the Moveable Column. Hauppoor is all right, and everybody very loyal. No news yet from Muzuffernugger. Get arrangements made for laying out Mail-carts to this; I am doing it at this end. Also for the re-establishment of Electric Telegraph. I have ordered the wire and posts to be collected. Get orders sent up about Rohilcund. It will take time to arrange matters. All will be quiet here in no time. Col. Greathed will find no enemy in the Doab, I believe. All are off to Rohilcund. Send us up some of the best boys of the Agra College for appointments. We ride out the storm with nearly 5 lacs in the Treasury, and lots more coming. Send orders for proclamations about arms. Wali Dad. Meerut Treasury full.

Sapte and Lyall[2] gone to join Moveable Column and reoccupy Bulundshuhur. I have given the latter Jt. Magte. powers. He has behaved very well. I hope it will be sanctioned. B. Sapte, C.S., A. C. Lyall, C.S.

FROM C. B. SAUNDERS, C.S. COMMR., DELHI,
TO F. WILLIAMS, C.S. COMMR., MEERUT.

(*Enclosure to above.*)

DEHLI, *Septr. 23rd*, 1857.

MY DEAR WILLIAMS,—I have just received your letter of the 22nd brought by your 4 Police Sowars, who, finding no Cavalry Picket on the Hindun, very properly came on here. A party of the Mooltan Horse went out yesterday to examine the bridge across the Hindun, but returned in the evening. You will be glad to hear that at length a column has been formed to proceed down the Doab. It will march from this to-morrow morning to Ghazeeoodeen Nugger, from thence the next day to Dadree, thence to Secundrabad, and then it will turn off to Malagurh to [attack] Wulleedad Khan, if he is still holding out. Moveable column formed.

[1] See enclosure following. [2] Sir Alred Lyall, G.C.S.I.

W. Clifford, C.S. B. Sapte, C.S. Clifford will accompany the Column from this until relieved by Sapte, who, I presume, is the proper person to be deputed for this duty. Greathed, I know, has arranged with you that Sapte should be ready to join any Moveable Column going down the Doab, and in your letter to poor Greathed's address of the 21st you mentioned that Sapte was all ready for a start. If therefore such be the case, it would be as well for him to try and join the Column at Dadree or Secundrabad before they get to Malagurh or to Boolondshuhur, as his knowledge of the localities and of the parties who ought to be secured and [punished] will be invaluable. Clifford can either return when Sapte joins, or after Malagurh is taken, and must use his discretion as to returning direct to Dehli or Meerut; or, if the roads are not safe, going on with the Column down country. Colonel Greathed will command the Column. In addition to the above, the Belooch Battalion above 300 strong march to-morrow morning for Meerut, and will greatly add to your strength. It is a good regiment, and the men are armed with Rifles. *The King is a prisoner here; and two of his sons, Mirza Moghul and Mirza Khizr Sultan, with his grandson Mirza Aboo Bukker, were taken prisoners yesterday by Hodson and shot.* Have you any good Officers over at Meerut who are anxious to be employed on this side of the Jumna? We want good men as Thannahdars, Tehsildars, etc., and must entertain men for the Police; but I am afraid it will be a difficult matter to get good men at present in this part of the country. I am sorry to say that poor General Nicholson died this morning in Camp from the effects of his wounds.

Colonel Greathed to command column. Beloch Battalion. King prisoner. His sons and grandson shot. Death of General Nicholson.

DCCXCVIII.

FROM F. WILLIAMS, C.S. COMMR., MEERUT, TO W. MUIR, C.S., AGRA.[1]

MEERUT, *Oct.* 15*th*, 1857.

Nawab of Rampore. MY DEAR MUIR,—I send you a slip of news received from Lahore to-day to be forwarded to you. There is a report in the City here to-day that the Nawab of Rampore has been made prisoner by a party from Bareilly and carried off to Bareilly, and that all the Nawab's people have openly mutinied against him and joined the rebels at Bareilly. Every Mahomedan in Rohilcund will make common cause with them. I think the news is very likely to be true, from the terms of a letter from a relative of the Nawab which I received from Rampore yesterday, which was full

[1] The reply to this letter is No. DLXXXVI., p. 90, vol. ii.—W. C.

of apprehension of things going wrong there. This makes the situation of Nynee Tal a ticklish one, cut off as it is from all help. 5000 men from Bareilly with guns have taken possession of Huldwanee[1] with above a lac of rupees worth of grain, which had unfortunately been left down there. A letter from Nynee Tal says that there is a party of Rebels at Kaleedoongee too, and that now no supplies can get up from below. Flour was 16 seers for a rupee, and would be soon twice as dear, with all the Rampore territory against them. It will be as much as they can do to hold their own there, and no time should be lost in re-inforcing them through the Hills from Mussooree, I think; the Goorkhas of Seharanpoor are very sickly, or it would be a good plan to send them up and across inside the Hills with mountain-train guns, ammunition, and supplies, sending other men to take their place at Seharanpoor. We should not let the poor ladies at Nynee Tal run a chance of falling into the hands of the rebels. I believe Ramsay would hold the place well if he did not think of going down into the plains to fight the enemy.[2] All quiet here. I congratulate you all on having the Mutineers that threatened you, so thoroughly beaten off.[3]

Naini Tal.

Major H. Ramsay.

---

8. BULANDSHAHR.

DCCXCIX.

FROM BRAND SAPTE, C.S., BOOLUNDSHUHR, TO W. MUIR, C.S., AGRA.

BOOLUNDSHUHR, *Oct.* 4, 1857.

MY DEAR MUIR,—Gave yours all right to Greathed last night. I have returned to Boolundshuhr, where I have 220 Beloochees, 200 Pathan Horse, and 2 R.A. Guns. I sent you an account of an action, or rather Reade, and hope it has reached. We took more ammunition than I thought, and lots of powder. Greathed will reach Allyghur to-morrow. I suppose the rascals will bolt on his approach, but I hope he'll come across the Bareilly Brigade, which has never yet once fought well. Greathed's advance will open the road clear through to Agra. I have the mail-cart running to his Camp, and the Dehli line is open all right. Wulli Dad has got away to Bareilly. I am catching his

[1] See No. CLX., p. 205, vol. i.—W. C.
[2] He did. See No. CLXVIII., pp. 218, 219, vol. i.—W. C.
[3] See No. CXLV., p. 186, vol. i.—W. C.

followers, and am going to hang his Tahseeldar to-morrow. Poor Home of the Engineers was blown up with the explosion at Malaghur and killed dead on the spot. He was to have had the Victoria Cross for blowing open the Cashmere Gate. Please tell them to send me my "Muff" (Mofussilite newspaper).

---

9. NAINI TÁL.

FROM R. ALEXANDER, C.S. COMMISSIONER, TO THE HONBLE. J. COLVIN, LT.-GOVR.

DCCC.

NAINI TAL, *Sept.* 1*st*, 1857.

MY DEAR MR. COLVIN,—I have no particular intelligence to communicate.

Haldwani threatened.

Our state here is as usual, save that we are again threatened with an attack from Bahcra, at which place and about it, report has it that some 2000 are assembled with the avowed object of an attack on Haldwani and this place. This threat has occasioned us to be on the *qui vive*, and to plant military posts about Katgodam and Haldwani. I do not anticipate bad results from the threat. I have but meagre accounts from Shahjehanpore and Budaon. The Nawab writes that the peace is well kept in Moradabad.

. . . .

DCCCI.

FROM SAME TO SAME.

NAINI TAL, *Sept.* 3*rd*, 1857.

King of Delhi appoints governors.

MY DEAR MR. COLVIN,—The Nawab of Rampore writes me that "Shooquas" from the King of Dehli have been received by Syud Mahomed Sheer Ali Khan of Umroha, investing him with the government of that Province, and by one Ghulam Rusool Khan (a former Kotwal of Dehli), investing him with the government of Hussanpore and Sumbhul. The former of these two persons is reported to have at once set up his Thannahs and Tehseels. A third Shooqua, it is said, has been received by Mujeedoodeen Ahmud Khan, (investing him) with the appointment of Moradabad, in reply to which the said recipient has applied for a force to control the Nawab of Rampore (which of course he cannot obtain from Dehli). In the meanwhile the intrigues within the district of Rampore, on the part of Mohamed Ali Khan's wife and others are such as to make the Nawab's position not less difficult than it has been from the commencement of these troubles. Sheoraj Sing of Kashipore sent me yesterday two letters from the Bijnore Hindoos, written in less heart than those I have previously received, and calling clamorously and almost despondingly for aid. I should fear that if the parties I have mentioned as having received appointments in Umroha and Hussanpore get any head, they may prove dangerous neighbours to the Hindoos in Bijnore. The present relation of these internal movements and commotions within Districts may hardly seem interesting and important enough to send you; my object, however, in sending it is to indicate the real necessity existing for *as early* a despatch of troops to restore tranquillity in the province as is consistent with what may be considered more urgent necessities elsewhere, for there cannot be doubt that delays augment the difficulties in the restoration of order, in almost the same ratio as they give scope to the exercise of the intentions and powers of those whose object is utter disorganisation. Having written to the Commander-in-Chief immediately after the loss of Rohilcund, and received his reply as to our prospect of getting relief, it is not, I conceive, my part to make further application, my first being known and registered. But doubtless your being advised of the internal state of Districts by reports such as this will give you the opportunity of judging of the relative state of different parts of the country, and so of the propriety of directing or demanding the march of troops in this or that direction. I therefore do not apologise for my troubling you with this report.

Intrigues in Rampore.

Bijnor Hindus.

Troops required.

. . . .

---

10. FROM ETAWAH.

DCCCIII.

FROM A. HUME,[1] C.S., MAGISTRATE OF ETAWAH, TO THE SECRETARY TO GOVT., N.W.P.

ETAWAH, *June 5th*, 3 *p.m.*

SIR,—I am happy to be able to report that order prevails throughout this district, except in one spot, Roora, not far from Rowayn; where a party of Thaquors are, or were yesterday,

Order in Etawah.

[1] Mr. Hume, Magt. of Etawah (where a regt. of the Gwalior Contingent was stationed).—W. M.

holding out against the Police who went to apprehend some of the criminals concerned in the late disturbances. This matter will, I hope, be settled to-day satisfactorily. The Thaquors of Bhurry, on hearing of the approach of Lieutnt. Coserat, fled across the Chumbul, whither they had long ago sent their wives and children; but as the Rajah of Rampoora of the Nagode territory has been threatening Sundows, Lt. Coserat has been pushed on to Oreyah; and as yesterday Lieutnt. Browne reported the probability of the mutiny of the two Companies at Oraiee, he has now been directed to advance with the 75 Paegah Horse (who, however, are good for little or nothing) to Jaloun, and place himself in communication with Browne.

Thakurs of Bharri. Lieutenant Coserat.

Rajah of Rampoora.

2. This day about 1 p.m. I received the message for the Governor-General, and sent it on with the news of the second affair at the Hindun to Oreyah by "Sandhnee Sowar,"[1] of the Soubah's, who happened to be going, and thence it will be sent as it can to Cawnpore. I have given the orders, and trust there will be no mistake. But I can get no "sandhnees," and nothing else will carry expresses properly. I have applied to Major Macpherson for 12 or 20, or any less number he can spare, and I hope that a telegraphic message may be sent to him explaining the expediency of his compliance with my request. I will then, if necessary, run the dak right through to Futtehpore, *via* Oreyah and Bhogneepor—5 "sandhnee" stages. I say if necessary, because the Natives who told us yesterday of Captn. Hayes' murder (confirmed this day) have this morning received notes by private hands professedly to announce the capture of Cawnpore on the night of the 3rd; we have, it is true, received no dak yesterday or to-day either from Cawnpore or any down country station, nor any dak to-day from Etah or farther up; but Brigadier Wheeler was entrenched,—had, I know, strong detachments of the 84th; and the report can, I think, scarcely be true.

Murder of Captain Hayes.

Reported capture of Cawnpore.

. . . .

(From the Original.)

DCCCIV.

FROM SAME TO SAME.

13th June 1857.

Order in Etawah.

SIR,—I have the honour to report the continuance of good order in my district up to half-past 5 p.m. yesterday (the 12th), but at that time the advance guard of a large body of Mutineers

[1] Swift camel-rider.

was moving on Oreyah, and I expect that ere now that town and its Tehseels have been, like Sicundra, looted and burned. I have received three several reports from Cawnpore. It appears that on the night of the 5th the Native troops, joined by the Peshwah's force, attacked the European Entrenchments with infantry, cavalry, and artillery, and that a ceaseless battle raged that night, thro' the 6th, 7th, and 8th, and was still going on on the 9th. One of the accounts says the Europeans had suffered little, but had cut up the Natives tremendously; the others assert that the Europeans, reduced to a very small number, and without ammunition, were being pounded into by the enemy's artillery, and were entirely hemmed in by the Natives. It is also reported that nearly a whole European Regiment has been murdered in detail between Benares and Cawnpore, that Sikh Mutineers murdering and plundering everywhere are pressing up the country.

Oriyah attacked.

Rebels successful at Cawnpore.

I recommend that, if it has not already been done, sufficient accommodation be instantly provided in the Agra Fort for all Europeans, that it be amply provisioned, that all weak points be strengthened, guns mounted, public records removed, and every reasonable precaution taken; if, as is just possible, the Jhansee and Cawnpore—joined with the Allahabad and Benares —Mutineers, hearing the bad news from Dehli, come straight upon Agra, you, unless well prepared, will be no better off than the Cawnpore people. We have determined to send off our ladies to Agra, as we mean to make a stand here, unless, which is very probable, the troops (their Officers have perfect faith in them, nevertheless) turn against us, in which case I shall get into some native fort and fight. I may be able to delay them a day or so. There is undoubtedly a large force now between Calpee and this place.

Mr. Hume's suggestion for safety of Agra.

---

11. FROM CAWNPORE.

DCCCVI.

FROM J. W. SHERER, C.S., TO W. MUIR, C.S.

(*A Kossid letter on a very small piece of thin paper closely written.*)

CAWNPORE, *Aug.* 30, 1857.

MY DEAR MUIR,[1]—

. . . .

And I have the greatest suspicions of another Deputy Collr.

[1] A great part of this letter is printed as No. CCCCLXXV., pp. 501–2, vol. i.—W. C.

Disloyalty of officials.

from Calpee. He was six weeks at Bithoor after the recapture of this place, and never communicated with me *once* till the army went the second time, and the danger was at his door. Our . . . . . . has gone to the bad; alas, ... have failed in the time of trial. One . . . . . .

Loyalty of Salámat Ali of Hatgaon.

have I found true in these parts, Salamut Ali, Moonsiff of Hutgaon, and he is superintending the police at Khaga and Hutgaon, with the assistance of . . . . who will insist on helping the Govt. now, and really is keeping the road open; *ας ι καννοτ πυνισ ίμ ι ρεκειvε ίς σερvισες ανδ σαι νοθινγ.*

He wrote to me to say he was a "Khyr Khwah," and I wrote back that well-wishers of the Govt. were expected to do something besides making expression of their sentiments. It is doubtful whether he himself was ever in Khaga till

Position at Cawnpore.

just now, but his son was in open rebellion. We are doing nothing whatever. Havelock is encamped on the parade ground; Neill lives near the Canal; and . . ., some Engineers and others, amongst them myself, live in the entrenchment.

Brown, . . ., Grant, . . ., dead of cholera.

Deaths by Cholera—Brown of the 56th, . . ., Grant of Sultanpore, Oude, . . ., but the disease has now quite disappeared.

Why not always send the Bankers letters to this place,

Dak arrangements.

or advices of bills given, to me? The mail-cart runs every day to Allahabad, and the Telegraph is all right. Shekoabad and Meeran kee Serai are now the only places to

Kossids.

be avoided, so the Kossids say. Pray do not promise Kossids more than 25 Rs. I never give more, and they are perfectly satisfied. I have two fat letters for Mr. Colvin, but Beadon especially told me not to send them till a good opportunity occurred—they are too large for the ordinary Kossid. Tell Clark I will try and arrange for regular runners

Concealment of letters.

for a light concealed dawk, between this and Orayah in Etawah, if he will manage the rest of the distance. The *λινινγ οφ α σόε μακς α γοοδ βαγ φορ α σμαλλ δαυκ.* . . . writes from somewhere in Etawah that he is all right; *ι κυεστιον ιτ vερι μυχ.*

(Sgnd.) J. W. S.

DCCCVII.

From Same to Same.

Cawnpore, *Sept.* 24, 1857, 6 *p.m.*

I am exceedingly obliged to you for your ample and interesting letters. I first telegraph their cream, and then send them bodily down country. Nixon gave you the go-by in the news of the assault on the 14th. Your letter came to-day, and his the night before last. His cossid came the whole distance in 3 days. News of assault of Delhi reaches Cawnpore from Agra in three days.

. . . .

Outram, as you will have heard from Col. Fraser, received no opposition after Mungulwara, found the bridge all right at Bunnee, and, when last heard of, was as jolly as possible, the evening of the 22nd his letter was dated, at Begum Gunj, 14 miles from Lucknow. Outram's advance on Lucknow.

. . . .

DCCCX.

From J. W. Sherer, C.S., to W. Muir, C.S., Agra.

Cawnpore, *October* 3, 1857.

My Dear Muir,—No further news from Lucknow. From native report we hear that there is still a large body of natives in Lucknow, and that last Tuesday (29th) there was a fight. What we cannot quite understand is that our troops in Alum Bagh do not seem to have any communication with those in the City. We are sending out provisions under a convoy of 300 men, and have sent for 150 men from Futtehpore to reinforce us. The Naval Brigade is expected at Allahabad to-morrow—which will disengage a few more troops. The country is much disturbed about here; 400 or 500 rascals have got into Bithoor again, and we hear that men are crossing at Calpee, but we do not yet know who they are. I send a letter giving latest Mirzapore news. Lucknow. Country disturbed.

. . . .

The Nawab of Banda has a large force at Chillatara on the other side of the Jumna, nearly opposite Futtehpore, but I fancy it is merely out of fear of our coming—when troops begin to come up, all will be well—but these pauses make the country very disturbed. Nawab of Banda.

. . . .

Monck Mason. I am very sorry about Monck Mason;[1] I knew him well. He was a most intelligent and determined officer.

. . . .

DCCCXII.

From Same to Same.

(A Kossid letter written on a scrap of thin paper.)

Cawnpore, *October* 10*th*. 1st Brigade.

My Dear Muir,—I have kept the kossid through the night in hopes of news from Lucknow, but not a word either from there or Alum Bagh. I gathered two more names of killed from a scrap yesterday which some one received from Domenichetti—Major Burck of H.M. 90th and Lieutenant Preston of the same corps.

Major Burck and Lieutenant Preston killed at Lucknow.

We are all tranquil here, and a strong native rumour prevails that Greathed has reached Futtehgurh. An army from the West, the approach of which every one is, strange enough, aware of, strikes amazement. No one came to Calpee. One of my spies saw a small body of horse cross over the day before yesterday, and, asking one of them who they were, the reply was that they were "Nanha's men, and had been to fetch the Gwalior troops." "Where are the Gwalior troops, then?" "Oh, they told us to go on and they would come presently." They must come quickly, now or never, for the red stream is setting in from the West.

Gwalior troops.

. . . .

I again assure you I am on my watch-tower, and a cloud of dust on the distant horizon shall be announced as soon as its form rises distinct from the rounding line.

DCCCXIII.

From Same to Same.

(A Kossid letter written on a scrap of the finest thin paper.)

Cawnpore, 5 *p.m.*, *October* 10*th*, 1857.

Your letter of the 4th has just come in, and the message been sent out. The letter will go by to-night's post.

[1] See No. LXXVIII., p. 116, vol. i.—W. C.

I now write for a special purpose; we have certain intelligence that the Nana intends to cross the Ganges, either to-morrow or the next day. He is accompanied only by a small body of horse, and Bruce and I are in great hopes the Colonel will be persuaded to send out a party to intercept him; there are nearly 800 men here now, so that they could easily be spared. However, if the expedition does not come off, or if he should slip through our fingers, it seems very desirable that Captain Macpherson should communicate with Scindia, and urge upon him how desirable it would be that he should secure his person and prevent his wandering about, spreading disaffection. It is almost certain the Nana wishes to go straight to Gwalior, but probably, if he was not favourably received, he would try to get down to Poonah. **Nana's intention.**

Would you kindly communicate all this at once to Colonel Fraser, for such notice as he may think proper to take of it?

This is his description—

"The Nana is 42 years of age. Hair black; complexion, light wheat coloured; large eyes; and fat round face; he is understood now to wear a beard; height, about 5 feet 8; he wears his hair very short (or at least did do so), leaving only so much as a small skull-cap would cover; he is full in person, and of powerful frame; he has not the Mahratta hooked nose with broad nostrils, but a straight well-shaped one; he has a servant, who never leaves his side, with a cut ear." **Personal description of the Nana.**

We are all serene here, and certainly nobody has come to Calpee yet. Besides, the stream is setting in; there are two or three bodies of our men between here and Allahabad. Not a word from Lucknow.

DCCCXIV.

FROM J. W. SHERER, C.S., TO W. MUIR, C.S. (confidential).

(This is a Kossid letter written on a very small scrap of thin paper.)

(Undated.)[1]

I ADD a secret only for Colonel Fraser and yourself just at present. *μαν σινγ ις αττεμπτινγ το τρεατ ὑιθ Ουτραμ θρο* **Man Singh.**

[1] There is a note in Sir W. Muir's hand, "7th October 1857, from Lucknow? 13th October, from Cawnpore?"

θις πλασε. θερε ις σομε ὀπε ἑ νιλλ ὑιθδραυ ἱς μεν τομορρου, πρελιμιναρι το σενδινγ α νακεελ. ιτ ις αβουτ τιμε, φορ ουρ γαρρισον σπεακ οφ εατινγ θειρ ὀρσες. Θις ωας ιν α λεττερ δατεδ θε 6th, *ρεκειυεδ γεςτερδαι, ματτερς μα ἀυε ιμπρουεδ σινσε θεν. Θε λεττερ οφ* 13 *δοες νοτ μεντιον συππλιες.* Lucknow killed and wounded. *Κιλλεδ ον* Sept. 25, 246, *ωουνδεδ ανδ μισσινγ* DCC.

DCCCXV.

From Same to Same.

(*A Kossid letter on a scrap of thin paper.*)

Cawnpore, 14*th October* 1857.

. . . .

I am afraid a sad mess is made of the telegraphing.

. . . .

All your letters are carefully sent down, and I saw a note from Lord Dunkellin to-day in which he said your letters were very welcome. We are all right here.

There is said to be a large body of men at Meeran Kee Serai.

. . . .

Native stories about Delhi. We were very much amused with their story about Dehli; they told one of the Kossids that the king of Puttiala had taken Dehli, and that at present he was favourable to the English, but his future conduct could not be foretold. There is a large body also of rebels still at Banda, but the Nawab has as much as he can do with the turbulent Zamindars. They have twice beaten back a post he attempted to establish on the Jumna, — not that they like us at all, — but that they have a taste for chaos in general, and its agreeable consequent, NO TAXES. A letter from Banda states that perpetual confusion reigns from flying reports that the "Gora log are coming." The accompanying letter will show that grief prevails in Reewan, but I believe in Osborne's star. I hope this will find you flushed with victory. Not a breath from Lucknow!

DCCCXVI.

FROM SAME TO SAME.

(*A Kossid letter on a scrap of thin paper.*)

October 14th, 1857.

I FORGOT to say in my letter to you, which I have just sent up, that the Nana is still at Futtehpore Chorasee, as he is afraid of being nabbed. His brother Appa Jee is said to be with the fugitives at Meeran Ki Serai. Probably he it was who fled from Boolundshuhur; we have near 1000 men here now.

Nana.

Appa Jee.

DCCCXVII.

FROM J. W. SHERER, C.S., TO W. MUIR, C.S.

(*A Kossid letter written on small piece of thin wrapped-up paper.*)

CAWNPORE, *October 16th*, 1857.

YOUR letter to Edmonstone dated the 10th reached here last night, but too late for the post. However, a telegram was at once sent off, and to-day, as your letter of the 11th has come in (10 a.m.), the two will go together, and give a complete account of the very brilliant affair,[1] on which you have my warmest congratulations. I have now the great pleasure of sending you a list of survivors in the Belee Guard, found there on the 25th September. You will be truly glad to find it so long, and even now not complete as regards the less prominent members of their little society.

. . . .

The Dehli fugitives have not yet advanced as far as Bithour, and it seems certain now, I think, they will cross into Oude. It seems a great pity they should be allowed to carry away so many guns and so much treasure, and, above all, so many elephants, which we want exceedingly; but still, unless they come within 20 miles, it would certainly not be right to go out against them. Besides the list from Oude, there is no news. They hold strong positions in the city, and do not mention that they are hard-up for supplies, but that, I fancy, must be the pinch. The Alum Bagh people are quite right, except that the camp-followers are much pressed for food. The Nana is still believed

Movements of Delhi fugitives.

Position at Lucknow, and at Alam Bagh.

Nana.

[1] Defeat of rebels at Agra, 10th October.—W. C.

to be at Futtehpore Chourassee. He has not ventured across the Doab yet. Matters are temporarily a little complicated down below, as you will see from enclosed letter, but the advance of troops will put all right. The sad delay in sending up troops causes the shedding of much precious blood. I cannot make out that any corps, except the 13th, has arrived from England yet. Upon my word, Greathed's men did nobly to fight so,—after a long march.

. . . .

This goes back by the Christian who brought the letter of the 11th.

DCCCXVIII.

From Same to Same.

Cawnpore, *October 18th*, 1857.

Cawnpore sends a force against the Delhi fugitives.

The Dehli fugitives had advanced so near, within 20 miles, and the report was so current that the Nana proposed to cross over and put himself at their head, that it became necessary to oppose their further progress; accordingly last night a force started on elephants, consisting of 325 Europeans each, and six guns with Royal Artillery men, about 60 Sowars and 100 musket men, new levies of Bruce's. Benson represents our Service, as Bruce wished me to watch the City and keep on the look-out. . . . .
. . . . I thought it not unlikely that the Bithoor people, some 50 Sowars and 100 Tulingas, hearing that our people were taking the upper road to Sheorajpore, might double back and harass the suburbs; but more men have come in this morning, and we could spare 100 rifles, to kick them out if they came. I had a great fight to effect this expedition.

. . . .

DCCCXX.

From Same to Same.

Cawnpore, *October 21st*, 1857.

. . . .

Convoy for Alam Bagh.

A convoy starts to-night for Alum Bagh 400 strong and 2 guns, carrying Bazaar stores for the camp-followers, and general supplies. We expect 6 lacs of treasure to-morrow under a good escort, and a wing of the 53rd is somewhere between here and Allahabad.

My news-writer at Banda reports that there was a battle near Banda on the 17th, between the Nawab and the Rana of Ajhegurh, and that the latter was defeated and taken prisoner by a soubahdar. The writer adds, there were 4 Sahibs with the Rana, of whom 1 was killed and the rest escaped in the direction of Nagode. Major Robertson was lying wounded in a village near Hurdeo Buksh's fort when Probyn first came here, but I fear he is since dead. He was in company with a Mr. Churcher; I will make further enquiries. I have written to Hurdeo Buksh to apprise him of the approach of the Dehli Column, and to beg him to arrest the Nawab of Furruckabad if he should fly into his part of the country. The Nawab is so great a coward that I have no doubt the mere movement of our Column down the Grand Trunk Road will drive him into exile. Hurdeo Buksh has written back that he will not fail to do so.

Battle near Banda.

Rana of Ajhegarh.

Major Robertson.

Hardeo Bakhsh.

Nawab of Farakhabad.

. . . .

DCCCXXI.

From Same to Same.

Cawnpore, *October 23rd*, 1857.

. . . .

The Dehli fugitives have not formed again since our demonstration, and small bodies of them, separating and dispersing amongst the villages, have been destroyed by the zamindars, only I fear on account of loot. We cannot trace the Gwalior people further than the Sinde river, which they do not seem to have been able to cross. My man at Calpee says the Goorserai Chief declares every day they will be in next morning, but they come not. The Calpee writer also adds that the Banda people have sent word they will join the Contingent at Calpee, but from another source we know that the Banda regiments want to cross Futtehpore into Oude without going to Futtehpore. But I do not see how they are to do this, for the scarlet stream is slowly flowing up the road, and it is not so easy to ford. . . . .

Delhi fugitives.

Banda regiments.

I cannot tell you exactly what troops are coming up country, for it is not known. But *ιου μαι ρελι ον θις, ονλι κινδλι ρεφραιν φρομ πριντινγ ιτ, θατ θερε ωιλλ βε ατ αλυμβαγ ανδ θις πλασε βι* 7th Nov. 2500 Europeans *ανδ μιλιταρι τραιν* quite *εξκλυσιυε οφ γρεατεδ'ς φορσε.* I heard from Greathed to-day; the letter was from Shekoabad. He hopes to be here by the 27th.

Strength of force collecting.

. . . .

DCCCXXII.

From Same to Same.

October 25th, 1 a.m.

Grant's column.

I have been woke up in the night with the agreeable intelligence that Brigadier Grant's column will be at Chobeepore, one march from this, to-morrow morning or rather this morning, for we have just passed into the 25th; so, as I cannot sleep, I will get my despatch ready, the Kossids liking nothing better than to start at earliest dawn. Grant met no opposition till the 23rd at Meeran ke Serai, then "he took 4 guns, and killed upwards of 200, chiefly sowars of the Irregular Cavalry, pursuing them to the Ganges, over which only one man escaped." Thus writes Lieut. Roberts.[1] There is no one else to overcome just at present; the road is perfectly clear between this and Peora, where the camp was yesterday (24th). There is no doubt the Gwalior Contingent is coming to Calpee; my spy, who left the night before last, reports that up to the time of his despatch no troops had arrived, but all was expectation, and the Goorserai Chief busy in completing his bridge over the Jumna. If they will come and be licked, all will be well, but they would very much complicate matters by holding on just now at Calpee. Kooer Singh (of Arrah) is reported to be on his way from Banda to join the G. C. at Calpee, but my Banda news is not good.

Action at Miran ke Serai.

Gwalior Contingent.

Kanwar Singh.

. . . .

I have seen Havelock's and Outram's despatches about Lucknow, the entry, etc. But, of course, we were not at liberty to take notes before they had been submitted to the C.-in-C.; as soon as ever they come up printed, however, I will forward you copies. The story is materially the same as we had gathered

[1] Now Lord Roberts.—W. C.

before. No opposition to speak of between Mungulwara and Alum Bagh; at the latter place, a battle on the 24th; sick, wounded, and camp-followers all left at Alum Bagh under a strong guard. Attack on the city on the 25th; canal easily crossed; deadly opposition in the suburbs; the Sikhs and 78th Highlanders alone reached Belee Guard that night with Havelock and Outram at their head. Next day great fighting for the rest of the troops to join their comrades, which they succeeded in doing without any General. The carnage was very dreadful, and the list I previously sent was a mere skeleton of the real one. Major Simmons of the 5th Fusiliers was killed, so was Hallyburton of the 90th, and Crump of the Artillery, and Major Bazeley, unattached. The wounded were very numerous, including young Havelock[1] and Tytler seriously, Outram himself, young Birch of the V. Cavalry, Lynch of the same, Palliser of the same, Major Stevenson of the Madras Fusiliers, etc. etc.

Fight at Alam Bagh.

Attack on city.

Officers killed and wounded.

. . . .

We *ἑαρ νο ρεσυλτς ιετ οφ Μαν σινγ's προποσαλς—βυτ θε βαττλε ις νου σιμπλι βετωεεν υς ανδ Μαν σινγ.* Brijus Kudr and Co. are as entirely out of the coach as Henri Cinq is out of that of France. We expect 400 of the 73rd Highlanders on the 27th; we have 600 effective men in the garrison, and there are 1100 men (including our convoy) at Alum Bagh, but I cannot tell what detachments are on the road, for we do not really know, Bruce does not, and the Colonel does not. The town is entirely in our favour here, but the district gets worse and worse. They see that we cannot spare men to go out into the Mofussil, and they fairly set us at defiance; but this will end immediately when a large force is permanently fixed here, and when parties can be detached to punish individual instances of outrage. Revenue has altogether ceased, tho' I have still more than a lakh due from June kists; but I mean to make capital of Grant's Column being here, unless our Gwalior friends cross the river. We are having a lovely and remarkably healthy autumn, and our convalescents are coming on nicely, but . . . . many of those who are fatally ill die without any of the consolations of religion.

Man Singh.

Troops at Cawnpore and in Lucknow.

Cawnpore town loyal, but district unsettled.

Revenue collections deficient.

Treatment of the sick.

. . . .

[1] Afterwards Sir Henry Havelock-Allan. He greatly distinguished himself in this Campaign.—W. C.

DCCCXXIII.

FROM SAME TO SAME.

CAWNPORE, *October 28th*, 1857, *before dawn.*

. . . .

Grant's Column.

Grant's column has not marched.

. . . .

Sir Colin Campbell.

Sir Colin Campbell will be here by the 1st.

. . . .

93rd Highlanders. Kanwar Singh at Calpee. Goorserai Chief. Oude the El Dorado of Badmashes.

400 of the 93rd Highlanders marched in yesterday. Splendid fellows, and in excellent heart and health, longing to have an early opportunity of distinguishing themselves. Kooer Singh with 12 or 1500 of the Banda rebels and 3 or 400 of his own men has arrived at Calpee. They are almost wholly without ammunition, and a wretched undisciplined rabble. The Goorserai Chief pays great court to them, and begs them to stay for the Gwalior Contingent, but they seem anxious to cross the Doab for the new El Dorado of Budmashes, Oude.

Gwalior Contingent. Order restored in Rewan.

The Gwalior Contingent on the 26th was at Mahoba, 25 miles off. What their meaning is in creeping on in this fashion it is hard to define. Osborne writes that order is entirely restored in Reewan.

. . . .

Road open to Calcutta.

Drummond starts to-day and Harington to-morrow. The road is quite open now to Calcutta for dawk garis.

DCCCXXV.

FROM SAME TO SAME.

(*A small-folded Kossid letter on small thin paper.*)

CAWNPORE, *October 31st*, 1857, *dawn.*

. . . .

Movements of the rebels.

All the rebels have left Banda. I told you 1200 had reached Calpee, and the rest had crossed into Futtehpore about 1500 strong with the two small Nagode guns.

It is believed they mean to run across and slip into Oudh, but there are several detachments on the road, and they will not be able to get safely across unless they play their cards very well. We shall hear fully to-day; they were at Ghazeepore yesterday. I cannot give you the details of reinforcements, as everybody was too much in a bustle to attend to me yesterday.

. . . .

You do not seem to have got my account of Wilson's trip to Sheorajpore. I did not go, as Bruce particularly wished me to look after the City for him, and he of course had to accompany his new levies. The force was 600 Europeans, 6 guns (light), and Bruce's odds and ends, Cavalry and Infantry. They reached Sheorajpore in the afternoon of the 18th, about 3. The enemy opened fire and did some damage. We returned, and the enemy's fire was silenced. Sheorajpur affair.

Our Artillery went on firing for a considerable time, and at last when the Infantry advanced there was not a soul to be found. Our force occupied the town that night, and next morning moved down towards the river. The guns got stuck in sandy lanes. There was a large body of the enemy on a sand-bank in the river without guns, and they could have been easily destroyed by the Enfield rifles, but Wilson would not separate a single man from his guns, and they escaped.

Our force returned through Bithoor; it did nothing, but the demonstration had an excellent effect, and the Dehli fugitives broke up—four of their guns falling afterwards, as you have heard, into Grant's hands.

DCCCXXVI.

From Same to Same.

1st Brigade, *November 3rd*, 1857.

. . . .

The Gwalior Contingent have not advanced beyond Jaloun. They cannot, I think, be seriously contemplating crossing the Jumna into the Doab, for every day is of the greatest value to them if they are, and yet they dawdle away as if the game were entirely in their own hands, but it may be *quos Deus vult perdere prius dementat.* Gwalior Contingent.

Banda rebels. The Banda fellows are roving about in Futtehpore district.

. . . .

As I write this, I hear the shrill whistle of the boatswain of the "Shannon." There are 100 men of the Naval Brigade here already, and more close by with Captain Peel and six 24-pounders. The first detachment brought in four 24-pounders.

Naval Brigade arrives at Cawnpore.

. . . .

Sir Colin is hourly expected. Some Cavalry and Horse Artillery have been left behind for him, and he will take command of the army at Alum Bagh.

Harington reached Benares all right yesterday morning.

I have refused, without express orders, to assist in setting up the mail-cart between this and Bhowgong. I told Mr. Phillips it is perfect insanity to attempt to risk the cart through the Furruckabad district just at present, and failure and loss of life will have the worst effects.

DCCCXXVII.

From Same to Same.

1st Brigade, Cawnpore, *November 4th*, 1857.

. . . .

Sir Colin arrives at Cawnpore. Sir Colin arrived yesterday, and stays over to-day. He will hold a levee this morning.

Near taken prisoner. He was as near as possible taken prisoner below Benares; he and his suite drove right into the 32nd Native Infantry. They turned the carriages round and galloped off as hard as they could.

. . . .

DCCCXXVIII.

From Same to Same.

Cawnpore, *November 8th*, 1857.

Chief at Cawnpore. I have little news, although the position of affairs here is daily becoming more interesting. The Chief is still at Bruce's house, pushing on every available man and gun towards Lucknow; the Naval Brigade has most of it gone with its heavy guns, and the 53rd have gone and some more Highlanders.

Naval Brigade.

General Windham is to command here. We have a good many accounts of the intentions of the Contingent, but I do not think they have yet left Jaloun. About 1000 men, mostly Dehli fugitives, have crossed back from Oudh, some passing towards Calpee and some towards Sheergurh Ghat. General Windham. Movements of Mutineers.

Then, curiously enough, it seems that the fellows who lost their guns at Kujooa are moving towards the Ganges by Nanamow, but not in a united body. My own impression about the Gwalior fellows is this, if they are left to themselves they will incline to getting into Oudh without coming within reach of our guns; but if the Nana gets a supremacy over them, they will either take up a position at Bithour or try their hands at our entrenchment.

Part of the military train are in—about 50 of them—and some small detachments with Colonel Barclay, but everything is swept into Oudh. I have had a letter, dated 27th October, from Willock in the Belee Guard. He was quite well. He mentions J. B. Thornhill as killed in the original garrison, as well as Ommaney. This, I fear, will be distressing news to Mrs. Muir. Poor Gonne was captured somewhere in the Mofusil, brought into Lucknow and beheaded the day before Outram got into the city. J. B. Thornhill, C.S., and Ommaney killed. Gonne, C.S., beheaded.

Grant is encamped on an open plain about 5 miles beyond Bunnee. On their way to occupy this position, the enemy, posted about in villages some little way off the road, gave trouble, but the villages were soon cleared, some of the enemy's cavalry cut up, and the rest of the forces as usual made off.

DCCCXXIX.

From Same to Same.

Cawnpore, *November* 11*th*, 1857.

Sir Colin is at Alam Bagh to-day, and it seems probable the attack will take place on the 13th. Sir Colin at Alam Bagh.

. . . .

The Gwalior Contingent movements we believe to be as follows:—The 1st division, about a thousand strong, arrived at Calpee on the 9th. I cannot make out yet with certainty how many batteries they have with them—perhaps two. The second division is expected to be at Calpee to-day or to-morrow. The Movements of Gwalior Contingent.

third division, with whom are the heavy guns, if I rightly interpret the conflicting accounts one always receives of such matters, seems not to have determined whether they will cross at Shergurh Ghat, nearly parallel with Jaloun, or follow the others to Calpee.

There is, humanly speaking, no apprehension for this place, whatever happens. There are so many troops on their way now, which could be detained, or recalled, or hurried on so as to concentrate here, that we could take care of ourselves in case of attack very well, and should be sufficiently formidable I think, by exaggerated reports, to deter them from coming here at all.

Still it is naturally a stirring time. The 2000 men I mentioned as having crossed at Sheorajpore are still there, I conceive, to cover the Nana's transit across the Doab. He came down to the Ghat last night, our spies say, but his heart failed and he returned to Futtehpore Chourasee.

The Nana.

We have just heard from the camp on the road to Lucknow that the rebels made an attack on Alum Bagh yesterday afternoon. However, Sir Colin will be there to-day with the whole force, and will rather astonish them.

Alam Bagh attacked.

There was some little alarm a day or two ago at Mirzapore; the 32nd with part of the Ramgurh force had got into the district. We have not heard yet how they got out of their troubles.

DCCCXXX.

From Same to Same.

Cawnpore, *November* 21*st*, 1857.

. . . .

Jackson, C.S.

Jackson has gone on to Lucknow to satisfy himself about the fate of his nephew and nieces. I am afraid from what I hear there are little grounds for hope. Bithour, Sheorajpore, Sheoler, Russoolabad, Dera Munyalpore, Leumdra, and Bhognapore are all lost for the present, and irregular collections are being made on account of the Nana.

The Nana.

But the gross oppression exercised by these disorganised bands of soldiers will ultimately greatly benefit our cause; the people will turn on them when our troops begin to move about.

. . . .

I have just heard definitely that the Calpee people are crossing. They have two regiments to guard the spare Magazine in the Fort at Calpee. **Gwalior Mutineers.**

DCCCXXXII.

From Same to Same.

Cawnpore, *November 27th*, 1857, *before dawn.*

At last news from Lucknow, but without details of any kind. A letter from Alum Bagh dated 24th, and mentioning the fighting as over, and headquarters and ladies, etc. as starting at once for Lucknow. Yesterday General Windham, having heard that the 1st Division of the Contingent really contemplated attack, moved in from his position on the Canal to the Pandoo Nuddee. He found the enemy posted on the opposite bank. The advance was very rapid, and the enemy was soon dislodged, leaving two 8-inch Howitzers and one 9-pounder in our hands. The General, not having at the time any news from Lucknow, could not encamp far from Cawnpore, and therefore returned in the afternoon. The 64th held the Dehli road all day, as there is a very considerable gathering at Chowbeepore, and Cawnpore itself was almost deserted. Neither Power nor myself was in action, as we cannot live out in the camp with the military chest in our hands, and the endless botherations of the commissariat, and so did not hear of the battle till it was over. Our loss was about 50 killed and wounded, I think. I only know yet of one officer killed, Capt. Day of the 88th. This regiment and the 34th distinguished themselves exceedingly, and so did the Rifle Brigade. The 82nd had not such opportunity as the others for coming out, but are said to be also a first-rate corps. A body of Cavalry made a feeble attempt at charging the 34th, but were knocked right and left out of their saddles, and appeared no more on the scene. **Lucknow.** **Action at Pandu Naddi.** **Captain Day killed.**

. . . .

DCCCXXXIII.

Memo. for Colonel Fraser.

State of things at Cawnpore.

5 *p.m.*, *December 4th*, 1857.

Sir Colin encamped on the Parade ground. Enemy between

Cawnpore. Subahdar's Tank and the Church. The Town, Church, Assembly Rooms, Theatre, Hotel, etc., all in the hands of the enemy. The Garrison inside the Fort. All the ladies and garrison of Lucknow left for Allahabad last night. Very little firing to-day. Sir James Outram at Alum Bagh with three thousand men. Communication entirely open with Futtehpore.

J. W. SHERER.

DCCCXXXIV.

FROM J. W. SHERER, C.S., TO W. MUIR, C.S.

CAWNPORE, *December* 10*th*, 1857.

I AM delighted to tell you that communication is restored, and, after not hearing from you for sixteen days, I have had three packets dated respectively 28th, 1st, and 2nd.

. . . .

It is perfectly true that poor John Thornhill is dead.

Mathauli prisoners. Nothing is known of the fate of the Muthowlie prisoners, but it is generally believed that they have all been put to death in Lucknow.

. . . .

DCCCXXXV.

FROM SAME TO SAME.

CAWNPORE, *December* 19*th*, 1857.

. . . .

Sir Colin. Brigadier Hope is still at Bithour, and Sir Colin here.

I am plagued to death with a disgusting Committee on the Crown jewels of Lucknow, which takes up time dreadfully. They have thrown their treasure and stamps into our hands without a single memo. of contents, and the trouble of arranging all this is inconceivable.

Crown jewels of Lucknow.

Martin Gubbins, C.S. I hear from Mrs. Gubbins that Martin Gubbins has been dangerously ill ever since he reached Allahabad, and he is not now considered out of danger.

Mrs. Gubbins and Miss Nepean were looking exceedingly well when they passed through here. In fact it was surprising how little ladies had suffered in health, apparently. But some of the men had aged fearfully.

Mr. Edwards has telegraphed up to me that he hopes you will be good enough to write at once to his wife to come down to Agra, as the Governor-General has directed an escort to be provided for ladies and children to Allahabad as soon as the road is open.

DCCCXXXVI.

FROM SAME TO SAME.

CAWNPORE, *December 23rd*, 1857, *before sunrise*.

. . . .

Sir Colin is still here, and Brigadier Hope at Bithour. The city is recovering, and I am establishing Thanas and Tuhseelees as fast as I can—not quite so fast, however, as the Calcutta people wish, for they have telegraphed up, "Why is not the Civil power more strongly established in the Cawnpore district?" But I know what I am about, and nothing does so much harm as pushing out establishments wholly unsupported which have to give in. There have been three Thanadars killed already in this district since July, besides two or three massacres of Bruce's police. Chester has been very ill, and is going home; F. Gubbins to succeed. Martin of the same name has had a dangerous attack on the brain, but is now better, though in a very weak state and not out of danger. He is lying at Allahabad. Jackson is going on very well. . . . . It was my horse that broke his leg; was not that unfortunate? I was so vexed.

Sir Colin. Civil government re-established at Cawnpore. Police officers killed. Chester, C.S. F. and M. Gubbins, C.S. Jackson, C.S.

. . . .

DCCCXXXVII.

FROM SAME TO SAME.

CAWNPORE, *December 24th*, 1857.

THE following is by telegraph from Accountant-General to Accountants of Agra and Punjab—"Statement of receipts and disbursements for 1856–57 urgently required. Please send also statement of loans, etc., for 1856–57."

The Commander-in-Chief left this morning. He has gone up the Trunk Road—I do not know where to—I suppose to

Commander-in-Chief.

John Power, C.S.

Futtehgurh. John Power accompanied him. A Thana and Tehseelee have been already established at Sheorajpore, and the materials for establishments at Bithour accompany the Chief, under John Power's directions, I being wholly tied by the leg by unadjusted accounts, uncounted treasure, and this abominable Jewel business.

. . . .

DCCCXXXVIII.

FROM SAME TO SAME.

CAWNPORE, *December 29th*, 1857.

Re-establishment of Civil government in Cawnpore District.

I HAVE been out with the Chief up the Trunk Road. All the Thanas and the Tehseelees are established along the Grand Trunk Road in my district, and the Wire floats out of it into Furruckabad. If we can only keep off invasion, I do not fear for permanent peace and order. The Chief must be to-day at Goorsehai Gunj. Brigadier Hope is following him, and is at Sheorajpore, I should say, now. Brigadier Walpole was at Ooriyah in Etawah the day before yesterday. His passage through unfrequented parts of this district did great good. He was accompanied by Captain Bradford, who has been appointed Joint-Magistrate here; and he did excellent service by hunting out and hanging several bad characters whose influence has tended to keep up ferment and disorder. I am promised a lakh this week, and I sincerely trust that a day of better things is now dawning.

Brigadier Hope.

Brigadier Walpole.

Captain Bradford.

As soon as the entrenchments are sufficiently completed to be safely confided to a few men, the Brigadier and myself and the military police under Thompson are all going a-gipsying into the district.

DCCCXXXIX.

FROM GENL. NEILL, CAWNPORE,
TO THE HONBLE. THE LT.-GOVERNOR, AGRA.

CAWNPORE, *7th September* 1857.[1]

. . . .

A great many of our Officers are yet alive and safe in Oude.

[1] A "Kossid letter" on thin paper and much folded.—W. C.

I have to-day heard of Captain Orr and Mr. Thornhill, with their wives and children, safe at Matouly near Seetapore. Capt. Gowan or Lt. Gowan, somewhere near Rohilcund, wrote to Genl. Havelock a most interesting letter as to what he could do, if empowered and with command of money, to raise and discipline men for us.

Officers in refuge: Orr, Thornhill, Gowan.

. . . .

76 Officers, 2025 Men (Europeans), left Allahabad or joined here previous to advance into Oude; in addition 326 men sent down sick to Allahabad, making a total of 645 killed or rendered *hors de combat*—this of Europeans only—between 7th July and 22nd August.

DCCCXLI.

FROM CAPT. CHALMERS, COMMISSARIAT, FORT AGRA, TO THE HON. THE LT.-GOVR.

I HAVE about 2000 Camels ready which might march day after to-morrow. I have given orders and made arrangements for the collection of hackeries as per your order of this morning, but of course no considerable number will be procured for four or five days. I also expect a good number additional camels within that time. Could not a Detacht. of Cavalry be left behind by Col. Greathed to overtake the Main Column by double marches?

14/10/57.

DCCCXLII.

FROM COLONEL WILSON, COMMANDING AT CAWNPORE, TO COLONEL FRASER, CHIEF COMMISSIONER AT AGRA, *October 20th.*

(*A Kossid despatch on a very small scrap of thin paper.*)

I HAVE received a message from the Governor-General, which I send you.

"Message." You are requested to forward the following message to Colonel Fraser, Chief Commissioner at Agra, with the utmost expedition. Message begins—"The presence of Colonel Greathed's column is urgently required in Oude, therefore do not

Greathed's Column hastened.

allow Lieutenant-Colonel Greathed to be detained at or near Agra an hour longer than is necessary. Allow him to exchange some of the sickly and weak European Infantry for some of your fresh men if he desires it. Let Colonel Greathed know that his cavalry are specially needed. The reinforcement of General Outram at Lucknow is the object which most presses, and you are requested to do everything in your power to hasten the accomplishment of this by Colonel Greathed."

FLETCHER MURPHY, Captain,
Staff Officer.

Duplicate (*true copy*).

I have sent two copies of this down the road direct to Colonel Greathed.

J. W. SHERER.

DCCCXLIV.

FROM CAPTAIN BRUCE TO COL. HUGH FRASER, C.B.

(*Kossid letter written on small thin paper.*)

CAWNPORE, 17*th October* 1857.

Sir J. Outram's communication with General at Delhi.

DEAR SIR,—I received a letter from General Outram dated 13th. Gathering from Mr. Muir's previous letters that Colonel Greathed would probably come down to Futtehgurh, I forwarded direct to its commander a copy of Sir J. Outram's requisition to the General at Dehli, a copy of which I had the honour to enclose to you on the 8th instant, reporting to General Outram that I had done so.

General Outram requires two brigades.

A good deal of Sir James' reply is taken up with instructions for the Officer Commanding the Dehli Column, with which it is now unnecessary to trouble you, but I think it right to mention that the General is still urgent for reinforcements—two strong brigades are at least required, one of which can be collected from troops now on their way up from Calcutta.

Position at Lucknow.

The General says, "In forcing our way from the Alum Bagh to the Residency with 2200 men our casualties were *σο ἑανι* that our sick, wounded, women, and children, amounting to upwards of *φιφτεεν* hundred, *καννοτ* be moved until we are greatly ρειυφορσεδ, nor could we obtain carriage for them while our communication with the well affected in the city is κυτ οφφ by the rebels, who still δομινεερ over it and συρρουνδ our position."

Being unable to ρεμονε the γαρρισον, the General's ὁλε φορσε is required to support it, and what is most to be apprehended is that the General's force will run ουτ of συππλιες. The road is pretty clear up to Alum Bagh (3 miles this side of Lucknow), and the detachment there can be φεδ from here, but from Alum Bagh to the General's ποσιτιον the ιντερυενινγ οβστακλες are too great to be overcome unless by a λαργε φορσε supported by αρτιλλερι.

H. Bruce.

DCCCXLVI.

From Capt. H. Bruce to Col. Fraser, C.B., Agra.

Cawnpore, *26th October* 1857.

Governor-General orders Colonel Fraser to send men to Cawnpore.

I have just received a Telegraphic Message from the Governor-General, in which His Lordship says, "I wish you to send this message to Col. Fraser, Agra. Received your letter of 12th, which says that a party of Col. Greathed's Column, consisting of 50 Cavalry, 200 Punjab Sikhs, and a detachment of Europeans, are sent to Alleeghur. I beg you to set free as much of this force as you possibly can, and to send it to Cawnpore, where every man is required, but especially Cavalry. Pray do not keep back from Cawnpore a single horseman you can spare. I also beg you to send to Dehli and Meerut, and to press General Penny to despatch as many remount horses to Cawnpore as he can spare, and to send with them as many of the Carabineers as he can spare. Tell him the Cavalry is urgently wanted."

Greathed's Column reaches Cawnpore.

Colonel Greathed's Column reached Cawnpore this morning, and will, I hope, move on towards Lucknow, reinforced by all the men who can be spared from this, on 28th. 200 of the Naval Brigade, a lot of Artillery, and 400 H.M. 93rd, and details, are between this and Allahabad. Any small party marching down had better be warned to avoid Bewar and Goorsahaigunge, as the Nawab of Futtehgurh could perhaps bring guns out on them. These two places can be avoided for encampments by arranging

Nawab of Fatehgarh hostile.

the marches so that the halts are made at Bhogong, Chabramow, and Meeran ke Serai.

The Comdr.-in-Chief leaves Calcutta to-morrow, and will be at Cawnpore on 1st or 2nd prox.

DCCCXLVII.

FROM CAPT. BRUCE, SUPT. OF POLICE (TO W. MUIR, C.S., AGRA ?)

CAWNPORE, *14th December* 1857.

MY DEAR SIR,—I received your Cossid's packet yesterday; the mail extract which you obligingly sent reached almost simultaneously with the packet from the eastward. The C.-in-C. is still encamped here, with one Brigade destroying the Nana's property at Bithoor. I fancy we shall all move in a day or two, but the route has not yet been determined upon. You will have heard from Mr. Sherer of the very good business we did with the Gwalior Contingent. *Every* gun they brought over the Jumna with them has been captured, besides 5 others, 4 of which are Horse Artillery ones, from Dehli I fancy. Altogether we have *parc*-ed 38 pieces of Cannon, Heavy and Field. Everything is quiet eastward except at Jounpore and Azimghur, where a lot of *Budmashes* have collected around 15 or 16 guns and threaten Colonel Longden's Column and the Goorkhas. Colonel Longden was obliged to fall back; but Colonel Franks, who now commands in those districts, has got a strong Brigade together, and by this time no doubt has established order. Any news I give you I beg may not be printed.

Commander-in-Chief at Cawnpore.

Artillery taken from Gwalior Contingent.

Disturbances in Jaunpore and Azimgarh.

Colonel Longden.

Colonel Franks.

Want of Police.

The great drawback now is the want of Police. We cannot take advantage of the defeat of rebels, because there are no properly constituted Police Officers to follow up with strong posts the movements of our armies. The Govt. do not seem to have decided what system to adopt, and individuals seem so bent upon bolstering the old plan, which I conceive *must* fail now, as it did before. Between all this indecision nothing is done, and in time the face of the country will be covered by Bandits. The proposition that was made to me did not seem to suit the times at all, and I therefore applied to join my Regt. His Exy. the C.-in-C. was pleased, however, to nominate me Dy. Qr.-Mr. Genl. and (*illegible*) his Headquarters.

DCCCLII.

From H. B. Harington, C.S., with Genl. Hope Grant's Column, to W. Muir, C.S., Agra.

(*From the Original.*)

Cawnpore, *October 27th*, 1857.

My Dear Muir,—

Your kind note deserved not only an earlier but an immediate reply.

. . . .

The Khareef harvest ought to be a most abundant one. During the whole time I have been in India I have never seen finer crops of bajrah, jawar, sugar-cane, etc., and I am glad to observe that the land was everywhere being prepared for the rabbie, tho' some of the poorer ryots told me that they feared they might not be able to purchase as much seed as they required, owing either to the flight of the village money-lender or to the disinclination to lend so long as there was no Court to which he could apply for the recovery of his money. With returning confidence in the stability of our rule the difficulty will, I trust, be overcome.

. . . .

It was a great pity that we were obliged to leave Futtehgurh in our rear in the occupation of the Nawab, who has doubtless given out that we were afraid to attack him; now, tho' he probably knows better, he will be believed by many, and the consequence will be a large addition to his numbers. He and his followers, as well as everybody else, took it for granted that after settling matters at Mynpoorie we should proceed to Futtehgurh: had we been able to do so we should have found the Fatehgarh. place deserted; and a wing of a Sikh Regiment with the 75 Queen's (the few men remaining of which are worn-out and require rest), with a few artillery, would not only have held the place against all comers, but would have so strengthened Bhewanee Singh's hands at Mynpoorie, and Hume's at Etawah, that I really believe it would have been quite unnecessary to send troops to either of these places. I am glad to find that everybody advocates the early occupation of Furruckabad; until Farakhabad. this is done every district in the Doab will remain in an unsettled state, and no regular communication by dak can be kept up between the stations on this and those on that side of the

Lucknow.

district. Sherer keeps you, I hear, well informed of all that is going on here. He has no late news from Lucknow, but we have every reason to believe that they are holding their own there, and that they have provisions sufficient to last them until the 10th proximo. I fully expect that, as soon as the fine force now collecting here for the relief of Lucknow commences its march, Man Singh's followers will desert him, and the C.-in-C., who is expected on Sunday or Monday, will have an easy victory. The troops are passing up the Grand Trunk Road; and they have already so many men in Calcutta that they do not know where to place them.

. . . .

Fatehgarh should be occupied.

I hear that owing to the closing of the Rohilkund markets grain is becoming very scarce below this; here is another strong reason for an early occupation of Futtehgurh, and another still stronger in my opinion is that as soon as that place is occupied by us the ladies at Agra may travel down the Great Trunk Road with the utmost safety.

. . . .

DCCCLIII.

FROM BRIG. HOPE GRANT, COMMANDING RELIEF COLUMN, TO W. MUIR, C.S., AGRA.

NAUGUNGE, *5th November* 1857.

MY DEAR MUIR,[1]—

. . . .

Attack on Hope Grant's Column repulsed.

We are close to Lucknow waiting for the C.-C., who has arrived at Cawnpore. We had another fight on the ground we are now encamped upon, the other day. About 1000 or 1200 had come to attack our rear and supplies, but it happened that I did not march that morning till daylight. They therefore attacked us in front without any guns, and were soon driven to the four winds. Another party I suppose came from Jellallabad near this, and brought out a 9-pounder of our own, which they early opened upon us. We took the gun and killed about 100.

I have a nice force now of nearly 5000 men.

[1] This and following letter written on tiny scraps of thin paper.—W. C.

DCCCLIV.

FROM BRIGADIER HOPE GRANT TO W. MUIR, C.S., AGRA.

[CAWNPORE ?], *8th December.*

MY DEAR MUIR,—Kindly forward the enclosed letters. We have relieved ladies and children, women and sick, from Lucknow, and they are safely on their way to Calcutta. We returned here and found the place besieged by the Gwalior force. We have given them a complete licking, have taken altogether 22 guns, and at this latter place have not lost altogether 50 men. Lucknow relieved.

We are moving up country.

DCCCLV.

FROM SAME TO SAME.

CAWNPORE, *13th December* 1857.

MY DEAR MUIR,[1]—Nothing new since I wrote the other day. Since coming to Cawnpore our force has taken 32 guns and Genl. Windham's 5, making altogether 37 guns. We have therefore drawn the teeth of the Gwalior force. Thirty-seven guns taken.

DCCCLVI.

FROM SAME TO SAME.

CAWNPORE, *16th December* 1857.

MY DEAR MUIR,—

. . . .

We shall soon be up your way, at least as far as Mynpoorie, to clear the country, and then in all probability into Oudh. I trust the road will soon be open between us. All the Lucknow garrison have been relieved—500 ladies, women, and children, some 700 sick and wounded, and nearly a million of jewels and treasure. . . . My love to poor good Jones, who I trust is doing well. Relief of Lucknow.

(Sgnd.).

[1] A Kossid letter written on small scrap of thin paper.—W. C.

DCCCLVII.

From James Power, C.S., Cawnpore.

Cawnpore, 18*th November* 1857.

My Dear Muir,—

. . . .

Herbert Harington.

Harington, it appears, is obliged to remain at Alum Bagh, and complains of a 24-pounder shot bowling through his tent as being a great nuisance. An unfortunate man, sick in hospital, was killed there a few days since.

Gwalior Mutineers.

Our young friends from Gwalior are still on their side of the Jumna; we *did* hear that their 1st Division had crossed on Sunday last, but it appears from our latest intelligence to be Kooer Singh's party and about 2000 of the Gwalior rebels, in search of "Russud," I suppose. These warriors had better make haste and come to Cawnpore if they wish to take it, for we are getting very strong in our fortifications, and our force is increasing daily.

. . . .

Macleod is here, and doing right good service as Engineer.

. . . .

E. Colvin dies at Calcutta. E. Hastings killed.

Poor Edward Colvin died in Calcutta a few days since, and my cousin Edward Hastings was killed at Ghazeepore.

I am appointed Joint here.

C. Jackson, C.S.

Coverley Jackson arrived here yesterday. He represents the "Board" of the Central Provinces.

DCCCLVIII.

From Same to Same.

Cawnpore, 19*th November* 1857.

My Dear Muir,—

. . . .

Kanwar Singh.

Kooer Singh's men and a few others of the Gwalior men in Bhogneepore, with two guns.

The Nana.

The Nana's men and miscellaneous Mutineers at Akbarpore, Sheolie, and Sheorajpore. The Gwalior Contingent had stated their intention to cross on the 19th (to-day), but it is thought they will not cross unless the Nana goes over to Calpee.

. . . .

DCCCLIX.

FROM MAJOR-GENERAL MANSFIELD, CHIEF OF THE STAFF, TO COLONEL FRASER, CHIEF COMMISSIONER, AGRA.

CAWNPORE, 14*th Decr.* 1857.

(*A Kossid letter on half-sheet of thin paper, folded very small.*)

SIR,—I am directed by the Commander-in-Chief to inform you of the total dispersion of the Gwalior Contingent, *37* of whose guns have been taken. I propose to move forward in two Columns. The stronger one up the Main Road towards Futtehgurh, and the second by Akbarpore, skirting the Jumna, and so to Mynpoorie. Sir James Outram has been left with a force of 4500 men in the immediate neighbourhood of Lucknow. A Column of *3* British Regts. is being organised at Benares to operate in the Jaunpore and Azimgurh districts; and Jung Bahadoor, by desire of the Governor-General, is about to move with *9000* Ghoorkhas towards Goruckpoor. His Lordship's arrangements in these respects are very complete. I have received Mr. Thornhill's Cossid of 4th Dec. His Excellency will move in a few days, as soon as he can equip the force under his immediate command with the necessaries of which it is destitute. The Nana is said to be about to fly to a distant part of Oudh. Our information coincides with yours. Will you kindly communicate the above to General Penny and to Sir John Lawrence, and inform the latter that we want $\chi\alpha\nu\alpha\lambda\rho\eta$? The Commander-in-Chief desires to have Mr. Raikes' assistance in Camp as soon as the road is open from Agra.

Rout of the Gwalior Contingent.

Sir James Outram.

Nine thousand Gurkhas.

The Nana.

Mr. Raikes.

DCCCLX.

FROM SAME TO SAME.

CAMP NEAR . . [*torn off*].

(*Duplicate.*)

(*A Kossid letter on thin paper, folded very small.*)

SIR,—The various Cossids have been received from Mr. Muir announcing Colonel Seaton's movements on Allygurh. Sir John Lawrence's views about Rohilcund will be forwarded by His Excellency to the Governor-General. This force is much in

Colonel Seaton's Column.

want of Boots and Tents, and a large store of both should be prepared at Agra, say (10,000) ten thousand pairs of the former and 500 of the latter.

Can you write to Scindia to intercept all fugitives from the Gwalior Contingent who have recrossed the Jumna, and lend a party of 200 Mahratta Horse, for whose fidelity he will *be responsible*, for service in the Cawnpore district? If the latter can be done I shall be obliged to you to communicate with me and with Brigadier Inglis, Comdg. at Cawnpore, as soon as possible on the subject. The Mahratta horsemen should be put in movement immediately. A Brigade marched this day for Mynpoorie, *via* Akbarpore, Etawah, etc.; and His Excellency hopes to leave Cawnpore for the N.-W. by the 22nd inst. In consideration of Colonel Seaton's advance, a *horse* dak should be organised towards Mynpoorie till the country admits of the use of mail-carts. Could you, if required, with the help of Jotee Pursad, get 400 swift riding Camels from Rajpootana speedily, and drivers, for whom security could be obtained from the influential Chiefs who may have remain(ed) loyal to our Government? The whole, if wanted, to be got together upon the Irregular Cavalry or Sillidar system.

Mahratta Horse asked from Scindia.

Colonel Seaton.

Joti Parsád.

Riding camels.

P.S.—Pray excuse the almost unpardonable abruptness of this *Cossid* letter.

DCCCLXI.

FROM GENERAL MANSFIELD, CHIEF OF THE STAFF, TO W. MUIR, C.S., AGRA.

FUTTEHGURH, *Janry. 8th*, 1858.

MY DEAR SIR,[1]—

. . . .

Police levies.

You are aware, I presume, of the formation which is now in progress of young Battalions, on the Punjab Police Model, at Cawnpore and Benares. H. E. has given the order for one to be raised at this place, and I think another will be put into shape at Mynpoorie. This organisation is not intended for any special purpose, but to be made available for every description of Service, and to be hereafter devoted to Army and Police purposes as Government may direct. It cannot but be useful in the course of six weeks to replace the British Troops, whose

[1] This letter is written in General Mansfield's own hand.

presence may be required at any hour in other quarters of the Empire; and, I take it, six weeks, if well employed by the Officers engaged in the duty, ought to render these raw battalions fit for district purposes. A good many guns and a vast quantity of Stores of every kind have been saved here.

Since writing the above, the sanction of H. E. has been given for the formation of the Mynpoorie Battalion. The escort with the Convoy, despatched from Agra, will be returned. Maiupúri Battalion sanctioned.

DCCCLXII.

From Capt. J. H. Smyth, R.H.A., Chief Staff Officer with Moveable Column, to W. Muir, C.S., Agra.[1]

Ukburpore, *Decr.* 22*nd*, 1857.

My Dear Sir,—As 2 Cossids are here, who are returning to Agra, I write to tell you what we are doing. We have 2500 men under Brigadier Walpole—a most efficient force, complete in Cavalry and guns. Capt. Bradford is doing his best to re-establish the Civil power; but, as there has been 7 months of misrule, the task will be difficult. Agents for the Nana (backed by the Raja of Mynpoorie, I think) have established his rule down here, and have been supported chiefly by the Mussulman population and the Chauhán (?) Rajpoots. We have succeeded in capturing Josee Sing, the Chief of the latter, and also a Mahommedan of note, who had been appointed to the district. The Tehseeldar Ahmedulla has fled. The great mart of Cajuere has been visited by a strong party from our Camp, and our presence was hailed with joy by the Traders; and though on our arrival the inhabitants fled, they soon returned and brought to the European soldiery all kinds of sweetmeats, milk, bread, etc., many of the shopkeepers refusing to take any payment. Having learned that the Takoors of Putra prevented supplies going to Cawnpore, and that they were backed by some of the Gwalior sepoys, we surrounded the village, caught the Heads of it and also 3 or 4 sepoys. As many of the Takoors did not join the enemy for several months, and not been at all active in opposing us (but rather passive spectators of the struggle), I am glad to find that Capt. Bradford does not think that it is

Captain Bradford.

The Nana.

Chauhán (?) Rajpúts. Josi Sing.

Takoors of Putra.

[1] From Walpole's force proceeding through Cawnpore and Etawah to re-establish authority.—W. M.

necessary to proceed with violence against them, and that he will do his utmost to warn them of the danger of not supporting us thoroughly. From what I have seen it is very necessary that some man [of] repute, and who is known down here, should be sent to put things to rights—our passing through the district is not sufficient—while the Mutineers hold Calpee and Jaloun.

. . . . . .

DCCCLXIII.

From Same to Same.

Etawah, *Decr.* 30*th*, 1857.

Rajah Zor Singh.

My Dear Sir,—We came in here yesterday. I have derived every assistance from the Row of Lucknow and Raja Zor Singh (?) of Pertaubnair. I think it would gratify these men if a letter was sent thanking them on the part of the Agra Government for the aid given to us. Colonel Walpole is precluded by the strictest orders from detaching any man from his force, neither can he remain here until Mr. Hume joins. We are directed to be at Mynpoorie not later than the 2nd of January. For several days past we have had no communication from the C.-in-C. (Private.) It is as well to inform you that His Excellency has determined to have no small posts that can possibly be done without—they are well known to be destructive to discipline, and in a certain way to lower the morale of the British soldier. I understand that the C.-in-C. proposes to establish Moveable Columns. I suppose that each garrison will be strong enough to afford these Columns in force sufficient to put down any opposition; and that they will be always on the move and at hand to assist the Civil power. Our garrisons, I conclude, will be—Allahabad, Futtehpore, Cawnpore, Futtehgurh, Mynpoorie or Agra, and Allygurh.

Commander-in-Chief's plans.

. . . .

Force at Calpee. People friendly.

I long to see the force at Calpee dispersed; while that body exists, the banks of the Jumna cannot be kept quiet. The people here seem very friendly to us. From Oryah to this the Country turned out to see us pass by, many saying they had never seen a European soldier before. Supplies for the soldiers, too, were freely brought in Camp.

DCCCLXV.

MEMORANDUM OF NEWS.

PUBLISHED UNDER THE AUTHORITY OF CAPT. H. BRUCE,
SUPT. OF POLICE.

No. 5. *Cawnpore, Friday* 20*th November* 1857.

. . . .

On the 13th ultimo two of the ex-King's sons—Mirza Jobrazshah and Mirza Bukhtawur Shah—were shot, pursuant to the sentence of the Military Commission before which they were arraigned (p. 199, vol. i.). **Mirza Jobraz Shah and Bukhtawur Shah shot.**

. . . .

LOCAL.—The Gwalior Contingent continue at Calpee, not being able to make up their minds to cross into the Doab. **Gwalior Contingent.**

That portion of the Dinapore Mutineers who were so severely handled by Capt. Peel, R.N., have joined the other party which moved from Banda direct upon Calpee, and the united number are encamped at Akbarpore, disheartened and much hampered by wounded. **Dinapore Mutineers.**

. . . .

A small Police post at Lucknow, to the westward, was attacked by an overwhelming number of the Nana's followers on the 17th inst. and forced to abandon the Thana, losing half their number, the casualties on both sides being equal.

. . . .

EUROPE.—Eleven steamers, with a further force of 5439, have left for India since the 26th September last. The Viceroy of Egypt has granted his free consent for the passage of troops through his dominions. 448 troops are already on their way out by the overland route. General Havelock has been created a K.C.B. and promoted to the rank of Major-General. **Havelock created K.C.B.**

The contributions to the India Relief Fund amount in England to 15 lakhs. **India Relief Fund.**

(Signed) S. THORNTON,
Deputy Collector and Deputy Magistrate.

DCCCLXVI.

Present Morning State of the Troops at Cawnpore Garrison under command of Colonel N. Wilson.

Cawnpore, *November* 1st.

Corps.	Field Officers.	Captains.	Subalterns.	Staff and Acting Staff.	Staff Sergeants.	Sergeants.	Drummers.	Rank and File.	Garrison Employ.	Regimental Employ.	Prisoners.	Sick.	Convalescent.	Total.	Remarks.
Royal Artillery . .	..	..	1	..	..	..	..	1	..	..	..	6	..	8	
Honble.Coy.'sEuropean Artillery . . .	..	1	1	..	..	2	5	11	..	..	..	4	1	25	
Her M.'s 5th Fusiliers .	1	..	1	1	2	4	1	66	..	..	..	29	2	107	
,, 8th (the King's) Regt. . . .	..	..	..	..	2	..	..	1	..	..	..	11	1	15	
Her M.'s 53rd Regt. .	..	..	3	1	..	6	2	151	..	..	..	7	..	170	
,, 64th Regt. .	1	2	5	5	4	16	11	257	9	19	7	31	4	373	
,, 75th Regt. .	..	..	..	..	..	1	..	..	..	..	..	14	..	15	
,, 78th Highlanders . . .	..	..	..	..	4	..	2	9	1	1	..	7	15	39	
Her M.'s 84th Regiment	..	..	..	..	..	1	..	33	2	1	..	21	28	86	
,, 90th Light Infantry . . .	..	..	1	1	1	..	11	34	..	5	..	26	26	105	
Her M.'s 93rd Highlanders . . .	1	2	13	4	..	22	9	248	..	..	..	17	..	316	
Madras Fusiliers . .	..	..	3	..	2	..	1	33	4	..	..	16	20	79	
Volunteer Cavalry .	..	..	..	..	..	..	..	1	..	..	..	3	..	4	
Invalid Artillery . .	..	..	..	..	..	2	..	18	..	..	..	1	..	21	
Native Artillery . .	..	..	..	..	1	4	..	14	..	..	..	1	..	20	
Seiks	..	..	..	..	1	2	..	26	..	..	..	2	..	31	
Officers of other Corps	..	2	3	9	..	..	..	.	..	..	..	..	..	14	
Nava Brigade . .	..	..	6	..	..	2	..	93	..	..	..	3	..	104	
Total strength	3	7	37	21	17	62	42	996	16	26	7	199	97	1532	

(Signed) Fletcher Murphy, Captain,
Brigade Major.

(*True Copy.*) (Signed) John W. Sherer,
Magistrate.

12. ALLAHABAD.

DCCCLXVII.

FROM C. CHESTER, C.S. COMMISSIONER, ALLAHABAD,
TO C. B. THORNHILL, C.S., AGRA.

ALLAHABAD, *August 27th*/57.

MY DEAR THORNHILL,[1]—

. . . .

The situation at *Λυκνοω* is *δεσπερατε*; may God in His mercy avert another catastrophe there. Desperate position of Lucknow.

. . . .

Court and Mayne are here, both well and working, like the true men they are. Court, C.S. Mayne, C.S.

. . . .

Bird held on at Gorukhpore alone, aided by friendly Rajahs, like a man. Bird at Gorakhpore.

DCCCLXVIII.

FROM C. CHESTER, C.S. COMMISSIONER, ALLAHABAD,
TO W. MUIR, C.S., AGRA.

ALLAHABAD, *Septr. 2nd*/57.

MY DEAR THORNHILL,[2]—

. . . .

Large reinforcements are coming from England, but all of them *via* the Cape, none overland. The British public don't yet understand the gravity of our situation. Troops from England.

DCCCLXIX.

FROM C. CHESTER, C.S., ALLAHABAD,
TO W. MUIR, C.S., AGRA.

ALLAHABAD, *Septr.* 4/57.

MY DEAR MUIR,[3]—Yours of the 20th with its enclosure to Beadon reached me yesterday; enclosure has been despatched to post. We shall never fail to honour your drafts. I have been

[1] Most of this letter has been printed in No. CCCCLXVI., vol. i. p. 494.

[2] Most of this letter is contained in No. DXXXVIII., pp. 539, 540, vol. i.

[3] A great part of this letter is printed in No. DXLII., pp. 541, 542, vol. i.

Treasure being sent from Allahabad to Agra.

ordered to send you 10 lakhs of treasure on first safe opportunity; meanwhile it is a deposit to your credit.

. . . .

Naval Brigade coming up.

Madras regiments are marching up the Trunk Road, and more Europeans coming on waggons. "Gamma" with Naval Brigade was at Rajmahal on 30th ulto.; should be here by 20th instant. What in the world will they do with 64-pounders? How move them?

Sweeper Police.

Capt. Bruce has established a Sweeper Police at Cawnpore with good effect.

. . . .

DCCCLXX.

C. Chester, C.S., to the Honble. J. R. Colvin, Lt.-Governor.

Allahabad, *Sept. 9th*/57.

My Dear Mr. Colvin,[1]—

. . . .

Poor Futtehpore, I cannot get a soldier for it, but am confident I could retake it with Darriao Singh's men if I were allowed to make the attempt.

The China force.

The China force does not make its appearance, but is daily expected in Calcutta.

Mayne, C.S.

Mayne is to go to Gopeegunge and manage the Allahabad Mirzapore Pergh: across Ganges. I have told Mr. Grant that I shall not be able to settle the Bundelcund districts without Mayne, and begged that he may be given back as soon as we are in a position to cross the Jumna.

Low caste levy.

We are trying hard to raise a low caste levy, but have not succeeded very well hitherto. We shall do better hereafter, I hope.

DCCCLXXI.

From C. Chester, C.S., to W. Muir, C.S., Agra.

Allahabad, *Sept. 28th*/57.

My Dear Muir,—

. . . .

Osborne still holds on at Rewah, tho' his position is far from secure, as the 50th at Nagode and the 52nd at Jubbulpore have mutinied, and Bundelcund and Baghelcund are in a very wild state. Ellis is at Punnah. The Rewah, Punnah, and Chickaree Rajahs are not disaffected, I believe, but overawed by so many mutinous regiments. The 7th and 8th regts. are still at Banda

[1] Other parts of this letter are printed in DCLXIII. of Series Twelfth.

and Nagode. The Nagode ladies are safe at Mirzapore, where wing of a Madras regt. is stationed.

We can learn nothing of the Jubbulpore ladies. For the last *six* days we have not heard a syllable from General Havelock's Army; the rebels have probably got into his rear in strength enough to cut off the communication. Naval Brigade was detained down below, and has not yet reached Benares. Edwards and Probyn have gone to Futtehpore as Judge, and Magte. and Colltr., respectively; between 3 and 400 Europeans are stationed there, and an entrenchment is being made. The Oudh scoundrels have possession of our trans-Gangetic Perghs. Can you answer the question contained in this note on the reverse of this paper?

DCCCLXXII.

[*The Note on the reverse.*]

BENARES, *Sept. 26th*, 1857.

MY DEAR SIR,—I am directed by the Lieutenant-Governor of the Central Provinces to request that you will (so far as may be practicable under present circumstances) take steps to ascertain whether there are at Mussourie and the other Hill Stations north of Meerut any considerable number of children of Europeans at school, etc., and whether it would be an object to the majority or many of the parents of these children to get them away from the Hills and placed in some more secure position.

O. M. G. WEBB (?),
Private Secretary, Lt.-Governor, C.P.

---

13. FROM THE MOVEABLE COLUMN.

DCCCLXXIII.

FROM WIGRAM CLIFFORD, C.S., TO W. MUIR, C.S., AGRA.

GAZEEOODEENUGGER, *Sept. 25th*, 1857.

MY DEAR MR. MUIR,[1]—

. . . .

Perhaps you will not yet have heard the sad news of Gen. Nicholson's death on the day before yesterday. He was certainly General Nicholson's death.

[1] The writer was shortly afterwards killed in action.

a splendid fellow, and had no doubt a glorious career before him but for that fatal wound. I am sorry this Column does not move on quicker. If Agra be really in danger, I think an urgent request from you would expedite its movements.[1] I am sorry I am not to go on to Agra, but Saunders wants Civilians here.—With kind regards to Mrs. Muir, very sincerely yours, (Sd.) WIGRAM CLIFFORD.

DCCCLXXIV.

FROM COL. E. H. GREATHED, COMMANDING THE MOVEABLE COLUMN, TO W. MUIR, C.S., AGRA.

CAMP SOMNA, *4th Octr.*

MY DEAR SIR,—The intelligence I have received to-day is that 3 Sepoy Regiments were at Hatrass yesterday; it seems uncertain whether they will come to Allygurh and join the insurgents, or whether they will make their way to Akberabad, and either make a stand there or go on to the Ram Ghaut. If they have taken the latter course, I am a march behind them; if either of the two former, I may hope to fall in with them. A Cossid who came in to my camp to-day from Dowar (?) 18th N.I., tells me that the people in Rohilcund are all on our side if supported by a small force. My orders, however, from General Wilson are not to cross the Ganges at present. When I have finished with the three regiments, which I fancy are the 18th and 68th and part of the Neemuch brigade, I will make the best of my way towards the force now at Muttra. It would be of great service to me to have the co-operation of the 250 Europeans with Mr. Cocks, and, if by moving towards Hatrass I could secure their junction, they would be of the greatest advantage, as I have only IIIIC available infantry. I will, however, write from Coel on this subject again. Now that a force is in this neighbourhood, the inhabitants of the country ought to refuse supplies to the Mutineers.

Rohilkhund loyal.

A. Cocks, C.S.

DCCCLXXV.

FROM SAME TO SAME.

CAMP ALLYGURH, *5th Octr.*

Capture of Aligarh.

MY DEAR SIR,—We marched in here this morning and cleared the town of the rabble who had driven out Govind Sing's

[1] See No. XC., p. 127, vol. i.—W. C.

people. Two 5-pounder guns fell into our hands. The Cavalry did most excellent service, and cut up fully 400 men with arms in their hands. I intend to march on Akberabad to-morrow morning, and hope to be able to inflict due chastisement on the Thakoor Mungul Singh and his adherents. My movements must be regulated by circumstances, and I am unable to say whether I shall go to Khasgunge or to Hatrass. I am in good hopes of intercepting some part of the rebel force, who appear to think of nothing but escape with their plunder.

DCCCLXXVI.

FROM COL. E. H. GREATHED, COMMG. MOVEABLE COLUMN, TO A. COCKS, C.S., CIVIL OFFICER, HATRASS.

CAMP AKBERABAD, *6th Octr.* 1857.

MY DEAR COCKS,—Many thanks for your two notes received last night, and for the news of the relief of Lucknow, which has, however, been purchased at the loss of some most excellent Officers. I came here this morning, and the Cavalry caught and cut up the two brothers Mungul and Mehtab Singh, and about 100 of their Rajpoot followers. **Mangal and Mehtab Singh killed.**

. . . .

We found 4 guns primed and loaded at the entrances. I march a short distance towards Hatrass to-morrow morning; my men and cattle are both weary. I shall make my way on towards Agra, and trust to meet you on your road to Allygurh. I cannot too strongly recommend the occupation of Coel as a military position; the force stationed in it might of course make excursions to such places as Atrolee, etc., with the greatest advantage. I have left 100 Punjab Infy. in the place as a temporary measure, but must withdraw them in a few days. I expect about 240 fresh Europeans, 50 Natives, and 20 gunners from Dehli, and I can wait for them at Agra as well as any other place. In a military point of view, I cannot say I like the idea of moving to attack Dholepore. I believe the fort is in good repair, and has guns of large calibre. We have any amount of guns at Agra, but no gunners; and if we were to sit down for a protracted period before Dholepore (I have just come from the siege of Dehli, and speak feelingly), the Gwalior force would most certainly have a strong inducement to come upon us. When I have the pleasure of seeing you, I will give you some other reasons for objecting to the idea of the siege of Dholepore. When I have been at Agra, it is quite clear that my line of

Koel as a military position.

Question of attacking Dholpore.

duty lies in putting myself in communication with General Havelock.

DCCCLXXVII.

FROM COL. E. H. GREATHED, COMMG. MOVEABLE COLUMN, TO W. MUIR, C.S., AGRA.

CAMP AKBERABAD, *7th Octr.*

MY DEAR MUIR,—My camp will be at Hatrass on the 9th *en route* to Agra. I hope to see Mr. Cocks at that place. I am glad to hear that Coel is to be occupied by a body of troops; it is a valuable military position. We were lucky in catching the twin rebel brothers yesterday, Mungul and Mehtab Singh. A great number of armed men were destroyed; but the villages appear all to be in arms against each other, and till they are deprived of their means of warfare there will be a great difficulty in telling friend from foe. I have issued the most stringent orders to prevent the villagers in the line of march from being injured; and if the inhabitants would come out of their villages, and sit down on the approach of troops, they need have no fear whatever of being molested by any one. I shall be at Agra on the 11th or 12th inst., and propose encamping on this side of the river and putting a guard on the bridge to prevent anyone from crossing without a pass. The Mutineer force which goes by the designation of the "Bareilly Brigade" has certainly gone down to Etah. The messenger who was sent round from Allygurh to Khasgunge and Secundra Raow came in this morning, and reports that not a Mutineer is to be seen on the Khasgunge Road. They have fairly run away from me; they had started for Coel when they heard of my force, and went back again to Secundra Raow. I am very glad to hear that Coel is to be held by a body of our troops; it is a most important military position, and very defensible.

Koel to be occupied.

Bareilly Brigade.

DCCCLXXXI.

FROM GEO. CAMPBELL, C.S., WITH GREATHED'S COLUMN, TO W. MUIR, C.S., AGRA.

AKRABAD, *Octr.* 7/57.

MY DEAR MUIR,—

. . . .

Atrowlee must not be left; but there is, I believe, no one of consequence there—a mere rabble of the town without guns or anything else—and throughout the rest of this district there is, I believe, nothing whatever for which a very small force will not suffice. I have thought it better not to go burning villages and that kind of thing more than I can help. . . . . .

DCCCLXXXII.

From Same to Same.

Camp Bijeyghur, *Octr. 8th*, 1857.

My Dear Muir,—We have made a move towards Agra. Col. Greathead has not marched more than 6 or 7 miles to this place to-day, intending to reach Hatrass to-morrow. Here we met the last news from Agra by letter from Kundowlee of yesterday that the Dholepore force had made a move on Agra.

. . . .

We have been perplexed by a letter from the Officer left at Coel to say that Cocks' Tehseeldar and the Civil Officials all left last night through apprehensions of a renewed attack of the Mahommedans, and that he wants assistance. Native officials flee from Koel.

. . . .

Greathed will send suitable assistance.

. . . .

The fact is that for two days, it having been given out that the Sikh detachment was under orders to evacuate the place, there was a panic in Coel among our friends, and it may be very likely preparations to return among our enemies; but, so far as I could make out, the stories of collections of Mahommedans were greatly exaggerated, and I cannot think that they can attack the Sikh garrison in the Mosque so soon, and with our Camp so near. It does, however, seem very strange the Tehseeldar having bolted without telling me a word of it. Panic in Koel.

. . . .

I have no doubt that Coel *must* be held, or we had better not have come at all, and think that when we march off to Agra 100 men will not suffice. So it will be well that the garrison is now to be made up to 250 Sikh Infantry and 50 Horse. Garrison to be strengthened.

. . . .

P.S.—Since writing, another telegraphic message has come, and Major Ouvry, commanding the Cavalry Brigade, has been to Greathed and got permission to push on to Agra with part of his force. He desires me to let you know that he expects to be Major Ouvry pushing on to Agra.

with you on the 10th (day after to-morrow) with the 9th Lancers, some Irregulars, and 2 troops of Horse Artillery (5 guns each), so I send this news off at once. . . . . His heart is in it, and he will come as quick as he can.

I have been again to Colonel Greathed, and he desires me to add from him that he will follow with the rest of the Column as quick as possible, and be, he hopes, at Kundowlee on the 10th.

(Sgnd.) G. C.

(*On reverse.*)

Major Ouvry, 2nd Dn. Gds., Comg. Caval. Brigade, is marching on Agra with 500 Cavalry and 2 troops of H.A.; H.M. 9th Lancers; 1, 2, 5 Punjab Cavry.; 2 troops H.A.: to be at 9th, Saidabad; 10th, Agra.

DCCCLXXXIV

From Major Ouvry, commanding Advance Cavalry Party of Greathed's Column.

Camp Sydabad, *Oct. 9th*, 11 *a.m.*

[*From Greathed's Force—day before battle of Agra*, 10*th Oct.* W. M.]

My Dear Sir,—I have seen and opened all the letters directed to Col. Greathed. This is the state of affairs. I left Byagurh Gurhi, which is about 6 miles from Akbarpore, at 10 p.m. last night, and have made a march of 26 miles, and am now encamped with a force of about 500 Sabres, including 200 of H.M. 9th Lancers, and two troops of Horse Artillery, on the road close by the 17th milestone from Agra. I fully understand the necessity of the case, and you may depend upon everything being done that is possible without rendering my force inefficient by precipitating exertions beyond endurance. Greathed is at Hatrass; he marched there this morning, but I do not think he can be at Agra before the day after to-morrow, as the hot weather before Dehli, and the fatigues of this Siege, have seriously affected the health of the men. I will give my force, which is in very efficient order, rest till 2 p.m., and then march at once to Kundowlee, when I hope you will send me an intelligent officer who knows the country well.

As for the rebels doing anything against the fort, of course that is impossible; so, if anything is to be done, perhaps you could form a junction with me with what force you can collect. I calculate on being at Kundowlee at 4.30 p.m. this day. The bearer of this, Capt. the Honble. E. Anson, will take any instructions from you; only, recollect that a march of 42 miles in the 24 hours renders horses very unfit for immediate exertion.

(From Major Ouvry, recd. 3 p.m., 9/10/57, by Captain Anson's hand.—W. M.)

DCCCLXXXV.

FROM GEORGE CAMPBELL, C.S., WITH GREATHED'S COLUMN, TO W. MUIR, C.S., AGRA.

CAMP BEWAR, *Wednesday morg., Oct.* 21/57.

MY DEAR MUIR,—The Nawab's people left this the day before yesterday, and we have met with no opposition. The people here are full of the news that the larger portion of the Regts. which retreated from Muttra, having gone towards Cawnpore, were 5 days ago defeated by our people at Sheorajpore (one march this side of Cawnpore) with great slaughter. They are said to have been all killed or dispersed except 300, who arrived as fugitives at Futtehgurh with 5 guns the day before yesterday, the rest of their guns (5 it is said) and all their ammunition having been captured.

Rumours of action at Sheorajpur.

. . . .

So far as is yet known, the Futtehgurh forces were still there—the Nawab's people (some of them are said to have bolted), the Seetapore Campoo, one of the Campoos from Dehli which originally stopped at Futtehgurh (half of them are said to have no muskets and many to be sick and wounded), and those who have come back from Cawnpore; they appear to have 20 or 25 guns. We are received here in a very friendly way, and all the people are ploughing their fields at the roadside in perfect confidence, apparently in ignorance of our looting propensities. I am afraid our friends are committing themselves in welcoming us more than they would have done if they knew we were not going to occupy the country; and I shall be much obliged if you will very particularly submit to Colonel Fraser my strong impressions that, if the rebels are again permitted to rule here and at Mynpoorie, the effect on our prestige must be *very* bad, and the confidence in us very greatly shaken. It will probably be some days before the Nawab takes courage to come on again (and I don't think the Regts. will come on at all), so I do earnestly trust that Col. Fraser will urge on the authorities

Composition of rebel force.

Attitude of the people.

G. Campbell's views as to occupation of the country.

at Cawnpore the great political necessity of occupying Futtehgurh the very moment the state of things at Lucknow renders it at all *possible*—not when it can *conveniently* be done, but whenever it can by any effort be effected. If things are easier at Lucknow as we get down, perhaps we may be permitted to turn back and do it. We might exchange some Cavalry for some fresh Infantry. Everything is going on right and well, so far.

DCCCLXXXVI.

FROM G. CAMPBELL, C.S., TO W. MUIR, C.S., AGRA.

CAMP GOORSAHAIGUNG, *Oct.* 22/57.

Column passes Fatehgarh.

MY DEAR MUIR,—We have made a double march, and are now on the Cawnpore side of Futtehgurh. We had no opposition, but surprised the Nawab's Thanah, and cut up some of them bolting. His Thanah was also at Meeran ke Serai with some guns this morning, but they have probably bolted, and we may get the guns. There seems no doubt whatever that the Dehli rebels have been defeated and dispersed towards Cawnpore, and we shall probably have no opposition on the way there. The people of the Futtehgurh district seem well-to-do; there has been little burning, and they are cultivating; but they seem

Attitude of people.

very glad to see us, and come out in the most friendly way. It is clear that *this* is not a hostile Sepoy country. I have not authentic news of what is going on at Futtehgurh, but 400

Movements of Mutineers.

Sepoys of the Seetapore Regt. went off this way last night, and others are said to have been crossing the Ganges yesterday. They say that the greater part of the dispersed Sepoys from Sheorajpore have gone south towards the Jumna, having been unable to get over the Ganges.

The Nawab's people are to-day breaking the Bridge between this and Futtehgurh.

DCCCLXXXVII.

FROM G. CAMPBELL, C.S., TO W. MUIR, C.S., AGRA.

CAMP MEERAN KE SERAI, near KANOUJ, *Oct.* 23, 1857.

MY DEAR MUIR,—Tho' the Cawnpore account of the victory of Sheorajpore is not so brilliant as that of the Natives', I am satisfied that the Dehli Regts. which went in that direction must have quite dispersed when they left some of their guns with the Nawab's Tehsildar here; and these latter, I am happy to say, we have got. I heard that they were here yesterday, and found from the people on the road that they had gone to Kanouj in the night, so got Ouvry with the advance guard to go on an expedition against them. Cavalry with 2 guns we took. We found them clearing out of Kanouj, but they had got the guns on the other side of the Kalee Nuddee, made a stand, and fired into the advance Cavalry. We soon, however, got up our two guns and opened on them, and after two or three rounds they bolted. We then rushed across the river with the Cavalry and followed them all the way up to the Ganges, ... so that *very* few escaped. A lot of Irregular Cavalry looking Mahommedans, some who looked like Resaldars, were killed. I have come back well drenched, having gone plump into the river. . . . . Meantime, however, I am sorry to say the plundering here has been *very bad*.

Dispersion of the Delhi Regiments. Major Ouvry, 9th Lancers. Action at Kanauj. Plundering by troops.

. . . .

This I am sorry for, because the Natives of this district appear to me particularly friendly to us. I never saw anything like it in the districts of which we have had *half* possession. They are altogether in a better state than elsewhere, and rush out to meet us. I hope this fact will be borne in mind with reference to future arrangements.

Attitude of people.

(*Duplicate: True Copy.*)

(Sd.) J. W. Power.

DCCCLXXXVIII.

From Brigadier Hope Grant, commanding Relief Column, to W. Muir, C.S., Agra.

Goorsaigunge, 22*nd Octr.* 1857.

My Dear Muir,—I received yours yesterday. You see we have got along pretty well, and are within 5 days' march of Cawnpore.

. . . .

I think our communications will be kept open; they all seem to have such a wholesome dread of us; and the country people seem charmed to have us back again. Think of the Futtehgurh force—some 5 or 6000 men and 20 guns—having all bolted. There seems not a doubt that we could have walked into the place without any opposition. The Rajah, I hear, means to poison himself. I marched 29 miles this morning—a pretty good stretch.

Country people welcome the English force. Fatehgarh.

. . . .

DCCCLXXXIX.

FROM BRIGADIER HOPE GRANT, C.B., COMMANDING RELIEF COLUMN, TO W. MUIR, C.S., AGRA.

KANAUJE, 23rd Octr.

MY DEAR MUIR,—

. . . .

Affair at Kanauj.

This morning we came upon about 300 of the rebels (unexpectedly for them), took 5 guns, and slaughtered about 200 of them.[1]

. . . .

Lucknow.

I meant to have chastised a great scoundrel in the shape of a Nawab who lives 6 or 8 miles from this, and who has 3000 men and some 3 or 4 guns, but the urgent letters I have from Cawnpore oblige me to go on as quickly as possible. Havelock is in distress, or at least wants relief; he is besieged in the Residency and two or three large Palaces, and is running very short of provisions. How fortunate that I shall just be in time, as he can hold out well till the 10th of next month. If the enemy stand no better than they have done here, he will soon be relieved. I shall get into Cawnpore by Monday next—3 days hence. The post, I think, will be quite safe. The crops and cultivation are beautiful all the way down.

. . . .

---

14. FROM CAPT. GOWAN (IN HIDING).

DCCCXCIII.

TO THE CHIEF CIVIL OR MILITARY AUTHORITY AT ALLYGURH.

ALLYGURH, 14th October 1857.

Refugee from Bareilly.

DEAR SIR,[2]—I am a refugee from Bareilly, who has been mercifully and wonderfully preserved by a gracious God through-

[1] This affair is described in Agra Memorandum of Intelligence of 25th Oct. 1857—No. DCXCI. of Series Twelfth. The corresponding description is omitted here.—W. C.

[2] This letter is written (no doubt for the sake of easy concealment) on a small piece of very thin paper, and bears marks of repeated folding. The action taken at Agra on receipt of the letter is stated in No. CLXV., p. 212, vol. i.—W. C.

out the rebellion. The Hindoo population have behaved very kindly to me and others, and continue to do so; but the Musulmans, aware that their time is but short now, appear to be leaving no stone unturned to apprehend me and others, either to destroy or keep us as hostages. I am therefore anxious to go to some of our Stations where troops are, and Allygurh is the nearest. For myself, being single, I could easily move from place to place, but there are helpless Women and Children at the same place (and at others), as I am, and for them I would gladly make an attempt to secure their safety and release from their present distressing condition, especially as all are badly off for clothing, and the cold weather is approaching. I have been trying to induce the large landholders and influential men around to join together and fight with the Musulmans, but can get them to do nothing but boast, and express their willingness to give aid, when that aid will not be required; so they have to pay the revenue to the rebels, and this though I have told them that they must not expect our Government to remit any portion of it, for that had they but joined together they might easily have put down their oppressors. Some few did make the attempt, but, not being joined by the rest, they succeeded in nothing but making the Musulmans their enemies, and now all have been made to pay something, and are being called upon to pay up the revenue due up to October, which, as there appears to be no probability of our forces moving to this side of the river before November or perhaps December, they will have to do.

Kind behaviour of the Hindu population.

Women and children in hiding.

Attitude of the large landholders.

Revenue paid to rebels.

I have no funds, and can procure but little money, otherwise I might raise a strong party of men to escort us across the river to some one of our Stations, for the peasantry are willing to assist us, and would gladly come with me if I could subsist them, and supply them with labourers to carry on their field labours. The Thakoors appear unwilling to furnish Escorts, but perhaps, if a purwanah were sent them from some Chief Civil or Military Authority to the effect that they can now best serve Government by escorting the various refugees across the river to some Military Station, they would afford the necessary aid; or if I could promise a handsome reward to a party of men, I could probably move the European families round about here without the assistance of the Thakoors, threatening them with the displeasure of the Govt. if they attempted to oppose our transit. I shall feel very much obliged to you for any news you can give me of the movements of our Troops, and how soon the rebels at Furruckabad will

Peasantry willing to assist refugees.

But funds required.

Absconded Sepoys at Bareilly.

be dealt with. There is a party of runaway Sepoys now at Bareilly, variously estimated at 5 or 600, who have demanded six months' pay from the rebel Chief there. These will probably remain until our Troops approach the Station, and then move elsewhere. Some 20,000 have passed by towards Lucknow, and will probably give us some trouble in Oude, as they are aware of the rewards offered by Government for their capture.

20,000 passed towards Lucknow.

J. G. Gowan, Captain,
Bengal Army.

---

15. FROM CALCUTTA.

DCCCXCIV.

From C. Beadon, C.S., to W. Muir, C.S., Agra.

Calcutta, *October 5th*, 1857.

My Dear Muir,—

. . . .

Death of Mr. Colvin.

Poor Mr. Colvin's death took us greatly by surprise. Though the medical certificate sent by Thornhill showed that there was no chance of his being able to resume his official duties on the restoration of order, yet no one was prepared to hear so soon that all was over. The loss of him at this time is a serious public calamity, as there is no one in the service so capable as he of organising a new administration on the ruins of the old one. . . . . Nothing whatever is settled as to the nomination of a successor to Colvin as Lieut.-Govr., though, now that Dehli is taken and we again possess ourselves of the districts of the Dehli and Meerut and Agra Divisions, it becomes essential that the G.-G. should come to a speedy decision on the subject. In a few days, when I have a little leisure, I will write to you on the subjects discussed in your first letter in which Lord Canning was much interested.

Punjab system recommended in reorganising Districts.

I certainly think that you will have to borrow much from the Punjab system in reorganising the system in those districts in which it has been entirely destroyed, and the more you can concentrate power in each district in the hands of one man the better. Tucker calls out vehemently for the abolition of the Civil Courts in all the districts of his division; and if the change be required there, much more is it wanted in the districts to the west of Allahabad.

Wilson has certainly managed the capture of Dehli to admiration, and the C.-in-C. is highly pleased with all he has done. He waited for the right moment, and then struck a blow with effect. General Wilson praised.

. . . .

At Lucknow, Maun Singh, who had professed loyalty up to the last, who had been in constant communication with the officers of Govt., who had protected British Officers and women, and who had received from Lawrence a promise of a Jageer of two lakhs in perpetuity, was actively engaged against us and was twice wounded! How can you account for such infatuation? Man Singh's defection.

. . . .

DCCCXCV.

From C. Beadon, C.S., to W. Muir, C.S., Agra.

Calcutta, 13*th October* 1857.

My Dear Muir,—Your letter of the 19th August was kept a long time by the Gov.-Genl., and was only returned to me yesterday by Genl. Low.

The policy to be adopted towards the Native States in regard to the support of troops for the protection of India must depend a good deal upon the manner in which it may be determined to reorganise the Bengal Army, upon the number of European troops of all arms which it may be thought necessary to keep in the country, upon the way in which they are to be distributed, and upon the extent to which local police battalions may be substituted for native regiments of the line, and for the irregular regiments of Cavalry and Infantry, which, except as to their complement of officers and the mode of their relief, have hitherto served as regiments of the line to all intents and purposes. It is evident, however, that we can have no more "Contingents" in the room of those which have followed the example of our own regular Sepoys, and that money payments must be substituted for service wherever this is practicable. I have little doubt, also, that the obligation of every State to contribute, according to its means and other circumstances, to the general defence of the country will be strictly enforced. But it will be impossible to apply one general Troops in Native States. "Contingents" condemned.

rule to all cases, especially where faithful service during these disturbances has established a peculiar claim to consideration and favour. You would not, for instance, think of dealing alike with Patiala and (——), with those who have shown that they are both able and willing to fulfil their treaty obligations, and those who may have been either unable or unwilling, or perhaps both.

Europeans alone to be relied on.

But, no doubt, the principle must be, that Europeans alone are to be relied on for the maintenance of our supremacy; and the internal and external defence of India against organised resistance to authority, and the extent to which it may be found necessary to increase the European force, must be the measure of our demands upon our native allies.

Removing Government from Agra.

I can see no reason for thinking of removing the seat of Govt. from Agra. It is to be on the great trunk line of railway from Calcutta to Lahore, and the Jumna then will be spanned by a masonry or iron bridge. There can be no doubt, I imagine, that a large European force will always be cantoned there, and that it will be the chief depôt for arms and military stores of all kinds between Calcutta and Lahore. Ultimately, too, there is every prospect that Agra will be joined to Bombay by a direct line of rail, by Ajmere to Ahmedabad.

Housing European troops.

The housing of the European troops during next hot season occupies the close attention of the C.-in-C. and the military authorities. We cannot afford to have a man in the Hills, and there is no time to provide permanent shelter for them in the plains, except of course where barracks already exist, either complete or in a state approaching completion. Many of them no doubt must be accommodated in thatched bungalows, or ranges of thatched barracks, which can be prepared for their reception in a comparatively short time.

Future supply of recruits.

With the assistance of the Seikhs and such local levies as can be raised from among the lower castes, I have no doubt we may manage to keep the peace next year, provided the military strength of the rebels is completely crushed and their leaders destroyed.

Jat Horse.

I shall be very glad to hear that your Jat Horse answer as well as their conduct at Hatrass and Allygurh seems to promise. You will have no difficulty in raising money as soon as the road is open from Agra to Cawnpore and the native merchants are able to correspond with regularity. Unless the Gwalior troops move towards Cawnpore, of which there now seems some likelihood, the column from Dehli ought completely to effect this object in the course of a few days. But, even now that Dehli has fallen, you can place no dependence on any class

Introduction of less privileged class to Army,

of men who sympathise with the Mutineers, and must depend entirely upon the inferior castes who have hitherto been excluded from the police as well as from the army.

including Aborigines. The Bhils.

I believe we might make much more of the aborigines in all parts of Central India than we have hitherto done. The Bheels have remained faithful, and done all that could be expected of them, considering their numbers.

Terms made with King of Delhi.

It strikes me as most unfortunate that any terms should have been made with the King of Dehli, who certainly deserved summary punishment, such as was righteously inflicted on his sons and grandson. However, we have yet to hear the circumstances under which a promise of his life was given to the wretched old man; and if it be a promise which must be kept (as no doubt it is, however imprudent and unauthorised), the Govt. will have to determine what is best to be done with him. I cannot doubt for a moment that the man is an arch ringleader and fully deserving of death, and I feel certain that to have hung him on the palace wall would have had the best effect throughout India, just as our omission to do so will be assuredly attributed to fear. The best thing now to do with him is to send him to Hong Kong, and give him a pittance enough to sustain life and no more.

Outram at Lucknow.

Outram's position at Lucknow is awkward, to say the least of it. He is *σεπαρατεδ φρομ ἱς ρεαρ γαρδ*, and *υναβλε το κομμυνικατε ουιθ θεμ*, but I have no doubt he will keep the enemy engaged till reinforcements arrive. There will be 1000 more Europeans at Cawnpore in a few days; and if Greathed's column can co-operate, or join them, and the whole march on Lucknow by the end of the month, the rebel force will be broken, and affairs in that quarter begin to take a favourable turn.

Oude the field for final struggle.

Oude is clearly to be the field for our final struggle with mutiny and rebellion, the remaining elements of which all tend in that direction as to a common focus. We shall have trouble, no doubt, in Central India, but it is in Oude where the great masses of our enemies will make their final stand, and where military operations on a large scale will have to be undertaken.

Central India.

Encomium on Wilson.

The capture of Dehli seems to have been admirably managed, and Wilson's first despatch is a model of clear description. We anxiously await further [details ?].

Christian Missions.

I do not believe that any restriction will be placed on Missionary operations, or on education, though the India House have shown some symptoms of fear on the subject. The firmer our power, the more confidently we may pursue the right course for the regeneration of the country without fear of temporary consequences. Still I think that the less the Govt. or its servants are directly concerned or connected with purely missionary objects the better.

Revenue collections.

I suppose you are collecting revenue again in the whole of the Dehli and Meerut divisions. The Agra division will be more difficult to restore to order, with Gwalior on one side and Furruckabad on the other, and Rohilcund must wait for some weeks before we can do anything there. Our troubles in Bengal are not quite over. The detachment of the 32nd at Deogurh mutinied last Friday, killing their officers, and the headquarters will no doubt follow suit. The infatuation of these people is incredible. The 93rd have all left Calcutta, and the 23rd and 82nd have begun to move. The 82nd goes to Patna to relieve the 10th, which will be moved on to the front.

Bengal still disturbed. Mutiny at Deogarh.

H.M.'s 93rd, 23rd, and 82nd.

DCCCXCVI.

From C. Beadon, C.S., to W. Muir, C.S., Agra.

Calcutta, *October 19th*, 1857.

My Dear Muir,—I heartily congratulate you and all at Agra upon Greathed's success against the Indore Mutineers, which I trust will have the effect of preventing any further attack upon Agra, and possibly of keeping the Gwalior Contingent quiet till means can be found to attack them. It will be a great point if Col. Greathed, reinforced by some of the fresh Europeans from Agra, can restore authority at Mynpoorie, and then march on Cawnpore, so as to be in time to give his valuable assistance to Outram in the reconquest of Oude, where now the final struggle with mutiny and rebellion will have to be fought.

Greathed's Column.

. . . .

British rule seems now to be more or less firmly established throughout the Meerut and Dehli divisions, and, now that all military resistance is overcome, you will be able to carry on by means of local levies, backed of course by the troops which are now at Dehli and Meerut, and which will be increased by further reinforcements from the Punjab. I trust Ramsay may be able to recover Rohilcund by means of his Goorkha army. There is a strong party in our favour there, and the force under Khan Buhadur is by all accounts most contemptible. Outram's position at Lucknow is, I trust, improving. It appears that most of the mutinous Sepoys have gone to their homes, and that the bulk of the host opposed to him consists of Ghazees and the retainers of the great Talookdars. . . . . The said Talookdars are preparing an attack upon Jaunpore and Azimgurh, where we ἀνε ονλι γοορκας το οπποσε θεμ. But I doubt if they will screw their courage to the striking point. The European troops are being pushed up to Cawnpore daily as fast as possible, and from thence to Alum Bagh. There will be 1000 more Europeans at Alum Bagh in the course of a week, and the force will be increased by 500 weekly till it is strong enough to do its work. When once we are fairly and fully in possession of the city, the rest will be comparatively easy work. The troops from England are now arriving daily; 100 men a day go up by the bullock train, and from the 1st Novr. the daily despatch will be 200, so that by Christmas we shall certainly have at and above Benares 8000 more Europeans than we now have, and with such a force success is everywhere certain. Goruckpore is still in the hands of Mahomed Husen, and he is threatening Chupra, but this I hope we shall be able to prevent. Grant can send a small force to Rewa to support the Raja, and put an end to the progress of rebellion in that quarter; but no doubt we shall have a vast deal of trouble in Bundelkund all through the cold weather. In the lower Provinces we are all right again, notwithstanding the mutiny of two companies of the 32nd N.I. They cannot do much mischief, and will very probably be intercepted before they get to the Soane. Except in Kooer Singh's Estates in Shahabad, all the Behar revenue has been paid up, and the opium advances are going on as usual.

European troops being hurried forward.

Troops from England.

Europeans at Benares.

Rewa.

Mutiny of the 32nd N.I.

DCCCXCVII.

From C. Beadon, C.S., to J. W. Sherer, C.S.

Calcutta, 28*th October* 1857.

My Dear Sherer,—The Dehli Column seems to have made a splendid march from Agra to Cawnpore.

. . . .

The Column, I suppose, will cross immediately into Oude, unless it is stopped by the Commander-in-Chief, who left yesterday by dawk with all his staff, for the purpose of taking the command in person. The demand for help from Lucknow is so urgent that I doubt whether the Column can remain at

Sir Colin Campbell.

Cawnpore; but if it does, there seems a likelihood of the Gwalior Contingent falling an easy prey to it. They are said to have left Gwalior about the 15th, and intend to cross the Jumna at Calpee with their Magazine and Siege Train. The Banda fellows will, I suppose, move on Futtehpore about the same time, and as the garrison there is weak, I fear our communications may be interrupted again for some days.

. . . .

Sir M. Jackson. Have you heard anything lately of Sir M. Jackson and his sisters? We are now very anxious about them, fearing that the Rajahs may not be able to protect them until our power is re-established in the province. I fear you may not have been able to forward the Cossid letters.

DCCCXCVIII.

(COPY.)

FROM G. F. EDMONSTONE, FOREIGN SECRETARY,
TO MR. SHERER, CAWNPORE.

CALCUTTA, *22nd October, Thursday,* 12/10 *p.m.*

Words 80.—*S. K.*

PLEASE send the following message by Cossid to Agra.

Message begins.—To Political Agent, Gwalior, Agra. Your message D/14th instant received. The Governor-General in Council requests that you will submit an explanation of the views with which you have acted in desiring Scindia to allow the rebels to leave Gwalior, and his Lordship in Council directs that no further step may be taken which may lead to encourage the advance of the Gwalior Troops upon Cawnpore. Message ends.

(Sgnd.) J. W. M. CEARNS,
Hd. asstt. in ch.

True Copy.

(Sgnd.) J. W. SHERER, Magte.

CAWNPORE E. T. OFFICE,
The 23rd Octr. /57.

DCCCXCIX.

(*COPY SERVICE TELEGRAM.*)

FROM THE GOVR.-GENL., CALCUTTA, TO THE CHIEF COMMISSIONER, AGRA, THROUGH MAGISTRATE OF CAWNPORE.

CALCUTTA, *Wednesday* 21*st October*, 9.30 *a.m.*

Words 136.—*S. K.*

LET it be known immediately at Dehli that Cavalry and Artillery horses which can be spared are required at Cawnpore or Allahabad, and that they are to be sent to Cawnpore as soon as ever that this can be done safely, an escort accompanying them. Probably it will not be necessary that any of the escort should proceed by forced marches. With reference to the arrangement of districts about Dehli, there is no objection to the employment of Military Officers in the charge of the districts, in the absence of a sufficient number of Civilians. I congratulate you on the success reported in your letter of the 11th, and thank Lieut.-Col. Greathed and yourself for it. You have been already requested to hasten his column downwards; I trust that this is done.

Cavalry and Artillery horses hurried down.

Military Officers may be employed in Delhi Division.

Greathed's Column hastened.

(Sgnd.) J. W. M. CEARNS.
Hd. asstt. in ch.

True Copy.

(Sgnd.) J. W. SHERER.

CAWNPORE E. T. OFFICE,
The 21*st Octr.* /57.

DCCCC.

FROM C. WINGFIELD, C.S. COMMISSIONER IN OUDH, TO W. MUIR, C.S., ALLAHABAD.

CAMP DAKEHREE, 7*th January* 1858.

MY DEAR MUIR,—Khyrooddeen went out this morning with a strong patrol to a distance of 13 miles north along the boundary Nullah, and ascertained beyond any doubt by enquiries of the villagers that Bala Rao entered the Nepaul Terai about four miles below the hills yesterday morning the 6th. Five or six hundred

Khairooddeen.

Bala Rao and followers enter Nepal.

sepoys, 150 cavalry, with two small guns mounted on bullocks, 50 Doolees and Dylees full of women, some elephants and camels, formed his retinue. They did not all go in a body, but continued passing at intervals from the night of the 5th up to this morning when the last detachment crossed.

Apprehended movement towards Bhojpore.

It was given out among them that Bala Rao meant to claim the protection of Jung Behadur, who was known to be at Tribinee on the Gunduk, as I have already told you, and the sepoys, who are said to be all Bhojepoor men, had the same object in view, but intended, if they failed in attaining it, to make their way to their homes. This intelligence may be confidently relied on. I shall move Capt. M'Mullin's Sikhs further to the east, as the sepoys, if they attempt to carry out their design of reaching their homes, will pass through the extreme east of this district. I have also written express to warn the authorities in Chupra, Ghazeepoor, Moteeharee, Azimgurh.

Further confirmation was also received to-day of the intelligence I had previously communicated to you, that Heera Lal's band of rebels was encamped in the villages in the Jungle north of Taolewa, 24 miles east of this—with them were several rebels of this district. They had refused to deliver up their arms, and the Nepaulese detachment was too weak to take them by force. But 50 sepoys, a separate party, had been disarmed.

No mention of Mahomed Hussun with Bala Rao—he is supposed to have gone westwards; probably he is afraid to trust himself to Jung Behadur, not being a co-religionist, and I know Jung Behadur suspected him of having put some Gurkhas to death at Goruckpoor.

General Grant marched towards Bhinga on the 6th. Brigadier Rowcroft is in his former position. I have been careful to warn the patrols against entering the Nepaulese territory, knowing the purpose of such a proceeding would be sure to be misrepresented to Jung Behadur.—Yours very sincerely,

C. Wingfield.

On further reflection I have telegraphed the above to Edmonstone.

APPENDICES

(TO VOL. II.)

I. Letter to Colonel G. B. Malleson, C.S.I., regarding the attack on Agra of 10th October 1857, commenting on the reference to this matter in Kaye and Malleson's Histories.

II. Statement, dated 7th October 1857, by Mr. C. B. Thornhill, C.S., Officiating Secretary to the Government of the North-West Provinces, *re* delegation, by the Honble. the Lieut.-Governor, to a Commission, of part of the current work of the Government during the outbreak.

III. Extract from letter of Lieut. Browne, dated October 1857, describing condition of the country between Agra and Meerut.

IV. List of Officers of Her Majesty's and the Honble. Company's Service, Civil Service, and others, who have been killed, also those who have died, since 10th May 1857, serving on the Bengal Establishment, as far as known in Agra up to 15th December 1857.

APPENDIX I.

LETTER TO COLONEL G. B. MALLESON, C.S.I., REGARDING THE ATTACK ON AGRA OF 10TH OCTOBER 1857, COMMENTING ON THE REFERENCE TO THIS MATTER IN KAYE AND MALLESON'S HISTORIES.

DEAN PARK HOUSE, EDINBURGH,
16th September 1896.

DEAR COLONEL MALLESON,—I happen to have preserved the MSS. volumes of correspondence and evidence which, after the battle of July, I kept every day for the Intelligence Department. They were returned to me after Sir John Kaye's death, and laid aside. Having lately had occasion to take them up, I was struck by the evidence they contain on the "surprise" of 10th October 1857. It was a surprise indeed, but not of the Intelligence Department.

For more than a month spies and informers had been employed by Major Macpherson and myself to bring intelligence from the Neemuch Mutineers as they advanced from Gwalior by Dholepore with the avowed object of attacking Agra; the evidence, etc., as in all such matters, being daily—and latterly often hourly—laid before Col. Fraser and Col. Cotton. As the time approached these became more frequent; and on Friday and Saturday (7th and 8th) the enemy was reported crossing the Kharee. On Saturday it became so close and threatening that I felt it was no longer a matter for the Intelligence spies in the midst of armed bands, and so on that evening, in sending on the evidence of approaching danger, I suggested to Cols. Fraser and Cotton the necessity "for a reconnoitring party and continuous military pickets." On Sunday (9th) consequently a mounted party was sent out; and writing on that day I find the report that "some hundreds of Sowars have already crossed the Kharee about 10 miles distant, are prowling about the country and obstructing the road. A reconnoitring party of our militia cavalry went out this morning. It was fired on at the river, and followed, though at a respectful distance, by the enemy's cavalry, and within a few miles of Agra."

I did not doubt that the Military authorities having thus followed one of my suggestions, had also followed the other for a continuous post of pickets, which, had they done, the hidden advance of Sunday night and surprise of Monday morning would have been impossible.

My communications with Col. Greathed had been several days before of the same urgent character; on the morning of the 8th I reported the near approach of the enemy, and said they were leaving supplies "at Kakaur, 8 or 10 miles off," and again in the afternoon an express with Col. Fraser's urgent call. On Sunday the 9th I wrote again that the force was crossing, and said that they may, "if they choose to risk the thing, cross over to-day, and to-morrow beard us in our Fort and plunder the City." Again in the afternoon I sent another express: "Our reconnoitring party has come in. Numbers of the cavalry have crossed the Kharee, and our party was fired on. 300 infantry about, had crossed. This all looks as if they meant to come. The cavalry are spreading over the country, and will be committing all kinds of excesses and outrages. Come quickly."

From all this you will see that timely information was given of the advance and imminence of the danger; that the service of spies had done its work, and that the outlook had passed from them into the hands of armed posts and pickets. Why the advice for these was not followed, so as to prevent a night and morning surprise, it is not for me to say.

I will only add that it is a matter of sincere regret to me that the records I have referred to (including daily correspondence with Dehli, Cawnpore, Havelock, etc.) were not in your hands when you drew up your History. My connection with the Intelligence Department is referred to by Kaye and yourself in the original work. It is not mentioned in your condensed work; but at p. 316 it is said that the rebels instead of being "as the Agra Authorities believed, etc." I should be glad if in future editions the imputation were confined to the failure of the "Military Authorities" to follow up the warnings of the Intelligence Department. What caused the failure of the Military outlook I never found out. But, trusting to it, the opening cannonade surprised me, as it did others, while sitting at breakfast with my friends Norman and Anson (our brother-in-law) in our quarters in the Fort.

If you ever were in this quarter, I should be only too glad to show you the ½-dozen vols., preserved as they were when leaving Agra.

W. MUIR.

APPENDIX II.

ORDERS OF THE HONOURABLE THE LT.-GOVERNOR, N.W.P REGARDING DISPOSAL OF CURRENT WORK AT HEAD-QUARTERS, JUNE 1857.

MEMORANDUM.

FORT AGRA, *the 7th October* 1857.

THE destruction of some of the papers which had not been brought on the records of the Government having taken place in the confusion consequent on the attack upon Agra by the Neemuch Mutineers, it seems desirable that the loss of one important document should as far as possible be remedied by a statement from the officiating Secretary, which I therefore now proceed to record.

On the 14th June, the time of the late Lieutenant-Governor having been for some days previously so completely occupied by pressing business connected with the outbreak, which admitted of no delay in its disposal, the ordinary current work had fallen very considerably into arrears. Mr. Colvin therefore determined to delegate this branch of the Government to a Commission, and dictated an order which I at once wrote out, and which was then signed by Mr. Colvin, to this effect, that, as the Lieutenant-Governor found his time so fully engrossed by matters of immediate and pressing urgency, the ordinary current business would, until further orders, be disposed of by a Commission, consisting of the following officers:—

Mr. E. A. Reade,
Mr. H. B. Harington,
Mr. W. Muir.

The first-named gentleman to dispose of all Revenue references; the second, those relating to the Judicial Branch; and Mr. Muir to take up the Public Works and General Departments. That in cases of doubt any question might be reserved for the special orders of the Lieutenant-Governor, but that the Secretary was to refer all cases in their respective Departments, as above detailed, to the Members of the Commission, and to receive and execute all orders passed by them, as though they had emanated from the Lieutenant-Governor.

With the concurrence of the Members of the Commission, this Memo. will be recorded in the proceedings of the Government of the North-Western Provinces.

(Signed) C. B. THORNHILL,
Officiating Secy. to Govt. N.W.P.

Approved.
(Sgnd.) E. A. READE, Sr. Mem. S. Bd. of Revenue.
H. B. HARINGTON.
W. MUIR.

. . . No. 190 A. . . .

Foreign Department, N.W.P.

D/ Agra, the 7th October 1857.

ORDER.—Ordered that a copy of the foregoing Memo. be sent to Mr. Muir for information.

(Sgnd.) C. B. THORNHILL,
Offg. Secy. to Govt. N.W.P.

Copd. B. M. GHOSE.

APPENDIX III.

STATE OF THE COUNTRY BETWEEN AGRA AND MEERUT, OCTOBER 1857.

Extract of Letter from W. Muir, C.S., dated 26th October 1857, Agra, to J. W. Sherer, C.S., Cawnpore.

. . . .

P.S.—Here is an extract from a letter of Lieut. Browne (of Jhansi), who has just left us to go home *via* Mooltan. He writes from Meerut, having travelled by horse dak. He reached, he says, "without meeting with the least obstruction on the road —all is so clear that a lady might travel alone almost. The traffic all along the road is going as if nothing had happened, and the people are very civil. Save for the bungalows and chowkies which have been destroyed, there are no signs of the late rebellion. Indeed, to look at the smiling face of the country, covered with the most luxuriant crops, it is difficult to realise the idea that such fearful events have occurred but the other day. The people are ploughing and sowing everywhere, and, though the curse of war is a heavy one, all must see that the country has been singularly blessed with a plentiful harvest. Meerut appears to have suffered but little, in appearance at least. The houses are all occupied, and there are all the usual signs of a large and busy cantonment."

This is very satisfactory; send it on as an enclosure to my letter.

(Sgnd.) W. M.

Gwalior news good. I will give it to-morrow. The Maharaja has done us noble service.

APPENDIX IV.

LIST OF OFFICERS OF HER MAJESTY'S AND THE HONOURABLE COMPANY'S SERVICE, CIVIL SERVICE, AND OTHERS, WHO HAVE BEEN KILLED, ALSO THOSE WHO HAVE DIED, SINCE THE 10TH MAY 1857, SERVING ON THE BENGAL ESTABLISHMENT, AS FAR AS KNOWN IN AGRA UP TO 15TH DECEMBER 1857.

LIST OF KILLED AND MISSING OF THE OFFICERS IN H.M.'S SERVICE, ALSO OF THOSE WHO HAVE DIED SINCE MAY 1857.

General Anson, died at Kurnaul of cholera.
„ Barnard, died before Delhi of cholera.
Major-General Sir H. Havelock, died at Lucknow.

6th Dragoon Guards.

Captain G. Wardlaw, killed at Gungaree.
Lieutenant Hudson, „ „
„ C. P. Rosser, killed at Dehli.
„ S. Vyse, died of wounds.
„ Wheatcroft, killed at Lucknow.
„ C. J. H. Ellis, died of cholera.
Assistant-Surgeon S. Moore, killed at battle of Hindun.

9th Lancers.

Lieut.-Colonel R. I. Pratt, died at sea.
Major R. A. Yule, killed at Dehli.
Captain L. French, killed at Agra.

8th Regiment Foot.

Lieutenant W. W. Pogson, killed at Dehli.
„ T. B. Grierson, died at Umballa.
„ W. R. Webb, killed at Dehli.
„ Vincent, killed at Cawnpore.
Ensign W. H. Mountsteven, killed.

10th Regiment Foot.

Captain C. Dunber, killed at Arrah.
Ensign H. J. Erskine, „

24th Regiment Foot.

Captain F. Spring, killed at Jhelum.
„ T. M. Greensill, killed before Dehli.

27th Regiment Foot.

Lieut. Colonel H. D'A. Kyle, died at Simla.

29th Regiment Foot.

Captain S. Fisher, commanding 15th Irr. Cavy., killed at Fyzabad, Oude.
„ J. E. Duncan, died at Calcutta.

32nd Regiment Foot.

Lieut.-Colonel W. Case, killed at Lucknow.
Captain J. Moore, } killed at Cawnpore.
Lieutenant F. Wainwright, } killed at Cawnpore.
Ensign E. C. Hill, } killed at Cawnpore.

52nd Regiment Foot.

Lieutenant Bradshaw, killed at Dehli.

53rd Regiment Foot.

Lieut.-Colonel T. S. Powell, C.B.

H.M.'s 1st Battalion 60th Rifles.

Captain F. Andrews, killed at Ghazioodeen Nugger.
Lieutenant Napier, died of wounds at Meerut.
„ Conyers, died at Allahabad.

61st Regiment Foot.

Captain R. Hunt, died at Kussowlie.
„ W. A. Dely, died at Landour.
Lieutenant T. Gabbitt, killed at Dehli.
„ Pattown, died at Simla.

75th Regiment Foot.

Colonel R. D. Halifax, died from exposure.
Captain Knox, killed at Dehli.
„ A. Chancellor, killed at Dehli.
Lieutenant A. Harrison.
„ C. R. Rivers, died of cholera.
„ J. R. S. Fitzgerald, killed at Dehli.
„ E. V. Briscoe, „ „
„ G. C. N. Faithfull, „ „
Ensign W. Crozier.
Surgeon J. Coglan, died of cholera.

84th Regiment Foot.

Captain E. Currie, died of wounds.
Lieutenant F. G. E. Saunders, killed at Cawnpore.

90th Regiment Foot.

Colonel R. R. Campbell, killed at Lucknow.

93rd Highlanders.

Captain Dalzell, killed at Lucknow.

Royal Artillery.

Captain Headly, killed at Lucknow.

Naval Brigade.

Midshipman Mr. A. Daniell.

List of Killed and Missing Officers of the Honble. East India Company's Service, also of those who have Died, since May 1857.

Artillery.

Colonel C. G. Dixon, died at Ajmere.
„ Sir H. M. Lawrence, K.C.B., killed at Lucknow.
„ F. Brind, killed at Sealkote.
„ J. L. Mowat, died of cholera near Dehli.
„ F. K. Bazeley, killed at Lucknow.
Major A. Robertson, gun carriage agent, died of wounds at Futtehgurh.
„ G. Larkins, killed at Cawnpore.
„ G. L. Cooper, killed at Lucknow.
„ V. Mackenzie, died of wounds.
Captain A. W. Hawkins, killed at Gwalior.
„ J. Mill, drowned in the Ghogra, Oude.
„ E. A. C. D'Oyly, killed at Agra.
Lieutenant W. Stewart, killed at Gwalior.
„ C. Dempster, killed at Cawnpore.
„ G. D. Willoughby, supposed to be murdered by villagers while escaping from Dehli.
„ H. G. Perkins, killed at the Hindun.
„ F. H. Turnbull, killed at Jhansi.
„ St. G. Ashe, killed at Cawnpore.
„ J. H. Lamb, died of wounds at Agra.
„ E. H. Hildebrand, killed before Dehli.
2nd Lieut. S. E. Townsend, killed at Nowgong.
„ „ J. N. Martin, } killed at Cawnpore.
„ „ G. W. M. Sotheby, } killed at Cawnpore.
„ „ J. H. Knox, died at Meerut.
„ „ T. E. Dickins, killed at Dehli.
„ „ J. A. H. Eckford, killed at Cawnpore.
„ „ W. Clephane, died at Umritsur.
„ „ W. T. Somerville, died before Dehli.

Engineers.

Captain E. Fraser, killed at Meerut.
„ P. F. S. Salkeld, died of wounds before Dehli.
„ F. Whiting, killed at Cawnpore.
Lieutenant K. Home, killed by explosion at Allygurh.

Lieutenant C. D. Innes, killed by explosion at Allahabad.
„ J. R. Monckton, killed at Futtehgurh.
„ O. C. Jervis, „ Cawnpore.
„ E. Walker, died at Dehli of cholera.
2nd Lieut. E. Jones, died of wounds before Dehli.
„ „ F. L. Tandy, killed at Dehli.
Ensign H. Rigby, died of cholera before Dehli.

Sappers and Miners.

Conductor R. Vernal, died of cholera before Dehli.
Overseer C. Hardy, „ „ „
„ J. Fullerton, „ „ „
„ W. McGilvray (Artillery) „ „
„ H. Cryan (Artillery) „ „

Cavalry.

1st Regiment—mutinied at Mhow.

Major A. Harris, killed at Mhow.
Captain Stewart Beatson, died at Cawnpore.

2nd Regiment—mutinied at Cawnpore.

Major E. Vibart, killed at Cawnpore.
Captain E. J. Seppings, killed at Cawnpore.
„ R. N. Jenkins, „ „
Lieutenant R. O. Quin, „ „
„ C. W. Quin, „ „
„ J. H. Harrison, „ „
„ W. J. Manderson, killed at Cawnpore.
„ F. S. M. Wren, „ „
„ M. G. Daniell, „ „
„ M. Balfour, „ „
Riding Master D. Walsh, „ „
Veterinary Surgeon E. G. Chalwin, „

3rd Regiment—mutinied in Meerut.

Lieutenant C. J. E. McNabb, killed at Meerut.
Veterinary Surgeon J. Phillips, „ „
„ „ C. J. Dawson.

4th Regiment—disarmed at Umballa.

Lieut.-Colonel T. Quin, died at Simla.
Lieutenant C. J. Hunt, killed at Mehidpore.
Veterinary Surgeon Jeffery, died at Umballa.

6th Regiment—part mutinied at Jullundur.

Captain A. Mactier, died at Jullundur.
Lieutenant F. G. Willock, died before Dehli.

7th Regiment—mutinied at Lucknow.

Cornet W. C. R. Raleigh, killed at Lucknow.

8th Regiment—disarmed at Lahore.

Lieut.-Colonel T. F. Tucker, missing at Futtehgurh.

9th Regiment—wing mutinied (annihilated).

None of the Officers killed.

10th Regiment—disarmed and mutinied.

Veterinary Surgeon V. Nelson, killed at Ferozepore.

EUROPEAN INFANTRY.

1st Regiment.

Major J. Pond, died.
Major G. O. Jacob, killed at Dehli.
Captain Howell, died of cholera at Dehli.
Lieutenant W. J. D. Cairns, died at Dehli.

2nd Regiment.

2nd Lieutenant S. Jackson, killed at Dehli.
" " D. Sheriff, " "

3rd Regiment—Agra Fort.

Major G. P. Thomas, died of wounds at Agra.

NATIVE INFANTRY.

1st Regiment—mutinied at Cawnpore.

Colonel Ewart, killed at Cawnpore.
Captain Athill Turner, killed at Cawnpore.
" F. Elms, " "
Lieutenant H. S. Smith, " "
" R. M. Satchwell, " "
" G. R. Wheeler, " "
" F. Redman, " "
Ensign J. C. Supple, " "
" C. Lindsay.

2nd Regiment—disarmed at Barrackpore.

Captain A. C. Lister, died.

3rd Regiment—mutinied at Phillour.

Lieutenant J. Yorke, killed.
" R. W. Alexander, killed.

6th Regiment—mutinied at Allahabad.

Captain J. Plunket, killed at Allahabad.
Lieutenant R. Stewart, " "
" G. H. Hawes, " "
Ensign G. L. Munro, " "
" G. S. Pringle, " "

7th Regiment—mutinied at Dinapore.

Lieutenant F. B. Boyd, died at Dunhoosa.

8th Regiment—mutinied at Dinapore.

Captain C. F. Simpson, killed by accident, Dehli.
Lieutenant G. H. Griffiths, died at Fort Mitchnie.

9th Regiment—mutinied at Allygurh and Mynpoorie.

Lieutenant S. Ross, died of cholera before Dehli.

10th Regiment—mutinied at Futtehgurh.

Lieut.-Colonel G. A. Smith, missing.
Major W. Lindsay, killed at Cawnpore.
Captain R. Munro, missing.
„ J. Phillot, „
„ F. D. O. Bignell, missing.
„ W. T. Phillimore, „
„ W. Law, killed at Dehli.
Lieutenant H. J. Fitzgerald, missing.
„ J. R. Simpson, „
„ C. W. Swetenham, „
Ensign D. Henderson, „
„ R. Eckford, „
„ R. S. Byrne, „

11th Regiment—mutinied at Meerut.

Lieut.-Colonel J. Finnis, killed at Meerut.

12th Regiment—mutinied at Nowgong and Jhansi.

Major Kirke, died from exposure.
Captain J. Dunlop.
Lieutenant J. H. Ewart, killed at Cawnpore.
Ensign S. B. Taylor.
Lieutenant J. H. Barber.

13th Regiment—mutinied at Lucknow.

Lieutenant E. W. Barwell, killed at Hansi.

14th Regiment—Jhelum (totally destroyed).

Lieutenant H. Smith, died at Jhelum.
„ C. Battine, killed at Cawnpore.

15th Regiment—mutinied at Nusseerabad.

Lieutenant J. Campbell, killed at Nusseerabad.

16th Regiment—disarmed at Lahore.

Lieutenant F. C. Angelo, D.P.W., killed at Cawnpore.
Ensign Marsh, killed in action near Allygurh.

17th Regiment—mutinied at Azimgurh.

Lieut.-Colonel R. McNair, died.
Lieutenant P. Hutchinson, killed.
„ R. P. Homfray, died from accident, Dehli.

18th Regiment—mutinied at Bareilly.

Major H. E. Pearson, missing.
Captain Richardson, „
„ Hathorn, „
Lieutenant Stewart, „
Ensign Dyson, „

19th Regiment—disbanded at Barrackpore.

Lieutenant Sir N. Leslie, Bart., killed in Sonthal District.

20th Regiment—mutinied at Meerut.

Captain J. H. Taylor, killed at Meerut.
„ D. McDonald, „ „
Lieutenant D. Henderson, „ „
„ W. Pattle, „ „
„ C. D. Barbor, killed near Allygurh.
„ M. A. Humphreys, killed before Dehli.

21st Regiment.

Lieutenant F. W. Brodie, killed at Mehidpore.

22nd Regiment—mutinied at Fyzabad, Oude.

Lieutenant Bright, killed near Fyzabad.
„ A. F. English.
„ T. E. Lindesay.
„ W. H. Thomas.
„ G. L. Cautley.
„ J. W. S. Anderson.
„ T. L. Ritchie.

23rd Regiment—mutinied at Mhow.

Lieut.-Colonel J. Platt, killed at Mhow.
Major and Bt.-Colonel C. Chester, killed at Dehli.
Captain Warden, died.
Lieutenant J. Fagan, killed at Mhow.
„ Hilliard, killed at Hissar.

25th Regiment—mutinied at Dinapore.

Major A. C. G. Sutherland, died at Akyab.
Captain C. G. Brodie, killed at Mehidpore.

26th Regiment—Lahore (totally destroyed).

Major B. Evans, died.
„ Spencer, killed.
Lieutenant Davidson, killed at Dehli.

27th Regiment—disarmed at Peshawur.

Captain G. T. Gowan, killed in Oude.
Lieutenant G. W. Fraser, missing.

28th Regiment—mutinied at Shajehanpore.

Captain Guise, killed at Benares.
Captain James, killed at Shahjehanpore.
„ H. W. T. Sneyd, killed at Shahjehanpore.
„ C. Lysaght, killed near Mohundee, on the road to Seetapore.
„ M. Salmon, „ „ „
Lieutenant A. Key, „ „ „
„ C. A. Robertson, „ „ „
„ C. F. Scott, „ „ „
„ W W. Pitt, „ „ „
„ G. W. Rutherford, „ „ „
Ensign Spens, and three other Ensigns, „ „

30th Regiment—mutinied at Nusseerabad.

Captain J. T. Lumsden, killed at Lucknow.

31*st Regiment—Saugor. Staunch and doing good service, having fought and beaten the Mutineers, 42nd Regiment and Irregular Cavalry, out of Saugor.*

Colonel A. Jack, C.B., killed at Cawnpore.
Captain T. C. Birch, killed at Allahabad.
Ensign U. G. P. Spens, blown up by accident in Bundelkund.

32nd Regiment—Sontal District.

Captain the Hon. E. P. Hastings, died at Shahabad.
„ C. R. G. Douglas, killed in Dehli.
Lieutenant E. J. Travers, killed before Dehli.

33rd Regiment—disarmed at Hosheyarpore.

Lieutenant J. Browne, killed before Dehli.

35th Regiment—disarmed at Sealkote.

Major Moorhouse, died at Allahabad.
Captain G. A. Crommelin, died at sea.

36th Regiment—mutinied at Jullundur.

Lieutenant Bagshaw, died of wounds at Jullundur.
Ensign W. R. Waudy, died at Dehli.

38th Regiment—mutinied at Dehli.

Lieut.-Colonel P. Goldney, missing at Fyzabad.
Major Hollings, died at Landour.
Captain H. C. Gardner, died at Kussowlie.
„ Gibbings, killed at Fyzabad, Oude.
Lieutenant A. J. Anderson, died in Europe.

39th Regiment—disarmed at Jhelum.

Lieutenant A. Procter, killed in Gwalior.

40th Regiment—mutinied at Dinapore.

Major C. E. Burton, killed at Kotah.
Lieutenant E. J. Wild, killed.

41st Regiment—mutinied at Seetapore, Oude.

Colonel Sibbald, killed at Bareilly.
Major F. W. Birch, killed at Seetapore.
Captain W. Williamson, killed at Cawnpore.
Lieutenant Smalley, killed at Seetapore.

42nd Regiment—mutinied at Saugor.

Lieut.-Colonel T. Dalyell, killed.
Lieutenant A. W. Murray, killed at Dehli.

44th Regiment—disarmed at Agra.

General Skardon, died.
Major G. M. Prendergast, died at Agra.
Lieutenant J. Smith, killed at Mozuffernuggur.

45th Regiment—mutinied at Ferozepore.

Lieutenant Trotter, died at Mussouri.
Ensign L. Wavell, died of coup de soleil.

46th Regiment—disarmed at Sealkote (totally destroyed).

Colonel Goldie, Mily. Auditor General, missing at Futtehgurh.
Captain W. L. M. Bishop, killed.
,, J. E. Sharpe, died.

48th Regiment—mutinied at Lucknow.

Major-General Sir H. M. Wheeler, killed at Cawnpore.
Lieutenant G. I. Bax, killed at Seetapore.

51st Regiment—disarmed and mutinied at Peshawur.

Lieut.-Colonel D. Ross, died in the Punjab.
Lieutenant J. C. Cooper, died at Peshawur.
,, A. B. Bowie, died.

52nd Regiment—mutinied at Jubbulpore.

Lieut.-Colonel Wiggens, killed at Cawnpore.
Captain F. M. H. Burlton, died of cholera at Agra Fort.
Lieutenant F. A. R. Macgregor, killed near Jubbulpore.

53rd Regiment—mutinied at Cawnpore.

Major W. Hillersdon, killed at Cawnpore.
Captain J. H. Reynolds, ,, ,,

Captain H. Belson, killed at Cawnpore.
Lieutenant Jellicoe, „ „
„ Armstrong, „ „
„ Master, „ „
„ Bridges, „ „
„ W. Prole, „ „
Ensign A. Dowson, „ „
„ Forman, „ „

54th Regiment—mutinied at Dehli.

Lieut.-Colonel J. P. Ripley, killed.
Major Blake, killed at Gwalior.
Captain C. W. Russell, killed before Dehli.

„ R. M. Smith, „ C. Burrowes, Lieutenant C. J. Butler, „ E. A. Edwards, „ W. Waterfield,	killed in Dehli.

Ensign C. B. Wheatly, killed before Dehli.
„ A. Angelo, killed between Dehli and Meerut.

55th Regiment—Nowshera.
(The men of this Corps have been totally destroyed.)

Lieut.-Colonel H. Spottiswoode, died.
Captain G. G. McBarnett, killed at Dehli.

56th Regiment—mutinied at Cawnpore.

Lieut.-Colonel S. Williams, Major W. R. Prout, Captain W. Halliday,	killed at Cawnpore.

„ J. Delamain, killed before Dehli.
„ G. Kempland.
Lieutenant Q. Battye, killed at Delhi.

„ C. R. Goad, „ W. A. Chalmers, „ H. Fagan, „ W. L. G. Morris, „ J. G. Warde, Ensign J. Henderson, „ R. Browne, „ R. Stevens,	killed at Cawnpore.

59th Regiment—disarmed at Umritsur.

Major J. G. Holmes, killed at Segowlie.

60th Regiment—mutinied at Umballa.

Lieutenant G. A. Doyne, died at Simla.

61st Regiment—mutinied at Jullundur.

Lieutenant J. Powys, killed at Jhansi.
Ensign H. Durnford, „ Jullundur.

62nd Regiment—disarmed.

Captain F. C. Hayes, killed near Bhowgong.
Lieutenant O. M'C. Span, died in Agra Fort.

64th Regiment—disarmed at Peshawur.

Major F. Knyvett, died.
Lieutenant G. Snell, killed at Seetapore, Oude.

65th Regiment—disarmed at Ghazeepore.

Colonel R. W. Wilson, died in Europe.
Brevet-Major Shirreff, killed at Gwalior.
Lieutenant E. Speke, killed at Dehli.

67th Regiment—disarmed at Agra.

Lieut.-Colonel Cotton, died at Dehra.
Lieutenant P. H. Jackson, killed at Cawnpore.
„ P. H. C. Burlton, killed at Muttra.

68th Regiment—mutinied at Bareilly.

Captain A. Skene, killed at Jhansi.
Lieutenant A. H. Alexander, killed at Allahabad.
„ W. H. Lumsden, killed before Dehli.
Ensign R. G. Tucker, killed at Bareilly.

69th Regiment—disarmed at Multan.

Major W. S. Menteath, died.

71st Regiment—mutinied at Lucknow.

Lieutenant A. P. Grant, killed at Lucknow.

72nd Regiment—mutinied at Neemuch.

Brigadier J. Handscomb, killed at Lucknow.
Lieutenant R. O. Dowda, killed at Augur.

73rd Regiment.

Ensign P. S. Codd.

74th Regiment—mutinied at Dehli.

Major Sir G. Parker, Bart., killed at Cawnpore.
Captain C. Gordon, killed in Dehli.
„ F. Burgess, killed at Jhansi.
„ J. W. B. Blagrave, died at Saugor.
Lieutenant M. Reveley, } killed in Dehli.
„ J. D. Smith, }
„ the Honble. H. Addington, killed in escaping from Dehli to Meerut.
„ H. Hyslop, „ „ „

Ensigns not joined.

Ensign Marchall D. Smith, ⎫
„ T. L. Bailiff, ⎪
„ A. S. Scott, ⎪
„ A. M. Cheek, ⎬ killed at Allahabad on their way up the country to join their corps.
„ Beaumont, ⎪
„ E. M. Smith, ⎪
„ C. G. Way, ⎭

UNATTACHED.

Lieutenant P. Mara, killed at Jounpore.
„ E. A. Powis, died from exposure, Buxar.

OFFICERS BELONGING TO THE MADRAS AND BOMBAY ARMIES.

General Neill, 1st Madras Fusiliers, killed at Lucknow.
Colonel Penny, Bombay Lancers, killed at Nusseerabad.
Captain Spottiswoode, „ „ „
Cornet Newbury.
Captain Gordon, Madras Army, killed at Jhansi.
Major Renaud, 1st Madras Fusiliers, died of wounds.
Lieut.-Colonel Cecil, died in Agra Fort.

PENSION ESTABLISHMENT.

Captain J. H. Ferris, died from exposure while being dragged to Gwalior.
Lieutenant F. Warwick, killed at Moradabad.
„ E. S. Whish, murdered at Darjeeling.

ECCLESIASTICAL DEPARTMENT.

Reverend M. J. Jennings, killed at Dehli.
„ E. T. R. Moncrieff, „ Cawnpore.
„ G. W. Coopland, „ Gwalior.
„ Hubbard, „ Dehli.
„ Hunter, „ Sealkote.
„ W. H. Haycock, „ Cawnpore.
„ F. Fisher, missing, Futteygurh.

MEDICAL ESTABLISHMENT.

Senior Surgeon Spilsbury, died at Calcutta.
„ „ J. Graham, killed at Sealkote.
Surgeon Garbett, killed at Cawnpore, Offtg. Superintending Surgeon.
„ H. H. Bowling, missing, 28th Regiment, Shahjehanpore.
Doctor Kirke, killed in Gwalior.
Surgeon Collyer, killed at Cawnpore, 53rd Regiment N.I.
Doctor R. Boyes, „ „ 2nd Lt. Cavalry.
Surgeon Newenham, „ „ 1st Regiment N.I.
„ W. A. Roffe, died at Calcutta.
Doctor Hay, killed at Bareilly.
„ H. Graham, killed at Sealkote.
„ R. Allan, missing, Cawnpore.

Doctor McEgan, killed in Jhansi.
" McAuley, " Cawnpore.
Assistant Surgeon Bowling, killed in Cawnpore, 56th Regiment N.I.
" " R. Lyell, killed in Patna.
" " H. P. Harris, killed in Cawnpore, Offtg. Civil Surgeon.
" " A. Dopping, killed in Dehli, 54th N.I.
" " J. Kirke, died at Attock.
" " James, killed at Augur, Gwalior.
" " T. H. Woodward, died at Dehli.
" " H. T. Cavey, killed at Mehidpore.
Doctor Hansbrow, killed at Bareilly.
" Mawe, died from exposure, 12th Regiment N.I.
Surgeon T. Smith, Invalid Establishment, killed at Meerut.

Civil Servants.

Honourable J. R. Colvin, Lieutenant-Governor, died at Agra.
Simon Fraser, Esq., Commissioner, killed at Dehli.
D. Robertson, Esq., Judge, Bareilly.
T. K. Lloyd, Esq., Magistrate, murdered at Humeerpore.
R. T. Tucker, Esq., Judge, Futtehpore.
G. D. Raikes, Esq., Judge, Bareilly.
R. B. Thornhill, Esq., Judge of Futtehpore, missing.
J. P. McWhirter, Esq., killed, Magistrate of Paneeput.
C. G. Hillersdon, Esq., Magistrate, Cawnpore.
J. R. Hutchinson, Esq., Magistrate, Dehli.
A. Galloway, Esq., Assistant Magistrate, Dehli.
G. J. Christian, Esq., Commissioner, Oude, missing.
J. Wedderburn, Esq., Magistrate, Hissar.
W. C. Watson, Esq., Magistrate, Allygurh, died at Agra.
M. Ricketts, Esq., Magistrate, Shahjehanpore.
J. McKillop, Esq., Magistrate, Cawnpore.
A. Johnstone, Esq., killed by a fall from his horse at Meerut.
J. G. Thomason, Esq., Deputy Commissioner, Oude, missing.
A. Block, Esq., " "
C. J. Jenkins, Esq., Assistant Magistrate, Futtehgurh, missing.
W. R. Moore, Esq., Magistrate.
D. Grant, Esq., Joint Magistrate, murdered at Humeerpore.
J. B. Thornhill, Esq., Assistant Commissioner, died at Lucknow.
A. C. Smith, Esq., Assistant, Rohilkund Division.
M. C. Ommaney, Esq., killed in Oude.
H. H. Greathed, Esq., died at Dehli.
E. T. Colvin, Esq., died at Calcutta.
H. B. Thornhill, Esq., killed in Oude.
R. M. Lowis, Esq., killed in Futtehgurh.
B. R. Cuppage, Esq., killed in Jaunpore.
H. E. Cockerell, Esq., killed in Bandah.
C. W. Cuncliffe, Esq., killed in Oude.
G. S. Benson, Esq., killed at Lucknow.
R. H. Pomeroy, Esq., killed.
Bransby H. Cooper, died at Mymensing.

List of People Killed at Meerut on the Night of the 10th May 1857.

Mrs. Captain Chambers, 11th Regiment N.I.
Mrs. „ Macdonald, 20th „ „
Mrs. Dawson and 2 children.
Mrs. Courtney and 3 „
Mr. V. Tregear (Inspector of Schools).
Pensioners McKinlay and Blanco.
Corporal Mortimer (Rifles).
„ Edwards and Private Fitzpatrick (Rifles) and wives.
Mr. Newland (Photographer).
Riding-master Langdale's child (Cavalry).
Overseer Sergeant Law (Cap Manufactory, Dum-Dum) and 2 children.
„ „ McPhee (Department Public Works).
„ „ Bingley „ „ „
„ „ Grant „ „ „ and wife.
„ „ Brooks „ „ „ „
Gunner Donohoe (Horse Artillery).
„ Connolly „ „
„ Benson „ „
„ Cairns „ „

List of People belonging to the late Dehli Magazine reported to have been Murdered in Dehli, on and after the 11th May 1857.

Conductor W. G. Shaw, wife and 4 children.
„ J. Nolan, wife and 5 children.
„ J. Scully, wife and 4 children.
Sub-Conductor R. N. Settle, wife and 3 children.
„ „ W. Crow, wife and 2 children.
„ „ G. Connor.
Mrs. E. Buckley and 3 children.
Mr. J. Smith, Head Clerk.
Sergeant B. Edwards, wife and 3 children.
„ P. Stewart and 1 child.
„ J. Hoyle.

List of Persons Murdered in Agra on the 5th and 6th July 1857.

Christie Leveret.
Alexander Derridon from Allygurh, his wife and 3 children.
B. A. Piaggio, Clerk in the Civil Auditor's Office.
J. Hawkins.
Louis Maxwell, a Government Pensioner.
Zacharias Parsick, Clerk in the Secretariat, and his mother.
John Anthony, Clerk in the Secretariat.
J. Lamborne and his daughter.
H. Hare and his son, Government Clerks.
J. Danselme, jun.
Mrs. Nowlan.
Mrs. Mathias, burnt to death.
C. R. Thornton, Assistant Patrol.

Major John Jacob, late of Scindia's Service.
F. C. Hubbard, Professor at the Agra College.
T. Delisle, Drummer 9th N.I.
G. Turvy, Bandmaster.
T. Allen, Pensioner.
Mr. Gray's mother-in-law.
R. Dennis, Compositor, Mofussilite Press.
Mrs. Dennis, „ „
Thakoor, a Catechist of the Kuttra Church.
Peter, living at the Kuttra Church.
Roostum, Christian living at the Kuttra Church.
Mr. Tandy, killed at Allygurh.
Mr. O'Connor, Mounted Militia, killed in action.
Mr. C. Horn, killed in action.
Mr. P. Horn, „ „
Mr. Carlton, „ „
Mr. R. Smith, „ „
Mons. Jourdan, „ „
Mr. Deeds, „ „
Mr. Wells, killed at Toll Gate, Mynpoorie Road.

MURDERED AT BHURTPORE.

Mr. A. Sharpley.

MURDERED AT DEHLI.

Mrs. McGuire, residing with Sergeant Edwards.
Mr. T. Davis, Commissioner's Office.
Mr. J. Davis, „ „
Miss Davis.
Mrs. Wilson and son.
Mrs. E. Ryley and 2 children.
Mrs. E. Prince.
Mrs. A. Ives.
Mr. and Mrs. Foulon (Department Public Works).
Mrs. Sheehan and 2 children (widow of late Riding-master Sheehan).
Mr. Hanly, wife and 4 children.
Mr. McNally.
Mrs. Colonel Foster.
Mrs. Captain Fuller.
Mrs. Hickey.
Mr. T. W. Collins (late Deputy Collector), wife and 4 children.
Mr. J. Staines and 2 children.
Mrs. E. P. Staines' son and daughter.
Mrs. A. M. Hunt and 3 children.
Mrs. Cochrane and 1 child.
Mrs. Leeson's 3 children.
Mrs. Thompson and 2 daughters (relict of late Rev. J. Thompson).
Mr. and Mrs. Thomas, Agent for Dawk Carriages.
Mr. McKay, Baptist Missionary.
The Rev. Father Zacharias, Catholic Priest.
Mr. J. A. Todd, Telegraph.
Mr. Bayley, Postmaster.
Mr. Dalton, P.O. Inspector.
Mr. and Mrs. George, 2 sons and a daughter.
Miss Jennings, daughter of Rev. R. M. Jennings.
Miss Clifford, staying with Rev. R. M. Jennings.
Rev. Mr. Sandys, Church Mission.
Rev. Mr. Koehe, „ „
Mr. F. Taylor, Principal of College.
Mr. Roberts and son, College.
Mr. R. Stewart, wife and 2 children, College.
Mr. and Mrs. Beresford and 5 daughters, Bank Secretary.
Mr. H. F. B. Churcher.
Mrs. Morgan and grandchild.
Mr. Clarke.
Mr. and Mrs. Burrows and 2 children.
Mr. and Mrs. Heatley and child, Dehli Gazette.
Mrs. Harton.
Mr. M. Daniells, Customs.
Master H. Herdon.
Master W. H. Herdon.
Mrs. Morley and 3 children.
Mr. and Mrs. Clarke and 1 child.
Mr. Nixon, Commissioner's Office.
Miss Lumley.

Overseer Sergeant Dennis, wife and 2 children.
Mr. J. Rennell, wife and 3 children.
Mr. P. Greenway, Clerk, Commissioner's Office.
Mr. and Mrs. Corbett and child.
Mr. Edward Marshall.
Mr. McNally.
Mr. Vere, Music Master, and wife.
Mr. Montreau, Commissioner's Office.
Mr. John Wilton.
Mr. T. Jones, Collector's Office.
Mr. T. Leonard, " "
Mr. W. Fleming, Commissioner's Office.
Mr. and Mrs. G. R. White and 4 children.
Mr. Aidwell, jun.
Infant child of Captain E. Fraser, Engineers, died from exposure on the road to Kurnaul.

MURDERED AT CAWNPORE.

Mrs. Major Larkins, Artillery, and children.
Mrs. Lieutenant Dempster, Artillery, and children.
Mrs. Major Vibart, 2nd Cavalry, and family.
Mrs. Captain Seppings, 2nd Cavalry, and family.
Mrs. Major Moore, H.M.'s 32nd Regiment.
Mrs. and Miss Wainwright, H.M.'s 32nd Regiment.
Mrs. Hill, H.M.'s 32nd Regiment.
Mrs. Colonel Ewart, 1st N.I., and child.
Mrs. Captain Turner, 1st N.I., and child.
Mrs. Dr. Newnham and children, 1st N.I.
Mrs. Captain Reynolds, 53rd Regiment N.I.
Mrs. Captain Belson and children, 53rd Regiment N.I.
Miss Campbell.
Miss Glasgow.
Miss —— Glasgow.
Mrs. Jellicoe and child, 53rd Regiment.
Mrs. Colonel Williams and 2 daughters, 56th Regiment.
Mrs. Major Prout.
Mrs. Captain Kempland and children, 56th Regiment.
Mrs. Jackson, 67th Regiment.
Lady Wheeler and 2 Misses Wheeler.
Mrs. Blair and 2 Misses Blair.
Mrs. Fraser.
Mrs. Evans.
Mrs. Darby and infant.
Miss Bisset.
Mrs. Swinton and 3 children. (?)
Miss Cripps.
—— Jack, Esq.
Mrs. Major Lindsay.
Mrs. Williamson and child.
Mrs. Moncrieff and baby.
Mrs. Dr. Allen.
Mrs. Dr. Harris.
Mrs. Dr. Boyes.
Miss Brightman.
Mrs. Dr. Bowling and child.
Mrs. Haycock.
Mrs. Chalwin.
Miss White, Mrs. Wade.
Mrs. G. Lindsay and 3 Misses Lindsay.
Mrs. Hillersdon and child.
Mr. Anderson.
Mr. Haycock.
Mr. Baines.
Mr. Nelson.
Mr. Latouche, Engineers.
Mr. Gum.
Mr. A. C. Heberden.
Mr. M. Miller.
Mr. Thomas.
Mr. H. D. Latouche.
Mrs. R. Hanna.
Mr. J. C. Bain.
Mr. W. Fersyth.
The Rev. Father Rooney.
Mrs. Anderson.
Mr. R. B. Cook.
Mr. Campbell.
Mr. and Mrs. Christie and family.
Mr. and Mrs. Fagan and family.
Mr. Shaw.

Mr. Sherman.
Mrs. J. Eckford.
The whole of the married women and children of H.M.'s 32nd Foot.
60 men of H.M.'s 84th Foot.
15 men of 1st E. B. Fusiliers.
70 men (invalids) of H.M.'s 32nd Foot.
59 Bengal Artillerymen (out of these, 4 men only escaped).
All married women and children of the 1st Company 6th Battalion Artillery.

List of the People Butchered at Cawnpore on the Night of the 16th July, taken from the Calcutta Papers of the 20th August.

Mr. Greenway.
Mrs. Greenway.
Miss Greenway.
H. Greenway.
Martha Greenway.
Jane Greenway.
Mr. F. Jacobie.
H. Jacobie.
Lucy Jacobie.
Hugh Jacobie.
Mrs. Tibbetts.
Miss Peter.
Miss Cooke.
Mrs. Borthwick.
Grace Kirk.
William Kirk.
Charlotte Kirk.
Mrs. White.
Mr. MacCullen.
Miss Sinclair.
John Greenway.
Mary Greenway.
Lizzy Homes.
Mrs. Sheridan.
William Sheridan.
Baby Sheridan.
Mrs. Wrixon.
Clara Wrixon.
Edmond Wrixon.
Eliza Bennett.
Mrs. Parbett.
Stephen Parbett.
Catherine Widlep.
Jane Widlep.
Thomas Widlep.
Mrs. Reed.
James Reed.
C. Reed.
Julia Reed.
Charles Reed.
Henry Simpson.
Miss Colgon.
Mrs. Kinliside.
Henry Kinliside.
Willis Kinliside.
Mrs. O'Brien.
Mrs. Green.
Edward Green.
Mrs. Crab.
John Fitzgerald.
Mrs. Jenkins.
Mrs. Peel.
George Peel.
Mrs. Moore.
Maria Conway.
G. Weston.
Mrs. Carroll.
Mrs. Battie.
Mrs. Johnson.
Jane Morfett.
Mrs. Pokeson.
Mr. C. Mackintosh.
Henry Brett.
Mrs. Domy.
Henry Duncan.
Mrs. Lery.
James Lery.
C. Lery.
Mrs. Norris.
Mr. Guthrie.
Catherine Guthrie.
Mrs. White.
Mrs. Wooller.
Tommy Wooller.
Susan Wooller.
Mrs. Cooper.
Mrs. Carroll.
Mrs. D. ——
Two Ayahs.
Mrs. Sanders.

William Sanders.
Margaret Fitzgerald.
Mary Fitzgerald.
Tom Fitzgerald.
Ellen Fitzgerald.
Mrs. Bell.
Alpen Bell.
Mrs. Murray.
Mrs. Jones.
Mrs. Russell.
Eliza Russell.
Sergeant Kelly, D.P.W., wife and child.
Sergeant J. Whelan, D.P.W., wife and 3 children.
Mr. Gilpin.
Sarah Gilpin.
Harriet Gilpin.
Sam Gilpin.
S. Gilpin.
Mrs. Walker.
Mrs. Copeman.
Emma Weston.
William James.
J. Gill.
James Cousins.
Mrs. Peter.
James Peter.
Mr. Baines.
Philip Baines.
Mrs. Fraser.
Mrs. Daly.
Miss Williams.
Mrs. Parrott.
Mary Peters.
Arthur Newman.
Charlotte Newman.
Mrs. Arhing.
Mr. Moore.
Miss White.
Mrs. Probett.
Charles Probett.
Emma Probett.
Louisa Probett.
Mrs. Seppings.
John Seppings.
W. Copeland, D.P.W.
Edward Seppings.
Mrs. Dupton.
Charles Dupton.
William Dupton.
Henry Dupton.
Miss Wallet.
Mrs. Hill.
Mrs. Raselier.
Mrs. Lindsay.
Francis Lindsay.
Caroline Lindsay.
Mrs. Scott.
Mrs. Mackinna.
Mrs. Willis.
Daniel Walker.
Mrs. Joshua Mackintosh.
Mrs. D. C. Mackintosh.
Mrs. Ame Walker.
Miss Burn.
Miss Burn.
Mrs. Dallas.
Miss O'Connor.
Lucy Lyell.
Mrs. Carter.
Harriett Pistol.
Elizabeth Saupore.
George Caley.
G. Caley.
Lucy Stake.
William Stake.
Miss Conway.
James Lewis.
Elizabeth West.
W. North.
Henry Williams.
Jervie Martindal.
Weston Dundi.
Baby Reed.
Mrs. Gillie.
T. A. Berrill, E.I. Railway.
Henry Berrill, „ „
Mrs. H. Berrill.
Miss Bella Berrill.

THE FOLLOWING IS A LIST OF THE FUTTEHGURH RESIDENTS, ALL SUPPOSED TO HAVE BEEN MURDERED AT CAWNPORE.

W. Copeland, D.P.W.
Mrs. Woolger.
Charles Woolger.
Thomas Woolger.
Mrs. Gillem.
Miss Seth.

Mr. Tucker.
Miss Tucker.
Louisa Tucker.
George Tucker.
L. Tucker.
Mrs Reen.
Mary Reen.
Catherine Reen.
Eliza Reen.
Lilly Reen.
Jane Reen.
Dina Reen.
Emiline Reen.
Mrs. Thomson.
Mr. Thornhill, } missing.
Mrs. Thornhill, }
Conductor Rohan and family.
J. Jones, killed in the Fort.
Hitchcock and wife.
Mr. J. J. Palmer, wife and family.
Miss Long.
Mrs. Maltby.
Mrs. Lewis.
Emma Lewis.
Eliza Lewis.
Mr. West.
3 Natives.
Mrs. Yaman.
Mr. Lupan.
Mrs. Heathcote.
Godfrey Loyd.
Baby Loyd.
Colonel Goldie.
Mrs. Goldie.
Mary Goldie.
Eliza Goldie.
Colonel Smith.
Mrs. Smith.
Mr. Rees.
Eliza Rees.
Jane Rees.
Mr. Roche, wife and 2 children.

THE FOLLOWING PERSONS WERE ALSO IN CAWNPORE AT THE TIME, AND IT IS TO BE FEARED HAVE MET THE SAME FATE.

Mr. H. Stacy, Dep. Collr.
Mr. and Mrs. MacLanders and child.
Mrs. Riding-master Walsh and family.
Frederick Palmer, Cutler to the Medical Depôt.
H. Palmer, Sub. Med. Est.
J. X. De Gama, Merchant.
Mr. Gee and family.
Mrs. Carmody.
Mr. Grey and family.
Lieutenant Reilly, Comm. Ord., and family.
Mr. De Russett, wife and family.
Mrs. Hagan.
Mr. and Mrs. Mackintosh and family.
Mr. T. Vaughan.
Mr. Wheelan, wife and 2 children.
Mr. Barlow.
Madame Rosenberg.
Mr. D. Hay and family.
Mr. D. Duncan and family.
Mr. Roach, Postmaster.
Mr. J. Schorn.
Mr. Shearin, wife and family.
Mr. Waterfield.
Mr. Bunny, Horse-breaker.
Mr. A. R. Johnstone, wife and child.
Margaret Stowell.
Mr. Little, Asst. to Mr. Hay.
Miss Grey.
Mr. Maxwell, Sub. Dept., Opium Agent.
Mrs. Shepherd and family (Mr. Shepherd escaped).
Apothecary Twoomy, Medical Dept.
Mrs. Collins.
Mr. Tritten.
Mr. Purcell.
Mr. Carr.
Mr. C. H. Peake, Telegraph Office.
Mr. Farmer, " "
Mr. R. Wrixon.
Rev. J. C. Freeman, Pres. Mission.
Rev. D. E. Campbell, " "

It must be remembered that this list does not include the soldiers of H.M.'s 32nd and 84th Foot and Artillery, and their wives and children, several hundred in number.

Rev. A. O. Johnson, Pres. Mission.
Rev. R. McMullen, „ „
Mrs. Freeman.
Mrs. Campbell and 2 children.
Mrs. Johnson.
Mrs. MacMullen.

Mr. Probett.
Mr. T. P. Collins.
40 Clerks, wives and children.
Mr. and Mrs. Alone and 2 children.
Mr. Lawrence and 5 children.
Mr. Davis and 4 children.

BAREILLY—
Mr. Smith and 5 children.
Mr. Jeffreys.
Mr. Barell.
Miss Thompson.
Mr. Wyatt, Deputy Collector.
Mr. Orr, „ „
Sergeant Hardy, wife and 5 children missing.

LAHORE—
Sergeant-Major 26th Regiment N.I.

SULTANPORE—
Mrs. Stroyan.
Mr. Black.

NEEMUCH—Wife of Staff Sergeant Supple, and children, burnt to death in boxes.

PATNA—Dr. Lyall.

MORADABAD—
Mrs. Warwick.
Mrs. Kitchen and son.
Mrs. Carbery.

BENARES—Mr. Jackson.

List of Persons Massacred at Jhansi.

Mr. C. Purcell.
Mr. J. Purcell.
Mr. A. Scott.
Mr. G. Young.
Mr. T. Munrowd.
Mr. W. Palgreyman.
Mr. Carshore, Collector of Customs.
Mr. G. D. Davies, father and mother.
Mr. Crawford.
Mr. Fleming.
Mrs. McEgan and three children.
Mr. and Mrs. Mutloo.
Mrs. Carshore and 4 children.
Sergeant Newton, wife and 4 children.
Mrs. Captain Powys and baby.
Sergeant Lucas.
Mrs. Langdale.
Mrs. Smalley.
Mr. Browne.
Miss Browne.
Mr. and Mrs. Thomas Wilton and 2 children.
Two Miss Wiltons.
Mr. and Mrs. R. Andrews and 3 children.
Mr. T. Andrews, Sudder Ameen.
Mr. and Mrs. J. Young.

Mr. and Mrs. D. T. Blyth and 3 children.
Sergeant and Mrs. Millard and 3 children.
Mr. W. Bennet.

HANSI—
Mrs. Major Milne and 2 children.
Mrs. Hallett.

SEGOWLEE—
Mrs. Major Holmes, killed.
Mr. Scott.

SEALKOTE—
Mrs. Hunter and child.

FYZABAD—
Sergeant-Major Busher, 22nd Regiment.
Mr. Hurst and Mr. Fitzgerald.

GWALIOR—
Sergeant-Majors Twicheum and Cronin.
Qr.-Master Sergeant Webb.
Mr. Collins.
Mrs. Stewart and children.

FUTTEHGURH—
Mrs. G. Smith.
Mrs. Major Robertson and 2 children and European maid.
Mrs. R. N. Lowis and child.
Mrs. Goldie and family.

Mrs. T. Tucker and 3 children.
Mrs. Fisher and 2 children.
Mrs. H. Collins, sen.
Mr. P. H. Churcher.

NUSSEERABAD—Mr. Paul and 6 children.

ALLAHABAD—
Mr. Boilard and family.
Mr. Fulow.
Mrs. M. Thomas.
Mr. C. B. Jones.
Mr. F. M. P. Jones.
Mrs. Major Ryres.
Mrs. J. H. Williams.
Mr. and Mrs. Hodson, died of cholera.
Mrs. Ed. Purcer, died of cholera.

SEETAPORE—
Mrs. Captain Gowan, 27th Regiment.
Mr. Christian, wife and family.

INDORE—
Mr. Murray.
Mr. and Mrs. McBeth and 7 children.
Mr. Payne.
Mr. and Mrs. Avery.
Mr. Brooke.
Mr. and Mrs. Norris.
Mr. Alphonge.
Mr. and Mrs. Bone. (?)
Mr. and Mrs. Butler and child.
Mrs. Beaurais. (?)
Mrs. Crawley.
Miss Crawley.
Mr. McMahon, Civil Engineer.
Mrs. Moran, wife of Overseer, D.P.W.
Mr. Butler, wife and child.
Mr. J. E. Martin, formerly of the Agra Bank, died from exposure, together with several Native Christians, Parsees, etc., names not known.

KOTAH—
Arthur Robert Burton.
Francis Clarke Burton.

AGRA, PRINTED BY J. A. GIBBON.

INDEX

VOLUME II